**Middle School 2-1**

기말고사 완벽대비

# 적중100

## 영어 기출 문제집

중**2**

시사 | 박준언

*Best Collection*

# 구성과 특징

교과서의 주요 학습 내용을 중심으로 학습 영역별 특성에 맞춰 단계별로 다양한 학습 기회를 제공하여 단원별 학습능력 평가는 물론 중간 및 기말고사 시험 등에 완벽하게 대비할 수 있도록 내용을 구성

## Words & Expressions

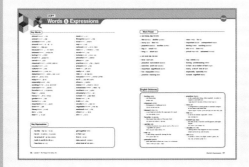

**Step1**  Key Words 단원별 핵심 단어 설명 및 풀이
Key Expression 단원별 핵심 숙어 및 관용어 설명
Word Power 반대 또는 비슷한 뜻 단어 배우기
English Dictionary 영어로 배우는 영어 단어

**Step2**  실력평가 단원별 수시평가 대비 주관식, 객관식 문제풀이

**Step3**  서술형 대비 학업성취도 및 수행능력평가 대비 서술형 문제풀이

## Conversation

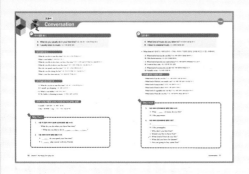

**Step1**  핵심 의사소통 의사소통에 필요한 주요 표현 방법 요약
핵심 Check 기본적인 표현 방법 및 활용능력 확인

**Step2**  대화문 익히기 상황에 따른 대화문 활용 및 연습

**Step3**  기본평가 시험대비 기초 학습 능력 평가

**Step4**  실력평가 단원별 수시평가 대비 주관식, 객관식 문제풀이

**Step5**  서술형 대비 학업성취도 및 수행능력평가 대비 서술형 문제풀이

## Grammar

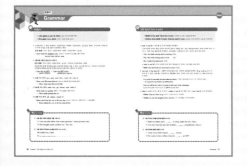

**Step1**  주요 문법 단원별 주요 문법 사항과 예문을 알기 쉽게 설명
핵심 Check 기본 문법사항에 대한 이해 여부 확인

**Step2**  기본평가 시험대비 기초 학습 능력 평가

**Step3**  실력평가 단원별 수시평가 대비 주관식, 객관식 문제풀이

**Step4**  서술형 대비 학업성취도 및 수행능력평가 대비 서술형 문제풀이

## Reading

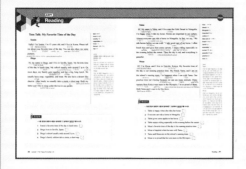

**Step1**  구문 분석 단원별로 제시된 문장에 대한 구문별 분석과 내용 설명
확인문제 문장에 대한 기본적인 이해와 인지능력 확인

**Step2**  확인학습A 빈칸 채우기를 통한 문장 완성 능력 확인

**Step3**  확인학습B 제시된 우리말을 영어로 완성하여 작문 능력 키우기

**Step4**  실력평가 단원별 수시평가 대비 주관식, 객관식 문제풀이

**Step5**  서술형 대비 학업성취도 및 수행능력평가 대비 서술형 문제풀이
교과서 구석구석 교과서에 나오는 기타 문장까지 완벽 학습

# Composition

## |영역별 핵심문제|

단어 및 어휘, 대화문, 문법, 독해 등 각 영역별 기출문제의 출제 유형을 분석하여 실전에 대비하고 연습할 수 있도록 문제를 배열

## |서술형 실전 및 창의사고력 문제|

학교 시험에서 점차 늘어나는 서술형 시험에 집중 대비하고 고득점을 취득하는데 만전을 기하기 위한 학습 코너

## |단원별 예상문제|

기출문제를 분석한 후 새로운 시험 출제 경향을 더하여 새롭게 출제될 수 있는 문제를 포함하여 시험에 완벽하게 대비할 수 있도록 준비

## |단원별 모의고사|

영역별, 단계별 학습을 모두 마친 후 실전 연습을 위한 모의고사

## on the textbook

교과서 파헤치기

- 단어Test1~2 영어 단어 우리말 쓰기와 우리말을 영어 단어로 쓰기

- 대화문Test1~2 대화문 빈칸 완성 및 전체 대화문 쓰기

- 본문Test1~5 빈칸 완성, 우리말 쓰기, 문장 배열연습, 영어 작문하기 복습 등 단계별 반복 학습을 통해 교과서 지문에 대한 완벽한 습득

- 구석구석지문Test1~2 지문 빈칸 완성 및 전문 영어로 쓰기

# Lesson 3

# Living a Healthy Life

## 의사소통 기능

- 능력 여부 묻기
  Do you know how to ride a longboard?

- 좋아하는 것 표현하기
  I enjoy riding my longboard because it reduces my stress.

## 언어 형식

- 사역동사
  It will **make** your eyes **feel** more comfortable.

- 조건을 나타내는 접속사 if
  **If** you massage yourself and stretch every day, you will feel healthier.

# Words & Expressions

## Key Words

- **activity** [æktívəti] 명 활동
- **advice** [ædváis] 명 조언, 충고(= tip)
- **already** [ɔːlrédi] 부 벌써, 이미
- **back** [bæk] 명 뒤쪽, 뒷부분
- **backward** [bǽkwərd] 부 뒤로(↔ forward)
- **behind** [biháind] 전 ~ 뒤에
- **bend** [bend] 동 구부리다
- **both** [bouθ] 대 둘 다
- **bowl** [boul] 명 그릇
- **comfortable** [kʌ́mfərtəbl] 형 편안한(↔ uncomfortable)
- **count** [kaunt] 동 세다
- **difficult** [dífikʌlt] 형 어려운(↔ easy)
- **download** [dáunlòud] 동 다운로드하다
- **exercise** [éksərsàiz] 동 운동하다
- **face** [feis] 동 ~을 마주보다[향하다] 명 얼굴
- **fall** [fɔːl] 동 넘어지다
- **fishing** [fíʃiŋ] 명 낚시
- **fresh** [freʃ] 형 신선한
- **habit** [hǽbit] 명 습관
- **healthy** [hélθi] 형 건강한, 건강에 좋은
- **hold** [hould] 동 유지하다
- **however** [hauévər] 부 그러나
- **life** [laif] 명 삶
- **light** [lait] 명 빛
- **like** [laik] 전 ~와 같은, ~처럼
- **lower** [lóuər] 동 ~을 낮추다, ~을 낮게 하다
- **massage** [məsɑ́ːʒ] 명 마사지 동 마사지를 하다
- **move** [muːv] 동 움직이다
- **nature** [néitʃər] 명 자연
- **neck** [nek] 명 목
- **place** [pleis] 동 놓다, 두다
- **position** [pəzíʃən] 명 자세
- **pour** [pɔːr] 동 붓다
- **pull** [pul] 동 당기다, 끌다
- **push** [puʃ] 동 밀다
- **put** [put] 동 놓다, 두다
- **reduce** [ridjúːs] 동 줄이다(↔ increase)
- **relax** [rilǽks] 동 (근육 등의) 긴장이 풀리다, 긴장을 풀다
- **second** [sékənd] 명 (시간 단위인) 초
- **shoulder** [ʃóuldər] 명 어깨
- **show** [ʃou] 동 보여[가르쳐] 주다
- **simple** [símpl] 형 간단한, 단순한(↔ complicated)
- **softly** [sɔ́ːftli] 부 부드럽게
- **step** [step] 명 걸음
- **stress** [stres] 동 스트레스를 받다[주다]
- **stretch** [stretʃ] 동 스트레칭하다
- **switch** [switʃ] 동 바꾸다(= change)
- **understand** [ʌndərstǽnd] 동 이해하다, 알다
- **usually** [júːʒuəli] 부 보통, 대개
- **waist** [weist] 명 허리
- **warm** [wɔːrm] 형 따뜻한(↔ cool)
- **way** [wei] 명 길

## Key Expressions

- **a little bit** 조금
- **at the same speed** 같은 속도로
- **be good for** ~에 좋다
- **be worried about** ~에 대해 걱정하다
- **block out** (빛을) 가리다[차단하다]
- **each other** 서로
- **from top to bottom** 위에서 아래까지
- **focus on** ~에 집중하다
- **for a few seconds** 몇 초 동안
- **get over** 회복[극복]하다
- **have a cold** 감기에 걸리다
- **loosen up** 몸을 풀어 주다
- **more than** ~ 이상
- **prepare for** ~을 준비하다
- **straighten up** 똑바로 하다
- **take a walk** 산책하다
- **team up with** ~와 협력하다, ~와 한 팀이 되다
- **three times a week** 일주일에 세 번
- **warm up** 준비 운동을 하다
- **what kind of** 어떤 종류의

## Word Power

※ 동사에 접미사 -able를 붙여 형용사가 되는 단어

☐ **comfort** → **comfortable** (편안한)

☐ **change** → **changeable** (바뀔 수 있는)

☐ **use** → **usable** (사용 가능한)

☐ **move** → **movable** (움직이는)

☐ **respect** → **respectable** (존경할 만한)

☐ **desire** → **desirable** (바람직한)

※ 접두사 un-은 형용사 · 부사 · 명사 앞에 붙어 부정이나 반대의 의미를 나타낸다.

☐ **comfortable** (편안한) → **uncomfortable** (불편한)

☐ **easy** (편한) → **uneasy** (불편한)

☐ **fair** (공평한) → **unfair** (불공평한)

☐ **friendly** (친절한) → **unfriendly** (불친절한)

☐ **happy** (행복한) → **unhappy** (행복하지 않은)

☐ **known** (알려진) → **unknown** (알려지지 않은)

## English Dictionary

☐ **advice** 조언
→ an opinion or suggestion about what someone should do
누군가에게 어떻게 하라고 알려 주는 말이나 제안

☐ **bend** 구부리다
→ to move your body so that it is not straight
몸을 움직여 구부리다

☐ **comfortable** 편안한
→ making you feel physically relaxed
당신을 신체적으로 편안함을 느끼게 하는

☐ **count** 세다
→ to say numbers in order
숫자를 순서대로 말하다

☐ **habit** 습관
→ something that a person does often in a regular and repeated way
사람이 규칙적으로 또는 반복적으로 자주 하는 행동

☐ **massage** 마사지
→ the action of rubbing and pressing a person's body with the hands to reduce pain in the muscles and joints
근육과 관절의 통증을 줄이기 위해 손으로 사람의 몸을 문지르고 누르는 행동

☐ **neck** 목
→ the part of the body between the head and the shoulders
머리와 어깨 사이의 신체 부위

☐ **position** 자세
→ the way someone stands, sits, or lies down
어떤 사람이 서거나 앉거나 눕는 방식

☐ **pull** 당기다
→ to hold something firmly and use force in order to move it or try to move it toward yourself
뭔가를 단단히 잡고 힘을 사용하여 움직이거나 자신을 향해 움직이려고 하다

☐ **reduce** 줄이다
→ to make something smaller in size, amount, number, etc.
어떤 것의 크기, 양, 수 등이 작아지게 하다

☐ **relax** (근육 등의) 긴장을 풀다
→ to cause something to become less tense, tight, or stiff
어떤 것이 긴장, 팽팽함 또는 경직성이 줄어들게 하다

☐ **simple** 간단한
→ not hard to understand or do
이해하거나 하기가 어렵지 않은

☐ **stretch** 스트레칭하다
→ to put your arms, legs, etc., in positions that make the muscles long and tight
근육이 길고 팽팽하게 하는 자세로 팔, 다리 등을 뻗다

☐ **switch** 바꾸다
→ to change or replace something with another thing
어떤 것을 다른 것으로 바꾸다

☐ **warm up** 준비 운동을 하다
→ to do gentle physical exercises to prepare your body for a sport or other activity
운동이나 다른 활동을 위해 당신의 몸을 준비하기 위해 가벼운 신체 운동을 하다

**01** 다음 중 〈보기〉와 같이 변화하는 단어가 <u>아닌</u> 것은?

┌─ 보기 ├─────────────┐
move – movable
└─────────────────────┘

① use      ② change

③ respect      ④ impress

⑤ comfort

**중요**

**02** 다음 빈칸에 알맞은 말이 바르게 짝지어진 것은?

┌─────────────────────┐
• Fruits are good _____ your health.

• You can focus _____ your studies better.
└─────────────────────┘

① at – in      ② for – on

③ on – at      ④ from – in

⑤ about – on

**서답형**

**03** 다음 짝지어진 단어의 관계가 같도록 빈칸에 알맞은 말을 쓰시오.

┌─────────────────────┐
strong : weak = cool : _____
└─────────────────────┘

**04** 다음 영영풀이에 해당하는 단어로 알맞은 것은?

┌─────────────────────┐
making you feel physically relaxed
└─────────────────────┘

① simple      ② comfortable

③ pleasure      ④ serious

⑤ popular

**서답형**

**05** 다음 우리말에 맞게 빈칸에 알맞은 말을 쓰시오.

┌─────────────────────┐
너희 둘 다 어린애들 같구나.

➡ _____ _____ you are acting like children.
└─────────────────────┘

**서답형**

**06** 다음 영영풀이에 해당하는 단어를 쓰시오.

┌─────────────────────┐
to do gentle physical exercises to prepare your body for a sport or other activity
└─────────────────────┘

➡ _____

**07** 다음 문장의 빈칸에 알맞은 것은?

┌─────────────────────┐
I hope you will get _____ your cold soon.
└─────────────────────┘

① from      ② over

③ off      ④ up

⑤ through

**서답형**

**08** 다음 빈칸에 공통으로 알맞은 말을 쓰시오.

┌─────────────────────┐
• He runs 100 meters in 13 _____s.

• He is a _____ year in middle school.
└─────────────────────┘

**01** 다음 짝지어진 두 단어의 관계가 같도록 빈칸에 알맞은 말을 쓰시오.

(1) before : after = backward : _____

(2) wrong : right = reduce : _____

(3) delicious : tasty = tip : _____

(4) appear : disappear = comfortable : _____

**02** 다음 우리말에 맞도록 빈칸에 알맞은 말을 쓰시오.

(1) 그들은 서로 쳐다보고 웃었다.
➡ They looked at _____ _____ and laughed.

(2) 나는 일주일에 세 번 이상 운동을 한다.
➡ I exercise _____ _____ three times a week.

(3) 그 문제는 조금 어렵다.
➡ The problem is _____ _____ _____ difficult.

**03** 다음 빈칸에 들어갈 알맞은 말을 〈보기〉에서 골라 쓰시오.

┌─ 보기 ─┐
download   count   reduce   ride

(1) I _____ my longboard when I'm stressed.

(2) The beautiful pictures _____ my stress.

(3) Tom, _____ to ten and open your eyes.

(4) Users can _____ the full image.

**04** 다음 괄호 안의 단어를 문맥에 맞게 고쳐 쓰시오.

(1) I want to eat something _____. (health)

(2) My bike is very old, but it is still _____. (move)

(3) We should wear _____ shoes for walking for a long time. (comfort)

**05** 다음 빈칸에 알맞은 말을 〈보기〉에서 골라 쓰시오.

┌─ 보기 ─┐
am worried about / prepare for / get over

(1) Do you know how to _____ a cold?

(2) I will _____ the English speech contest.

(3) I _____ the math quiz on Monday.

**06** 다음 영영풀이에 해당하는 단어를 주어진 철자로 시작하여 쓰시오.

(1) s_____ : to put your arms, legs, etc., in positions that make the muscles long and tight

(2) h_____ : something that a person does often in a regular and repeated way

(3) s_____ : to change or replace something with another thing

(4) r_____ : to cause something to become less tense, tight, or stiff

# Conversation

## 1 능력 여부 묻기

**A** Do you know how to play basketball? 너는 농구를 어떻게 하는지 아니?

**B** Yes, I do. / No, I don't. 응, 알아. / 아니, 몰라.

■ Do you know how to+동사원형 ~?은 '너는 ~를 어떻게 하는지 아니?'라는 뜻으로, 어떤 일을 할 수 있는지 물을 때 사용하는 표현이다.

• A: Do you know how to do rock climbing? 너는 암벽 등반을 어떻게 하는지 아니?
  B: Yes, I do. 응, 알아.

### 상대방의 능력 여부를 묻는 표현

• Do you know how to + 동사원형 ~? 너는 ~하는 방법을 아니?
• Can you + 동사원형 ~? 너는 ~할 수 있니?
• Are you able to + 동사원형 ~? 너는 ~할 수 있니?
• Are you good at ~? 너는 ~를 잘하니?

### 능력을 나타내는 표현

• I know how to + 동사원형 ~. 나는 ~하는 방법을 알아.
• I can + 동사원형 ~. 나는 ~할 수 있어.
• I'm able to + 동사원형 ~. 나는 ~할 수 있어.
• I'm good at ~. 나는 ~을 잘해.

### 능력 여부에 답하기

〈긍정〉 Yes, I do. / Yes, I can. / I'm good at ~. / Yes, I know how to + 동사원형 ~. / Sure. / Of course.

〈부정〉 No, I don't. / No, I can't. / I'm not good at ~. / No, I don't know how to + 동사원형 ~. / No, I'm poor at ~.

## 핵심 Check

1. 다음 우리말과 일치하도록 빈칸에 알맞은 말을 쓰시오.

(1) **A**: Do you know _____ _____ fix a computer? (컴퓨터를 어떻게 고치는지 아니?)

    **B**: I'm _____ _____ _____ fixing machines. (난 기계 고치는 일을 잘 못해.)

(2) **A**: Do you know how to make potato salad? (너는 감자 샐러드를 어떻게 만드는지 아니?)

    **B**: No, I don't know _____ _____ _____ it. (아니, 나는 그것을 만드는 방법을 몰라.)

## 2 좋아하는 것 표현하기

**A** Kate, what do you enjoy doing to be healthy?

Kate, 너는 건강해지기 위해 무엇을 하는 걸 즐기니?

**B** I enjoy riding a bike. 나는 자전거 타는 것을 즐겨.

■ I enjoy ~(very much).는 '나는 ~하는 것을 (매우) 즐겨.'라는 뜻으로, 자신이 좋아하는 것을 말하는 표현이다.

• A: Amy, what do you enjoy doing to be healthy? Amy, 너는 건강해지기 위해 무엇을 하는 걸 즐기니?

B: I enjoy growing vegetables. 나는 채소 기르는 것을 즐겨.

### 좋아하는 것 말하는 표현

• I enjoy -ing ~. 나는 ~하는 것을 즐겨.

• I like ~. 나는 ~하는 것을 좋아해.

• I love ~. 나는 ~하는 것을 정말 좋아해.

• I feel great when I ~. 나는 ~할 때 기분이 좋아.

### 관심을 나타내는 표현

• Sounds cool. / That's great. / That's interesting! / How interesting!

• A: I enjoy watching birds. 나는 새를 관찰하는 것을 즐겨.

B: How interesting! 정말 흥미롭구나!

### 핵심 Check

2. 다음 우리말과 일치하도록 빈칸에 알맞은 말을 쓰시오.

(1) A: _____ do you _____ _____ do after school? (넌 방과 후에 무엇 하기를 좋아하니?)

B: I enjoy _____ a bike. (난 자전거 타는 것을 즐겨.)

(2) A: David, _____ do you _____ _____ to be healthy?

(David, 너는 건강해지기 위해 무엇을 하는 것을 즐기니?)

B: I enjoy _____. (나는 낚시를 즐겨.)

(3) A: What _____ _____ _____ in your free time? (너는 여가 시간에 무엇을 하니?)

B: I _____ _____ cartoons. I post them on the Internet.

(나는 만화 그리는 것을 즐겨. 나는 그것들을 인터넷에 게시하지.)

A: _____ interesting! (정말 흥미롭구나!)

🎤 **A. Listen & Speak 1 - A - 1**

> **B:** ❶I want to eat something healthy. Do you have any advice?
>
> **G:** I often eat fresh salad. ❷It makes me feel good.
>
> **B:** Really? ❸Do you know how to make it?
>
> **G:** Yes, it's quite simple. ❹First, cut many vegetables into small pieces. ❺Next, put them into a bowl. Then, pour some lemon juice on them. Finally, mix everything together.
>
> **B:** That's it? I should try it.

> **B:** 나는 건강에 좋은 것을 먹고 싶어. 말해 줄 조언이 있니?
>
> **G:** 나는 신선한 샐러드를 자주 먹어. 그것은 나를 기분 좋게 만들어.
>
> **B:** 정말? 그것을 어떻게 만드는지 아니?
>
> **G:** 응, 아주 간단해. 먼저, 많은 채소들을 작은 조각으로 잘라. 다음으로 그것들을 그릇에 담아. 그런 다음, 레몬주스를 조금 부어. 마지막으로 모든 것을 함께 섞어.
>
> **B:** 그게 다야? 한번 해 봐야겠다.

❶ -thing으로 끝나는 부정대명사는 형용사가 뒤에서 수식한다.
❷ It=fresh salad / make me feel good: 나를 기분 좋게 만들다
❸ Do you know how to+동사원형 ~?: ~하는 방법을 아니?(능력 여부 묻기)
❹ cut A into B: A를 B로 자르다
❺ put A into B: A를 B에 넣다 / them: small pieces

**Check(√) True or False**

(1) The girl knows how to make fresh salad.　　　　　　　　　　　　　T ☐ F ☐

(2) The first step in making fresh salad is to put vegetables into a bowl.　　T ☐ F ☐

🎤 **Conversation B**

> **Karl:** Hana, ❶what's the matter?
>
> **Hana:** Well, ❷I'm stressed about the test next week.
>
> **Karl:** I understand. I ride my longboard when I'm stressed. ❸Do you know how to ride a longboard?
>
> **Hana:** No, I don't.
>
> **Karl:** Let's go out! I can teach you. Put one foot on the board and push hard with the other.
>
> **Hana:** Like this? Wow! This is fun. ❹I feel better already.
>
> **Karl:** See? ❺I enjoy riding my longboard because it reduces my stress.
>
> **Hana:** That's great!

> **Karl:** 하나야, 무슨 일 있니?
>
> **하나:** 음, 다음 주에 있을 시험 때문에 스트레스를 받아.
>
> **Karl:** 난 이해돼. 나는 스트레스를 받을 때 롱보드를 타. 넌 롱보드를 어떻게 타는지 아니?
>
> **하나:** 아니, 몰라.
>
> **Karl:** 나가자! 내가 가르쳐 줄 수 있어. 한 발을 보드 위에 올려놓고 다른 한 발로 세게 밀어.
>
> **하나:** 이렇게? 와! 이거 재밌다. 벌써 기분이 좋아졌어.
>
> **Karl:** 봤지? 나는 롱보드를 타는 것이 나의 스트레스를 줄여 주기 때문에 즐겨.
>
> **하나:** 정말 멋진데!

❶ What's the matter?: 슬픔, 불만족, 실망의 원인에 대해 묻기
❷ be stressed about: ~에 대해 스트레스를 받다
❸ Do you know how to + 동사원형 ~? = Can you + 동사원형 ~?
❹ feel better: 기분이 더 좋아지다
❺ I enjoy + (동)명사 ~: 나는 ~하는 것을 즐긴다.(좋아하는 것 말하기) / it=riding my longboard / reduce: 줄이다

**Check(√) True or False**

(3) Hana doesn't know how to ride a longboard.　　　　　　　　T ☐ F ☐

(4) Karl listens to music to reduce his stress.　　　　　　　　　T ☐ F ☐

### Listen & Speak 1 - A - 2

B: ❶People say that we should walk more than 10,000 steps every day to be healthy. I can't count the number of my steps easily.

G: You can use this smartphone app. ❷Do you know how to use it?

B: No. ❸Can you show me?

G: Sure. First, download the app. Then, walk with your smartphone. Later, you can check the number of steps you took.

B: Thank you. ❹I will start using it today.

❶ more than: ~ 이상 / to be: to부정사의 부사적 용법 중 목적 ❷ Do you know how to + 동사원형 ~?: 너는 ~하는 방법을 아니? (능력 여부 묻기) ❸ Can you + 동사원형 ~?: ~해 줄래? ❹ it = a smartphone app

### Listen & Speak 2 - A - 1

G: ❶What do you enjoy doing after school?

B: ❷I enjoy cooking healthy food.

G: ❸Sounds cool. What can you make?

B: I can make salad, Bibimbap, and vegetable juice.

❶ What do you enjoy -ing?: 너는 무엇을 ~하기를 즐기니? (좋아하는 것 묻기) / after school: 방과 후에 ❷ I enjoy -ing ~. 나는 ~하는 것을 즐긴다. (좋아하는 것 말하기) / healthy: 건강에 좋은 ❸ Sounds cool.: 관심을 나타내는 표현이다.

### Listen & Speak 2 - A - 2

B: ❶What do you do on weekends?

G: I take pictures.

B: ❷What kind of pictures do you usually take?

G: ❸I enjoy taking pictures of nature, like trees and flowers. ❹The beautiful pictures reduce my stress.

❶ on weekends: 주말에 ❷ What kind of: 어떤 종류의 ❸ I enjoy -ing ~: 나는 ~하는 것을 즐긴다 / take a picture: 사진을 찍다 / like: ~같은 ❹ reduce one's stress: 스트레스를 줄이다

### Listen & Speak 2 - A - 3

G: Do you have a puppy?

B: Yes. Her name is Coco. I really like her.

G: ❶What do you do with her?

B: I enjoy ❷taking a walk with her. ❸It makes me healthy.

❶ with: ~와 함께 / her = Coco ❷ take a walk: 산책하다 ❸ It = taking a walk with her / make + 목적어 + 형용사: ~을 …하게 만들다 / healthy: 건강한

### Conversation A

B: Tomorrow, I have an English speaking contest. ❶I started preparing for the contest two weeks ago. ❷I enjoy speaking in English, but I am worried about the contest. I cannot sleep well.

❶ start+to부정사[동명사]: ~하기 시작하다 / prepare for: ~을 준비하다 / two weeks ago: 2주 전 ❷ enjoy+동명사: ~하는 것을 즐기다 / be worried about: ~에 대해 걱정하다

### Wrap Up - ❶

B: ❶You look sick. ❷What's the matter?

G: ❸Well, I have a cold.

B: ❹Did you see a doctor?

G: Not yet. ❺Do you know how to get over a cold?

B: Well, I usually drink warm water when I have a cold. It makes me feel better.

G: Sounds good. I will try it.

❶ look+형용사: ~하게 보이다 ❷ What's the matter? = What's wrong? = What's the problem? = What happened? ❸ have a cold: 감기에 걸리다 (=catch[get/take] a cold) ❹ see a doctor: 병원에 가 보다 ❺ get over: 회복하다

### Wrap Up - ❷

B: My family enjoys many activities. My dad enjoys fishing. ❶Early in the morning, he goes to the lake and comes back with some fish. ❷My mom enjoys drawing pictures. ❸She likes to draw beautiful mountains and lakes. My brother and I enjoy playing soccer.

❶ early in the morning: 이른 아침 / come back: 돌아오다 ❷ draw a picture: 그림을 그리다 ❸ lake: 호수

● 다음 우리말과 일치하도록 빈칸에 알맞은 말을 쓰시오.

### Listen & Speak 1-A-1

B: I want to eat _____ _____ . Do you _____ any _____ ?

G: I _____ _____ fresh salad. It _____ me feel _____ .

B: Really? Do you know _____ _____ make it?

G: Yes, it's quite simple. First, _____ many vegetables _____ small pieces. Next, _____ them _____ a bowl. Then, _____ some lemon juice on them. Finally, _____ everything together.

B: That's it? I _____ _____ it.

### Listen & Speak 1-A-2

B: People say that we should walk _____ _____ 10,000 steps every day _____ _____ healthy. I can't _____ the number of my _____ easily.

G: You _____ _____ this smartphone app. Do you know _____ _____ _____ it?

B: No. _____ you _____ me?

G: Sure. First, _____ the app. Then, walk _____ your smartphone. Later, you can _____ the number of steps you took.

B: Thank you. I _____ start _____ it today.

### Listen & Speak 2 - A - 1

G: _____ do you enjoy _____ after school?

B: I _____ _____ healthy food.

G: _____ cool. What _____ you make?

B: I _____ _____ salad, Bibimbap, and vegetable juice.

### Listen & Speak 1-A-1

B: What do you do _____ _____ ?

G: I _____ pictures.

B: _____ _____ of pictures do you usually _____ ?

G: I enjoy _____ pictures _____ nature, _____ trees and flowers. The beautiful pictures _____ my stress.

해석

B: 나는 건강에 좋은 것을 먹고 싶어. 말해 줄 조언이 있니?
G: 나는 신선한 샐러드를 자주 먹어. 그것은 나를 기분 좋게 만들어.
B: 정말? 그것을 어떻게 만드는지 아니?
G: 응. 아주 간단해. 먼저, 많은 채소들을 작은 조각으로 잘라. 다음으로 그것들을 그릇에 담아. 그런 다음, 레몬 주스를 조금 부어. 마지막으로 모든 것을 함께 섞어.
B: 그게 다야? 한번 해 봐야겠다.

B: 사람들은 우리가 건강해지기 위해서 매일 10,000 걸음 이상을 걸어야 한다고 말해. 나는 내 걸음 수를 쉽게 셀 수 없어.
G: 너는 이 스마트폰 앱을 사용할 수 있어. 어떻게 사용하는지 아니?
B: 아니. 내게 보여줄 수 있니?
G: 물론. 먼저 앱을 다운로드해. 그런 다음 스마트폰을 가지고 걸어. 나중에 네가 걸은 걸음 수를 확인할 수 있어.
B: 고마워. 오늘부터 그것을 쓰기 시작해야겠어.

G: 너는 방과 후에 뭐 하는 걸 즐기니?
B: 나는 건강에 좋은 음식을 요리하는 것을 즐겨.
G: 멋지구나. 너는 무엇을 만들 수 있니?
B: 나는 샐러드, 비빔밥 그리고 야채 주스를 만들 수 있어.

B: 너는 주말에 무엇을 하니?
G: 나는 사진을 찍어.
B: 너는 보통 어떤 종류의 사진을 찍니?
G: 나는 나무와 꽃 같은 자연의 사진을 찍는 것을 좋아해. 그 아름다운 사진들은 내 스트레스를 줄여주거든.

## Listen & Speak 2-A-3

G: Do you have a _____?

B: Yes. _____ name is Coco. I _____ like her.

G: What do you do _____ her?

B: I _____ _____ a walk with her. It _____ me _____.

## Conversation A

B: Tomorrow, I _____ an English _____ contest. I started _____ _____ the contest two weeks _____. I enjoy _____ _____ English, but I am worried _____ the contest. I _____ _____ well.

## Conversation B

Karl: Hana, what's the _____?

Hana: Well, I'm _____ _____ the test next week.

Karl: I understand. I _____ my longboard _____ I'm stressed. Do you know _____ _____ _____ a longboard?

Hana: No, I don't.

Karl: Let's _____ _____! I _____ teach you. _____ one foot _____ the board and _____ hard _____ the other.

Hana: _____ this? Wow! This is fun. I _____ _____ already.

Karl: See? I enjoy _____ my longboard _____ it reduces my stress.

Hana: That's great!

## Wrap Up 1

B: You look _____. _____ the matter?

G: Well, I have a _____.

B: Did you _____ a doctor?

G: Not _____. Do you know how to _____ _____ a cold?

B: Well, I usually drink _____ water _____ I have a cold. It _____ me _____ better.

G: Sounds good. I _____ _____ it.

## Wrap Up 2

B: My family _____ many activities. My dad enjoys _____. _____ in the morning, he goes to the lake and _____ _____ with some fish. My mom _____ _____ pictures. She likes _____ beautiful mountains and lakes. My brother and I _____ soccer.

해석

G: 너는 강아지를 기르고 있니?

B: 응. 그녀의 이름은 코코야. 난 코코를 아주 좋아해.

G: 너는 코코와 함께 무엇을 하니?

B: 난 코코와 산책하는 걸 즐겨. 그것은 나를 건강하게 만들어.

B: 내일 영어 말하기 대회가 있어. 나는 2주 전에 대회를 준비하기 시작했어. 나는 영어로 말하는 것을 즐기지만, 난 그 대회가 걱정돼. 나는 잠을 잘 못 자.

Karl: 하나야, 무슨 일 있니?

하나: 음, 다음 주에 있을 시험 때문에 스트레스를 받아.

Karl: 난 이해돼. 나는 스트레스를 받을 때 롱보드를 타. 넌 롱보드를 어떻게 타는지 아니?

하나: 아니, 몰라.

Karl: 나가자! 내가 가르쳐 줄 수 있어. 한 발을 보드 위에 올려놓고 다른 한 발로 세게 밀어.

하나: 이렇게? 와! 이거 재밌다. 벌써 기분이 좋아졌어.

Karl: 봤지? 나는 롱보드를 타는 것이 나의 스트레스를 줄여주기 때문에 즐겨.

하나: 정말 멋진데!

B: 너 아파 보여. 무슨 일 있니?

G: 음, 감기에 걸렸어.

B: 병원에 가봤니?

G: 아직. 넌 감기가 나아지는 방법을 아니?

B: 음, 나는 감기에 걸렸을 때 보통 따뜻한 물을 마셔. 그것은 내 기분을 좋아지게 해.

G: 좋아. 한번 해 볼게.

B: 우리 가족은 많은 활동을 즐겨. 우리 아빠는 낚시를 즐기셔. 이른 아침, 그는 호수에 가셔서 약간의 물고기를 가지고 돌아오셔. 우리 엄마는 그림 그리기를 즐기셔. 그녀는 아름다운 산과 호수를 그리는 것을 좋아하셔. 나의 형과 나는 축구를 즐겨.

**01** 다음 대화의 빈칸에 알맞은 것은?

> A: Do you know _____ healthy juice?
> B: Yes, I do.

① when to make     ② how to make
③ what to make     ④ where to make
⑤ how to do

**02** 다음 대화의 빈칸에 들어갈 말로 적절하지 <u>않은</u> 것은?

> A: Kate, what do you enjoy doing to be healthy?
> B: I enjoy _____.

① fishing     ② jogging
③ playing catch     ④ riding a bike
⑤ playing computer games

**03** 다음 문장과 바꿔 쓸 수 있는 것은?

> Do you know how to fix the watering can?

① Are you fixing the watering can?
② Can you fix the watering can?
③ Can I fix the watering can?
④ May I fix the watering can?
⑤ Did you fix the watering can?

**04** 다음 대화의 ⓐ~ⓓ를 자연스러운 대화가 되도록 바르게 배열하시오.

> ⓐ What do you do with her?
> ⓑ Yes. Her name is Coco. I really like her.
> ⓒ Do you have a puppy?
> ⓓ I enjoy taking a walk with her. It makes me healthy.

➡ _____

> healthy 건강한

> take a walk 산책하다

[01~05] 다음 대화를 읽고, 물음에 답하시오.

Karl: Hana, what's the matter?

Hana: Well, I'm stressed ___ⓐ___ the test next week. (①)

Karl: I understand. I ride my longboard when I'm stressed. Do you know how ⓑride a longboard?

Hana: No, I don't. (②)

Karl: Let's go out! I can teach you. (③) Put one foot on the board and push hard ___ⓒ___ the other. (④)

Hana: Like this? Wow! This is fun. (⑤)

Karl: See? I enjoy ⓓride my longboard because ⓔit reduces my stress.

Hana: That's great!

**01** 위 대화의 ①~⑤ 중 다음 문장이 들어갈 알맞은 곳은?

> I feel better already.

①　　　②　　　③　　　④　　　⑤

**02** 위 대화의 빈칸 ⓐ와 ⓒ에 알맞은 말이 바르게 짝지어진 것은?

① for – to
② of – with
③ on – from
④ from – into
⑤ about – with

**서답형**

**03** 위 대화의 밑줄 친 ⓑ와 ⓓ를 알맞은 형태로 각각 고쳐 쓰시오.

ⓑ _____　ⓓ _____

**서답형**

**04** 위 대화의 밑줄 친 ⓔ가 가리키는 것을 영어로 쓰시오.

➡ _____

**05** 위 대화를 읽고, 답할 수 <u>없는</u> 질문은?

① Why is Hana stressed?
② What does Hana do when she's stressed?
③ Did Hana know how to ride a longboard?
④ Does Karl teach Hana how to ride a longboard?
⑤ Why does Karl enjoy riding his longboard?

[06~08] 다음 대화를 읽고, 물음에 답하시오.

B: You look sick. ⓐWhat's the matter?

G: Well, I have a cold.

B: Did you see a doctor?

G: Not yet. ⓑDo you know how to get over a cold?

B: Well, I usually drink warm water when I have a cold. ⓒIt makes me feel better.

G: Sounds good. I will try it.

**06** 위 대화의 밑줄 친 ⓐ와 바꿔 쓸 수 <u>없는</u> 것은?

① What's wrong?
② What happened?
③ How have you been?
④ What's the problem?
⑤ Is there something wrong?

**07** 위 대화의 밑줄 친 ⓑ의 의도로 알맞은 것은?

① 제안하기　　　② 주제 정하기

③ 능력 여부 묻기　　④ 위로하기

⑤ 반문하기

**서답형**

**08** 위 대화의 밑줄 친 ⓒ가 의미하는 것을 우리말로 쓰시오.

➡ _____

[09~11] 다음 대화를 읽고, 물음에 답하시오.

> B: ⓐI want to eat healthy something. Do you have any advice?
> G: I often eat fresh salad. ⓑIt makes me feel good.
> B: Really? ⓒDo you know how to make it?
> G: Yes, it's quite simple. First, cut many vegetables into small pieces. Next, put them into a bowl. Then, pour some lemon juice on them. Finally, mix everything together.
> B: That's it? I should try it.

**서답형**

**09** 위 대화의 밑줄 친 ⓐ에서 어법상 어색한 부분을 고쳐 문장을 다시 쓰시오.

➡ _____

**서답형**

**10** 위 대화의 밑줄 친 ⓑ가 의미하는 것을 영어로 쓰시오.

➡ _____

**11** 위 대화의 밑줄 친 ⓒ와 의미가 같은 문장은? (2개)

① Can you make it?

② Why don't you make it?

③ Are you good at making it?

④ When did you make it?

⑤ Are you interested in cooking?

[12~14] 다음 글을 읽고, 물음에 답하시오.

> B: Tomorrow, I have an English speaking contest. I started preparing ___ⓐ___ the contest two weeks ago. I enjoy speaking in English, ___ⓑ___ I am worried ___ⓒ___ the contest. I cannot sleep well.

**12** 위 글의 빈칸 ⓐ와 ⓒ에 알맞은 말이 바르게 짝지어진 것은?

① at – of　　　② for – about

③ with – for　　④ of – at

⑤ from – over

**13** 위 글의 빈칸 ⓑ에 알맞은 것은?

① so　　　② but

③ and　　　④ for

⑤ or

**14** 위 글의 글쓴이의 심경으로 알맞은 것은?

① bored　　　② excited

③ stressed　　④ pleased

⑤ happy

[01~04] 다음 대화를 읽고, 물음에 답하시오.

B: People say that we should walk more than 10,000 steps every day to be healthy. I can't count the number of my steps easily.

G: You can use this smartphone ⓐ . ⓑDo you know how to use it?

B: No. Can you show me?

G: Sure. First, download the ⓒ . Then, walk with your smartphone. Later, you can check the number of steps you took.

**01** How many steps do people say we should walk every day to be healthy? Answer in English.

➡ _____

**02** 위 대화의 밑줄 친 ⓑ를 해석하고, 이와 바꿔 쓸 수 있는 표현을 2개 쓰시오.

(1) 해석: _____

(2) 같은 표현: _____

_____

**03** 위 대화의 빈칸 ⓐ와 ⓒ에 공통으로 들어갈 단어를 다음 영영풀이를 참조하여 쓰시오. (세 글자)

> a computer program designed to do a particular job, especially one that you can use on a smartphone

➡ _____

**04** What is the first step in using the smartphone app? Answer in English.

➡ _____

[05~08] 다음 대화를 읽고, 물음에 답하시오.

B: What do you do on weekends?

G: I take pictures.

B: What kind of pictures do you usually take?

G: I enjoy ⓐtake pictures of nature, ⓑlike trees and flowers. The beautiful pictures _____ ⓒ my stress.

**05** 위 대화의 밑줄 친 ⓐ를 알맞은 형태로 고쳐 쓰시오.

➡ _____

**06** What does the girl enjoy doing? Answer in English.

➡ _____

**07** 위 대화의 밑줄 친 ⓑ를 두 단어로 바꿔 쓰시오.

➡ _____

**08** 위 대화의 빈칸 ⓒ에 다음 영영풀이에 해당하는 단어를 주어진 글자로 시작하여 쓰시오

> to make something smaller in size, amount, number, etc.

➡ r_____

# Grammar

## ① 사역동사

> - It will **make** your eyes **feel** more comfortable. 그것은 너의 눈을 더 편안하게 할 것이다.
> - I will **let** you **ride** my new longboard. 나는 네가 나의 새 롱보드를 타게 해 줄게.
> - The massage will **help** you **(to) feel** better. 마사지는 너의 기분이 좋아지도록 도울 것이다.

■ 사역동사 make, have, let은 「사역동사+목적어+목적격 보어(동사원형)」의 형태로 '(목적어)에게 ~하게 하다'라는 의미로 목적어의 행동을 설명한다.

　① let: ~ 하도록 허락하다 / I will **let** you **go**. 네가 가도록 허락해 줄게.

　② have: ~ 하도록 하다 / I will **have** my brother **clean** my room. 나는 내 남동생이 내 방을 치우도록 할 것이다.

　③ make: ~ 하게 시키다 / My mom **makes** me **do** the dishes. 엄마는 내가 설거지를 하도록 시킨다.

■ help는 목적격 보어로 동사원형이나 to부정사 둘 다 사용할 수 있다.

　- I **helped** Julia **(to) cook** breakfast for the family. 나는 Julia가 가족을 위해 아침식사를 요리하는 것을 도왔다.

■ get은 목적격 보어로 to부정사를 사용한다.

　- He **got** our dreams **to come** true. 그는 우리의 꿈이 실현되게 했다.

■ have는 목적어와 목적격 보어가 능동 관계이면 동사원형을, 수동 관계이면 과거분사형을 쓴다.

　- I **had** him **repair** my computer. 나는 그에게 내 컴퓨터를 고치게 했다.

　- I **had** my computer **repaired**. 나는 내 컴퓨터를 수리시켰다.

## 핵심 Check

1. 다음 괄호 안에서 알맞은 것을 고르시오.

　⑴ The heat makes the ice ( melt / to melt ).

　⑵ Parents often don't let their children ( doing / do ) what they want.

　⑶ The secretary had the phone ( rings / ring ) at lunchtime.

　⑷ He got her ( come / to come ) to the meeting.

## ② 조건을 나타내는 접속사 if

- **If** you massage yourself and stretch every day, you will feel healthier.
  매일 마사지를 하고 스트레칭을 하면, 너는 더 건강하게 느껴질 것이다.

- **If** it is sunny tomorrow, we can go for a bike ride.
  내일 날씨가 맑으면, 우리는 자전거를 타러 갈 수 있다.

- He will get sick **if** he doesn't stop eating fast food.
  패스트푸드 먹는 것을 멈추지 않으면, 그는 병에 걸릴 것이다.

■ 접속사 if는 두 개의 절을 연결하는 접속사이며, '만약 ~하면'이라는 의미로 조건을 나타낸다. if가 이끄는 종속절은 주절의 앞이나 뒤에 올 수 있다.

- **If** we take a taxi, we can get there in ten minutes.
  만약 우리가 택시를 타면, 우리는 그곳에 10분 후에 도착할 수 있다.

- You can win the contest **if** you practice hard. 만약 네가 열심히 연습한다면, 너는 대회에서 우승을 할 수 있다.

■ 조건을 나타내는 접속사 if가 이끄는 절에서는 미래의 일을 나타내는 경우에도 동사는 현재시제를 쓴다.

- **If** it will be sunny tomorrow, we will play soccer. (X)

- **If** it **is** sunny tomorrow, we will play soccer. (○) 만약 내일 날씨가 맑으면, 우리는 축구를 할 것이다.

■ '만약 ~하지 않는다면'이라는 의미의 「if+주어+don't[doesn't]+동사원형 ~」은 「unless+주어+동사의 현재형 ~」으로 바꿔 쓸 수 있다.

- **If** he does**n't** study hard, he can't get a high score.
  = **Unless** he studies hard, he can't get a high score.
  만일 그가 열심히 공부하지 않는다면, 그는 높은 점수를 얻을 수 없다.

### 핵심 Check

2. 다음 괄호 안에서 알맞은 것을 고르시오.

(1) If I see her, I ( give / will give ) it to her.

(2) ( If / Because ) you arrive early, you will get a good seat.

(3) If she ( takes / will take ) the subway, she will be there on time.

(4) Unless you ( drink / don't drink ) some water, you will feel very thirsty.

**01** 다음 우리말과 같도록 주어진 단어들을 바르게 배열하시오.

go to a movie 영화 보러 가다

(1) 프랑스에 간다면, 나는 에펠탑을 방문할 거야. (France / I / to / if / go)

➡ _____, I will visit the Eiffel Tower.

(2) 내일 비가 오면 난 영화 보러 갈 거야. (rains, if, tomorrow, it)

➡ _____, I will go to a movie.

**02** 다음 문장에서 어법상 어색한 부분을 찾아 바르게 고쳐 쓰시오.

(1) The dress makes her to look slim.

_____ ➡ _____

(2) She had her son to write the teacher a letter.

_____ ➡ _____

(3) She won't let me to go there.

_____ ➡ _____

**03** 다음 두 문장이 같은 뜻이 되도록 빈칸에 알맞은 말을 쓰시오.

leave 떠나다, 출발하다
miss 놓치다

(1) If you don't leave now, you will miss the school bus.

= _____ _____ _____ now, you will miss the school bus.

(2) Unless it rains tomorrow, I will go camping.

= _____ _____ _____ _____ tomorrow, I will go camping.

**04** 다음 주어진 문장을 〈보기〉와 같이 바꾸어 쓸 때, 빈칸에 알맞은 말을 쓰시오.

┌─ 보기 ─┐

I cleaned my hands.

➡ My teacher made me clean my hands.

(1) I went out after dinner.

➡ My mother let _____.

(2) The children played outside.

➡ He had _____.

(3) The bear stood on the ball.

➡ Mr. Brown made _____.

**01** 다음 문장의 빈칸에 알맞은 것은?

> She had me _____ my work.

① to do
② starting
③ finish
④ done
⑤ be finished

**02** 다음 빈칸에 공통으로 알맞은 것은?

> • I'm not going to work tomorrow _____
>   I don't feel well.
> • I'm not sure _____ he will enter the
>   speech contest.

① if
② so
③ that
④ since
⑤ whether

**03** 다음 문장의 빈칸에 알맞지 <u>않은</u> 것은?

> Eating chocolate can make you _____.

① fat
② happy
③ smile
④ feel better
⑤ feeling good

**04** 다음 문장의 빈칸에 알맞은 것은?

> If you pass the test, you _____ study
> more.

① has to
② don't
③ had to
④ were to
⑤ won't have to

서답형
**05** 다음 문장에서 어법상 <u>어색한</u> 부분을 찾아 바르게 고쳐 쓰시오.

> Lisa makes me to do her homework.

_____ ➡ _____

**06** 다음 문장의 빈칸에 알맞은 것은?

> If you _____ straight two blocks, you
> will find our school.

① will go
② were
③ go
④ must be
⑤ went

서답형
**07** 다음 주어진 어구를 이용하여 우리말을 영어로 옮기시오.
(필요시 어형 변경할 것)

> 나는 엄마가 설거지하시는 것을 도와 드렸다.
> (do the dishes)

➡ _____

중요
**08** 다음 우리말과 같도록 할 때, 빈칸에 알맞은 것은?

> 만약 내일 그가 오지 않으면, 나는 매우 슬플 것
> 이다.
> = _____, I will feel very sad.

① If he comes tomorrow
② If he won't come tomorrow
③ If he doesn't come tomorrow
④ Unless he won't come tomorrow
⑤ Unless he doesn't come tomorrow

**09** 다음 문장의 빈칸에 알맞지 <u>않은</u> 것은?

> My mother _____ me clean the room.

① let  ② had

③ wanted  ④ made

⑤ helped

**10** 다음 두 문장의 의미가 같도록 빈칸에 알맞은 것은?

> If you don't eat breakfast, you can't focus on your studies.
> = _____ you eat breakfast, you can't focus on your studies.

① When  ② While

③ Because  ④ Unless

⑤ Although

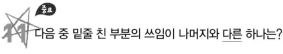

**11** 다음 중 밑줄 친 부분의 쓰임이 나머지와 <u>다른</u> 하나는?

① I <u>made</u> him wash the dishes.

② Please <u>make</u> me laugh.

③ I <u>made</u> him carry the box.

④ My mom <u>made</u> me some snacks.

⑤ His advice <u>made</u> me do the work.

서답형

**12** 다음 문장에서 어법상 어색한 부분을 찾아 바르게 고쳐 쓰시오.

> If it will rain tomorrow, I will not go there, either.

_____ ➡ _____

**13** 다음 문장의 빈칸에 알맞은 것은?

> If it _____, we'll play soccer outside.

① won't rain  ② don't rain

③ doesn't rain  ④ didn't rain

⑤ hadn't rained

서답형

**14** 다음 우리말과 일치하도록 주어진 표현을 이용하여 영작하시오.

> 그의 미소는 항상 나를 미소 짓게 만든다.
> (make)

➡ _____

**15** 다음 빈칸에 공통으로 알맞은 것은?

> • I'll _____ him to see a doctor.
> • How can I _____ him to help me?

① let  ② make

③ get  ④ have

⑤ help

**16** 다음 세 문장의 뜻이 같도록 빈칸에 들어갈 말을 순서대로 짝지은 것은?

> Be careful, or you'll be in danger.
> = _____ you are careful, you'll be in danger.
> = _____ you are careful, you won't be in danger.

① If – If  ② If – Unless

③ Unless – If  ④ As – If

⑤ Unless – As

**17** 다음 빈칸에 알맞은 말이 바르게 짝지어진 것은?

> Her mother _____ the girl _____ care of her little sister.

① let – to take  ② had – take
③ helped – taking  ④ had – to take
⑤ made – taking

**서답형**

**18** 다음 두 문장이 같은 뜻이 되도록 빈칸에 알맞은 말을 쓰시오.

> If you don't stop shouting, they will call the police.
> = Unless _____ _____ shouting, they will call the police.

**중요**

**19** 다음 밑줄 친 부분 중 어법상 어색한 것은?

① She made me <u>come</u> early.
② My sister let me <u>to go</u> home early.
③ Sumi asked me <u>to call</u> her right now.
④ I will make her <u>go</u> to the party.
⑤ My mother helped me <u>do</u> my homework.

**서답형**

**20** 다음 우리말과 같도록 주어진 단어를 바르게 배열하여 문장을 완성하시오.

> Judy는 남동생에게 수학 공부를 하도록 시킨다.
> (makes / brother / study / her / math / Judy)

➡ _____

**중요**

**21** 다음 중 어법상 어색한 것은?

① If he helps me, I can carry this easily.
② If you don't have breakfast, you will feel hungry soon.
③ If you will leave now, you can get there on time.
④ If she makes a lot of money, she will buy a car.
⑤ If school finishes early today, we'll go to the movies.

**서답형**

**22** 다음 두 문장의 의미가 같도록 빈칸에 알맞은 말을 쓰시오.

> If you don't like the food, you don't have to pay.
> = _____, you don't have to pay.

**서답형**

**23** 다음 우리말과 일치하도록 주어진 어구를 바르게 배열하시오.

> 아버지는 내가 무거운 가방 드는 것을 도와 주셨다.
> (me / heavy / my father / bag / carry / helped / the)

➡ _____

**24** 다음 대화의 밑줄 친 부분과 쓰임이 같은 것은?

> A: Why do you like bright colors?
> B: Because they <u>make</u> me feel happy.

① He <u>made</u> me a toy boat.
② She <u>made</u> us coffee.
③ Wine is <u>made</u> from grapes.
④ She <u>makes</u> her own clothes.
⑤ My mom <u>made</u> me stop playing games.

**01** 다음 빈칸에 알맞은 말을 〈보기〉에서 골라 쓰시오. (필요시 어형을 바꿀 것)

┌─ 보기 ─┐
help   get   carry   show
└────────┘

(1) He helped me _____ the heavy bag.

(2) I couldn't _____ the car to start this morning.

(3) Please let me _____ you with your homework.

(4) I have lots of pictures _____ _____ you.

**02** 다음 빈칸에 알맞은 말을 〈보기〉에서 골라 쓰시오. (문장의 앞에 오는 경우 대문자로 쓰시오.)

┌─ 보기 ─┐
when   if   unless
└────────┘

(1) _____ you don't leave now, you will miss the last train.

(2) We had a big party _____ Sarah came home.

(3) _____ you start now, you'll be late for the meeting.

**03** 다음 문장에서 어법상 어색한 부분을 찾아 바르게 고쳐 쓰시오.

(1) I let Tom to explain why he was late.

_____ ➡ _____

(2) The hot milk will make you fell asleep easily.

_____ ➡ _____

(3) The teacher had his students played outside.

_____ ➡ _____

**04** 접속사 if를 사용하여 다음 두 문장을 한 문장으로 고쳐 쓰시오. (단, 종속절이 주절의 앞에 오는 문장으로 바꿀 것)

(1) I am late for class. My teacher gets very angry.

➡ _____

(2) The weather is nice. I always walk to school.

➡ _____

(3) It rains on weekends. We watch TV.

➡ _____

[05~06] 다음 주어진 말을 이용하여 우리말을 영작하시오.

**05**
┌──────────────────────────────┐
│ 엄마는 내가 밤에 밖에 나가는 것을 허락하지 않 │
│ 으신다. (let, night)           │
└──────────────────────────────┘

➡ _____

**06**
┌──────────────────────────────┐
│ 나는 남동생에게 TV를 끄도록 했다.  │
│ (make, turn)                  │
└──────────────────────────────┘

➡ _____

**07** 다음 우리말과 일치하도록 빈칸에 알맞은 말을 넣어 문장을 완성하시오.

(1) 네가 만일 열심히 공부한다면, 너는 그 시험에 합격할 거야.

➡ _____, you'll pass the exam.

(2) 만일 내일 비가 오면 우리는 집에 있을 것이다.

➡ _____ tomorrow, we'll stay home.

**08** 다음 문장에서 어법상 어색한 부분을 찾아 바르게 고쳐 문장을 다시 쓰시오.

(1) Finally, the police let the thief goes.

➡ _____

(2) Love makes people to do unusual things.

➡ _____

(3) I got my dog wear strange glasses.

➡ _____

(4) My English teacher helps us writing a diary every day.

➡ _____

**09** 다음 문장에서 어법상 어색한 것을 찾아 바르게 고쳐 쓰시오.

(1) You'll be happy if you'll pass the exam.

_____ ➡ _____

(2) If I won't be free tomorrow, I'll see you on Saturday.

_____ ➡ _____

**10** 다음 〈보기〉와 같이 문장을 바꿔 쓰시오. (단, make, let을 사용할 것)

┌─ 보기 ─
My mom: Clean your room.
➡ My mom made me clean my room.
└─

(1) My parents: Play computer games every Friday.

➡ _____

(2) My teacher: Wash your hands.

➡ _____

(3) My mom: Don't go out.

➡ _____

**11** 다음 문장에서 어법상 어색한 부분을 바르게 고쳐서 문장을 다시 쓰시오.

(1) If it will rain tomorrow, we won't go hiking.

➡ _____

(2) Unless you don't hurry, you will miss the train.

➡ _____

**12** 다음 우리말과 일치하도록 주어진 어구를 바르게 배열하시오.

(1) Eddie는 남동생에게 그의 장난감을 갖고 놀게 한다. (lets / play / his toys / Eddie / his brother / with)

➡ _____

(2) 그녀는 아이들에게 영어 공부를 시킨다.
(English / makes / she / children / study / her)

➡ _____

(3) 아빠는 우리에게 일요일마다 아침을 요리하게 한다. (breakfast / Dad / us / Sundays / cook / on / has)

➡ _____

**13** 다음 주어진 단어를 바르게 배열하여 문장을 완성하시오.

┌─────────────────────────
(she / will / if / study / the exam / , / she / fail / doesn't / hard)
└─────────────────────────

➡ _____

# Reading

## Loosen Up!

At school you sit for many hours. Do you get tired? Why don't you
massage yourself and stretch?

Let's begin with the eyes. Close your eyes and massage them softly
with your fingers. It will relax your eyes. When you finish, cover your
eyes with your hands to block out the light. It will make your eyes feel
more comfortable.

Next, massage your neck. Put your fingers on the back of your neck.
Draw small circles with your fingers to massage your neck. Massage
from top to bottom. The massage will help you feel better.

loosen up 몸을 풀어 주다
massage 마사지하다
stretch 스트레칭하다
softly 부드럽게
finger 손가락
relax 편안하게 하다
finish 끝나다
cover 가리다
comfortable 편안한
neck 목
back 뒤쪽, 뒷부분
draw 그리다
circle 원

 확인문제

● 다음 문장이 본문의 내용과 일치하면 T, 일치하지 않으면 F를 쓰시오.

1 To massage your eyes softly with your fingers will relax your eyes.

2 We cover our eyes with our arms to block out the light.

3 We draw small circles with our fingers to massage our neck.

4 The neck massage will help you feel better.

Let's work on your waist. Team up with a friend. Stand close to each
other and face your partner. Hold each other's wrists. Slowly stretch
your head and body backward. Hold that position for three seconds.
Then, slowly pull each other to a standing position. You and your
partner should move at the same speed. If you don't, both of you will
fall!

Place the top of your right foot on the desk behind you. Then, slowly
bend your left leg and lower yourself. Hold it for a few seconds and
slowly straighten up. This position will loosen up your right leg.
Switch your legs and repeat the exercise.

How do you feel now? If you massage yourself and stretch every day,
you will feel healthier. Also, you can focus on your studies better.

waist 허리
close 가까이
face ~을 마주보다
slowly 천천히
wrist 손목
position 자세
pull 끌어당기다
fall 넘어지다
behind ~ 뒤에
bend 구부리다
lower 낮추다
hold 유지하다
switch 바꾸다
repeat 반복하다
exercise 운동
healthy 건강한
study 공부

**확인문제**

● 다음 문장이 본문의 내용과 일치하면 T, 일치하지 않으면 F를 쓰시오.

1  To work on your waist, you have to team up with a friend. ☐

2  If two people move at the same speed, they will fall. ☐

3  After we place the top of our right foot on the desk behind us, we slowly bend our right leg and lower ourselves. ☐

4  If you massage yourself and stretch every day, you can focus on your studies better. ☐

● 우리말을 참고하여 빈칸에 알맞은 말을 쓰시오.

**1** _____ school you sit _____ many hours.

**2** Do you _____ _____ ?

**3** _____ _____ you massage _____ and stretch?

**4** _____ begin _____ the eyes.

**5** _____ your eyes and _____ them softly _____ your fingers.

**6** It _____ _____ your eyes.

**7** _____ you finish, _____ your eyes _____ your hands to _____ _____ the light.

**8** It will _____ your eyes _____ more _____ .

**9** Next, _____ your neck.

**10** _____ your fingers _____ the back of your neck.

**11** _____ small circles _____ your fingers _____ massage your neck.

**12** Massage _____ top _____ bottom.

**13** The massage will _____ you _____ better.

**14** _____ work on your _____ .

**15** _____ with a friend.

**1** 학교에서 너는 오랜 시간에 걸쳐 앉아 있다.

**2** 여러분은 피곤한가?

**3** 마사지와 스트레칭을 하는 게 어떤가?

**4** 눈부터 시작하자.

**5** 눈을 감고 손가락으로 눈을 부드럽게 마사지해라.

**6** 그것은 여러분의 눈을 편안하게 해줄 것이다.

**7** 끝나면, 빛을 차단하기 위해 손으로 눈을 가려라.

**8** 그것은 여러분의 눈을 더 편안하게 해줄 것이다.

**9** 다음으로, 여러분의 목을 마사지해라.

**10** 여러분의 목 뒤에 손가락을 대라.

**11** 여러분의 목을 마사지하기 위해 손가락으로 작은 원을 그려라.

**12** 위에서 아래로 마사지해라.

**13** 마사지는 여러분의 기분이 좋아지도록 도울 것이다.

**14** 허리 운동을 하자.

**15** 친구와 짝을 이루어라.

**16** Stand close to _____ _____ and _____ your partner.

**17** _____ each other's wrists.

**18** Slowly _____ your head and body _____.

**19** _____ that position _____ three seconds.

**20** Then, slowly _____ each other _____ a standing position.

**21** You and _____ partner should move _____ the same speed.

**22** _____ you don't, _____ _____ you will fall!

**23** _____ the top of your right foot _____ the desk _____ you.

**24** Then, slowly _____ your left leg and _____ yourself.

**25** _____ it for _____ _____ seconds and slowly straighten _____.

**26** This position will _____ _____ your right leg.

**27** _____ your legs and _____ the exercise.

**28** _____ do you _____ now?

**29** If you _____ yourself and _____ every day, you will _____.

**30** Also, you can _____ _____ your studies _____.

**16** 서로 가까이 서서 여러분의 파트너를 마주 보아라.

**17** 서로의 손목을 잡아라.

**18** 천천히 여러분의 머리와 몸을 뒤로 뻗어라.

**19** 3초 동안 그 자세를 유지해라.

**20** 그리고 나서, 천천히 서로 선 자세로 끌어 당겨라.

**21** 너와 너의 파트너는 같은 속도로 움직여야 한다.

**22** 그렇지 않으면, 너희 둘 다 넘어질 것이다!

**23** 여러분의 뒤에 있는 책상 위에 오른쪽 발등을 올려놓아라.

**24** 그리고 나서, 천천히 왼쪽 다리를 구부리고 몸을 낮추어라.

**25** 몇 초 동안 그 자세를 유지하다가 천천히 몸을 펴라.

**26** 이 자세는 여러분의 오른쪽 다리를 풀어 줄 것이다.

**27** 다리를 바꿔서 운동을 반복해라.

**28** 지금 기분이 어떤가?

**29** 매일 마사지와 스트레칭을 하면, 여러분은 더 건강해지는 것을 느낄 것이다.

**30** 또한, 여러분은 공부에 더 집중할 수 있을 것이다.

● 우리말을 참고하여 본문을 영작하시오.

**1** 학교에서 여러분은 오랜 시간에 걸쳐 앉아 있다.

➡ _____

**2** 여러분은 피곤한가?

➡ _____

**3** 마사지와 스트레칭을 하는 게 어떤가?

➡ _____

**4** 눈부터 시작하자.

➡ _____

**5** 눈을 감고 손가락으로 눈을 부드럽게 마사지해라.

➡ _____

**6** 그것은 여러분의 눈을 편안하게 해줄 것이다.

➡ _____

**7** 끝나면, 빛을 차단하기 위해 손으로 눈을 가려라.

➡ _____

**8** 그것은 여러분의 눈을 더 편안하게 해줄 것이다.

➡ _____

**9** 다음으로, 여러분의 목을 마사지해라.

➡ _____

**10** 여러분의 목 뒤에 손가락을 대라.

➡ _____

**11** 여러분의 목을 마사지하기 위해 손가락으로 작은 원을 그려라.

➡ _____

**12** 위에서 아래로 마사지해라.

➡ _____

**13** 마사지는 여러분의 기분이 좋아지도록 도울 것이다.

➡ _____

**14** 허리 운동을 하자.

➡ _____

**15** 친구와 짝을 이루어라.

➡ _____

**16** 서로 가까이 서서 여러분의 파트너를 마주 보아라.

➡ _____

**17** 서로의 손목을 잡아라.

➡ _____

**18** 천천히 여러분의 머리와 몸을 뒤로 뻗어라.

➡ _____

**19** 3초 동안 그 자세를 유지해라.

➡ _____

**20** 그러고 나서, 천천히 서로 선 자세로 끌어 당겨라.

➡ _____

**21** 너와 너의 파트너는 같은 속도로 움직여야 한다.

➡ _____

**22** 그렇지 않으면, 너희 둘 다 넘어질 것이다!

➡ _____

**23** 여러분의 뒤에 있는 책상 위에 오른쪽 발등을 올려놓아라.

➡ _____

**24** 그러고 나서, 천천히 왼쪽 다리를 구부리고 몸을 낮추어라.

➡ _____

**25** 몇 초 동안 그 자세를 유지하다가 천천히 몸을 펴라.

➡ _____

**26** 이 자세는 여러분의 오른쪽 다리를 풀어 줄 것이다.

➡ _____

**27** 다리를 바꿔서 운동을 반복해라.

➡ _____

**28** 지금 기분이 어떤가?

➡ _____

**29** 매일 마사지와 스트레칭을 하면, 여러분은 더 건강해지는 것을 느낄 것이다.

➡ _____

**30** 또한, 여러분은 공부에 더 집중할 수 있을 것이다.

➡ _____

[01~05] 다음 글을 읽고, 물음에 답하시오.

At school you sit ⓐ_____ many hours. Do you ___ⓑ___ tired? Why don't you massage yourself and stretch?

Let's begin with the eyes. Close your eyes and massage ⓒthem softly with your fingers. It will relax your eyes. When you finish, cover your eyes with your hands to block _____ⓓ_____ the light. ⓔIt will make your eyes feel more comfortable.

**01** 위 글의 빈칸 ⓐ와 ⓓ에 알맞은 말이 바르게 짝지어진 것은?

① in – up      ② by – off
③ for – out      ④ over – into
⑤ during – over

**02** 위 글의 빈칸 ⓑ에 알맞은 것은?

① go     ② get     ③ put
④ take     ⑤ have

서답형
**03** 위 글의 밑줄 친 ⓒ가 가리키는 것을 찾아 영어로 쓰시오.

➡ _____

서답형
**04** 위 글에서 다음 영영풀이에 해당하는 단어를 찾아 쓰시오.

> to put your arms, legs, etc., in positions that make the muscles long and tight

➡ _____

**05** 위 글의 밑줄 친 ⓔIt이 의미하는 것은?

① 스트레칭을 하는 것
② 눈을 감는 것
③ 손으로 눈을 비비는 것
④ 손가락으로 눈을 마사지하는 것
⑤ 빛을 차단하기 위해 손으로 눈을 가리는 것

[06~10] 다음 글을 읽고, 물음에 답하시오.

Let's work on your waist. Team up with a friend. Stand close to each other and ⓐface your partner. Hold each other's wrists. Slowly stretch your head and body backward. Hold that position ___ⓑ___ three seconds. Then, slowly pull each other to a standing _____ⓒ_____. You and your partner should move at the same speed. _____ⓓ_____ you don't, both ___ⓔ___ you will fall!

**06** 위 글의 밑줄 친 ⓐ와 쓰임이 같은 것은?

① She looks thin in the face.
② She'll face with a difficult decision.
③ I turned the chair to face him.
④ The man is wiping his face.
⑤ The birds build their nests in the rock face.

서답형
**07** 위 글의 빈칸 ⓑ와 ⓔ에 알맞은 말을 쓰시오.

ⓑ _____     ⓔ _____

**08** 위 글의 빈칸 ⓒ에 다음 영영풀이에 해당하는 단어를 쓰시오.

> the way someone stands, sits, or lies down

➡ _____

**09** 위 글의 빈칸 ⓓ에 알맞은 것은?

① As    ② If
③ That    ④ While
⑤ When

**10** 위 글의 내용과 일치하지 <u>않는</u> 것은?

① 친구와 함께 협력한다.
② 서로 가까이 서서 파트너를 마주 본다.
③ 서로의 손목을 잡는다.
④ 천천히 머리와 몸을 뒤로 뻗는다.
⑤ 두 사람이 같은 속도로 움직이면 둘 다 넘어진다.

[11~15] 다음 글을 읽고, 물음에 답하시오.

①Place the top of your right foot on the desk behind you. Then, ②slowly ⓐbend your left leg and lower ③itself. Hold it ④for a few seconds and ⓑslow straighten ____ ⓒ ____. This position will loosen ____ ⓓ ____ your right leg. Switch your legs and ⑤repeat the exercise.

**11** 위 글의 밑줄 친 ①~⑤ 중 어법상 <u>틀린</u> 것은?

①    ②    ③    ④    ⑤

**12** 위 글의 밑줄 친 ⓐ의 영영풀이로 알맞은 것은?

① to add something to something else
② to change or replace something with another thing
③ to move your body so that it is not straight
④ to put something or someone in a particular place or position
⑤ to extend your arm, leg, etc., in order to reach something

**13** 위 글의 밑줄 친 ⓑ를 알맞은 형태로 고쳐 쓰시오.

➡ _____

**14** 위 글의 빈칸 ⓒ와 ⓓ에 공통으로 알맞은 것은?

① on    ② out
③ off    ④ up
⑤ over

**15** 위 글의 다리를 풀어 주는 방법을 순서대로 배열하시오.

> ⓐ 다리를 구부리고 몸을 낮춘 상태로 몇 초 동안 유지한다.
> ⓑ 뒤에 있는 책상 위에 오른쪽 발의 윗부분을 올려놓는다.
> ⓒ 천천히 왼쪽 다리를 구부리고 몸을 낮춘다.

➡ _____

[16~20] 다음 글을 읽고, 물음에 답하시오.

> Let's begin with the eyes. Close your eyes and massage them ⓐsoft with your fingers. ⓑIt will relax your eyes. When you finish, _____ⓒ_____ your eyes with your hands ⓓblock out the light. ⓔ그것은 너의 눈을 더 편안하게 해줄 것이다.

**서답형**

**16** 위 글의 밑줄 친 ⓐ를 알맞은 형태로 고쳐 쓰시오.

➡ _____

**서답형**

**17** 위 글의 밑줄 친 ⓑIt이 가리키는 것을 우리말로 쓰시오.

➡ _____

**18** 문맥상 위 글의 빈칸 ⓒ에 알맞은 것은?

① open      ② rub
③ cover      ④ close
⑤ massage

**19** 위 글의 밑줄 친 ⓓ의 형태로 알맞은 것은?

① block      ② blocks
③ blocking      ④ to block
⑤ to blocking

**서답형**

**20** 위 글의 밑줄 친 ⓔ의 우리말에 맞게 주어진 어구를 이용하여 문장을 완성하시오.

> It will _____.

[21~23] 다음 글을 읽고, 물음에 답하시오.

> Next, massage your neck. ___ⓐ___ your fingers on the back of your neck. ___ⓑ___ small circles with your fingers ⓒto massage your neck. ___ⓓ___ from top to bottom. ⓔThe massage will help you feeling better.

**21** 위 글의 빈칸 ⓐ, ⓑ, ⓓ에 알맞은 말이 바르게 짝지어진 것은?

① Draw – Massage – Put
② Put – Draw – Massage
③ Massage – Put – Draw
④ Draw – Put – Massage
⑤ Put – Massage – Draw

**중요**

**22** 위 글의 밑줄 친 ⓒ와 쓰임이 같은 것은?

① The boy wants to drink juice.
② He loves to play outside.
③ She dressed up to meet her boyfriend.
④ To swim in this river is dangerous.
⑤ My plan is to travel around Thailand.

**서답형**

**23** 위 글의 밑줄 친 ⓔ에서 어법상 틀린 부분을 찾아 바르게 고쳐 쓰시오.

_____ ➡ _____

**[24~27]** 다음 글을 읽고, 물음에 답하시오.

Let's work on your ____ⓐ____ . Team up with a friend. ①Stand close to each other and face your partner. ②Hold each other's wrists. Slowly stretch your head and body ③forward. ④Hold that position for three ⓑ seconds. Then, slowly ⑤pull each other to a standing position. You and your partner ____ⓒ____ move at the same speed. If you don't, both of you ____ⓓ____ fall!

**서답형**

**24** 위 글의 빈칸 ⓐ에 다음 영영풀이에 해당하는 단어를 쓰시오.

> the area around the middle of the body between the ribs and the hips

➡ _____

**25** 위 글의 밑줄 친 ①~⑤ 중 문맥상 단어의 쓰임이 어색한 것은?

① ② ③ ④ ⑤

**26** 위 글의 밑줄 친 ⓑ와 뜻이 같은 것은?

① I agreed to speak second.
② The light flashes every 5 seconds.
③ He was the second to arrive.
④ Milan is Italy's second largest city.
⑤ Fill the second bowl with warm water.

**중요**

**27** 위 글의 빈칸 ⓒ와 ⓓ에 알맞은 말이 바르게 짝지어진 것은?

① might – will     ② would – can
③ must – may     ④ could – will
⑤ should – will

**[28~31]** 다음 글을 읽고, 물음에 답하시오.

( ① ) Place the top of your right foot on the desk behind you. ( ② ) Then, slowly bend your left leg and lower ⓐyou. ( ③ ) This position will ____ⓑ____ your right leg. ( ④ ) Switch your legs and repeat the exercise. ( ⑤ )

**중요**

**28** 위 글의 ①~⑤ 중 다음 문장이 들어갈 알맞은 곳은?

> Hold it for a few seconds and slowly straighten up.

① ② ③ ④ ⑤

**서답형**

**29** 위 글의 밑줄 친 ⓐ를 알맞은 형태로 고쳐 쓰시오.

➡ _____

**서답형**

**30** 위 글에서 다음 영영풀이에 해당하는 단어를 찾아 쓰시오.

> to make a change from one thing to another

➡ _____

**31** 위 글의 빈칸 ⓑ에 알맞은 것은?

① get over        ② put on
③ block out       ④ focus on
⑤ loosen up

[01~04] 다음 글을 읽고, 물음에 답하시오.

At school you sit for many hours. Do you get tired? ⓐ(you / why / massage / don't) yourself and stretch?

Let's begin with the eyes. Close your eyes and massage them softly with your fingers. It will relax your eyes. When you finish, cover your eyes with your hands to block out the light. ⓑIt will make your eyes feel more comfortably.

**01** 위 글의 빈칸 ⓐ 안의 단어들을 바르게 배열하시오.

➡ _____

**02** 위 글에서 다음 영영풀이에 해당하는 단어를 찾아 쓰시오.

to rub or press someone's body in a way that helps muscles to relax or reduces pain in muscles and joints

➡ _____

**03** 위 글의 밑줄 친 ⓑ에서 어법상 틀린 부분을 찾아 바르게 고쳐 쓰시오.

_____ ➡ _____

**04** What can we do to block out the light? Answer in English.

➡ _____

[05~08] 다음 글을 읽고, 물음에 답하시오.

Next, massage your neck. Put your fingers on the back of your neck. Draw small circles with your fingers ⓐmassage your neck. Massage ___ⓑ___ top to bottom. ⓒ마사지는 여러분의 기분이 나아지도록 도울 것이다.

**05** 위 글의 밑줄 친 ⓐ를 알맞은 형태로 고쳐 쓰시오.

➡ _____

**06** 위 글의 빈칸 ⓑ에 알맞은 말을 쓰시오.

➡ _____

**07** 위 글의 밑줄 친 ⓒ의 우리말에 맞도록 주어진 어구를 바르게 배열하시오.

(you / will / the massage / help / better / feel)

➡ _____

**08** 목을 마사지하는 방법을 순서대로 배열하시오.

ⓐ 목을 마사지하기 위해 손가락으로 작은 원을 그린다.
ⓑ 위에서부터 아래로 마사지한다.
ⓒ 목 뒷부분에 손가락을 댄다.

➡ _____

[09~12] 다음 글을 읽고, 물음에 답하시오.

Place the top of your right foot on the desk behind you. Then, slowly bend your left leg and ___ⓐ___ yourself. Hold ⓑit for a few seconds and slowly straighten ___ⓒ___. ⓓThis position will loosen up your right leg. Switch your legs and repeat the exercise.

**09** 위 글의 빈칸 ⓐ에 다음 영영풀이에 해당하는 단어를 주어진 철자로 시작하여 쓰시오.

| to move something down from higher up |
| --- |

➡ l_____

**10** 위 글의 밑줄 친 ⓑ가 의미하는 것을 우리말로 구체적으로 쓰시오.

➡ _____

**11** 위 글의 밑줄 친 ⓒ에 '똑바로 하다'라는 의미가 되도록 할 때 빈칸에 알맞은 말을 쓰시오.

➡ _____

**12** 위 글의 밑줄 친 ⓓ를 우리말로 옮기시오.

➡ _____

[13~16] 다음 글을 읽고, 물음에 답하시오.

Let's work on your waist. Team up with a friend. Stand close to each other and ___ⓐ___ your partner. Hold each other's wrists. Slowly stretch your head and body backward. Hold ⓑthat position for three seconds. ⓒThen, slowly push each other to a standing position. You and your partner should move at the same speed. If you don't, both of you will fall!

**13** 위 글의 빈칸 ⓐ에 다음 영영풀이에 해당하는 단어를 주어진 철자로 시작하여 쓰시오.

| to stand or sit with your face and body turned toward something or someone |
| --- |

➡ f_____

**14** 위 글의 밑줄 친 ⓑ가 의미하는 것을 우리말로 구체적으로 쓰시오.

➡ _____

**15** 위 글의 밑줄 친 ⓒ에서 문맥상 단어의 쓰임이 어색한 것을 찾아 바르게 고쳐 쓰시오.

_____ ➡ _____

**16** If two people don't move at the same speed, what will happen?

➡ _____

해석

### Enjoy Writing C

My Plan to Be Healthier

Here is my plan to be healthier.
Here is + 단수 명사 ~: 여기 ~이 있다

1. I will exercise more than three times a week.
            ~ 이상        일주일에 세 번

2. I will eat breakfast every day.
                        매일

If I exercise more than three times a week, I will become stronger. Also, if
조건을 나타내는 접속사 if(~한다면)                              become+형용사: ~해지다

I eat breakfast every day, I will feel better in the morning. I will change my
                              기분이 좋아지다

habits, and it will make me live a healthy life.
            사역동사 make+목적어+목적격 보어(동사원형): ~을 ...하게 하다

구문해설  • healthy: 건강한  • exercise: 운동하다  • change: 바꾸다  • habit: 습관

더 건강해지기 위한 나의 계획
여기 더 건강해지기 위한 나의
계획이 있다.

1. 나는 일주일에 세 번 이상
운동을 할 것이다.

2. 나는 매일 아침을 먹을 것이
다. 일주일에 세 번 이상 운
동을 하면 더 강해질 것이
다. 또한, 매일 아침을 먹으
면 아침에 기분이 나아질 것
이다. 나는 습관을 바꿀 것
이고, 그것은 나를 건강한
삶을 살게 할 것이다.

### Project - Step 2

Do you know how to stretch your shoulders? Our stretching exercise is
            how+to부정사: 어떻게 ~하는지                              ~라고 불리다

called "Number Stretching." First, make a number "1" with your arm to warm
                                            목적을 나타내는 to부정사의 부사적 용법(~하기 위해)

up. Then, make a number "2" with your arms. It will stretch your shoulders.
                              ~으로

Now, make a number "3". If you move your arms in a circle, it will feel nice.
                                                            feel+형용사: ~하게 느끼다

Finally, make a number "4". It is a little bit difficult, but it will be good for
                              조금                              ~에 좋다

your shoulders.

구문해설  • stretch: 스트레칭하다  • shoulder: 어깨  • warm up: 준비 운동을 하다  • circle: 원
        • finally: 마지막으로  • difficult: 어려운

여러분은 어깨를 어떻게 스
트레칭하는지 아는가? 우리
의 스트레칭 운동은 "숫자 스
트레칭"이라고 부른다. "첫 번
째, 준비 운동을 하기 위해 팔
로 숫자 "1"를 만들어라. 그런
다음, 팔로 숫자 2를 만들어라.
그것은 여러분의 어깨를 쫙 펴
줄 것이다. 이제 숫자 3을 만들
어라. 팔을 동그랗게 움직이면
기분이 좋아질 것이다. 마지막
으로, 숫자 4를 만들어라. 그것
은 조금 어렵긴 하지만, 여러
분의 어깨에 좋을 것이다.

### Wrap Up - Writing

Sumi: I feel stressed these days. What should I do?
                        요즘

Jiae: When I get stressed, I listen to music. It makes me feel better. If you don't
            스트레스를 받다        사역동사 make+목적어+목적격 보어(동사원형): ~을 ...하게 하다

      know how to download music, I will show you.
            다운로드하는 방법

구문해설  • listen to: ~을 듣다  • feel better: 기분이 더 좋아지다  • show: 보여주다, 가르쳐 주다

수미: 나는 요즘 스트레스를
받고 있어. 어떻게 해야
하지?
지애: 스트레스를 받을 때, 나
는 음악을 들어. 그건 내
기분을 좋아지게 해. 음
악을 다운로드하는 방법
을 모르면, 내가 가르쳐
줄게.

# 영역별 핵심문제

**01** 다음 중 짝지어진 단어의 관계가 <u>다른</u> 것은?

① warm : cool    ② difficult : easy

③ heavy : light    ④ switch : change

⑤ backward : forward

**02** 다음 영영풀이에 해당하는 단어는?

> to move your body so that it is not straight

① pull    ② bend

③ place    ④ push

⑤ stretch

**03** 다음 우리말과 같도록 빈칸에 알맞은 말을 쓰시오.

> 새로운 과학 프로젝트를 위해, 우리는 친구들과 협력할 필요가 있다.
> ➡ For the new science project, we need to _____ with friends.

**04** 다음 영영풀이에 해당하는 단어를 쓰시오.

> the action of rubbing and pressing a person's body with the hands to reduce pain in the muscles and joints

➡ _____

**05** 다음 빈칸에 공통으로 알맞은 것은?

> • What is the best _____ to get to City Hall?
> • I don't know the _____ to the stadium.

① tip    ② part

③ way    ④ top

⑤ choice

**06** 다음 빈칸에 알맞은 말이 바르게 짝지어진 것은?

> • You have to loosen _____ your arms and legs before swimming.
> • The trees in the park block _____ a lot of sunlight.

① of – in    ② over – at

③ to – off    ④ from – on

⑤ up – out

**07** 다음 대화의 빈칸에 알맞지 <u>않은</u> 것은?

> A: What do you enjoy doing after school?
> B: _____

① I like to go hiking.

② I enjoy playing soccer.

③ I enjoy cooking healthy food.

④ I'm interested in science.

⑤ I enjoy listening to music.

**08** 다음 대화의 빈칸에 알맞은 것은?

> A: How about making paper flowers?
> B: That sounds great. But I don't know _____.

① what to make them
② how to make them
③ how to use them
④ where to get there
⑤ what to use them

**09** 다음 대화의 빈칸에 알맞은 것은?

> A: _____
> B: I enjoy listening to pop music.

① Can you play music?
② Why don't you listen to music?
③ What kind of music do you like?
④ Do you want to listen to music?
⑤ What's your favorite sport?

**10** 다음 대화의 빈칸에 들어갈 말로 알맞은 것은?

> A: Are you good at solving math problems?
> B: No, I _____ math.

① am going to
② can get
③ am not good at
④ feel so good
⑤ am looking forward to

**11** 다음 대화의 순서를 바르게 배열하시오.

> (A) I enjoy cooking healthy food.
> (B) I can make salad, Bibimbap, and vegetable juice.
> (C) What do you enjoy doing after school?
> (D) Sounds cool. What can you make?

➡ _____

**[12~15]** 다음 대화를 읽고, 물음에 답하시오.

> B: I want to eat something healthy. Do you have any advice?
> G: I often eat fresh salad. It makes me ⓐfeel good.
> B: Really? Do you know how ⓑmake it?
> G: Yes, it's quite simple. __(A)__, cut many vegetables __ⓒ__ small pieces. __(B)__, put them into a bowl. Then, pour some lemon juice on them. __(C)__, mix everything together.
> B: That's it? I should try it.

**12** 위 대화의 밑줄 친 ⓐ와 ⓑ를 알맞은 형태로 쓰시오.

ⓐ _____ ⓑ _____

**13** 위 대화의 빈칸 ⓒ에 알맞은 것은?

① by    ② on    ③ for
④ into    ⑤ with

**14** 위 대화의 빈칸 (A)~(C)에 들어갈 말을 순서대로 나열한 것은?

① Second – Finally – Third
② First – Two – Third
③ First – Then – Finally
④ First – Finally – After then
⑤ Finally – First – End

**15** 위 대화를 읽고, 다음 물음에 완전한 문장으로 답하시오.

> Q: What is the second step in making fresh salad?
> A: _____
> _____

## Grammar

**16** 다음 빈칸에 공통으로 알맞은 것은?

> • He _____ me cook dinner.
> • Mom _____ me clean up my room.

① gave      ② wanted
③ made      ④ enjoyed
⑤ asked

**17** 다음 중 〈보기〉의 밑줄 친 부분과 쓰임이 같은 것은?

┌─ 보기 ┐
I want to know if it will rain tomorrow.
└────┘

① If he comes back, I will tell him about it.
② I won't go there if is cold tomorrow.
③ If you turn right, you can see the building.
④ You may go home early if you don't feel well.
⑤ I doubt if the baby can understand your words.

**18** 다음 밑줄 친 부분의 쓰임이 나머지와 다른 것은?

① Let me tell you about my teacher.
② I made him do his homework last night.
③ The students have many books to read.
④ I helped my dad wash his car.
⑤ My teacher had the students play outside.

**19** 다음 문장에서 어법상 어색한 부분을 바르게 고쳐서 문장을 다시 쓰시오.

> What do you do if he visits your home tomorrow?

➡ _____

**20** 다음 중 어법상 어색한 문장은?

① Mom let me go to bed early.
② Mr. Han told me go home early.
③ He made the children wash his car.
④ Jack will help you find the bicycle.
⑤ It lets you know about the price.

**21** 다음 빈칸에 공통으로 알맞은 것은?

> • You will get one free _____ you buy this.
> • I wonder _____ she is really a middle school student.

① as        ② if
③ that      ④ since
⑤ whether

**22** 다음 주어진 어구를 바르게 배열하여 문장을 완성하시오.

> 그녀는 아이들에게 축구를 하게 한다.
> (soccer / she / the children / play / has)

➡ _____

**23** 다음 〈보기〉의 밑줄 친 부분의 의미와 같은 것은?

┌─ 보기 ┐
He made me do my math homework.
└────┘

① She made it after all.
② I want to make money to buy the ring.
③ She made pasta for her little son.
④ They make the students do voluntary service at school.
⑤ You have to make an effort to be happy.

## 24 다음 밑줄 친 부분 중 어법상 어색한 것은?

① Unless he <u>is</u> late, we will start on time.

② Don't open the box until he <u>says</u> it's safe.

③ I'll go swimming if it <u>will be</u> sunny.

④ She will be happy when he <u>sends</u> her some flowers.

⑤ I'll wait here until the concert <u>is</u> over.

## 25 다음 문장에서 어법상 어색한 부분을 찾아 고쳐 쓰시오.

> Nothing will make me changing my mind.

_____ ➡ _____

## 26 다음 두 문장을 접속사 if를 써서 한 문장으로 바꿔 쓰시오.

> Jenny does not get up now. She will miss the train.

➡ _____

_____

## 27 다음 빈칸에 들어갈 말이 나머지 넷과 다른 것은?

① Mike will stay at home _____ it is cold.

② You can stay at home _____ you're tired.

③ She'll watch TV _____ she finishes her work early.

④ He'll buy a necktie for his dad _____ he goes shopping.

⑤ I think _____ Anderson won't come back.

Reading

**[28~31]** 다음 글을 읽고, 물음에 답하시오.

> At school you sit (A)[for / during] many hours. Do you get tired? Why don't you massage (B)[itself / yourself] and stretch?
> Let's begin ___ⓐ___ the eyes. ①<u>Close</u> your eyes and ②<u>massage</u> them softly ___ⓑ___ your fingers. It will ③<u>relax</u> your eyes. When you finish, ④<u>open</u> your eyes with your hands (C)[blocking / to block] out the light. It will ⓒ(feel / eyes / make / your) more ⑤<u>comfortable</u>.

## 28 위 글의 괄호 (A)~(C)에서 알맞은 것이 바르게 짝지어진 것은?

① for – itself – blocking

② for – yourself – to block

③ during – itself – blocking

④ during – yourself – blocking

⑤ during – itself – to block

## 29 위 글의 빈칸 ⓐ와 ⓑ에 공통으로 알맞은 말을 쓰시오.

➡ _____

## 30 위 글의 밑줄 친 ①~⑤ 중 흐름상 적절하지 않은 것은?

①       ②       ③       ④       ⑤

## 31 위 글의 괄호 ⓒ 안의 단어들을 순서대로 바르게 배열하시오.

➡ _____

**[32~35]** 다음 글을 읽고, 물음에 답하시오.

Let's ⓐ<u>work</u> on your waist. Team __(A)__ with a friend. (①) Stand close to each other and ⓑ<u>face</u> your partner. (②) Hold each other's __(B)__ . (③) Slowly ⓒ<u>stretch</u> your head and body backward. (④) Then, ⓓ<u>slowly</u> pull each other to a standing position. (⑤) You and your partner should move at the same speed. If you don't, both of you ⓔ<u>fall</u>!

**32** 위 글의 빈칸 (A)에 알맞은 것은?

① on                  ② in
③ out                 ④ up
⑤ down

**33** 위 글의 빈칸 (B)에 다음 영영풀이에 해당하는 단어를 쓰시오. (복수형으로 쓸 것)

> the part of your body where your hand joins your arm

➡ _____

**34** 위 글의 ①~⑤ 중 다음 문장이 들어갈 알맞은 곳은?

> Hold that position for three seconds.

①        ②        ③        ④        ⑤

**35** 위 글의 밑줄 친 ⓐ~ⓔ 중 어법상 어색한 것은?

① ⓐ        ② ⓑ        ③ ⓒ        ④ ⓓ        ⑤ ⓔ

**[36~39]** 다음 글을 읽고, 물음에 답하시오.

ⓐ<u>너는 너의 어깨를 스트레칭하는 방법을 아니?</u> Our stretching exercise is called "Number Stretching." __(A)__ , make a number "1" with your arm to warm up. __(B)__ , make a number "2" with your arms. ⓑ<u>It</u> will stretch your shoulders. Now, make a number "3". If you move your arms in a circle, it will feel nice. __(C)__ , make a number "4". It is a little bit difficult, __ⓒ__ it will be good for your shoulders.

**36** 위 글의 밑줄 친 ⓐ의 우리말과 일치하도록 빈칸에 알맞은 말을 쓰시오.

> Do you know _____ _____ _____ your shoulders?

**37** 위 글의 빈칸 (A)~(C)에 알맞은 말을 〈보기〉에서 골라 차례대로 쓰시오.

┌─ 보기 ──────────────┐
│   Finally   First   Then   │
└────────────────────────┘

(A) _____  (B) _____  (C) _____

**38** 위 글의 밑줄 친 ⓑ가 가리키는 것을 우리말로 쓰시오.

➡ _____

**39** 위 글의 빈칸 ⓒ에 알맞은 것은?

① so                  ② and
③ for                 ④ but
⑤ also

## 단원별 예상문제

출제율 95%

**01** 다음 〈보기〉와 같이 변화하는 단어는?

┌─ 보기 ─┐

use → usable

① create
② act
③ comfort
④ attract
⑤ impress

출제율 90%

**02** 다음 짝지어진 단어의 관계가 같도록 빈칸에 알맞은 말을 쓰시오.

simple : complicated = top : _____

출제율 100%

**03** 다음 빈칸에 알맞은 말이 바르게 짝지어진 것은?

• I want to focus _____ losing weight.
• Straighten _____ your shoulders when you walk.

① in – on
② at – up
③ of – off
④ into – for
⑤ on – up

출제율 90%

**04** 다음 영영풀이에 해당하는 단어는?

to become or to cause something to become less tense, tight, or stiff

① bend
② switch
③ reduce
④ relax
⑤ prepare

출제율 90%

**05** 다음 우리말에 맞게 빈칸에 알맞은 말을 쓰시오.

(1) 몇 초 동안 수프를 저어라.
➡ Stir the soup for _____ _____ _____.

(2) 나는 항상 저녁 식사 후에 산책을 한다.
➡ I always _____ _____ after dinner.

(3) 너는 보통 어떤 종류의 사진을 찍니?
➡ _____ _____ _____ pictures do you usually take?

출제율 100%

**06** 다음 대화의 밑줄 친 부분의 의도로 알맞은 것은?

A: Do you know how to make healthy juice?
B: No, I don't.

① 의견 동의하기
② 도움 요청하기
③ 능력 여부 묻기
④ 제안이나 권유하기
⑤ 선호에 대해 묻기

출제율 90%

**07** 다음 대화의 빈칸에 알맞지 않은 것은?

A: What do you do in your free time?
B: _____
A: How interesting!

① I ride a bike in the park.
② I hate to study English and math.
③ I take pictures of animals.
④ I enjoy drawing cartoons.
⑤ I play badminton with my sister.

[08~11] 다음 대화를 읽고, 물음에 답하시오.

B: People say that we should walk more than 10,000 steps every day ⓐbe healthy. I can't count the number of my steps easily.

G: You can use this smartphone app. ⓑ(you / how / do / it / use / know / to)?

B: No. Can you show me?

G: Sure. First, download the app. Then, walk with your smartphone. ⓒLate, you can check the number of steps you took.

B: Thank you. I will start using ⓓit today.

출제율 95%

**08** 위 대화의 밑줄 친 ⓐ를 알맞은 형태로 고쳐 쓰시오.

➡ _____

출제율 90%

**09** 위 대화의 괄호 ⓑ 안의 단어들을 바르게 배열하시오.

➡ _____

출제율 100%

**10** 위 대화의 밑줄 친 ⓒ를 알맞은 형태로 고치시오.

➡ _____

출제율 95%

**11** 위 대화의 밑줄 친 ⓓ가 가리키는 것을 영어로 쓰시오.

➡ _____

출제율 95%

**12** 다음 빈칸에 들어갈 말로 알맞은 것은?

| She won't let me _____ home early. |
| --- |

① to go
② going
③ went
④ will go
⑤ go

출제율 100%

**13** 다음 중 어법상 어색한 것은?

① We can make the robots work better.
② My father made my dog stand up.
③ The house is the biggest in our town.
④ It makes students practicing their English a lot.
⑤ Swimming is the most interesting activity for me.

출제율 95%

**14** 다음 문장의 빈칸에 알맞은 것은?

| If it _____ tomorrow, we won't go fishing. |
| --- |

① rain
② rains
③ rained
④ will rain
⑤ would rain

출제율 90%

**15** 다음 글의 밑줄 친 ①~⑤ 중 어색한 것은?

| Sanghui ①loves ②repairing machines. She can ③make any broken machine ④working again. And Mr. Han makes children run away by ⑤shouting at them. |
| --- |

①     ②     ③     ④     ⑤

**16** 다음 우리말을 영어로 바르게 옮긴 것은? 출제율 95%

> 나는 날씨가 좋으면 주말마다 낚시하러 간다.

① I go fishing on weekends because the weather is good.
② The weather is good, so I go fishing on weekends.
③ As the weather is good, I will go fishing on weekends.
④ If the weather will be good, I go fishing on weekends.
⑤ I go fishing on weekends if the weather is good.

**17** 다음 빈칸에 들어갈 말이 바르게 짝지어진 것은? 출제율 100%

> • I was late _____ the bus broke down.
> • I can finish that work _____ I have three days.

① when – how
② when – where
③ if – because
④ because – that
⑤ because – if

**18** 다음 우리말과 같도록 빈칸에 알맞은 말을 써서 문장을 완성하시오. 출제율 90%

> 만약 이번 일요일에 날씨가 맑으면, 우리는 소풍을 갈 것이다.
> = _____ _____ _____ sunny this Sunday, we _____ _____ on a picnic.

**19** 다음 우리말과 같은 뜻이 되도록 빈칸에 알맞은 말을 쓰시오. (필요하면 어형을 바꾸시오.) 출제율 85%

> 선생님은 Martin이 반 아이들 앞에서 그 이야기를 읽도록 하셨다. (have)

➡ The teacher _____ the story in front of the class.

**[20~23]** 다음 글을 읽고, 물음에 답하시오.

> (①) Place the ____ⓐ____ of your right foot ____ⓑ____ the desk behind you. (②) Then, slowly bend your left leg and lower yourself. (③) Hold it for ____ⓒ____ seconds and slowly straighten up. (④) Switch your legs and repeat the exercise. (⑤)

**20** 위 글의 빈칸 ⓐ에 다음 영영풀이에 해당하는 단어를 쓰시오. 출제율 85%

> an upper surface of something

➡ _____

**21** 위 글의 빈칸 ⓑ에 알맞은 것은? 출제율 95%

① at
② with
③ in
④ on
⑤ for

**22** 위 글의 빈칸 ⓒ에 알맞은 것은? 출제율 100%

① few
② little
③ much
④ a little
⑤ a few

**23** 위 글의 ①~⑤ 중 다음 문장이 들어갈 알맞은 곳은? 출제율 95%

> This position will loosen up your right leg.

①  ②  ③  ④  ⑤

**[24~26]** 다음 글을 읽고, 물음에 답하시오.

Do you know how ___ⓐ___ stretch your shoulders? Our stretching exercise is called "Number Stretching." First, make a number "1" with your arm ___ⓑ___ warm up. Then, make a number "2" with your arms. It will stretch your shoulders. Now, make a number "3". If you move your arms in a circle, it will feel nice. Finally, make a number "4". It is a little bit difficult, but it will be good ___ⓒ___ your shoulders.

**24** 위 글의 빈칸 ⓐ와 ⓑ에 공통으로 알맞은 말을 쓰시오.

➡ _____

**25** 위 글에서 다음 영영풀이에 해당하는 단어를 찾아 쓰시오.

> to do an exercise or set of exercises done to prepare for a sport or other activity

➡ _____

**26** 위 글의 빈칸 ⓒ에 알맞은 말을 쓰시오.

➡ _____

**[27~30]** 다음 글을 읽고, 물음에 답하시오.

___ⓐ___ the top of your right foot on the desk behind you. Then, slowly ___ⓑ___ your left leg and lower yourself. ___ⓒ___ it for a few seconds and slowly straighten ___ⓓ___. This position will ___ⓔ___. Switch your legs and repeat the exercise.

How do you feel now? If you massage yourself and stretch every day, you will feel healthier. ___ⓕ___, you can focus ___ⓖ___ your studies better.

**27** 위 글의 빈칸 ⓐ~ⓒ에 알맞은 말을 〈보기〉에서 골라 쓰시오.

> ┤ 보기 ├
>
> hold   place   bend

ⓐ _____   ⓑ _____   ⓒ _____

**28** 위 글의 빈칸 ⓓ와 ⓖ에 알맞은 말이 바르게 짝지어진 것은?

① up – on   ② on – in
③ in – of   ④ off – to
⑤ on – about

**29** 위 글의 빈칸 ⓔ에 알맞은 것은?

① tighten your right foot
② relax your left leg
③ make your left leg strong
④ straighten up your position
⑤ loosen up your right leg

**30** 위 글의 빈칸 ⓕ에 알맞은 것은?

① But   ② And
③ Or   ④ Also
⑤ So

[01~02] 괄호 안의 단어를 바르게 배열하여 대화를 완성하시오.
(필요하면 어형을 바꿀 것)

 01

A: (how / do / massage / know / you / to)
legs?
B: Yes, I do.

➡ _____

02

A: Kate, what do you enjoy doing to be
healthy?
B: (catch / enjoy / I / play).

➡ _____

03 다음 대화의 밑줄 친 말을 주어진 표현을 이용하여 영작하
시오.

A: Are you good at solving math problems?
B: No, 나는 수학을 잘 못해. (be good at)

➡ _____

 04 자연스러운 대화가 되도록 (A)~(D)의 순서를 바르게 배열
하시오.

(A) Sounds cool. What can you make?
(B) I can make salad, Bibimbap, and
vegetable juice.
(C) I enjoy cooking healthy food.
(D) What do you enjoy doing after school?

➡ _____

05 다음 문장에서 어법상 어색한 부분을 고쳐 다시 쓰시오.

(1) I will have my brother cleaned my room.

➡ _____

(2) Inhui made her daughter did the dishes.

➡ _____

(3) My mother let me to watch the TV drama.

➡ _____

06 다음 괄호 안의 어구를 이용하여 우리말을 영어로 옮기시오.

(1) 열이 있으면 너는 의사의 진찰을 받아야 한다.
(have, you, a, fever, should, see, doctor)

➡ _____

(2) 내일 비가 오면 난 영화 보러 갈 거야.
(rains, tomorrow, it, go, a movie)

➡ _____

(3) 파란색에 노란색을 섞으면 초록색이 된다.
(add, to, blue, green, yellow, you, become)

➡ _____

07 다음 주어진 어구를 바르게 배열하시오.

(1) (makes / my / clean / mother / my / me /
room)

➡ _____

(2) (librarian / find / the / a / helped / book /
me)

➡ _____

(3) (safely / her / they / go / let)

➡ _____

Let's begin with the eyes. Close your eyes and massage them softly with your fingers. It will relax your eyes. When you finish, cover your eyes with your hands to block out the light. ⓐIt will make your eyes feel more comfortable.

Next, massage your neck. Put your fingers on the back of your neck. Draw small circles with your fingers to massage your neck. Massage from top to bottom. ⓑ마사지는 여러분의 기분이 좋아지도록 도울 것이다.

**08** How do we massage our eyes with our fingers? Answer in English.

➡ _____

**09** 위 글의 밑줄 친 ⓐ를 우리말로 옮기시오.

➡ _____

**10** What can we do to massage our neck? Answer in English.

➡ _____

**11** 위 글의 밑줄 친 ⓑ의 우리말에 맞도록 괄호 안의 어구를 순서대로 배열하시오.

(will / the / feel / help / you / better / massage)

➡ _____

[12~15] 다음 글을 읽고, 물음에 답하시오.

ⓐHere are my plan to be healthier.
1. I will exercise more than three times a week.
2. I will eat breakfast every day.
   If I exercise more than three times a week, I will become stronger. Also, if I eat breakfast every day, I will feel better in the morning. I will change my habits, and ⓑit will ⓒ (healthy / live / a / me / make / life).

**12** 위 글의 밑줄 친 ⓐ에서 어법상 틀린 부분을 찾아 바르게 고쳐 쓰시오.

_____ ➡ _____

**13** How many times a week does the writer plan to exercise? Answer in English.

➡ _____

_____

**14** 위 글의 밑줄 친 ⓑit이 가리키는 것을 우리말로 쓰시오.

➡ _____

**15** 위 글의 괄호 ⓒ 안의 단어들을 바르게 배열하시오.

➡ _____

**01** 다음 주어진 표현을 보고, 자신이 할 수 있는 일에 ∨표 한 후, 〈보기〉와 같이 대화문을 완성하시오.

- shop on the Internet (   )
- cook instant noodles (   )

> ┤ 보기 ├
>
> A: Do you know how to make fresh salad?
> B: Yes, I know how to make fresh salad. / No, I don't know how to make fresh salad.

(1) A: _____
　　B: _____
(2) A: _____
　　B: _____

**02** 다음과 같은 상황이 벌어진다면 어떨지 상상하여 〈보기〉와 같이 쓰시오.

- get an A on the math test
- go to Paris
- it is sunny tomorrow
- find an abandoned dog on the street　　　　　　　　* abandoned dog: 유기견

> ┤ 보기 ├
>
> If I get an A on the math test, I will be very happy.

(1) _____
(2) _____
(3) _____

**03** 다음 〈보기〉의 사역동사들을 이용하여 문장을 4개 쓰시오. (필요시 형태를 바꿀 것)

> ┤ 보기 ├
>
> let　　make　　help　　have

(1) _____
(2) _____
(3) _____
(4) _____

# 단원별 모의고사

**01** 다음 영영풀이에 해당하는 단어로 알맞은 것은?

> either of the two parts of the body between the top of each arm and the neck

① hip
② waist
③ back
④ chest
⑤ shoulder

**02** 다음 중 밑줄 친 우리말 뜻이 잘못된 것은?

① Massage from top to bottom.
　　위에서부터 아래까지
② I think you should see a doctor.
　　병원에 가다
③ For a few seconds nobody said anything.
　　오랫동안
④ You and your partner should move at the same speed. 같은 속도로
⑤ Both of my sisters moved even farther away from home. 둘 다

**03** 다음 빈칸에 공통으로 알맞은 것은?

> • She has a pretty _____.
> • Stand close to each other and _____ your partner.

① step
② store
③ place
④ face
⑤ switch

**04** 다음 짝지어진 두 단어의 관계가 같도록 빈칸에 알맞은 말을 쓰시오.

> hungry : full = complicated : _____

**05** 다음 영영풀이에 해당하는 단어를 주어진 철자로 시작하여 쓰시오.

> an opinion or suggestion about what someone should do

➡ a_____

**06** 다음 대화의 밑줄 친 부분과 의미가 같은 것은?

> A: Do you know how to download photos from the Internet?
> B: Yes. I do. I'm good at using computers.

① Do you want to download photos?
② Can I download photos from the Internet?
③ May I download photos from the Internet?
④ Would you mind downloading photos from the Internet?
⑤ Can you download photos from the Internet?

**07** 다음 밑줄 친 말과 바꿔 쓸 수 있는 것을 모두 고르면?

> A: What do you enjoy doing to be healthy?
> B: I enjoy riding a bike.

① I can ride a bike.
② I like to ride a bike.
③ I want to ride a bike.
④ I will ride a bike.
⑤ I feel great when I ride a bike.

[08~11] 다음 대화를 읽고, 물음에 답하시오.

Karl: Hana, what's the matter?

Hana: Well, I'm stressed about the test next week.

Karl: I understand. I ride my longboard ⓐ I'm stressed. ⓑ<u>Do you know how to ride a longboard?</u>

Hana: No, I don't.

Karl: Let's go out! I can teach you. Put one foot on the board and push hard with ⓒ .

Hana: Like this? Wow! This is fun. I feel better already.

Karl: See? I enjoy riding my longboard ⓓ it reduces my stress.

Hana: That's great!

**08** 위 대화의 빈칸 ⓐ와 ⓓ에 알맞은 말이 바르게 짝지어진 것은?

① if – as
② when – because
③ as – for
④ if – before
⑤ while – because of

**09** 위 대화의 밑줄 친 ⓑ와 의미가 <u>다른</u> 것을 <u>모두</u> 고르시오.

① Can you ride a longboard?
② Are you riding a longboard?
③ Are you good at riding a longboard?
④ How can I ride a longboard?
⑤ Are you able to ride a longboard?

**10** 위 대화의 빈칸 ⓒ에 알맞은 것은?

① two
② others
③ the other
④ the second
⑤ the others

**11** Explain how to ride the longboard. Answer in Korean.

➡ _____

**12** 다음 문장의 빈칸에 알맞은 것은?

> Why don't you cook some soup _____ you're hungry?

① and
② but
③ if
④ where
⑤ because

**13** 다음 문장에서 어법상 <u>틀린</u> 부분을 찾아 고쳐 쓰시오.

> Brian makes his dad feels comfortable.

_____ ➡ _____

**14** 다음 문장의 빈칸에 알맞은 것은?

> The police officer let the children _____ the road.

① cross
② crossing
③ to cross
④ to crossing
⑤ crossed

**15** 다음 밑줄 친 ①~⑤ 중 어법상 <u>틀린</u> 것은?

> My father <u>will buy</u> <u>me</u> <u>a computer</u> <u>if</u> I
> ① ② ③
> <u>will get</u> a perfect score <u>in the final exam.</u>
> ④ ⑤

**16** 다음 괄호 안에 주어진 단어를 이용하여 우리말을 영어로 옮기시오. (필요하면 어형을 바꿀 것)

> 나의 형은 나에게 방을 청소하라고 시켰다.
> (have)

➡ _____

**17** 다음 두 문장의 뜻이 같도록 빈칸에 알맞은 말을 쓰시오.

> If you don't hurry up, you will miss the bus.
> = _____ you hurry up, you will miss the bus.

**18** 다음 중 밑줄 친 make의 쓰임이 다른 하나는?

① He made the dog sit down.
② Mom made him some tea.
③ It makes you have more energy.
④ The Reading Club makes you read faster.
⑤ She made us work again.

**19** 다음 중 어법상 어색한 것은?

① I'll phone you if I'll have time.
② If you don't have a ticket, you can't come in.
③ We can be in Seoul by 10 if we catch the first train.
④ If you don't give me my money, I'm going to the police.
⑤ If it is sunny tomorrow, we'll have the party outside.

**[20~21]** 다음 글을 읽고, 물음에 답하시오.

> Place the ⓐbottom of your right foot on the desk behind you. Then, slowly ⓑbend your left leg and ⓒlower yourself. ⓓHold it for a few seconds and slowly ⓔstraighten up. This position will _____ your right leg. Switch your legs and repeat the exercise.

**20** 위 글의 밑줄 친 ⓐ~ⓔ 중 문맥상 어색한 것은?

① ⓐ    ② ⓑ    ③ ⓒ    ④ ⓓ    ⑤ ⓔ

**21** 위 글의 빈칸에 알맞은 것은?

① block out          ② team up
③ fasten up          ④ loosen up
⑤ get along with

**[22~23]** 다음 글을 읽고, 물음에 답하시오.

> Next, massage your neck. ⓐ your fingers on the back of your neck. Draw small circles with your fingers to massage your neck. ⓑ위에서 아래로 마사지해라. The massage will help you feel better.

**22** 문맥상 위 글의 빈칸 ⓐ에 알맞은 것은?

① Put           ② Pull
③ Bend          ④ Move
⑤ Cover

**23** 위 글의 밑줄 친 ⓑ의 우리말에 맞게 주어진 단어를 바르게 배열하시오.

> (bottom / to / massage / top / from)

➡ _____

[24~27] 다음 글을 읽고, 물음에 답하시오.

Let's work on your waist. Team up with a friend. Stand close to each other and __(A)__ your partner. Hold each other's wrists. Slowly __(B)__ your head and body backward. Hold that position __ⓐ__ three seconds. Then, slowly __(C)__ each other to a standing position. You and your partner should move __ⓑ__ the same speed. ⓒIf you won't, both of you will fall!

**24** 위 글의 빈칸 (A)~(C)에 알맞은 말이 바르게 짝지어진 것은?

① face – pull – stretch

② pull – stretch – face

③ stretch – face – pull

④ face – stretch – pull

⑤ pull – face – stretch

**25** 위 글의 빈칸 ⓐ와 ⓑ에 알맞은 말이 바르게 짝지어진 것은?

① at – in          ② during – at

③ for – at         ④ for – with

⑤ during – with

**26** 위 글에서 다음 영영풀이에 해당하는 단어를 찾아 쓰시오.

the way someone stands, sits, or lies down

➡ _____

**27** 위 글의 밑줄 친 ⓒ에서 어법상 틀린 부분을 찾아 바르게 고쳐 쓰시오.

_____ ➡ _____

[28~30] 다음 글을 읽고, 물음에 답하시오.

At school you sit for many hours. (①) Do you get tired? (②) Why don't you massage yourself and stretch?

(③) Let's begin with the eyes. (④) Close your eyes and massage them softly with your fingers. (⑤) When you finish, cover your eyes with your hands to block __ⓐ__ the light. ⓑIt will make your eyes to feel more comfortable.

**28** 위 글의 ①~⑤ 중 주어진 문장이 들어갈 알맞은 곳은?

It will relax your eyes.

①          ②          ③          ④          ⑤

**29** 위 글의 빈칸 ⓐ에 알맞은 것은?

① up          ② out

③ off          ④ into

⑤ over

**30** 위 글의 밑줄 친 ⓑ에서 어법상 틀린 부분을 찾아 바르게 고쳐 쓰시오.

_____ ➡ _____

# To Be a Global Citizen

## 🗣 의사소통 기능

- 의도 묻기
  Are you going to eat all of that?

- 희망 표현하기
  I hope we can save the Earth.

## 🗣 언어 형식

- 주격 관계대명사
  Global citizens are people **who** try to understand different cultures.

- something/anything/nothing/everything + 형용사
  You did **something wonderful**.

# Words & Expressions

## Key Words

- **adult** [ədʌ́lt] 명 어른
- **aim** [eim] 동 ~을 목표로 삼다, 지향하다
- **alongside** [əlɔ́ŋsaid] 전 ~ 옆에, 나란히
- **American** [əmérikən] 형 미국의 명 미국인
- **awesome** [ɔ́:səm] 형 굉장한, 감탄할 만한, 엄청난
- **bag** [bæg] 명 가방
- **campaign** [kæmpéin] 명 캠페인, 조직적 활동
- **celebrate** [séləbrèit] 동 (특별한 날·경사 등을) 축하하다, 기념하다
- **citizen** [sítəzən] 명 시민
- **communicate** [kəmjú:nəkèit] 동 의사소통하다
- **community** [kəmjú:nəti] 명 공동체
- **education** [èdʒukéiʃən] 명 교육
- **environment** [inváiərənmənt] 명 자연환경, 환경
- **far** [fɑ:r] 부 멀리 형 먼
- **fight** [fait] 명 싸움 동 싸우다
- **flood** [flʌd] 명 홍수
- **garden** [gɑ́:rdn] 명 정원
- **gather** [gǽðər] 동 모으다
- **global** [glóubəl] 형 전 세계적인, 지구상의
- **hold** [hould] 동 (회의, 시합 등을) 열다
- **hunger** [hʌ́ŋgər] 명 기아, 배고픔
- **hurt** [hə:rt] 동 다치게 하다

- **international** [ìntərnǽʃənəl] 형 국제적인
- **join** [dʒɔin] 동 참여하다
- **Kenyan** [kénjən] 형 케냐의
- **lantern** [lǽntərn] 명 랜턴, 등불, 등
- **leave** [li:v] 동 남기다
- **messy** [mési] 형 엉망진창의
- **nothing** [nʌ́θiŋ] 대 아무것도 ~ 아니다
- **plate** [pleit] 명 접시
- **poor** [puər] 형 가난한
- **produce** [prədjú:s] 동 생산하다
- **protect** [prətékt] 동 보호하다
- **raise** [reiz] 동 (자금 등을) 모금하다
- **recycle** [ri:sáikl] 동 (폐기물을) 재활용하다
- **save** [seiv] 동 살리다, 구하다
- **sell** [sel] 동 팔다
- **send** [send] 동 보내다, 전하다
- **share** [ʃɛər] 동 같이 쓰다, 공유하다
- **site** [sait] 명 (인터넷의) 사이트
- **take** [teik] 동 가져가다
- **trash** [træʃ] 명 쓰레기
- **upload** [ʌplóud] 동 업로드하다, 올리다
- **upset** [ʌ́pset] 형 당황한
- **waste** [weist] 동 낭비하다, 허비하다

## Key Expressions

- **be going to 동사원형** ~할 것이다
- **be good at** ~을 잘하다
- **care about** ~에 관심을 가지다
- **care for** ~을 돌보다, 신경 쓰다
- **die of** ~으로 죽다
- **do volunteer work** 자원 봉사를 하다
- **go well** 잘 되다
- **in need** 어려움에 처한
- **send+간접목적어(사람)+직접목적어(사물)** ···에게 ~을 보내다

- **share A(사물) with B(사람)** A를 B와 나누다[나눠 가지다]
- **take a shower** 샤워를 하다
- **thanks to** ~ 덕분에
- **throw away** ~을 버리다
- **turn down the heat** (실내) 온도를 낮추다
- **turn on** (전등·불·텔레비전·라디오 등을) 켜다
- **watch out (for)** (~에 대해서) 조심하다

## Word Power

※ 서로 반대되는 뜻을 가진 단어

- □ **far**(멀리; 먼) ↔ **near**(가까운)
- □ **sell**(팔다) ↔ **buy**(사다)

- □ **poor**(가난한) ↔ **rich**(부유한)
- □ **arrive**(도착하다) ↔ **leave**(떠나다)

※ 서로 비슷한 뜻을 가진 단어

- □ **gather**(모으다) : **collect**(모으다)
- □ **save**(살리다, 구하다) : **rescue**(구출하다, 구조하다)

- □ **global**(전 세계적인) : **worldwide**(세계적인)
- □ **upset**(당황한) : **worried**(걱정스러운, 당황하는)

## English Dictionary

- □ **adult** 어른
  → a grown-up person 성인이 된 사람

- □ **aim** ~을 목표로 삼다, 지향하다
  → to plan or hope to achieve something
  어떤 것을 성취하는 것을 계획하거나 희망하다

- □ **alongside** 옆에, 나란히
  → along the side of something, or close to the side of it
  어떤 것의 옆을 따라서 혹은 옆에 가까이

- □ **celebrate** (특별한 날·경사 등을) 축하하다, 기념하다
  → to do something enjoyable on a special occasion
  특별한 경우에 즐거운 어떤 것을 하다

- □ **communicate** 의사소통하다
  → to share or exchange information or emotion with someone 다른 사람과 정보나 감정을 나누거나 교환하다

- □ **community** 공동체
  → a group of people who live in the same area or who are similar in some way
  같은 지역에 사는 사람들이나 어떤 방식으로 비슷한 사람들의 모임

- □ **education** 교육
  → the activity of teaching or training students in school, etc. 학교 등에서 학생들을 가르치거나 훈련시키는 활동

- □ **environment** 자연환경, 환경
  → the nature where there are land, sea, air, plants, and animals 육지, 바다, 공기, 식물 및 동물이 있는 자연

- □ **fight** 싸우다
  → to contend in a battle or physical combat
  전투나 육체적 싸움으로 다투다

- □ **flood** 홍수
  → an overflow of water 물의 넘쳐흐름

- □ **garden** 정원
  → a place where you can grow plants
  식물을 기를 수 있는 장소

- □ **gather** 모으다
  → to bring people together or collect things together
  사람이나 사물을 함께 모이도록 하다

- □ **global** 전 세계적인, 지구상의
  → including the whole world 전 세계를 포함하는

- □ **hurt** 다치게 하다
  → to injure or cause pain to a part of someone's body
  어떤 사람의 신체 일부에 부상을 입히거나 고통을 유발하다

- □ **lantern** 랜턴, 등불, 등
  → a lamp in a metal frame with glass sides and with a handle on top so you can carry it
  금속 테두리와 유리로 된 옆면 그리고 위에 손잡이가 달려 갖고 다닐 수 있는 램프

- □ **messy** 엉망진창의
  → untidy or dirty 깔끔하지 못하거나 더러운

- □ **raise** (자금 등을) 모금하다
  → to collect money for a particular purpose
  특정한 목적을 위해 돈을 모으다

- □ **recycle** (폐기물을) 재활용하다
  → to process used or waste materials so as to make suitable for reuse
  사용된 재료나 폐기물을 재사용에 알맞게 되도록 처리하다

- □ **sell** 팔다
  → to give goods in exchange for money
  돈과 교환하여 물건을 주다

- □ **upload** 업로드하다
  → to send documents or programs from your computer to a larger system using the Internet
  인터넷을 사용해서 문서나 프로그램을 컴퓨터에서 더 큰 시스템으로 보내다

- □ **upset** 당황한
  → emotionally disturbed or agitated
  감정적으로 매우 교란되거나 동요된

- □ **waste** 낭비하다, 허비하다
  → to fail to use time, money, energy, etc. fully or in the sensible or useful way
  시간, 돈, 에너지를 완전히 또는 합리적이거나 유용한 방법으로 사용하지 못하다

**서답형**

**01** 다음 짝지어진 두 단어의 관계가 같도록 빈칸에 알맞은 단어를 쓰시오.

> more : less – _____ : near

[02~03] 다음 빈칸에 들어갈 말로 적절한 것은?

**02**

> The heavy rain resulted in the _____.

① flood      ② earthquake
③ drought      ④ weather
⑤ environment

**03** 중요

> A very large _____ is called a city.

① population      ② experience
③ site      ④ community
⑤ situation

[04~05] 다음 영영 풀이에 해당하는 단어를 고르시오.

**04**

> to send documents or programs from your computer to a larger system using the Internet

① take      ② leave
③ update      ④ upload
⑤ post

**05**

> a person who lives in a country or town legally

① adult      ② citizen
③ lawyer      ④ village
⑤ community

 중요

**06** 밑줄 친 부분의 의미가 잘못된 것은?

① Will you plant roses in your garden this year? (정원)
② Charlie entered a Kenyan middle school. (케냐의)
③ The town will hold a festival this year. (잡다, 쥐다)
④ She saw the light of a lantern in the distance. (등불, 등)
⑤ Many workers come from poor areas. (가난한)

**서답형**

[07~08] 다음 밑줄 친 부분과 의미가 가장 가까운 것을 주어진 철자로 시작하여 쓰시오.

**07**

> Teaching and learning is the most important thing to change the world.

➡ E_____

**08**

> He wants to be the CEO of a worldwide company.

➡ g_____

**서답형**

**09** 다음 주어진 우리말에 맞게 빈칸을 채우시오.

(1) 어떤 종류의 가방을 원해?
   ➡ What _____ of _____ do you want?

(2) 그들은 사과를 판매한다.
   ➡ They _____ some apples.

**01** 다음 우리말에 맞게 주어진 단어를 바르게 배열하시오.

(1) 차들이 우리와 나란히 움직이고 있다.
(moving, us, the cars, alongside, are)
➡ _____

(2) 같은 나라의 시민들은 같은 국적을 가지고 있다.
(citizens, the, nationality, the, of, same, country, same, have)
➡ _____
_____

(3) 그 폭우로 홍수가 났다.
(the flood, rain, heavy, in, the, resulted)
➡ _____

(4) 우리는 궁핍한 사람들을 돕기 위해 모금하기로 결정했다.
(to, for, needy, decided, we, people, the, raise, money)
➡ _____
_____

**02** 다음 빈칸에 알맞은 단어를 〈보기〉에서 골라 쓰시오. (형태 변화 가능)

┌─ 보기 ┤
communicate   leave   gather   celebrate
└─────────────

(1) We _____ with each other in English.
(2) He has _____ information on the Internet.
(3) She _____ my birthday last year.
(4) He _____ food on his plate yesterday.

**03** 주어진 단어를 활용하여 빈칸에 알맞은 말을 넣으시오.

(1) They will suffer from _____ and air pollution. (hungry)
(2) This is not a _____ but an international issue. (nation)

**04** 다음 〈보기〉에서 빈칸에 공통으로 들어갈 단어를 골라 쓰시오.

┌─ 보기 ┤
take   be   care   look
└─────────────

• She wanted to _____ for him for two weeks until he got better.
• He should _____ about others' feeling.

**05** 다음 주어진 우리말에 맞게 빈칸을 채우시오. (철자가 주어진 것도 있음)

(1) 그는 어려운 수학 문제 푸는 것을 잘한다.
➡ He _____ difficult math problems.
(2) 네 도움 덕분에 나는 그것을 할 수 있었다.
➡ _____ your help, I was able to do it.
(3) 너는 실내 온도를 낮출 거니?
➡ Are you _____ to _____ _____ the heat?
(4) 그들은 크리스마스와 새해를 함께 기념해.
➡ They c_____ Christmas and New Year's Day together.

**1** 의도 묻기

**Are you going to eat all of that?** 너 그걸 다 먹을 거니?

■ 의도나 계획을 묻는 표현으로 'Are you planning to 동사원형 ~?', 'Are you going to 동사원형 ~?', 'Are you trying to 동사원형 ~?' 등이 있으며, '너는 ~할 계획이니?' 또는 '너는 ~할 거니?'의 의미로 쓰인다.

■ 'I'm planning to 동사원형 ~.'은 '나는 ~할 계획이다.'라는 의미이며 미래의 계획이나 의도에 대해 사용하는 표현으로 to 다음에 동사원형이 온다. 비슷한 표현으로 'I'm going to 동사원형~.', 'I'll 동사원형 ~.' 등이 있다.

### 의도 묻기

• Are you planning to 동사원형 ~? 너는 ~할 거니?

• Are you trying to 동사원형 ~?

• What are you going to do? 너는 무엇을 할 거니?

• Are you going to 동사원형 ~?

• Do you have a plan to 동사원형 ~?

### 의도 표현하기

• I'm planning to 동사원형 ~.

• I will 동사원형 ~.

• I'm going to 동사원형 ~.

### 핵심 Check

1. 다음 우리말과 일치하도록 빈칸에 알맞은 말을 쓰시오. (철자가 주어진 것도 있음)

   (1) **A:** Are _____ p_____ _____ take a dance class? (너는 무용 수업을 받을 계획이니?)

   **B:** Yes, I _____. (응. 그래.)

   (2) **A:** _____ _____ _____ planning _____ _____ this weekend?
   (이번 주말에 무엇을 할 계획이니?)

   **B:** _____ planning _____ visit my grandparents. (조부모님을 방문할 계획이야.)

2. 대화의 순서를 알맞게 배열하시오.

   (A) I'm planning to go hiking. How about you?

   (B) What are you doing this afternoon?

   (C) I'm going to play table tennis.

   ➡ _____

**②** **희망 표현하기**

**I hope we can save the Earth.** 나는 우리가 지구를 살리기를 바라.

■ 소망을 표현할 때는 동사 want나 hope를 사용할 수 있다. want와 hope는 둘 다 to부정사를 사용한다. 또한 hope는 that절을 목적어로 사용할 수도 있다.

■ 자신이 희망하는 바를 표현할 때에는 'I hope (that) I can ~.(나는 ~할 수 있기를 바라.)', 'I hope to ~.(나는 ~하고 싶어.)', 'I want to ~.(나는 ~하고 싶어.)', 'I'd like to ~.(나는 ~하고 싶어.) 등으로 말할 수 있다.

• I hope that I can read books to the children. 나는 아이들을 위해 책을 읽어줄 수 있기를 바라.

= I hope to read books to the children.

• I hope I can stay with him. 나는 그와 같이 머무르기를 바라.

= I hope to stay with him.

**희망 표현하기**

• I hope (that) 주어 can 동사 ~. 나는 ~하기를 바라.　　• I hope to 동사원형 ~. 나는 ~하고 싶어.

• I want to 동사원형 ~.　　• I'd like to 동사원형 ~.

**핵심 Check**

3. 다음 우리말과 일치하도록 빈칸에 알맞은 말을 쓰시오. (철자가 주어진 것도 있음)

(1) **A:** _____ _____ p_____ to take a swimming lesson after school?
(방과 후에 수영 강습 받을 거니?)

**B:** Yes, I hope _____ _____ in the sea. (네, 바다에서 수영하고 싶거든요.)

(2) **A:** Is this present for Mina? (이 선물이 미나를 위한 것이야?)

**B:** Yes. _____ _____ _____ will like it.
(그래. 나는 그녀가 그것을 좋아하기를 바라.)

4. 주어진 문장과 바꿔 쓸 수 있는 것을 모두 고르시오.

• I hope that I can go on a picnic with my family.

① I want to go on a picnic with my family.

② I need to go on a picnic with my family.

③ I hope to go on a picnic with my family.

④ I should go on a picnic with my family.

⑤ I can go on a picnic with my family.

### Listen & Speak ① A-1

B: Did you watch the news ❶about the flood?

G: Yes, I ❷did. They said ❸a lot of people ❹lost their homes.

B: My club ❺is going to send them some money.

G: How can you do ❻that? Are you going to ❼raise money, Andy?

B: Yes. We're going to make pencil cases and ❽sell them.

B: 홍수에 대한 뉴스를 보았니?
G: 응, 보았어. 많은 사람들이 집을 잃었다고 하더라.
B: 우리 동아리는 그들에게 약간의 돈을 보낼 거야.
G: 그것을 어떻게 할 수 있니? 돈을 모금할 거니, Andy?
B: 응. 우리는 필통을 만들어서 그것들을 팔 거야.

❶ about the flood은 '홍수에 대한'의 의미로 앞의 the news를 수식하고 있다. flood: 홍수
❷ 'Did you ~?'로 질문하고 있으므로, 대답으로 'Yes, I did.' 또는 'No, I didn't.'가 나올 수 있다.
❸ said 뒤에는 접속사 that이 생략되어 있다. a lot of: 많은 (= lots of = many)
❹ lost는 lose(잃다)의 과거형이다. (lose-lost-lost)
❺ 'be going to 동사원형 ~'은 '~할 것이다'의 의미로 의도를 나타낼 때 사용하는 표현이다.
❻ 여기서 that은 앞 문장의 'to send them some money'를 의미한다.
❼ raise: (자금 등을) 모으다, 모금하다
❽ sell은 접속사 and에 의해 make와 병렬 구조를 이루고 있다. them은 pencil cases를 의미한다.

**Check(√) True or False**

(1) Because of the flood, a few people lost their homes.     T ☐ F ☐

(2) The girl didn't watch the news about the flood.     T ☐ F ☐

### Listen & Speak ② A-1

G: ❶What are you doing, Jason?

B: I'm making a poster about ❷global hunger. ❸Many people are dying of hunger.

G: ❹That's too bad. I didn't know that.

B: I hope ❺more people ❻care about global hunger.

G: 무엇을 하고 있니, Jason?
B: 세계의 기아 문제에 대한 포스터를 만드는 중이야. 많은 사람들이 기아로 죽어가고 있어.
G: 정말 안됐다. 난 몰랐어.
B: 더 많은 사람들이 세계의 기아 문제에 관심을 갖기를 바라.

❶ 현재진행형(be동사의 현재형+동사ing)을 사용하여, 지금 진행하고 있는 일이 무엇인지 질문하고 있다.
❷ global: 전 세계적인, 지구상의(= worldwide) hunger: 기아, 배고픔
❸ people은 '사람들'이라는 의미로 much가 아닌 many로 수식한다. dying은 die의 현재분사형이다. hunger: 기아, 배고픔
❹ 'That's too bad.'는 유감을 표현하는 말로 'I'm sorry to hear that.(그 말을 들으니 유감이다.)'으로 바꾸어 쓸 수 있다.
❺ hope와 more 사이에 접속사 that이 생략되어 있다.
❻ care about: ~에 관심을 가지다 global: 전 세계적인, 지구상의

**Check(√) True or False**

(3) The boy wants many people to care about global hunger.     T ☐ F ☐

(4) The girl didn't know that many people are dying of hunger.     T ☐ F ☐

### Listen & Speak ① A-2

B: Do you have any plans for the summer vacation, Suji?

G: Yes. ❶I'm going to the Philippines ❷to ❸do some volunteer work with my family.

B: Oh, ❹I went there and helped some children study last year. ❺Are you going to do that, too?

G: Yes. And I'll also paint walls with the children.

B: That ❻sounds nice.

❶ be going to 동사원형: ～할 것이다(의도나 계획을 말하는 표현)
❷ to부정사의 부사적 용법 중 목적(～하기 위해서)의 의미로 사용되었다.
❸ do volunteer work: 자원 봉사를 하다
❹ went와 helped는 접속사 and로 연결되어 있는 동사 병렬구조이고, last year(작년에)라는 과거 시간의 부사구가 있기 때문에 과거형 동사로 사용되었다. there는 to the Philippines를 의미한다.
❺ Are you going to 동사원형 ～?: 너는 ～할 계획이니?, 너는 ～할 거니? (= Are you planning to 동사원형 ～?)
❻ sound+형용사: ～하게 들리다

### Listen & Speak ① B-1

A: ❶Are you going to ❷take a short shower?

B: ❸Yes, I am.

❶ Are you going to 동사원형 ～?: ～할 거니?(의도나 계획 묻기)
❷ take a shower: 샤워하다
❸ 'Are you ～?'로 질문하였으므로 'Yes, I am.' 또는 'No, I'm not.'으로 대답할 수 있다.

### Listen & Speak ② B-1

A: I hope ❶people don't throw away trash.

B: I hope so, too. ❷Let's ❸hold a Keep the World Clean campaign.

A: ❹That's a good idea.

❶ hope와 people 사이에 접속사 that이 생략되어 있다. throw away: ～을 버리다 trash: 쓰레기
❷ Let's 동사원형: ～하자 / 어떤 활동을 함께 하자고 제안할 경우에는 'Why don't we+동사?' 혹은 'Let's+동사'를 사용할 수 있다.
❸ hold: (회의, 시합 등을) 열다
❹ 'That's a good idea.(좋은 생각이야.)'는 상대방이 말한 의견에 대해 동의하는 표현이다.

### Listen & Speak ② A-2

G: Dad, my class ❶decided to make a vegetable ❷garden.

M: A vegetable garden? ❸What will you grow there, Sena?

G: Carrots. ❹We'll grow them and share them with others.

M: That's a good idea.

G: I hope ❺the carrots grow well.

❶ decide는 동명사가 아닌 to부정사(to 동사원형)를 목적어로 취하는 동사이다.
❷ garden: 정원
❸ What will you grow there?: 거기서 무엇을 기를 거니? (= What are you going to grow there? = What are you planning to grow there?)
❹ grow와 share는 접속사 and로 연결되어 있는 동사 병렬구조이다. them은 carrots를 의미한다. others: 다른 사람들
❺ hope와 the carrots 사이에 접속사 that이 생략되어 있다. hope는 목적어로 to부정사와 that절을 취할 수 있다. grow: 기르다, 재배하다

### Wrap Up 1

B: ❶What's your plan for the weekend, Sumin? Are you going to do ❷anything special?

G: Yes. ❸On Saturday, ❹I'm going to visit my grandmother.

B: ❺How about on Sunday?

G: I have no plans for Sunday. Why?

B: I'm going to ❻do volunteer work at the library on Sunday. ❼Would you like to come with me?

❶ What's your plan for the weekend?: 너의 주말 계획은 뭐니?(= What are you going to do this weekend? = What are you planning to do this weekend?)
❷ '-thing', '-body', '-one'으로 끝나는 대명사는 형용사가 뒤에서 수식한다.
❸ 요일 앞에는 전치사 on을 사용한다.
❹ I'm going to 동사원형: 나는 ～할 거야. (의도 표현)
❺ How about on Sunday?: 일요일은 어때? (= What about on Sunday?)
❻ do volunteer work: 자원 봉사를 하다
❼ Would you like to 동사원형 ～?: ～할래?(요청, 제안하는 표현)

● 다음 우리말과 일치하도록 빈칸에 알맞은 말을 쓰시오.

### Listen & Speak 1 A

1. B: Did you watch the news _____ _____ _____?
   G: Yes, _____ _____. They said a _____ of people _____ their homes.
   B: My club is going _____ _____ them some money.
   G: _____ can you do that? _____ _____ going _____ _____ money, Andy?
   B: Yes. We're _____ _____ make pencil cases and _____ them.

2. B: Do you have any _____ for the summer _____, Suji?
   G: Yes. I'm _____ _____ the Philippines to _____ some volunteer work _____ my family.
   B: Oh, I _____ there and _____ some children study last year. _____ _____ _____ _____ _____ that, too?
   G: Yes. And I'll also _____ _____ with the children.
   B: That sounds nice.

### Listen & Speak 1 B

1. A: Are you going _____ _____ a short shower?
   B: Yes, I _____. / No, _____ _____.

2. A: Are you _____ _____ _____ bottles?
   B: Yes, _____ _____. / No, I'm not.

### Listen & Speak 2 A

1. G: _____ are you doing, Jason?
   B: I'm _____ a poster _____ global _____. Many people are _____ of hunger.
   G: That's _____ _____. I didn't know that.
   B: I _____ more people _____ _____ _____ hunger.

해석

1. B: 홍수에 대한 뉴스를 보았니?
   G: 응, 보았어. 많은 사람들이 집을 잃었다고 하더라.
   B: 우리 동아리는 그들에게 약간의 돈을 보낼 거야.
   G: 그것을 어떻게 할 수 있니? 돈을 모금할 거니, Andy?
   B: 응. 우리는 필통을 만들어서 그것들을 팔 거야.

2. B: 여름 방학에 어떤 계획이 있니, 수지야?
   G: 응. 나는 나의 가족들과 봉사활동을 하러 필리핀에 갈 거야.
   B: 오, 나는 작년에 그곳에 가서 몇몇 아이들이 공부하는 것을 도와줬어. 너도 그렇게 할 거니?
   G: 응, 그리고 나는 또한 아이들과 벽화를 그릴 거야.
   B: 정말 좋겠다.

1. A: 너는 샤워를 짧게 할 거니?
   B: 응, 그럴 거야. / 아니, 그러지 않을 거야.

2. A: 너는 병을 재활용할 거니?
   B: 응, 그럴 거야. / 아니, 그러지 않을 거야.

1. G: 무엇을 하고 있니, Jason?
   B: 세계의 기아 문제에 대한 포스터를 만드는 중이야. 많은 사람들이 기아로 죽어가고 있어.
   G: 정말 안됐다. 난 몰랐어.
   B: 더 많은 사람들이 세계의 기아 문제에 관심을 갖기를 바라.

2. **G:** Dad, my class decided _____ _____ a vegetable _____.

   **M:** A _____ _____? What _____ you grow there, Sena?

   **G:** Carrots. We'll _____ them and _____ them _____ others.

   **M:** That's a good idea.

   **G:** I _____ the carrots _____ well.

### Listen & Speak 2 B

1. **A:** I _____ people _____ _____ _____ trash.

   **B:** I _____ _____, too. _____ _____ a Keep the World Clean _____.

   **A:** That's a good idea.

2. **A:** _____ _____ _____ _____ hurt animals.

   **B:** I hope _____, too. _____ _____ a Love Animals campaign.

   **A:** That's a good idea.

### Wrap Up

1. **B:** _____ _____ _____ for the weekend, Sumin? _____ you going _____ _____ _____ _____?

   **G:** Yes. _____ Saturday, I'm _____ _____ visit my grandmother.

   **B:** How _____ _____ Sunday?

   **G:** I _____ no plans for Sunday. Why?

   **B:** I'm _____ _____ _____ _____ _____ at the library on Sunday. Would you _____ _____ _____ _____ with me?

   **G:** Sure.

2. **G:** My club is _____ _____ _____ a green campaign _____ school next Friday.

   **B:** _____ _____ a green campaign?

   **G:** It's a campaign to _____ the environment. Many students _____ _____ _____ the streets. We hope _____ _____ that.

   **B:** I _____ your campaign _____ well.

   **G:** Thanks. I hope so, too.

2. **G:** 아빠, 우리 반은 채소밭을 가꾸기로 했어요.
   **M:** 채소밭? 거기서 무엇을 기를 거니, 세나야?
   **G:** 당근이요. 우리는 그것을 길러서 사람들과 나눌 거예요.
   **M:** 좋은 생각이구나.
   **G:** 당근이 잘 자랐으면 좋겠어요.

1. **A:** 나는 사람들이 쓰레기를 버리지 않기를 바라.
   **B:** 나도 그렇게 생각해. '세상을 깨끗하게 하라'라는 캠페인을 열자.
   **A:** 좋은 생각이야.

2. **A:** 나는 사람들이 동물을 해치지 않기를 바라.
   **B:** 나도 그렇게 생각해. '동물을 사랑하라'라는 캠페인을 열자.
   **A:** 좋은 생각이야.

1. **B:** 너의 주말 계획은 뭐니, 수민아? 특별한 걸 할 거니?
   **G:** 응. 토요일에 할머니를 방문할 거야.
   **B:** 일요일은 어때?
   **G:** 일요일은 아무 계획 없어. 왜?
   **B:** 나는 일요일에 도서관에서 봉사활동을 할 거야. 나와 함께 갈래?
   **G:** 물론이지.

2. **G:** 우리 동아리는 다음 주 금요일에 학교에서 그린 캠페인을 열 거야.
   **B:** 그린 캠페인이 뭐야?
   **G:** 환경을 보호하기 위한 캠페인이야. 많은 학생들이 길에 쓰레기를 버려. 우리는 그걸 멈추길 바라.
   **B:** 네 캠페인이 잘 되길 바라.
   **G:** 고마워. 나도 그러길 바라.

[01~03] 다음 대화의 빈칸에 알맞은 말은?

## 01

A: Are you going to take a shopping bag?
B: _____

① Yes, I do.
② No, I don't.
③ Yes, I go.
④ Yes, I am.
⑤ No, you aren't.

## 02

A: _____
B: I hope so, too. Let's hold a Love Animals campaign.

① I hope to keep the world clean.
② I'm going to the Philippines to do some volunteer work.
③ I hope people don't hurt animals.
④ I hope that more people care about global hunger.
⑤ I want to turn down the heat.

## 03

B: What's your plan for the weekend, Sumin? Are you _____ do anything special?
G: Yes. On Saturday, I'm _____ visit my grandmother.

① going to
② going
③ planning
④ want
⑤ have to

## 04 자연스러운 대화가 되도록 순서대로 배열하시오.

(A) Carrots. We'll grow them and share them with others.
(B) Dad, my class decided to make a vegetable garden.
(C) A vegetable garden? What will you grow there, Sena?
(D) That's a good idea.

➡ _____

[01~03] 다음 대화를 읽고 물음에 답하시오.

> G: _____ (A) _____, Jason?
> B: I'm making a poster ⓐ global hunger.
>   Many people are dying ⓑ hunger.
> G: _____ (B) _____ I didn't know that.
> B: I hope more people care ⓒ global hunger.

**01** 빈칸 (A)에 알맞은 말을 고르시오.

① What are you planning to do
② What did you do
③ What are you going to do
④ What are you doing
⑤ What will you make

**02** 빈칸 (B)에 알맞은 말을 <u>모두</u> 고르시오.

① I want to cook food.
② I'm sorry to hear that.
③ Let's hold a Keep the World Clean campaign.
④ I usually like to make a poster.
⑤ That's too bad.

**03** 빈칸 ⓐ~ⓒ에 알맞은 말로 짝지어진 것은?

|   | ⓐ | ⓑ | ⓒ |
|---|---|---|---|
| ① | about | about | for |
| ② | at | of | for |
| ③ | about | about | at |
| ④ | about | of | about |
| ⑤ | for | for | at |

**04** 다음 중 짝지어진 대화가 <u>어색한</u> 것은?

① A: Are you going to turn down the heat?
  B: No, I'm not.
② A: I hope to solve this problem.
  B: I hope so, too.
③ A: Are you going to raise money?
  B: Yes, we are.
④ A: I hope the air gets cleaner. Let's hold a Plant More Trees campaign.
  B: That's too bad.
⑤ A: Are you planning to take a swimming lesson after school?
  B: Yes, I hope to swim in the sea.

[05~06] 다음 대화를 읽고 물음에 답하시오.

> G: Dad, my class decided to make a vegetable garden.
> M: A vegetable garden? What will you grow there, Sena?
> G: ⓐCarrots. We'll grow ⓑthem and share ⓒthem with ⓓothers.
> M: That's a good idea.
> G: I hope ⓔthey grow well.

서답형
**05** 다음 영영풀이에 해당하는 단어를 대화에서 찾아 쓰시오.

> a place where you can grow plants

➡ _____

**06** 밑줄 친 ⓐ~ⓔ 중 가리키는 것이 <u>다른</u> 것을 고르시오.

① ⓐ    ② ⓑ    ③ ⓒ
④ ⓓ    ⑤ ⓔ

**07** 밑줄 친 부분과 바꾸어 쓸 수 있는 문장을 <u>모두</u> 고르시오.

> **A:** <u>Are you going to take a shopping bag?</u>
> **B:** Yes, I am.

① Do you hope to take a shopping bag?
② Are you planning to take a shopping bag?
③ Do you take a shopping bag?
④ Are you trying to take a shopping bag?
⑤ Do you want to take a shopping bag?

**08** 빈칸에 알맞은 말을 고르시오.

> **A:** I hope the air gets cleaner.
> **B:** I hope so, too. _____

① Let's hold a Plant More Trees campaign.
② Let's hold a Love Animals campaign.
③ Let's hold a Save Water campaign.
④ I'm making a poster about global hunger.
⑤ I hope your campaign goes well.

**[09~12]** 다음 대화를 읽고 물음에 답하시오.

> **Karl:** Jiho, isn't that too much? Are you going to eat all of that? (①)
> **Jiho:** I'm not sure, but Bulgogi is my favorite. (①)
> **Karl:** Hey! Look at the campaign poster. "Think, Eat, Save!" (②)
> **Jiho:** What does that mean?
> **Karl:** It means "Think first before you eat and save the Earth." (③)
> **Jiho:** I think I took too much Bulgogi. (④)
> **Karl:** Okay. That's a good idea.

> **Jiho:** We ate it all. My clean plate makes me feel good. (⑤)
> **Karl:** Let's not waste ___(A)___ now on. I hope we can save the Earth.

**서답형**

**09** 위 대화의 ①~⑤ 중 다음 주어진 말이 들어갈 알맞은 곳은?

> Let's share it.

①      ②      ③      ④      ⑤

**서답형**

**10** 다음 영영풀이에 해당하는 단어를 대화에서 찾아 쓰시오.

> to fail to use time, money, energy, etc. fully or in the sensible or useful way

➡ _____

**11** 빈칸 (A)에 알맞은 것은?

① to            ② from
③ at            ④ of
⑤ with

**12** 위 대화의 내용과 일치하지 <u>않는</u> 것을 <u>모두</u> 고르시오.

① "Think, Eat, Save!" is on the campaign poster.
② Jiho is sure that he is going to eat all of Bulgogi.
③ Jiho likes Bulgogi.
④ They left some food.
⑤ Karl hopes to save the Earth.

[01~03] 다음 대화를 읽고 물음에 답하시오.

B: What's your plan for the weekend, Sumin?
Are you ___(A)___ to do anything special?

G: Yes. On Saturday, I'm ___(B)___ to visit my grandmother.

B: How about on Sunday?

G: I have no ___ⓐ___ for Sunday. Why?

B: I'm ___(C)___ to do volunteer work at the library on Sunday. Would you like to come with me?

G: Sure.

**01** (A)~(C)에 공통으로 들어갈 알맞은 말을 두 개 쓰시오. (주어진 철자로 시작할 것)

➡ (1) g_____ (2) p_____

**02** 빈칸 ⓐ에 알맞은 말을 대화에서 찾아 쓰시오. (복수형으로 쓸 것)

➡ _____

**03** According to the dialog, what will Sumin do on the weekend? (Answer in English)

➡ On Saturday, _____,
and on Sunday, _____
_____.

**04** 대화 속 괄호 안의 단어를 바르게 배열하시오.

A: (own, you, your, cup, going, are, use, to, ?)
B: Yes, I am.

➡ _____

[05~07] 다음 대화를 읽고 물음에 답하시오.

B: Did you watch the news about the flood?

G: Yes, I did. They said a lot of people lost their homes.

B: 우리 동아리는 그들에게 약간의 돈을 보낼 거야.

G: ___(A)___ can you do that? Are you going to raise money, Andy?

B: Yes. We're going to make pencil cases and sell them.

**05** 다음 영영풀이에 해당하는 단어를 대화에서 찾아 쓰시오.

| an overflow of water |
| --- |

➡ _____

**06** 밑줄 친 우리말을 주어진 단어를 이용하여 영작하시오.

➡ _____

(going, some, them)

**07** 빈칸 (A)에 알맞은 의문사를 쓰시오.

➡ _____

**08** 밑줄 친 우리말을 주어진 단어를 이용하여 영작하시오.

A: 나는 사람들이 쓰레기를 버리지 않기를 바라.
(away, don't, hope, trash)

B: I hope so, too. Let's hold a Keep the World Clean campaign.

A: That's a good idea.

➡ _____

# Grammar

교과서

## 1 주격 관계대명사

- Global citizens are people **who** try to understand different cultures.
  세계 시민이란 다른 문화를 이해하려고 노력하는 사람들이다.
- I want to live in a house **that** is not far from the school.
  나는 학교에서 멀지 않은 집에서 살고 싶다.

### ■ 주격 관계대명사

앞에 오는 명사를 대신하고 뒤에 오는 절을 선행사에 연결해 주는 대명사와 접속사 역할을 함께하는 것을 관계대명사라고 한다. 관계대명사에는 'who, which, that'이 있다. 관계대명사 뒤에 동사가 나오고 관계대명사가 이끄는 절에서 'who, which, that'이 주어 역할을 할 때 이를 주격 관계대명사라고 한다. 주격 관계대명사가 이끄는 절은 앞에 나온 명사인 선행사를 수식해 준다.

### ■ 주격 관계대명사의 종류

| 선행사 | 관계대명사 |
|---|---|
| 사람 | who |
| 사물·동물 | which |
| 사람·사물·동물 | that |

### ■ 관계대명사로 문장 연결하기

① 두 문장에서 동일한 대상을 가리키는 단어를 찾는다.

- The man is my friend. He is working in the garden.

② 뒤 문장의 대명사를 관계대명사(who, which, that)로 바꾼다.

- He is working in the garden.
  → who is working in the garden

③ 관계대명사가 이끄는 문장을 선행사 바로 뒤에 붙여 쓴다.

- The man **who** is working in the garden is my friend.

*cf.* '주격 관계대명사＋be동사'는 생략할 수 있다.

*e.g.* The man (**who is**) working in the garden is my friend.

### 핵심 Check

1. 괄호 안에서 알맞은 것을 고르시오.

   (1) I like the girl (which / who) is wearing a red ribbon.

   (2) I like the house which (has / have) big windows.

   (3) Ann is the girl (that / which) has blue eyes.

## ② something/anything/everything/nothing + 형용사

- You did **something wonderful**. 너는 멋진 일을 했구나.
- Sam didn't do **anything bad**. Sam은 나쁜 일을 하지 않았다.

■ '형용사+명사'의 어순

명사의 상태나 성격을 나타내는 형용사는 보통 명사 앞에 와서 명사를 꾸며 준다.

- Tom is a **good boy**.
- Ms. Jang is a **nice teacher**.
- This is a very **difficult problem**.

■ 형용사가 뒤에서 꾸며 주는 단어

'something, anything, nothing, everything'처럼 -thing으로 끝나거나 -body, -one으로 끝나는 부정대명사는 형용사가 뒤에서 꾸며 준다.

- I want to eat **something sweet**. 나는 뭔가 단 것이 먹고 싶다.
- Is there **anything interesting**? 뭐 재미있는 것 있니?
- I have **nothing special** to do this weekend. 이번 주말에 해야 할 특별한 일이 없어.
- I did **everything wrong**. 나는 모든 것을 잘못했다.

*cf.* 'something'은 긍정문에, 'anything'은 부정문과 의문문에 주로 쓰인다.

### 핵심 Check

**2.** 괄호 안에서 알맞은 것을 고르시오.

(1) There is (nothing strange / strange nothing) here.

(2) Peter didn't eat (delicious anything / anything delicious) today.

(3) They are holding (anything bright / something bright).

**3.** 주어진 단어를 바르게 배열하여 문장을 완성하시오.

(1) I need to drink _____. (cool, something)

(2) There is _____ here. (exciting, nothing)

(3) Do you have _____? (sweet, anything)

**01** 다음 문장에서 어법상 <u>어색한</u> 부분을 바르게 고쳐 쓰시오.

(1) Global citizens are people which try to understand different cultures.

_____ ➡ _____

(2) This is wonderful something.

_____ ➡ _____

(3) I know the girl which is wearing a white dress.

_____ ➡ _____

(4) Kate didn't eat delicious anything yesterday.

_____ ➡ _____

**02** 다음 빈칸에 들어갈 말로 알맞은 것은?

> There is a huge clock _____ called Big Ben.

① who　　　　② who is　　　　③ which
④ which is　　⑤ which are

**03** 두 문장을 한 문장으로 만들 때 빈칸에 알맞은 말을 <u>모두</u> 고르시오.

> • I need a woman.
> • She can take care of my baby.
> ➡ I need a woman _____ can take care of my baby.

① whose　　　② who　　　③ which
④ that　　　　⑤ what

**04** 다음 빈칸에 들어갈 말로 알맞은 것은?

> Global citizenship education is _____ for the world.

① useful anything　　　② useful something
③ something useful　　④ anything useful
⑤ useful nothing

**01** 다음 중 어법상 <u>어색한</u> 문장은?

① I saw strange something outside.
② I know a girl who wants to be a news reporter.
③ Ben is my neighbor who works in a hospital.
④ Sandra doesn't want to sell anything expensive.
⑤ Look at the dog that is very fat.

**서답형**

**02** 다음 우리말에 맞게 주어진 단어를 알맞은 순서로 배열하시오.

(1) 너는 유명한 누군가를 아니?
(do / famous / you / anybody / know)?
➡ _____

(2) 나는 뭔가 다른 것을 해보고 싶다.
(I / want / different / to / something / do).
➡ _____

(3) 너는 무언가 새로운 게 있니?
(have / anything / do / new / you)?
➡ _____

(4) 그는 어제 어떤 아름다운 사람을 만났다.
(he / yesterday / met / beautiful / someone).
➡ _____

**서답형**

**03** 다음 대화를 읽고 빈칸에 알맞은 관계대명사를 쓰시오. (that은 제외할 것)

> A: The lion _____ is in the cage looks sick.
> B: Yes, we should tell this to an animal doctor _____ takes care of animals.

**서답형**

**04** 다음 괄호 안에서 알맞은 단어를 고르시오.

(1) Laura was the first woman (who / which) became the president of the country.
(2) Students (who is / who are) good at painting will gather and paint on some walls of schools and parks.
(3) Dave first gave it to the girl (whose / who) was studying history.

**05** 다음 우리말에 맞게 알맞게 영작한 것은?

> 옆집에 사는 소녀는 Jenny다.

① Jenny is the girl which live next door.
② The girl which lives next door is Jenny.
③ The girl who live next door is Jenny.
④ Jenny lives next door who is the girl.
⑤ The girl who lives next door is Jenny.

**중요**

**06** 다음 문장에서 주격 관계대명사가 쓰인 문장은?

① Ann is the girl whom I was talking to.
② I know a chef who makes great food.
③ I like your jacket whose design is unique.
④ Amy is the girl whose dad is a doctor.
⑤ Jim is the boy who I made friends with.

**07** 〈보기〉의 밑줄 친 부분과 쓰임이 같은 것은?

┌─ 보기 ─┐
I admire the actress <u>who</u> helps the poor.
└────────┘

① <u>Who</u> won the prize this semester?
② She asked me <u>who</u> you are.
③ Can you tell me <u>who</u> is late for the meeting?
④ He is the man <u>who</u> takes care of some dogs.
⑤ Let me guess <u>who</u> you are thinking of.

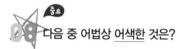

**08** 다음 중 어법상 어색한 것은?

① The company will hire a man that can speak English.
② I met an old lady that showed me the way to the station.
③ This is the girl who gave me the doll.
④ He has two daughters who is doctors.
⑤ I dislike the man that is wearing glasses.

**서답형**

**09** 어법상 틀린 부분을 찾아 바르게 고치시오.

(1) We have special nothing this weekend.

_____ ➡ _____

(2) Is there something interesting?

_____ ➡ _____

(3) Harry lives in a house who are 100 years old.

_____ ➡ _____

**10** 다음 빈칸에 들어갈 알맞은 것은?

┌──────────────────────────────┐
There are many people _____ want to take part in the festival.
└──────────────────────────────┘

① who            ② which
③ whose          ④ of which
⑤ whom

**11** 다음 두 문장을 한 문장으로 바꿀 때 빈칸에 들어갈 말로 바르게 짝지어진 것은?

┌──────────────────────────────┐
• I have two books.
• The books have many beautiful pictures.
➡ I have two books _____ many beautiful pictures.
• Do you know the man?
• He is wearing a hat.
➡ Do you know the man _____ wearing a hat?
└──────────────────────────────┘

① who have – who is
② who have – which is
③ which have – who is
④ which has – who are
⑤ which has – which is

**12** 다음 중 어법상 알맞은 것은?

① I like the girl which lives next door.
② Kate sent me a book who was written by Lee Sang.
③ I would like you to meet Ms. Ha whom is a great teacher.
④ Give me the phone whose is on the table.
⑤ They brought my mom the flowers that made her happy.

**서답형**

**13** 다음 괄호 안에서 알맞은 것을 고르시오.

(1) They enjoy reading books (who / which) are about Abraham Lincoln.

(2) He has two nephews (who / which) live in Rome.

(3) We prepared the surprise party (who / which) was for my daughter.

(4) She is going to meet the woman (who / which) studied abroad with her.

**14** 다음 빈칸에 들어갈 알맞은 것은?

I enjoy watching the movie _____ is scary.

① who              ② which
③ whom             ④ whose
⑤ of which

**서답형**

**15** 다음 우리말에 맞게 주어진 단어를 이용하여 영작하시오.

나는 뭔가 단 것이 먹고 싶다.
(sweet, something)

➡ _____

**서답형**

**16** 다음 우리말에 맞도록 빈칸에 들어갈 알맞은 말을 쓰시오.

우리는 키가 큰 누군가를 찾고 있다.
➡ We are looking for _____ _____.

**서답형**

**17** 다음 밑줄 친 부분과 바꿔 쓸 수 있는 말을 한 단어로 쓰시오.

There are many people that want to visit Rome.

➡ _____

**18** 다음 우리말을 바르게 영작한 것은?

미진이는 뜨거운 뭔가를 마시기를 원한다.

① Mijin wants to drink something hot.
② Mijin wants to drink hot something.
③ Mijin wants to drink to something hot.
④ Mijin wants to drink for hot something.
⑤ Hot something is wanted to Mijin.

**19** 다음 두 문장을 한 문장으로 바르게 바꿔 쓴 것은?

• I like to collect stamps.
• They were made in 1900s.

① I like to collect stamps who were made in 1900s.
② I like to collect stamps of which were made in 1900s.
③ I like to collect stamps which were made in 1900s.
④ I like to collect stamps which made in 1900s.
⑤ I like to collect stamps who made in 1900s.

**20** 다음 빈칸에 들어갈 알맞은 것은?

There is _____ interesting on TV now.

① a talk show      ② a drama
③ the news         ④ a movie
⑤ nothing

**서답형**

**21** 괄호 안에서 알맞은 것을 고르시오.

(1) He is the boy (who / whose) broke the window.

(2) A nurse is a person (which / that) looks after the sick.

**01** 다음 문장에서 어법상 틀린 부분을 찾아 바르게 고쳐 쓰시오.

> Did the thief take valuable anything?

➡ _____

**02** 다음 문장에서 어법상 어색한 부분을 고쳐 문장을 다시 쓰시오.

(1) Both paintings show a couple which are dancing.

➡ _____
_____

(2) In 1883, Renoir completed two paintings whose look very similar.

➡ _____
_____

(3) Jake is wearing a hat who look very old.

➡ _____

**03** 다음 문장에서 어법상 잘못된 부분을 찾아 바르게 고쳐 쓰시오.

(1) Sally enjoys drinking the tea who smells sweet.

_____ ➡ _____

(2) Kirk wants to live in a house who are not far from the station.

_____ ➡ _____

(3) Picasso is the famous painter whom is loved the most.

_____ ➡ _____

**04** 〈보기〉의 문장을 참고하여, 그림을 보고 관계대명사를 이용하여 문장을 완성하시오.

— 보기 —

Sumi is talking to a girl who is wearing glasses.

(1) Jiho is watering the plant _____ _____ yellow flowers.

(2) The girl _____ _____ cleaning the floor is Mina.

(3) Jinsu is reading a book _____ _____ a red cover.

**05** 두 문장을 관계대명사를 이용하여 한 문장으로 쓰시오. (that은 사용하지 말 것)

(1) Yesterday I met a girl.
+ She is from Mexico.

➡ _____

(2) I want to buy a smartphone.
+ It has a large screen.

➡ _____
_____

(3) John read an article.
+ It was written by his friend.

➡ _____
_____

**06** 주어진 단어와 'something, anything, nothing'을 이용하여 대화를 완성하시오.

> A: Do you have any plans this weekend?
> B: I have (1)_____ _____ to do this weekend. (special) Why?
> A: I'm planning to eat (2)_____ _____ with Jenny this weekend. (nice) Can you join us?
> B: Sure.

**07** 우리말과 일치하도록 주어진 어구를 알맞은 순서로 배열하시오.

(1) 선생님께서 뭔가 다른 것에 대해 말씀하셨다.
(something / talked / about / the / teacher / different)

➡ _____

(2) Sam은 그에게 너무 큰 신발을 신고 있다.
(Sam / big / that / is wearing / shoes / are / too / for him)

➡ _____

(3) 너는 여름 방학 동안 어떤 특별한 것을 할 거니?
(the summer / are / special / you / going / during / to / vacation / do / anything / ?)

➡ _____
_____

**08** 다음 글에서 어법상 틀린 부분을 찾아 바르게 고쳐 쓰시오.

> My group made a poster which aim to help people understand different cultures. We'll hold an Around the World Cultural Festival. If you want to do special something for other people, join us!

_____ ➡ _____
_____ ➡ _____

**09** 다음 대화의 밑줄 친 우리말에 맞도록 괄호 안의 단어들을 순서대로 바르게 배열하시오.

> A: I can't solve this science problem. Can you do me a favor?
> B: No, I can't. It's too difficult. <u>우리보다 더 똑똑한 누군가가 필요해.</u> (us / than / need / we / smarter / someone)

➡ _____

**10** 다음 문장을 어법에 맞게 고쳐 쓰시오.

(1) There is strange something on the roof of the house.

➡ _____
_____

(2) He liked to draw ballet dancers which was moving.

➡ _____
_____

(3) He fell in love with a lady which taught music at the nursing home.

➡ _____
_____

# Reading

教科書 (교과서)

## Global Citizenship Education

This is the Global Citizenship Education site. Global Citizenship Education helps us grow as global citizens. Global citizens are people who try to understand different cultures. They also care for people in need and work for a better world. Please share your global citizenship education experiences here.

Hello. I am Minhee from Korea. I am a member of the Global Community Club. My club aims to communicate with people from around the world. A week ago we produced a video about the lantern festival in our village. We uploaded it to the Internet and amazingly, we got nearly 5,000 hits. Click here for our video.

↳ **Alice:** Wow, your lantern festival looks fantastic!

↳ **Sunan:** We have a water festival in our village. I'd like to make a video like yours.

**Glossary (우측 단어)**

- global 세계적인, 지구의
- citizenship 시민 의식, 시민권
- education 교육
- site 사이트, 장소
- citizen 시민
- share 나누다, 공유하다
- care for 돌보다, 보살피다
- in need 어려움에 처한
- community 공동체, 사회
- aim 목표로 하다, 조준하다
- communicate 의사소통하다
- produce 생산하다
- lantern 등불, 등
- upload 올리다, 탑재하다

확인문제

● 다음 문장이 본문의 내용과 일치하면 T, 일치하지 <u>않으면</u> F를 쓰시오.

1  Global Citizenship Education helps us grow as global citizens. ☐

2  Global citizens try to understand their own cultures first. ☐

3  Global citizens are people who are in need. ☐

4  Global citizens work for a better world. ☐

5  Minhee is a member of the Global Community Club. ☐

6  Minhee's club aims to communicate with their neighbors. ☐

7  Minhee's club produced a video about the lantern festival in their village. ☐

Hi, my name is Jo. I am from Australia. A few weeks <u>ago</u>, my teacher
〜 전에

<u>showed</u> <u>us</u> <u>pictures of students</u> in Kenya. <u>Sadly</u>, they were all using
수여동사  간접목적어       직접목적어        문장 전체를 수식하는 부사

<u>plastic bags</u> <u>to carry</u> their books. My class decided <u>to raise</u> money to
비닐봉지   목적을 나타내는 to부정사              (자금 등을) 모으다, 모금하다

send <u>them</u> new school bags. We <u>sold</u> cookies and drinks and raised 600
= students in Kenya        sell의 과거형

dollars. We hope the Kenyan students <u>are happy with</u> the new bags.
        We hope와 the Kenyan 사이에는 두 문장을      〜에 기뻐하다
        연결해 주는 접속사 that이 생략되어 있다.

└, **Wang:** <u>Awesome</u>! I'm sure they will like the bags.
        굉장한

└, **Kozo:** You did <u>something wonderful</u>!
        something / anything / nothing+형용사 → 형용사가 뒤에서 수식


I am Afig from Malaysia. My school started a wall painting campaign

<u>to make our village look</u> better. Students <u>who</u> <u>are good at</u> painting
to부정사의 부사적 용법, 사역동사+목적어+동사원형      주격 관계대명사  〜을 잘하다

<u>gathered</u> and <u>painted</u> on some walls of schools and parks. Thanks to
모으다 V1        V2

this campaign, our village <u>looks</u> <u>much</u> nicer. Now everyone can enjoy
        'look(보이다)'은 감각동사로 뒤에 형용사가 온다.  비교급을 강조하는 부사

walking alongside the painted walls.
enjoy는 동명사를 목적어로 취함

└, **Junho:** What a nice idea!
        'It is a very nice idea.'라는 문장을 'What+a+형용사+명사(+주어+동사)!'
        어순의 감탄문으로 바꾼 것이다.

**raise** (돈을) 모으다, 기르다, 키우다
**Kenyan** 케냐의; 케냐인, 케냐어
**awesome** 감탄할 만한, 엄청난
**gather** 모이다
**campaign** 캠페인
**alongside** 〜 옆에, 〜와 나란히
**be good at** 〜을 잘하다, 〜에 능숙하다
**thanks to** 〜 덕분에

---

📎 **확인문제**

● 다음 문장이 본문의 내용과 일치하면 T, 일치하지 <u>않으면</u> F를 쓰시오.

1   Jo is from Austria. ☐

2   Jo's teacher showed students pictures of Kenyan students. ☐

3   The Kenyan students were using school bags to carry books. ☐

4   Jo's class decided to raise money to send the Kenyan students new school bags. ☐

5   Afig's school started a wall painting campaign. ☐

6   Students who are interested in painting gathered and painted. ☐

7   Thanks to this campaign, their school looks much nicer. ☐

8   Now everyone can enjoy walking alongside the painted walls. ☐

● 우리말을 참고하여 빈칸에 알맞은 말을 쓰시오.

**1** _____ _____ Education

**2** _____ _____ the Global Citizenship Education site.

**3** Global Citizenship Education _____ _____ _____ as global citizens.

**4** Global citizens are people _____ _____ _____ different cultures.

**5** They also _____ _____ people _____ _____ and work for a better world.

**6** Please _____ your global citizenship education _____ here.

**7** Hello. I am Minhee _____ _____.

**8** I am _____ _____ _____ the Global Community Club.

**9** My club aims _____ _____ _____ people from around the world.

**10** A week ago we produced a video _____ _____ _____ _____ in our village.

**11** We _____ _____ to the Internet and amazingly, we got nearly _____ _____.

**12** Click here _____ _____ _____.

**13** Alice: Wow, your lantern festival _____ _____!

**14** Sunan: We have _____ _____ in our village.

**15** I'd like to make a video _____ _____.

---

**1** 세계 시민 교육

**2** 이곳은 세계 시민 교육 사이트 입니다.

**3** 세계 시민 교육은 우리가 세계 시민으로 자라도록 도와줍니다.

**4** 세계 시민은 다른 문화를 이해 하려고 노력하는 사람들입니다.

**5** 그들은 또한 어려움에 처한 사 람들을 보살피고 더 나은 세상 을 위해서 일합니다.

**6** 당신의 세계 시민 교육 경험을 이곳에 공유해 주세요.

**7** 안녕. 나는 한국의 민희야.

**8** 나는 세계 공동체 동아리의 회 원이야.

**9** 우리 동아리는 전 세계의 사람 들과 소통하는 것을 목표로 해.

**10** 일주일 전에 우리는 우리 마을 의 등 축제에 관한 비디오를 제 작했어.

**11** 우리는 그것을 인터넷에 올렸는 데, 놀랍게도 거의 5,000개의 조회 수를 획득했어.

**12** 우리 비디오를 보려면 이곳을 클릭해.

**13** Alice: 와, 너희 등 축제는 환상 적으로 보인다!

**14** Sunan: 우리 마을에는 물 축제 가 있어.

**15** 나도 너희 것과 같은 비디오를 만들고 싶어.

**16** Hi, _____ _____ is Jo.

**17** I _____ _____ Australia.

**18** A few weeks ago, my teacher _____ _____ _____ of students in Kenya.

**19** Sadly, _____ _____ _____ using plastic bags _____ _____ _____ _____.

**20** My class decided _____ _____ _____ to send them new school bags.

**21** We sold cookies and drinks and _____ _____ _____.

**22** We hope the Kenyan students _____ _____ _____ the new bags.

**23** Wang: _____! _____ _____ they will like the bags.

**24** Kozo: You did _____ _____!

**25** I am Afig _____ Malaysia.

**26** My school started _____ _____ _____ campaign to make our village _____ _____.

**27** Students who _____ _____ _____ painting _____ and _____ on some walls of schools and parks.

**28** _____ _____ this campaign, our village looks _____ _____.

**29** Now everyone can enjoy _____ _____ the _____ walls.

**30** Junho: _____ _____ _____ _____ _____!

16 안녕, 내 이름은 Jo야.

17 나는 호주 출신이야.

18 몇 주 전에, 선생님이 우리에게 케냐에 있는 학생들의 사진을 보여주셨어.

19 슬프게도, 그들은 모두 책을 들고 다니기 위해서 비닐 봉지를 사용하고 있었어.

20 우리 반은 그들에게 새로운 책가방을 보내기 위해서 기금을 모금하기로 결정했어.

21 우리는 쿠키와 음료를 팔아서 600달러를 모았어.

22 우리는 케냐의 학생들이 그들의 새 가방을 좋아하기를 바라.

23 Wang: 멋지다! 분명 그들이 가방을 좋아할 거야.

24 Kozo: 훌륭한 일을 했구나!

25 난 말레이시아의 Afig야.

26 우리 학교는 우리 마을을 좀 더 좋아 보이게 하기 위해서 벽화 캠페인을 시작했어.

27 그림을 잘 그리는 학생들이 모여서 학교와 공원 벽에 그림을 그렸어.

28 이 캠페인 덕분에, 우리 마을은 훨씬 멋져 보여.

29 이제 모든 사람들이 그림이 그려진 벽을 따라서 산책하는 것을 즐길 수 있어.

30 Junho: 정말 멋진 생각이다!

● 우리말을 참고하여 본문을 영작하시오.

**1** 세계 시민 교육

➡ _____

**2** 이곳은 세계 시민 교육 사이트입니다.

➡ _____

**3** 세계 시민 교육은 우리가 세계 시민으로 자라도록 도와줍니다.

➡ _____

**4** 세계 시민은 다른 문화를 이해하려고 노력하는 사람들입니다.

➡ _____

**5** 그들은 또한 어려움에 처한 사람들을 보살피고 더 나은 세상을 위해서 일합니다.

➡ _____

**6** 당신의 세계 시민 교육 경험을 이곳에 공유해 주세요.

➡ _____

**7** 안녕. 나는 한국의 민희야.

➡ _____

**8** 나는 세계 공동체 동아리의 회원이야.

➡ _____

**9** 우리 동아리는 전 세계의 사람들과 소통하는 것을 목표로 해.

➡ _____

**10** 일주일 전에 우리는 우리 마을의 등 축제에 관한 비디오를 제작했어.

➡ _____

**11** 우리는 그것을 인터넷에 올렸는데, 놀랍게도 거의 5,000개의 조회 수를 획득했어.

➡ _____

**12** 우리 비디오를 보려면 이곳을 클릭해.

➡ _____

**13** Alice: 와, 너희 등 축제는 환상적으로 보인다!

➡ _____

**14** Sunan: 우리 마을에는 물 축제가 있어.

➡ _____

**15** 나도 너희 것과 같은 비디오를 만들고 싶어.

➡ _____

**16** 안녕, 내 이름은 Jo야.

➡ _____

**17** 나는 호주 출신이야.

➡ _____

**18** 몇 주 전에, 선생님이 우리에게 케냐에 있는 학생들의 사진을 보여주셨어.

➡ _____

**19** 슬프게도, 그들은 모두 책을 들고 다니기 위해서 비닐 봉지를 사용하고 있었어.

➡ _____

**20** 우리 반은 그들에게 새로운 책가방을 보내기 위해서 기금을 모금하기로 결정했어.

➡ _____

**21** 우리는 쿠키와 음료를 팔아서 600달러를 모았어.

➡ _____

**22** 우리는 케냐의 학생들이 그들의 새 가방을 좋아하기를 바라.

➡ _____

**23** Wang: 멋지다! 분명 그들이 가방을 좋아할 거야.

➡ _____

**24** Kozo: 훌륭한 일을 했구나!

➡ _____

**25** 난 말레이시아의 Afig야.

➡ _____

**26** 우리 학교는 우리 마을을 좀 더 좋아 보이게 하기 위해서 벽화 캠페인을 시작했어.

➡ _____

**27** 그림을 잘 그리는 학생들이 모여서 학교와 공원 벽에 그림을 그렸어.

➡ _____

**28** 이 캠페인 덕분에, 우리 마을은 훨씬 멋져 보여.

➡ _____

**29** 이제 모든 사람들이 그림이 그려진 벽을 따라서 산책하는 것을 즐길 수 있어.

➡ _____

**30** Junho: 정말 멋진 생각이다!

➡ _____

[01~03] 다음 글을 읽고 물음에 답하시오.

```
http://www.globalcitizen.com
SHARE        VIDEO        HELP        CAMPAIGN
```

**Global Citizenship Education**

This is the Global Citizenship Education site. Global Citizenship Education helps us grow ⓐas global citizens. Global citizens are people who try to understand different cultures. ⓑThey also care for people in need and work for a better world. Please share your global citizenship education experiences here.

**01** 위 글의 종류로 알맞은 것을 고르시오.

① e-mail from the education website
② review of the education experiences
③ article about the education site
④ writing posted on the website
⑤ summary of the citizenship education experience

**02** 위 글의 밑줄 친 ⓐas와 같은 의미로 쓰인 것을 고르시오.

① As she was tired, she soon fell asleep.
② He runs as fast as you.
③ He is famous as a singer.
④ As you know, he is honest.
⑤ As we go up, the air grows colder.

서답형
**03** 위 글의 밑줄 친 ⓑThey가 가리키는 것을 본문에서 찾아 쓰시오.

➡ _____

[04~06] 다음 글을 읽고 물음에 답하시오.

Hello. I am Minhee from Korea. I am a member of the Global Community Club. My club aims ⓐto communicate with people from around the world. A week ago we produced a video about the lantern festival in our village. We uploaded it ____ⓑ____ the Internet and amazingly, we got nearly 5,000 hits. Click here ____ⓒ____ our video.

**04** 아래 보기에서 위 글의 밑줄 친 ⓐto communicate와 to부정사의 용법이 같은 것의 개수를 고르시오.

┌─── 보기 ───┐
① I was glad to meet him at the party.
② He expected to go to Europe.
③ I have some pictures to show you.
④ It is good for the health to eat breakfast.
⑤ Do you want to go there?
└────────────┘

① 1개    ② 2개    ③ 3개    ④ 4개    ⑤ 5개

**05** 위 글의 빈칸 ⓑ와 ⓒ에 들어갈 전치사가 바르게 짝지어진 것은?

① to – for          ② from – in
③ on – from        ④ to – by
⑤ from – for

**06** 위 글의 제목으로 알맞은 것을 고르시오.

① Join the Global Community Club!
② How to Communicate with Netizens
③ How about Producing a Video?
④ The Most Famous Club in Our School
⑤ Let Me Introduce Our Club Activity

[07~09] 다음 글을 읽고 물음에 답하시오.

I am Afig from Malaysia. My school started a wall painting campaign to make our village look better. Students who are good at painting gathered and painted on some walls of schools and parks. Thanks to this campaign, our village looks ____ⓐ____ nicer. Now everyone can enjoy walking alongside the painted walls.

└, Junho: ⓑWhat a nice idea!

**07** 위 글의 요지로 알맞은 것을 고르시오.

① Afig의 학교는 다양한 캠페인을 시작했다.

② 그림을 잘 그리는 학생들은 봉사활동을 통해 보람을 얻을 수 있다.

③ 학교와 공원 벽에는 그림을 그려야 한다.

④ Afig의 학교는 벽화 캠페인으로 마을을 더 보기 좋게 만들었다.

⑤ 그림이 그려진 벽을 따라서 산책하는 것은 즐겁다.

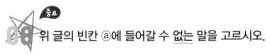
**08** 위 글의 빈칸 ⓐ에 들어갈 수 없는 말을 고르시오.

① very　　② much　　③ even

④ still　　⑤ a lot

**서답형**

**09** 위 글의 밑줄 친 ⓑ를 (1) How로 시작하는 감탄문과 (2) 평서문으로 고치시오.

➡ (1) _____

(2) _____

[10~12] 다음 글을 읽고 물음에 답하시오.

Hello. I am Minhee from Korea. I am a member of the Global Community Club. My club aims to communicate with people from around the world. A week ago we produced a video about the lantern festival in our village. We uploaded it to the Internet and amazingly, we got nearly 5,000 ____ⓐ____ s. Click here for our video.

└, Alice: Wow, your lantern festival looks fantastic!

└, Sunan: We have a water festival in our village. I'd like to make a video ⓑlike yours.

**서답형**

**10** 주어진 영영풀이를 참고하여 빈칸 ⓐ에 철자 h로 시작하는 단어를 쓰시오.

| a single visit to a website |
| --- |

➡ _____ s

**11** 위 글의 밑줄 친 ⓑlike와 다른 의미로 쓰인 것을 고르시오.

① She's wearing a dress like mine.

② Do you like your new house?

③ He drinks like a fish.

④ I cannot cook well like you.

⑤ She looks like an actress.

**중요**
**12** 위 글의 내용과 일치하지 않는 것은?

① 민희는 세계 공동체 동아리의 회원이다.

② 세계 공동체 동아리는 전 세계의 사람들과 소통하는 것을 목표로 한다.

③ 세계 공동체 동아리는 민희네 마을의 등 축제에 관한 비디오를 제작했다.

④ Alice는 등 축제가 환상적으로 보인다고 했다.

⑤ Sunan은 자기 마을의 물 축제에 관한 비디오를 만들었다.

[13~15] 다음 Sunan이 살고 있는 태국의 송크란 축제를 소개하는 글을 읽고 물음에 답하시오.

Where: In Thailand
When: from April 13th to 15th
Why: To celebrate the traditional Thai New Year and ⓐhave fun
What you can do at the festival:
• Enjoy the big water fight ___ⓑ___ is very popular
• Watch Songkran parade ___ⓒ___ shows Thai culture and traditions
• Taste traditional Thai food

**13** 위 글의 밑줄 친 ⓐhave fun과 바꿔 쓸 수 있는 말을 모두 고르시오.

① have a good time
② make fun of it
③ help yourself
④ enjoy yourself
⑤ make a funny face

서답형
**14** 위 글의 빈칸 ⓑ와 ⓒ에 공통으로 들어갈 말을 쓰시오.

➡ _____

**15** 다음 중 태국의 송크란 축제에 대한 설명과 일치하지 않는 것은?

① 4월 13일부터 15일까지 열린다.
② 전통적인 태국의 설날을 축하하는 축제이다.
③ 물싸움은 금지되어 있다.
④ 송크란 퍼레이드는 태국의 문화와 전통을 보여 준다.
⑤ 전통적인 태국 음식을 맛볼 수 있다.

[16~19] 다음 글을 읽고 물음에 답하시오.

Hi, my name is Jo. I am from Australia. (①) A few weeks ago, my teacher showed us pictures of students in Kenya. (②) Sadly, they were all using plastic bags ⓐto carry their books. (③) We sold cookies and drinks and raised 600 dollars. (④) We hope the ___ⓑ___ students are happy with the new bags. (⑤)

중요
**16** 위 글의 흐름으로 보아, 주어진 문장이 들어가기에 가장 적절한 곳은?

My class decided to raise money to send them new school bags.

①          ②          ③          ④          ⑤

**17** 위 글의 밑줄 친 ⓐto carry와 to부정사의 용법이 다른 것을 모두 고르시오.

① She needs someone to talk with.
② I am sorry to hear the bad news.
③ I use the computer to get information.
④ This book is easy to read.
⑤ To study English is interesting.

서답형
**18** 본문의 한 단어를 변형하여 위 글의 빈칸 ⓑ에 들어갈 알맞은 말을 쓰시오.

➡ _____

**19** 위 글을 읽고 대답할 수 없는 질문은?

① Where is Jo from?
② A few weeks ago, what did Jo's teacher show to the students?
③ Did the students in the pictures use school bags to carry their books?
④ Where did Jo's class sell cookies and drinks?
⑤ How much did Jo's class raise?

[20~23] 다음 글을 읽고 물음에 답하시오.

Hi, my name is Jo. I am from Australia. A few weeks ago, my teacher showed us pictures of students in Kenya. Sadly, they were all ①using plastic bags ②to carry their books. My class decided ③raising money to send ⓐthem new school bags. We sold cookies and drinks and ④raised 600 dollars. We hope the Kenyan students are happy with the new bags.

∟ **Wang:** Awesome! I'm sure they will like the bags.

∟ **Kozo:** You did ⑤something wonderful!

**20** 위 글의 주제로 알맞은 것을 고르시오.

① the pictures of the Kenyan students
② using plastic bags to carry the books
③ raising money to send new school bags
④ how to sell cookies and drinks
⑤ the difficulty of raising money

**서답형**

**21** 위 글의 밑줄 친 ①~⑤ 중 어법상 **틀린** 것을 찾아 고치시오.

_____ ➡ _____

**서답형**

**22** 위 글의 밑줄 친 ⓐthem이 가리키는 것을 본문에서 찾아 쓰시오.

➡ _____

**23** 위 글을 읽고 알 수 **없는** 것을 고르시오.

① Jo의 출신 국가
② Jo의 선생님이 보여주신 사진의 숫자
③ 사진의 학생들이 책가방으로 사용한 것
④ Jo의 반이 기금을 모금한 방법
⑤ Jo의 반이 모은 기금의 액수

[24~26] 다음 Sunan이 살고 있는 태국의 송크란 축제를 소개하는 글을 읽고 물음에 답하시오.

To my friend Minhee,

Hi, Minhee. I want to let you ①knowing about Songkran, a big festival in Thailand. It ②is held from April 13th to 15th. People ③hold this festival to celebrate the traditional Thai New Year and have fun. At the festival, you can enjoy the big water fight ④which is very popular. You can also watch Songkran parade ⑤that shows Thai culture and traditions. For food, you can taste traditional Thai food. If you want to experience something special, come and enjoy the Songkran festival.

From Sunan

**서답형**

**24** 위 글의 밑줄 친 ①~⑤ 중 어법상 **틀린** 것을 찾아 고치시오.

_____ ➡ _____

**25** 다음 빈칸에 들어갈 알맞은 말을 고르시오.

Sunan is _____ Minhee to come to Thailand and enjoy the Songkran festival.

① visiting
② calling
③ ordering
④ forcing
⑤ inviting

**26** 다음 중 송크란 축제에서 할 수 있는 것을 **모두** 고르시오.

① 물싸움
② 장기 자랑
③ 퍼레이드 구경
④ 민속 씨름
⑤ 태국 전통 음식을 맛보기

[01~03] 다음 글을 읽고 물음에 답하시오.

This is the Global Citizenship Education (A)[cite / site]. Global Citizenship Education helps us (B)[grow / growing] as global citizens. Global citizens are people who try to understand different cultures. They also ⓐcare for people in need and (C)[work / working] for a better world. Please share your global citizenship education experiences here.

**01** 위 글의 괄호 (A)~(C)에서 문맥이나 어법이나 알맞은 낱말을 골라 쓰시오.

➡ (A) _____ (B) _____ (C) _____

**02** 위 글을 읽고 Global citizens의 정의를 우리말로 쓰시오.

➡ (1) _____
  (2) _____
  _____

**03** 위 글의 밑줄 친 ⓐcare for와 바꿔 쓸 수 있는 말을 쓰시오.

➡ _____

[04~06] 다음 글을 읽고 물음에 답하시오.

Hello. I am Minhee from Korea. I am a member of the Global Community Club. My club aims to communicate with people from around the world. A week ago we produced a video about the lantern festival in our village. We uploaded it to the Internet and amazingly, ⓐ거의 5,000 조회 수를 획득했어. Click here for our video.

ㄴ Alice: ⓑWow, your lantern festival looks like fantastic!

ㄴ Sunan: We have a water festival in our village. ⓒI'd like to make a video like yours.

**04** 위 글의 밑줄 친 ⓐ의 우리말에 맞게 주어진 어휘를 이용하여 5 단어로 영작하시오.

| we, got |
| --- |

➡ _____

**05** 위 글의 밑줄 친 ⓑ에서 어법상 틀린 부분을 찾아 고치시오.

_____ ➡ _____

**06** 다음 빈칸 (A)와 (B)에 알맞은 단어를 넣어 위 글의 밑줄 친 문장 ⓒ가 말하고 있는 내용을 완성하시오.

Sunan wants to (A)_____ _____ _____ about a water festival in their village like (B)_____ _____ produced a video about the lantern festival in their village.

[07~10] 다음 글을 읽고 물음에 답하시오.

Hi, my name is Jo. ①I am from Australia. A few weeks ago, my teacher ②showed us pictures of students in Kenya. Sadly, they were all using plastic bags ③to carry their books. My class decided to raise money ⓐto send them new school bags. We sold cookies and drinks and ④raised 600 dollars. ⑤We hope the Kenyan students to be happy with the new bags.

**07** 다음 질문에 대한 알맞은 대답을 주어진 단어로 시작하여 쓰시오. (4 단어)

> Q: What were the Kenyan students in the pictures using to carry their books?
> A: They _____ .

➡ _____

**08** 다음 문장에서 위 글의 내용과 <u>다른</u> 부분을 찾아서 고치시오.

> Jo's class raised 600 dollars to send the Kenyan students new plastic bags by selling cookies and drinks.

_____ ➡ _____

**09** 위 글의 밑줄 친 ①~⑤ 중 어법상 틀린 것을 찾아 고치시오.

_____ ➡ _____

**10** 위 글의 밑줄 친 @를 3형식으로 고치시오.

➡ _____

**[11~12]** 다음 글을 읽고 물음에 답하시오.

> I am Afig from Malaysia. My school started a wall painting campaign to make our village look better. @그림을 잘 그리는 학생들이 모여서 학교와 공원 벽에 그림을 그렸어. Thanks to this campaign, our village looks much nicer. Now everyone can enjoy walking alongside the painted walls.

**11** 다음 질문에 대한 알맞은 대답을 주어진 단어로 시작하여 쓰시오. (5 단어)

> Q: Why did Afig's school start a wall painting campaign?
> A: To _____ .

**12** 위 글의 밑줄 친 @의 우리말에 맞게 한 단어를 보충하여, 주어진 어휘를 알맞게 배열하시오.

> gathered and painted / students / some walls / on / good / who / painting / schools and parks / are / of

➡ _____
_____

**[13~14]** 다음 글을 읽고 물음에 답하시오.

> To my friend Minhee,
> Hi, Minhee. I want to let you know about Songkran, a big festival in Thailand. It is held from April 13th to 15th. People hold this festival to celebrate the traditional ___@___ New Year and have fun. At the festival, you can enjoy the big water fight which is very popular. You can also watch Songkran parade that shows ___ⓑ___ culture and traditions. For food, you can taste traditional ___ⓒ___ food. If you want to experience something special, come and enjoy the Songkran festival.
> From Sunan

**13** 다음 빈칸 (A)와 (B)에 알맞은 단어를 넣어 송크란 축제에 대한 소개를 완성하시오.

> Songkran is held to celebrate the traditional (A)_____ _____ of Thailand. At the festival, you can enjoy the big (B)_____ _____ .

**14** 본문의 한 단어를 변형하여 위 글의 빈칸 @~ⓒ에 공통으로 들어갈 알맞은 말을 쓰시오.

➡ _____

교과서

# 구석구석

## Conversation B

**Karl:** Jiho, isn't that too much? <u>Are you going to</u> eat all of that?
= Are you planning to 동사원형 ~?: 너는 ~할 거니?

**Jiho:** I'm not sure, but Bulgogi is my <u>favorite</u>.
(형) 좋아하는 (명) 좋아하는 것, 여기서는 명사

**Karl:** Hey! Look at the campaign poster. "Think, Eat, Save!"

**Jiho:** <u>What does that mean?</u>
의미를 묻는 표현

**Karl:** It means "Think first before you eat and save the Earth."
'It means ~.'를 사용해서 설명할 수 있다. 몰라서 설명을 하지 못하는 경우에는 'I'm sorry. but I don't know what it means.'

**Jiho:** I think I took too much Bulgogi. <u>Let's share it.</u>  또는 'I'm not sure what it means.'
Let's 동사원형: ~하자  등으로 답한다.

**Karl:** Okay. That's a good idea.

**Jiho:** We ate it all. My clean plate <u>makes me feel good</u>.
make+목적어+동사원형: …가 ~하도록 만들다 feel+형용사: ~하게 느끼다

**Karl:** Let's not waste food from now on. I hope we can save the Earth.

구문해설 • **look at:** ~을 보다 • **share:** 같이 쓰다, 공유하다 • **waste:** 낭비하다, 허비하다
• **from now on** 앞으로는, 이제부터 • **save** 살리다, 구하다

## Project

**A:** <u>What kind of</u> activity do you like?
어떤 종류의

**B:** <u>What do you think about</u> sending shoes to poor children?
~하는 게 어때?

**C:** Good. I hope they are happy with them.

**D:** Let's make a poster about the activity to find <u>people</u> <u>who want to help</u>.
선행사  주격 관계대명사절(people을 수식)

Sending Shoes of Hope

Why: To help poor children <u>who don't have shoes</u>
주격 관계대명사절로 선행사 poor children을 수식

How: 1. Bring shoes from home.

2. Draw pictures or write caring words on them.

3. Send them to children in need.

When: July 3rd

If you want to do <u>something special</u> for the world, join us!
-thing+형용사

구문해설 • **activity** 활동 • **be happy with** ~에 만족하다 • **bring** 가져오다 • **caring** 배려하는
• **in need** 어려움에 처한

해석

Karl: 지호야, 너무 많지 않니? 너 그걸 다 먹을 거니?

지호: 잘 모르겠어, 그렇지만 불고기는 내가 가장 좋아하는 음식이야.

Karl: 저기! 캠페인 포스터를 봐. "생각하라, 먹어라, 구하라!"

지호: 저게 무슨 뜻이야?

Karl: 그것은 먹기 전에 먼저 생각하고 지구를 살리자는 뜻이야.

지호: 나 불고기를 너무 많이 담아온 것 같아. 나눠 먹자.

Karl: 그래. 좋은 생각이야.

지호: 우리 다 먹었네. 내 깨끗한 그릇을 보니 기분이 좋아.

Karl: 이제부터 음식을 낭비하지 말자. 나는 우리가 지구를 살리기를 바라.

A: 어떤 활동을 하고 싶니?
B: 가난한 아이들에게 신발을 보내는 게 어때?
C: 좋아. 그들이 그것들을 좋아하길 바라.
D: 도움을 주고 싶어 하는 사람들을 찾기 위해서 이 활동에 대한 포스터를 만들자.
희망의 신발 보내기
왜: 신발이 없는 가난한 아이들을 돕기 위해
어떻게:
1. 집에서 신발을 가져오세요.
2. 신발에 그림을 그리거나 배려의 말을 쓰세요.
3. 그것들을 어려움에 처한 아이들에게 보내세요.
언제: 7월 3일
세상을 위해 뭔가 특별한 일을 하고 싶다면, 우리와 함께 해요!

**01** 〈보기〉에 주어진 두 단어의 관계가 나머지와 <u>다른</u> 것을 고르시오.

┌─ 보기 ┌─
ⓐ gather – collect
ⓑ global – worldwide
ⓒ save – rescue
ⓓ upset – worried
ⓔ far – near
└─

① ⓐ     ② ⓑ     ③ ⓒ     ④ ⓓ     ⑤ ⓔ

**02** 밑줄 친 단어와 의미가 같은 것을 고르시오.

┌─────────────────────────┐
That movie is <u>awesome</u>.
└─────────────────────────┘

① impressive          ② interesting
③ awful               ④ boring
⑤ popular

**03** 그림을 보고 대화의 빈칸에 어울리는 단어를 고르시오.

┌─────────────────────────┐
A: Are you going to _____ all your
  food?
B: Yes, I am.
└─────────────────────────┘

① hold     ② take     ③ lose
④ leave    ⑤ finish

**04** 다음 〈보기〉의 단어를 사용하여 자연스러운 문장을 만들 수 <u>없는</u> 것은? (형태 변화 가능)

┌─ 보기 ┌─
campaign    bag    garden    trash
└─

① Do you need plastic _____ for food?
② This park will be closing in ten minutes.
   You must not leave the _____ behind.
③ Do you often have a _____ with your
   friends?
④ I want you to participate in our new
   _____.
⑤ Will you plant roses in your _____?

**05** 다음 대화의 빈칸에 알맞은 단어를 고르시오.

┌─────────────────────────┐
A: I hope people don't waste water.
B: I hope so, too. Let's hold a _____
   Water campaign.
A: That's a good idea.
└─────────────────────────┘

① Hold     ② Save     ③ Hope
④ Eat      ⑤ Waste

**[06~08]** 다음 대화를 읽고 물음에 답하시오.

B: Do you have any plans for the summer
   vacation, Suji?
G: Yes. I'm ___(A)___ (go) to the Philippines
   ___(B)___ (do) some volunteer work with my
   family.
B: Oh, I went there and ___(C)___ (help) some
   children study last year. 너도 그렇게 할 거니?
G: Yes. And I'll also paint walls with the
   children.
B: That sounds nice.

**06** 빈칸 (A)~(C)를 주어진 단어를 이용하여 채우시오.

➡ (A) _____ (B) _____ (C) _____

**07** 밑줄 친 우리말을 주어진 단어를 이용하여 영작하시오.

➡ _____

(too, that, going, 7단어)

**08** 위 대화를 읽고 답할 수 <u>없는</u> 질문을 고르시오.

① When did the boy go to the Philippines?
② Where is the girl planning to go for the summer vacation?
③ What did the boy do in the Philippines?
④ Does the boy have any plans for the summer vacation?
⑤ When is the girl going to go to the Philippines?

[09~10] 다음 대화를 읽고 물음에 답하시오.

B: Did you watch the news about the flood?
G: Yes, I did. They said a lot of people lost their homes.
B: My club is going to send them some money.
G: How can you do that? Are you going to raise money, Andy?
B: Yes. <u>우리는 필통을 만들어서 그것들을 팔 거야.</u>

**09** 다음 영영풀이에 해당하는 단어를 대화에서 찾아 쓰시오.

> to collect money for a particular purpose

➡ _____

**10** 밑줄 친 우리말을 주어진 단어를 이용하여 영작하시오.

➡ _____

(and, going)

[11~12] 주어진 문장 이후에 이어질 대화의 순서를 바르게 배열하시오.

**11**

> My club is going to hold a green campaign at school next Friday.

> (A) It's a campaign to protect the environment. Many students throw trash on the streets. We hope to stop that.
> (B) What is a green campaign?
> (C) Thanks. I hope so, too.
> (D) I hope your campaign goes well.

➡ _____

**12**

> What are you doing, Jason?

> (A) That's too bad. I didn't know that.
> (B) I'm making a poster about global hunger. Many people are dying of hunger.
> (C) I hope more people care about global hunger.

➡ _____

Grammar

**13** 우리말에 맞게 주어진 단어를 이용하여 영어로 쓰시오.

> 세상을 위해 뭔가 특별한 일을 하고 싶다면, 우리와 함께 해!
>
> (if / want / special / something / for)

➡ _____,
   join us!

**14** 다음 두 문장을 관계대명사를 이용하여 한 문장으로 쓰시오. (that은 쓰지 말 것)

(1) • He is the student.
    • He won the speech contest.
    ➡ _____

(2) • I know the man.
    • He was looking for his dog.
    ➡ _____

(3) • He wrote a novel.
    • It became a best-seller.
    ➡ _____

**15** 빈칸에 알맞은 것은?

> There is a lady _____ to see you.

① who want          ② who wants
③ which wanted      ④ who wanting
⑤ which to want

**16** 빈칸에 공통으로 들어갈 말은?

> • Look at the man _____ is wearing blue jeans.
> • There are animals _____ live in the water.

① who      ② that      ③ what
④ which    ⑤ whose

**17** 밑줄 친 부분의 쓰임이 다른 것은?

① Which one is his laptop computer?
② Can you tell me which book she wants to buy?
③ I don't know which car is Tom's.
④ She asked me which hat was mine.
⑤ Do you know the house which has a beautiful garden?

**18** 주어진 문장을 어법상 바르게 고친 것이 아닌 것은?

① They are holding bright something.
   ➡ They are holding something bright.
② I invited Tom and his cat who live near my house.
   ➡ I invited Tom and his cat which live near my house.
③ Terry is the girl which went there alone.
   ➡ Terry is the girl that went there alone.
④ If you find sharp something, you should not touch it.
   ➡ If you find something sharp, you should not touch it.
⑤ I like the house whom has big windows.
   ➡ I like the house which has big windows.

**19** 다음 문장에서 틀린 것을 고치시오.

> Prepare activities that helps people understand the country's culture.

_____ ➡ _____

## 20 다음 중 어법상 바르지 <u>않은</u> 것은 몇 개인가?

- She knows a guy who is selling cars.
- Ben is my neighbor which works in a hospital.
- I want to buy a bag that has many pockets.
- I know the man and his dog that are taking a walk in the park.
- We should take care of the cats which doesn't have a home.

① 1개          ② 2개          ③ 3개
④ 4개          ⑤ 5개

## 21 다음 빈칸에 들어갈 형태로 알맞은 것은?

Minsu has a cat _____ cute.

① who is          ② that are
③ who are         ④ which is
⑤ which are

## 22 다음 문장에서 <u>틀린</u> 곳을 찾아 바르게 고쳐 쓰시오.

(1) Students that is good at painting gathered and painted on some walls of schools and parks.

➡ _____

(2) A musician is a person which play music.

➡ _____

(3) The man is my friend that are working in the garden.

➡ _____

## 23 다음 중 어법상 바르지 <u>않은</u> 것은?

① He told me that I could be somebody more important.
② She needs somebody strong.
③ I think I ate something bad.
④ My sister likes to eat something sweet.
⑤ There's interesting nothing on TV tonight.

## 24 다음 중 어법상 올바른 문장을 고르시오.

① There is exciting nothing in that room.
② My grandfather told funny something to us.
③ Mr. Kim sent me an email who was written in French.
④ He is a baker who makes the best apple pie in my town.
⑤ I saw him making beautiful something.

---

**Reading**

**[25~26]** 다음 글을 읽고 물음에 답하시오.

This is the Global Citizenship Education site. Global Citizenship Education helps us grow as global citizens. Global citizens are people ___ⓐ___ try to understand different cultures. They also care for people in need and work for a better world. Please share your global citizenship education experiences here.

## 25 위 글의 빈칸 ⓐ에 들어갈 알맞은 말을 <u>모두</u> 고르시오.

① which          ② who
③ whom           ④ what
⑤ that

**26** 위 글의 내용과 일치하지 <u>않는</u> 것은?

① 세계 시민 교육은 우리가 세계 시민으로 자라도 록 도와준다.

② 세계 시민은 다른 문화를 이해하려고 노력하는 사람들이다.

③ 세계 시민은 어려움에 처한 사람들을 보살핀다.

④ 세계 시민은 더 나은 세상을 위해서 일한다.

⑤ 세계 시민은 교육 경험을 공유하는 사람들이다.

**[27~28]** 다음 글을 읽고 물음에 답하시오.

Hello. I am Minhee from Korea. I am a member of the Global Community Club. My club aims to communicate with people from around the world. A week ago we produced a video about the lantern festival in our village. We uploaded it to the Internet and amazingly, we got nearly 5,000 hits. Click here for our video.

└ **Alice:** Wow, your lantern festival looks fantastic!

└ **Sunan:** We have a water festival in our village. I'd like to make a video like yours.

**27** 본문의 내용과 일치하도록 다음 빈칸 (A)와 (B)에 알맞은 단 어를 쓰시오.

Minhee's club made a video about (A)_____ _____ _____ in their village, and Sunan wants to produce a video about (B)_____ _____ _____ in their village.

**28** 위 글을 읽고 대답할 수 <u>없는</u> 질문은?

① What is the aim of Minhee's club?

② What did Minhee's club produce?

③ How long did it take to make a video about the lantern festival?

④ How many hits did Minhee's club video get?

⑤ What does Alice think of the lantern festival?

**[29~30]** 다음 글을 읽고 물음에 답하시오.

Hi, my name is Jo. I am from Australia. A few weeks ago, my teacher showed us pictures of students in Kenya. Sadly, they were all using plastic bags to carry their books. ⓐ우리 반은 그들에게 새로운 책가방을 보내기 위해서 기금을 모금하기로 결정했어. We sold cookies and drinks and raised 600 dollars. We hope the Kenyan students are happy with the new bags.

**29** 위 글의 밑줄 친 ⓐ의 우리말에 맞게 한 단어를 보충하여, 주어진 어휘를 알맞게 배열하시오.

new school bags / money / decided / my class / to send / to / them

➡ _____

_____

**30** 위 글의 제목으로 알맞은 것을 고르시오.

① Fund Raising for Sending School Bags

② Pictures of the Kenyan Students

③ The Weak Point of Using Plastic Bags

④ How to Raise Money Effectively

⑤ The Strong Point of New School Bags

**01** 출제율 100%

다음 〈보기〉와 같은 관계가 되도록 빈칸에 알맞은 말을 쓰시오.

보기

China – Chinese

(1) America – _____

(2) Kenya – _____

**02** 출제율 90%

다음 밑줄 친 부분과 의미와 가장 가까운 것을 주어진 철자로 시작하여 쓰시오.

We should not harm any animals.

➡ h_____

**03** 출제율 95%

다음 우리말 해석에 맞게 빈칸을 완성하시오.

(1) My house is _____ from yours.
(우리 집은 너희 집에서 멀다.)

(2) The _____ can change a culture. (환경은 문화를 바꿀 수 있다.)

(3) I want to become an _____ lawyer. (나는 국제 변호사가 되고 싶다.)

**04** 출제율 90%

다음 중 단어의 영영풀이가 바르지 않은 것은?

① celebrate: to do something enjoyable on a special occasion

② environment: the nature where there are land, sea, air, plants, and animals

③ community: a group of people who live in the same area or who are similar in some way

④ fight: to contend in a battle or physical combat

⑤ gather: to share or exchange information or emotion with someone

**[05~08]** 다음 대화를 읽고 물음에 답하시오.

Karl: Jiho, isn't that too much? (A)너 그걸 다 먹을 거니?

Jiho: I'm not sure, but Bulgogi is my favorite. (①)

Karl: Hey! Look at the campaign poster. "Think, Eat, Save!" (②)

Jiho: What does that mean?

Karl: It means "Think first before you eat and save the Earth."

Jiho: I think I took too much Bulgogi. (③) Let's share it. (④)

Karl: Okay. That's a good idea.

Jiho: (⑤) My clean plate makes me feel good.

Karl: Let's not waste food from now on. I hope we can ____(B)____ the Earth.

**05** 출제율 100%

위 대화의 ①~⑤ 중 주어진 문장이 들어갈 알맞은 곳은?

We ate it all.

① ② ③ ④ ⑤

**06** 출제율 90%

밑줄 친 (A)와 의미가 같도록 주어진 단어를 이용해 문장을 완성하시오.

➡ _____

(of, going, that)

**07** 출제율 90%

빈칸 (B)에 들어갈 알맞은 말을 위 대화에서 찾아 쓰시오.

➡ _____

**08** 출제율 90%

다음 영영풀이에 해당하는 단어를 대화에서 찾아 쓰시오.

the nature where there are land, sea, air, plants, and animals

➡ _____

[09~11] 다음 대화를 읽고 물음에 답하시오.

G: ⓐ<u>My club is going to hold a green campaign at school next Friday.</u> (①)

B: What is a green campaign? (②)

G: (③) It's a campaign to ___(A)___ the environment. Many students ___(B)___ trash on the streets. (④)

B: I hope your campaign ___(C)___ well. (⑤)

G: Thanks. I hope so, too.

**09** 위 대화의 ①~⑤ 중 주어진 문장이 들어갈 알맞은 곳은?

> We hope to stop that.

①      ②      ③      ④      ⑤

**10** 밑줄 친 ⓐ와 같은 의미를 가진 문장으로 쓰고자 한다. 괄호 안에 주어진 단어를 알맞게 배열하시오

(1) (a, club, to, hold, campaign, at, planning, my, Friday, is, green, next, school)

   ➡ _____

   _____

(2) (next, hold, green, at, my, school, will, Friday, a, campaign, club)

   ➡ _____

   _____

**11** 빈칸(A)~(C)를 〈보기〉에 주어진 단어를 이용해서 채우시오. (형태 변화 가능)

┌─── 보기 ───
come   go   protect   raise
send   throw   visit

➡ (A) _____ (B) _____ (C) _____

**12** 다음 대화의 (A)~(D)에 어울리는 말을 골라 쓰시오.

B: Did you watch the news about the flood?

G: Yes, I did. They said a lot of people (A)[lose / lost / are going to lose] their homes.

B: My club is going to (B)[spend / sell / send] them some money.

G: How can you do that? Are you going to (C)[raise / rise / arise] money, Andy?

B: Yes. We're going to make pencil cases and (D)[sell / to sell / selling] them.

➡ (A) _____ (B) _____ (C) _____

   (C) _____

**13** 다음 대화의 흐름상 어색한 것을 고르시오.

Karl: Jiho, isn't that too much? Are you going to eat all of that?

Jiho: ①I'm not sure, but Bulgogi is my favorite.

Karl: Hey! Look at the campaign poster. "Think, Eat, Save!"

Jiho: ②What does that mean?

Karl: ③It means "Think first before you eat and save the Earth."

Jiho: ④I think I took too much Bulgogi. Let's share it.

Karl: Okay. That's a good idea.

Jiho: We ate it all. My clean plate makes me feel good.

Karl: ⑤Let's waste food from now on. I hope we can save the Earth.

①      ②      ③      ④      ⑤

**14** 다음 문장의 빈칸에 알맞은 것은?

> Do you know the girl _____ is sitting on the bench?

① when    ② who    ③ what
④ which    ⑤ whose

**15** 다음 빈칸에 공통으로 들어갈 말로 알맞은 것은?

> • I want to buy a backpack _____ has many big pockets.
> • The girl _____ is standing under the tree looks like my sister.

① that    ② who    ③ which
④ she    ⑤ it

**16** 다음 두 문장을 관계대명사를 이용하여 한 문장으로 바꾸시오.

> • The man is my friend.
> • He is working in the garden.

➡ _____

**17** 다음 중 어법상 어색한 것은?

① I want to buy something special for my mom.
② Did I do anything wrong?
③ Mr. Jackson is planning to eat something nice in the evening.
④ They have nothing special to do this weekend.
⑤ If you want to experience special something, come and enjoy the Songkran festival.

**18** 다음 글에서 어법상 어색한 것을 찾아 바르게 고치시오.

> My advice is to always think before you speak, especially when you want to say bad something about someone else.

_____ ➡ _____

**19** 다음 문장에서 생략된 관계대명사를 보충하여 다시 쓰시오.

> I will buy the novels written by Ernest Hemingway.

➡ _____

**20** 다음 글의 빈칸에 들어갈 말이 알맞게 짝지어진 것은?

> • Thery are many pets ___(A)___ require a lot of care and attention.
> • My role model is a woman ___(B)___ won a gold medal in the Olympics.

① that – which    ② who – who
③ which – who    ④ who – which
⑤ which – which

**[21~23]** 다음 글을 읽고 물음에 답하시오.

> This is the Global Citizenship Education site. ⓐ세계 시민 교육은 우리가 세계 시민으로 자라도록 도와줍니다. Global citizens are people who try to understand different cultures. They also care for people in need and work for a better world. Please ___ⓑ___ your global citizenship education experiences here.

**21** 위 글의 밑줄 친 ⓐ의 우리말에 맞게 주어진 어휘를 이용하여 9 단어로 영작하시오.

> as

➡ _____

**22** 다음 영영풀이를 참고하여 위 대화의 빈칸 ⓑ에 철자 s로 시작하는 단어를 쓰시오. <sub>출제율 90%</sub>

> have in common or use in common

➡ _____

**23** 위 글을 읽고 대답할 수 <u>없는</u> 질문은? <sub>출제율 95%</sub>

① What site is this?

② How does Global Citizenship Education help us grow as global citizens?

③ What do global citizens try to understand?

④ Whom do global citizens care for?

⑤ What do global citizens work for?

[24~26] 다음 글을 읽고 물음에 답하시오.

Hello. I am Minhee from Korea. I am a member of the Global Community Club. ⓐ우리 동아리는 전 세계의 사람들과 소통하는 것을 목표로 해. A week ago we produced a video about the lantern festival in our village. We uploaded ⓑit to the Internet and amazingly, we got nearly 5,000 hits. Click here for our video.

└ **Alice:** Wow, your lantern festival looks fantastic!

└ **Sunan:** We have a water festival in our village. I'd like ⓒto make a video like yours.

**24** 위 글의 밑줄 친 ⓐ의 우리말에 맞게 한 단어를 보충하여, 주어진 어휘를 알맞게 배열하시오. <sub>출제율 95%</sub>

> to / world / club / around / aims / people / the / communicate / from / my

➡ _____

_____

**25** 위 글의 밑줄 친 ⓑit이 가리키는 것을 본문에서 찾아 영어로 쓰시오. <sub>출제율 90%</sub>

➡ _____

**26** 아래 보기에서 위 글의 밑줄 친 ⓒto make와 to부정사의 용법이 다른 것의 개수를 고르시오. <sub>출제율 100%</sub>

> ┤ 보기 ├
> ① She went there <u>to meet</u> him.
> ② Did he promise <u>to study</u> hard?
> ③ It's time <u>to start</u> from the station.
> ④ Is there something wrong <u>to correct</u>?
> ⑤ What do you need <u>to make</u> the food?

① 1개 ② 2개 ③ 3개 ④ 4개 ⑤ 5개

[27~28] 다음 글을 읽고 물음에 답하시오.

I am Afig from Malaysia. My school started a wall painting campaign to make our village look better. Students who are good at _____ⓐ_____ gathered and painted on some walls of schools and parks. Thanks to this campaign, our village looks _____ⓑ_____ nicer. Now everyone can enjoy walking alongside the _____ⓒ_____ walls.

**27** 위 글의 빈칸 ⓐ와 ⓒ에 paint를 각각 알맞은 형태로 쓰시오. <sub>출제율 95%</sub>

➡ ⓐ _____ ⓒ _____

**28** 빈칸 ⓑ에 들어갈 수 <u>없는</u> 것은? <sub>출제율 95%</sub>

① far ② very

③ even ④ still

⑤ a lot

[01~02] 주어진 영영풀이에 해당하는 단어를 이용하여 다음 대화의 빈칸을 채우시오. (내용상이나 어법상 단어 추가 가능)

**01**

A: Are you going _____ bottles?
B: Yes, I am.

to process used or waste materials so as to make suitable for reuse

➡ _____

**02** 중요

A: I hope people _____ animals.
B: I hope so, too. Let's hold a Love Animals campaign.
A: That's a good idea.

to injure or cause pain to a part of someone's body

➡ _____

**03** 괄호 안의 단어를 이용하여 밑줄 친 우리말을 바르게 영작하시오. (if로 시작할 것)

W: Every day, many students leave some food on their plates. So, our club is going to hold a campaign about it. 만약 여러분이 접시에 담은 음식을 다 먹는다면, 작은 선물을 받을 것이다. I hope many students join our campaign.

➡ _____

_____

(finish, small, if, get, gift, all)

**04** 다음 우리말에 맞게 주어진 단어를 이용하여 빈칸에 들어갈 알맞은 말을 쓰시오.

(1) 우리 계획에는 잘못된 것이 있어.
➡ There is _____ _____ with our plan. (wrong, something)

(2) 거기에 재미있는 게 있니?
➡ Is there _____ _____ there? (anything, interesting)

(3) 우리는 중요한 모든 것을 복사해야 한다.
➡ We must take a copy of _____ _____. (important, everything)

**05** 중요 다음 문장에서 어법상 틀린 부분을 찾아 바르게 고쳐 쓰시오.

(1) This is the girl who like to play the violin.
_____ ➡ _____

(2) The man which teach English is my father.
_____ ➡ _____

**06** 다음 두 문장을 관계대명사를 이용하여 한 문장으로 바꾸시오.

(1) • I like my house.
• It is by the lake.
➡ _____

(2) • Look at my dog.
• It is playing with a ball.
➡ _____

**07** 다음 문장은 생략 가능한 부분이 있다. 생략하여 문장을 다시 쓰시오.

> Look at the bird that is flying in the sky.

➡ _____

**[08~10]** 다음 글을 읽고 물음에 답하시오.

> Hello. I am Minhee from Korea. I am a member of the Global Community Club. My club aims to communicate with people from around the world. A week ago we produced a video about the lantern festival in our village. We (A)[uploaded / downloaded] it to the Internet and amazingly, we got (B)[near / nearly] 5,000 hits. Click here for our video.
> └ **Alice:** Wow, your lantern festival looks fantastic!
> └ **Sunan:** We have a water festival in our village. I'd like (C)[to make / making] a video like yours.

**08** 위 글의 괄호 (A)~(C)에서 문맥이나 어법상 알맞은 낱말을 골라 쓰시오.

➡ (A) _____ (B) _____ (C) _____

**09** 다음 빈칸 (A)와 (B)에 알맞은 단어를 넣어 Global Community Club에 대한 소개를 완성하시오. (본문의 단어를 이용할 것.)

> It is a club whose ___(A)___ is to communicate with people from around the world. The club members made a video introducing a local festival and ___(B)___ it to the Internet.

➡ (A) _____ (B) _____

**10** 다음 문장에서 위 글의 내용과 다른 부분을 찾아서 고치시오.

> A week ago Minhee's club made a video about the lantern festival in the world.

_____ ➡ _____

**[11~13]** 다음 글을 읽고 물음에 답하시오.

> I am Afig from Malaysia. My school started a wall painting campaign ⓐ우리 마을을 더 좋아 보이게 하기 위해서. Students who are good at painting gathered and painted on some walls of schools and parks. Thanks to ⓑthis campaign, ⓒour village looks very nicer. Now everyone can enjoy walking alongside the painted walls.

**11** 위 글의 밑줄 친 ⓐ의 우리말에 맞게 주어진 어휘를 이용하여 6 단어로 영작하시오.

> to, better

➡ _____

**12** 다음 빈칸 (A)와 (B)에 알맞은 단어를 넣어 ⓑthis campaign에 대한 설명을 완성하시오.

> It is a (A)_____ _____ campaign which Afig's school started, and students who (B)_____ well gathered and painted on some walls of schools and parks.

➡ (A) _____ (B) _____

**13** 위 글의 밑줄 친 ⓒ에서 어법상 틀린 부분을 찾아 고치시오.

_____ ➡ _____

**01** 다음 그림을 보고 여름 방학에 하려고 계획하는 일에 대한 대화의 빈칸을 완성하시오. (주어진 단어를 활용할 것)

Karen – vegetable garden

Yuri – do volunteer work, library

Yuri: Do you have any plans for _____, Karen?

Karen: Yes. _____. (going) How about you?

Yuri: _____. (planning)

Karen: That's a good idea.

**02** 〈보기〉를 참고하여 주어진 단어와 관계대명사를 이용하여 사람을 묘사하는 문장 3개를 만드시오.

보기

A thief is a person who steals things.

a thief / a musician / a dentist / a genius / a patient

steals things / sees a doctor / plays music / takes care of your teeth / is very intelligent

**03** 다음 세계 시민 교육을 실천하기 위해 어떤 활동을 할지에 관한 내용을 바탕으로 세계 시민 교육 활동의 참가자를 모집하는 공고문을 만드시오.

A: What kind of activity do you like?

B: What do you think about sending shoes to poor children?

C: Good. I hope they are happy with them.

D: Let's make a poster about the activity to find people who want to help.

| Why | To help poor children who don't have (A) |
| --- | --- |
| How | 1. Bring shoes from home. |
|  | 2. (B) pictures or (C) caring words on them. |
|  | 3. Send them to children in (D) . |
| When | July 3rd |

If you want to do something (E) for the world, join us!

# 단원별 모의고사

**01** 주어진 문장의 밑줄 친 hold의 뜻과 같은 의미로 쓰이지 않은 것을 고르시오.

> A: I hope the air gets cleaner.
> B: I hope so, too. Let's <u>hold</u> a Plant More Trees campaign.
> A: That's a good idea.

① I <u>held</u> a party this morning.
② The kite festival is <u>held</u> every year.
③ He <u>held</u> her by the arm.
④ The fans <u>held</u> an online contest last year.
⑤ We <u>held</u> a celebration for his promotion.

**02** 다음 우리말 해석에 맞게 빈칸을 완성하시오. (철자가 주어진 경우 그 철자로 시작할 것)

(1) Tickets are $2 for a_____ and $1 for children. (티켓은 어른은 2달러이고 아이들은 1달러이다.)

(2) Tom a_____ to be back to work in time, but was _____. (Tom은 제시간에 직장에 돌아가려고 목표했지만 늦었다.)

(3) We should know the value of _____. (우리는 교육의 가치를 알아야 한다.)

(4) Members of the charity r_____ money for people _____ _____. (그 자선 단체 회원들은 어려움에 처한 사람들을 위해 모금한다.)

**[03~04]** 다음 글을 읽고 물음에 답하시오.

> W: Every day, many students ___(A)___ some food on their plates. So, our club is going to ___(B)___ a campaign about it. If you ___(C)___ all the food on your plate, you will get a small gift. <u>나는 많은 학생들이 우리 캠페인에 참여하기를 바란다.</u>

**03** 다음 〈보기〉에서 빈칸 (A)~(C)에 들어갈 단어를 골라 쓰시오.

> ┌─ 보기 ├─
> hold   hope   mean   save   volunteer
> leave   finish   hurt   get

➡ (A) _____ (B) _____ (C) _____

**04** 괄호 안의 단어를 이용하여 밑줄 친 우리말을 바르게 영작하시오.

➡ _____

(join, hope, many)

**[05~06]** 다음 대화를 읽고 물음에 답하시오.

> B: Did you watch the news about the flood?
> G: Yes, I did. They said a lot of people lost their homes.
> B: My club is going to send them some money.
> G: How can you do that? Are you going to raise money, Andy?
> B: Yes. We're going to make pencil cases and sell them.

**05** 다음 영영풀이에 해당하는 단어를 대화에서 찾아 쓰시오.

> to give goods in exchange for money

➡ _____

**06** 위 대화를 읽고 답할 수 없는 질문을 고르시오.

① Did the boy watch the news about the flood?
② Why did many people lose their homes?
③ Is the boy a member of the club?
④ How will the boy raise the money?
⑤ Does the girl know how to make pencil cases?

**[07~09]** 다음 대화를 읽고 물음에 답하시오.

B: What's your plan ⓐfor the weekend, Sumin? Are you going to do ⓑspecial anything? (①)

G: Yes. (②) ⓒOn Saturday, ⓓI was going to visit my grandmother.

B: ⓔHow about on Sunday? (③)

G: (④) I have no plans for Sunday. Why?

B: I'm going to ___(A)___ volunteer work at the library on Sunday. (⑤)

G: Sure.

**07** 위 대화의 ①~⑤ 중 주어진 말이 들어갈 알맞은 곳은?

> Would you like to come with me?

① ② ③ ④ ⑤

**08** ⓐ~ⓔ 중 어법상 어색한 부분을 모두 골라 고치시오.

➡ _____

_____

**09** 위 대화의 빈칸 (A)에 알맞은 말을 대화에서 찾아 쓰시오.

➡ _____

**[10~11]** 다음 대화를 읽고 물음에 답하시오.

G: What are you doing, Jason?

B: I'm making a poster about global hunger. Many people are (A)die of hunger.

G: That's too bad. I didn't know that.

B: (B)더 많은 사람들이 세계의 기아 문제에 관심을 갖기를 바라.

**10** 밑줄 친 (A)를 알맞은 형으로 고치시오.

➡ _____

**11** 괄호 안의 단어를 이용하여 밑줄 친 우리말을 바르게 영작하시오.

➡ _____

(care, global, hope, more)

**12** ⓐ~ⓔ 중 어법상 어색한 부분을 모두 골라 고치시오.

G: Dad, my class decided ⓐmaking a vegetable garden.

M: A vegetable garden? ⓑWhat will you grow there, Sena?

G: Carrots. We'll grow them and share ⓒit ⓓby others.

M: That's a good idea.

G: I hope the carrots grow ⓔgood.

➡ _____

_____

**13** 다음 괄호 안의 단어를 알맞은 곳에 넣어 문장을 다시 쓰시오.

(1) She wanted to do something. (different)

➡ _____

(2) I did nothing last year. (special)

➡ _____

(3) Your daughter will never do anything again. (stupid)

➡ _____

**14** 두 문장을 한 문장으로 바꾸어 쓸 때 빈칸에 알맞은 말은?

- She bought an expensive watch.
- It was made in Switzerland.
➡ She bought an expensive watch _____ made in Switzerland.

① which
② which were
③ who was
④ which was
⑤ who

**15** 다음 중 어법상 틀린 문장을 바르게 고친 것이 아닌 것은?

① The film who was based on a true story impressed many people.
➡ The film which was based on a true story impressed many people.
② We need delicious something.
➡ We need something delicious.
③ Look at the girl who are playing the violin on the stage.
➡ Look at the girl who is playing the violin on the stage.
④ The car who is parked here is mine.
➡ The car which is parked here is mine.
⑤ Is there strong somebody to carry this box?
➡ Is there strong anybody to carry this box?

**16** 다음 문장의 빈칸에 알맞은 말을 쓰시오.

Abraham Lincoln was the sixteenth President _____ succeeded in freeing black slaves.

➡ _____

**17** 다음 글을 읽고 밑줄 친 부분을 바르게 고치시오.

Sori has bought the latest cell phone. The cell phone whose has a camera is really small. My cousin who live in California has the same cell phone.

➡ _____ ➡ _____
_____ ➡ _____

**18** 다음 두 문장을 한 문장으로 알맞게 바꾼 것은?

- I bought a car.
- It was made in Germany.

① I bought a car which made in Germany.
② I bought a car who was made in Germany.
③ I bought a car who made in Germany.
④ I bought a car which was made in Germany.
⑤ I bought a car that made in Germany.

**19** 다음 중 어법상 어색한 것은?

① There are people who make noises in public places.
② She lives in the house which has seven bedrooms.
③ He has the dog that has brown eyes.
④ Summer is the season that comes after spring.
⑤ I read the letter who was written in French.

**[20~21]** 다음 글을 읽고 물음에 답하시오.

This is the Global Citizenship Education site. Global Citizenship Education helps us grow as global citizens. Global citizens are people who try ⓐto understand different cultures. ⓑ그들은 또한 어려움에 처한 사람들을 보살핀다 and work for a better world. Please share your global citizenship education experiences here.

**20** 위 글의 밑줄 친 ⓐto understand와 to부정사의 용법이 같은 것을 모두 고르시오.

① She worked hard to pass the test.
② What's the fast way to buy the ticket?
③ It is important to finish your work.
④ She decided to meet her sister.
⑤ He was happy to meet her.

**21** 위 글의 밑줄 친 ⓑ의 우리말에 맞게 한 단어를 보충하여, 주어진 어휘를 알맞게 배열하시오.

for / they / care / need / people / also

➡ _____

**[22~23]** 다음 글을 읽고 물음에 답하시오.

Hello. I am Minhee from Korea. (①) I am a member of the Global Community Club. (②) My club aims to communicate with people from around the world. (③) We uploaded it to the Internet and amazingly, we got nearly 5,000 hits. (④) Click here for our video. (⑤)
└ **Alice:** Wow, your lantern festival looks fantastic!
└ **Sunan:** We have a water festival in our village. I'd like to make a video like ⓐyours.

**22** 위 글의 흐름으로 보아, 주어진 문장이 들어가기에 가장 적절한 곳은?

A week ago we produced a video about the lantern festival in our village.

①        ②        ③        ④        ⑤

**23** 위 글의 밑줄 친 ⓐyours가 가리키는 것을 영어로 쓰시오.

➡ _____

**[24~25]** 다음 글을 읽고 물음에 답하시오.

I am Afig from Malaysia. My school started a wall painting campaign to make our village (A)[look / to look] better. Students who are good at painting gathered and painted on some walls of schools and parks. Thanks to this campaign, our village looks much nicer. Now everyone can enjoy (B)[to walk / walking] alongside the painted walls.
└ **Junho:** (C)[How / What] a nice idea!

**24** 위 글의 괄호 (A)~(C)에서 어법상 알맞은 낱말을 골라 쓰시오.

➡ (A) _____ (B) _____ (C) _____

**25** 위 글을 읽고 대답할 수 없는 질문은?

① Where is Afig from?
② What did Afig's school start?
③ Who gathered and painted?
④ How many students joined it?
⑤ Where did the students paint?

# Interesting Facts Are Around Us

교과서
# Words & Expressions

## Key Words

- **adult**[ədʌ́lt] 명 성인, 어른
- **again**[əgén] 부 다시
- **average**[ǽvəridʒ] 명 보통, 평균
- **bite**[bait] 동 물다
- **blood**[blʌd] 명 피
- **bone**[boun] 명 뼈
- **completely**[kəmplíːtli] 부 완전히
- **during**[djúəriŋ] 전 ~ 동안, ~ 중에
- **enough**[inʌ́f] 형 충분한
- **expand**[ikspǽnd] 동 팽창하다
- **false**[fɔːls] 형 거짓의
- **female**[fíːmeil] 명 여성, 암컷
- **fewer**[fjúːər] 형 (**few**의 비교급) 보다 적은
- **gravity**[grǽvəti] 명 중력
- **grow**[grou] 동 (사람 · 동식물 등이) 자라다, 성장하다
- **guess**[ges] 동 추측하다
- **heat**[hiːt] 명 열, 열기
- **inventor**[invéntər] 명 발명가
- **item**[áitəm] 명 항목, 물품

- **lay**[lei] 동 (새 · 곤충 등이) [알을] 낳다
- **lightning**[láitniŋ] 명 번개, 벼락
- **male**[meil] 명 남성, 수컷
- **Mars**[maːrz] 명 화성
- **metal**[métl] 명 금속
- **mosquito**[məskíːtou] 명 모기
- **next**[nekst] 형 다음의 부 그 다음에
- **produce**[prədjúːs] 동 (자식 · 새끼를) 낳다
- **rest**[rest] 동 쉬다, 휴식하다
- **same**[seim] 형 같은, 똑같은
- **strike**[straik] 동 부딪치다, 충돌하다
- **tongue**[tʌŋ] 명 혀
- **topic**[tápik] 명 화제, 주제
- **toward**[tɔːrd] 전 (위치 · 방향) ~쪽으로
- **twice**[twais] 부 두 번, 두 배
- **Venus**[víːnəs] 명 금성
- **weaken**[wíːkən] 동 약화시키다, 약화되다
- **weigh**[wei] 동 무게가 ~ 나가다, 무게를 달다
- **whale**[hweil] 명 고래

## Key Expressions

- **a few** 약간의, 조금
- **be full of** ~로 가득 차다
- **due to** ~ 때문에
- **find out** 알아보다, 찾아보다
- **go away** 사라지다
- **in fact** 사실상, 실제로

- **join together** ~와 이어지다
- **on average** 평균적으로
- **over and over** 여러 번, 몇 번이고
- **such as** ~와 같은
- **up to** (특정한 수 또는 정도) ~까지
- **with time** 시간이 지남에 따라

## Word Power

※ 뒤에 접미사 'en'을 붙여 형용사가 동사로 바뀌는 단어

- □ **bright**(밝은) → **brighten**(밝히다)
- □ **dark**(어두운) → **darken**(어둡게 하다)
- □ **straight**(똑바른) → **straighten**(똑바르게 하다)
- □ **weak**(약한) → **weaken**(약화시키다)

- □ **broad**(넓은) → **broaden**(넓어지다)
- □ **deep**(깊은) → **deepen**(깊게 하다)
- □ **short**(짧은) → **shorten**(줄이다, 짧아지다)
- □ **tight**(꽉 조인) → **tighten**(꽉 조이다)

※ 서로 반대되는 뜻을 가진 단어

- □ **false**(거짓의) ↔ **true**(사실인)
- □ **same**(같은, 똑같은) ↔ **different**(다른)

- □ **female**(여성, 암컷) ↔ **male**(남성, 수컷)
- □ **weaken**(약화시키다, 약화되다) ↔ **strengthen**(강화하다)

※ 서로 비슷한 뜻을 가진 단어

- □ **enough**(충분한) : **sufficient**(충분한)
- □ **next**(다음의) : **following**(다음의, 다음에 계속되는)

- □ **guess**(추측하다) : **estimate**(평가하다, 추정하다)
- □ **topic**(화제, 주제) : **subject**(주제, 당면 과제)

## English Dictionary

- □ **average** 보통, 평균
  → the usual amount, extent, quality, number, etc.
  보통[평균]의 양, 정도, 질, 수 등

- □ **bite** 물다
  → to seize or grasp something with teeth
  이를 이용해 무언가를 붙잡거나 움켜잡다

- □ **blood** 피
  → a red fluid in living things
  살아있는 것 안에 있는 빨간 액체

- □ **bone** 뼈
  → a white piece of tissue providing structural support for the body
  몸에 구조적 지지를 제공하는 하얀 조직

- □ **completely** 완전히
  → to a complete degree or to the full or entire extent
  완전한 정도로 또는 완전히 또는 전적으로

- □ **expand** 팽창하다
  → to increase in size, number, or importance
  크기, 수 또는 중요성에서 증가하다

- □ **false** 거짓의
  → not real, because it is not true
  진실이 아니기 때문에 사실이 아닌

- □ **female** 여성, 암컷
  → the gender which has the ability to give birth to children
  아이를 낳을 수 있는 성

- □ **gravity** 중력
  → the force that a planet pulls things towards the center of it
  행성이 그것의 중심 쪽으로 당기는 힘

- □ **inventor** 발명가
  → a person who creates something that does not exist
  존재하지 않는 어떤 것을 창조하는 사람

- □ **male** 남성, 수컷
  → the gender which does not give birth
  출산할 수 없는 성

- □ **metal** 금속
  → a hard substance such as lead, iron, gold, etc.
  납, 철, 금 등과 같은 단단한 물질

- □ **mosquito** 모기
  → a small flying insect which bites and sucks blood
  물고, 피를 빠는 날아다니는 작은 곤충

- □ **rest** 쉬다, 휴식하다
  → to spend a period of time relaxing or sleeping after doing something tiring
  무엇인가 피곤한 일을 한 후에 쉬거나 자면서 일정한 시간을 보내다

- □ **strike** 부딪치다, 충돌하다
  → to come or bring into heavy contact with someone or something
  어떤 사람이나 물체와 강하게 접촉하다

- □ **weigh** 무게가 ~ 나가다, 무게를 달다
  → to find how heavy a person or thing is
  사람이나 물건이 얼마나 무거운지 알아보다

## Interesting Facts Are Around Us

Welcome to "Ask Dr. Lawrence"! The world is full of interesting
things. Take this quiz and find out how much you know about them.
Are you ready?

Quiz

1. The Eiffel Tower gets taller during the summer.

2. Babies have fewer bones than adults.

3. Only female mosquitoes bite people.

4. Lightning never strikes the same place twice.

5. The elephant is the biggest animal on the Earth.

6. There is no gravity in space.

1. Metal expands in heat. Due to summer heat, the metal of the Eiffel
   Tower expands. In summer, the Eiffel tower gets 15cm taller than in
   winter.

2. Adults have 206 bones, but babies have about 300 bones. With time,
   some of the babies' bones join together, so adults have fewer bones
   than babies.

---

**female** 여성의, 암컷의; 여성, 암컷

**mosquito** 모기

**strike** 치다, 때리다

**gravity** 중력

**be full of** ~로 가득 차다
(= be filled with)

**false** 거짓의

**metal** 금속

**expand** 팽창하다, 확장하다

**due to** ~ 때문에

**with time** 시간이 지남에 따라

---

📎 **확인문제**

● 다음 문장이 본문의 내용과 일치하면 T, 일치하지 <u>않으면</u> F를 쓰시오.

1　The world is full of interesting things. ☐

2　Due to winter cold, the metal of the Eiffel Tower expands. ☐

3　In winter, the Eiffel tower gets 15cm taller than in summer. ☐

4　Adults have 206 bones, but babies have about 300 bones. ☐

5　With time, some of the babies' bones join together. ☐

6　Adults have more bones than babies. ☐

3. Only female mosquitoes will bite you. <u>They</u> need blood to produce

'알을 낳기 위하여'라는 의미로 to부정사의 부사적 용법

They = female mosquitoes

eggs. <u>After a female mosquito gets enough blood</u>, she'll <u>rest</u> for a

부사절 / after는 부사절 접속사    쉬다, 휴식하다

few days and <u>lay</u> her eggs.

lay–laid–laid. 놓다. (새·곤충·어류가) (알을) 낳다

4. Lightning can strike the same place <u>over and over again</u>. The Empire

반복해서

State Building gets hit by lightning 23 times a year on <u>average</u>.

보통, 평균

5. <u>The biggest</u> animal on the Earth is the blue whale. It can <u>weigh</u>

최상급: the+형용사-est    'weigh'는 '~만큼 무게가 나가다'라는 동사

<u>up to</u> 180 tons and <u>grow up to</u> 30 meters long. Its tongue <u>alone</u> can

up to'는 '~까지'라는 의미로, 'weigh up to'가    'grow up to'는 '~까지 자라다'라는 의미이다.    ~만으로도
게 쓰여 '~까지 무게가 나가다'라는 의미로 쓰였다.

weigh <u>as much as</u> an average African elephant.

as+부사+as: 원급비교

6. <u>In fact</u>, there is gravity everywhere in space. <u>As</u> you get farther from

사실    'as'는 '~함에 따라'라는 의미의 접속사로 쓰였다.

the Earth, the gravity of the Earth <u>weakens</u>, <u>but</u> it never goes away

weaken: 약해지다    'but'은 등위접속사로, 앞문장과
반대되는 내용을 연결해 준다.

<u>completely</u>. When you get closer to another planet, <u>such as</u> <u>Mars</u> or

완전히    'such as'는 '~와 같은'이라는 의미로, 'like'와 바꿔 쓸 수 있다.    화성

Venus, <u>its</u> gravity becomes stronger than that of the Earth.

금성    'another planet'을 가리키는 소유격

Which of these quiz <u>items</u> is <u>the most interesting</u> to you? There will

항목    3음절 이상의 형용사는 앞에 the most를 붙여 최상급을 만듦

be another quiz soon. Guess <u>what the next topic will be</u>. See you next

'의문사(what)+주어(the next topic)+동사(will be)'의
간접의문문으로 'guess'의 목적어

month.

rest 쉬다, 휴식을 취하다

lightning 번개

average 평균의

whale 고래

weigh 무게가 나가다, ~의 무게를 달다

tongue 혀

up to ~까지

weaken 약화시키다

completely 완전히

Mars 화성

Venus 금성

item 항목, 물품

 확인문제

● 다음 문장이 본문의 내용과 일치하면 T, 일치하지 <u>않으면</u> F를 쓰시오.

1 Female mosquitoes need blood to produce eggs. ☐

2 Lightning never strikes the same place twice. ☐

3 The elephant is the largest animal on the Earth. ☐

4 The blue whale can weigh up to 180 tons. ☐

5 The blue whale's tongue alone can weigh as much as an average African elephant. ☐

6 As you get farther from the Earth, the gravity of the Earth weakens, and it goes away completely. ☐

● 우리말을 참고하여 빈칸에 알맞은 말을 쓰시오.

**1** _____ _____ Are _____ Us

**2** _____ _____ "Ask Dr. Lawrence"!

**3** The world _____ _____ _____ interesting things.

**4** Take this quiz and find out _____ _____ _____ _____ about them.

**5** Are you _____?

**6** _____

**7** The Eiffel Tower _____ _____ during the summer.

**8** Babies have _____ bones _____ adults.

**9** _____ female mosquitoes _____ people.

**10** Lightning _____ _____ the same place twice.

**11** The elephant is _____ _____ _____ on the Earth.

**12** There is _____ _____ in space.

**13** Metal expands _____ _____.

**14** _____ _____ summer heat, the metal of the Eiffel Tower _____.

**15** In summer, the Eiffel tower _____ 15cm _____ _____ in winter.

**16** _____ have 206 bones, but babies have _____ 300 bones.

**17** _____ _____, some of the babies' bones _____ _____, so adults have fewer bones than babies.

---

**1** 흥미로운 사실들은 우리 주위에 있다

**2** "Lawrence 박사에게 물어 보세요"에 오신 것을 환영합니다!

**3** 세상은 흥미로운 것들로 가득 차 있습니다.

**4** 퀴즈를 풀어보고 그것들에 대해 얼마나 아는지 알아보세요.

**5** 준비 됐나요?

**6** 퀴즈

**7** 에펠 타워는 여름에 키가 더 커진다.

**8** 아기들은 어른보다 더 적은 수의 뼈를 가지고 있다.

**9** 암컷 모기만이 사람을 문다.

**10** 번개는 결코 같은 곳을 내리치지 않는다.

**11** 코끼리는 지구에서 가장 큰 동물이다.

**12** 우주에는 중력이 없다.

**13** 금속은 열에 팽창한다.

**14** 여름의 열기 때문에, 에펠 타워의 금속은 팽창한다.

**15** 여름에 에펠 타워는 겨울보다 15센티미터 정도 더 커진다.

**16** 어른은 206개의 뼈를 가지고 있고, 아기는 대략 300개의 뼈를 가지고 있다.

**17** 시간이 흐르면서, 아기의 몇몇 뼈들은 붙는다. 그래서 어른들은 아기보다 더 적은 수의 뼈를 가지고 있다.

**18** _____ _____ _____ will bite you.

**19** They need blood _____ _____ _____ .

**20** After a female mosquito gets _____ _____ , she'll _____ for a few days and _____ her eggs.

**21** Lightning can strike the same place _____ _____ _____ _____ .

**22** The Empire State Building _____ _____ _____ lightning 23 times a year _____ _____ .

**23** _____ _____ _____ on the Earth is the blue whale.

**24** It can weigh _____ _____ 180 tons and grow _____ _____ 30 meters _____ .

**25** Its tongue _____ can weigh _____ _____ _____ an average African elephant.

**26** _____ _____ , there is gravity everywhere in space.

**27** As you _____ _____ from the Earth, the gravity of the Earth _____ , but it never goes away _____ .

**28** When you _____ _____ to another planet, _____ _____ Mars or Venus, its gravity becomes stronger than _____ _____ the Earth.

**29** _____ of these quiz items is _____ _____ _____ to you?

**30** There will be _____ _____ soon.

**31** Guess _____ _____ _____ _____ _____ .

**32** _____ _____ next month.

**18** 오직 암컷 모기만이 당신을 물 것이다.

**19** 그들은 알을 생산하기 위해서 피가 필요하다.

**20** 암컷 모기는 충분히 흡혈을 한 뒤, 며칠 동안 쉬고 알을 낳는다.

**21** 번개는 같은 곳을 반복해서 칠 수 있다.

**22** 엠파이어스테이트 빌딩은 한 해 평균 스물세 번 번개를 맞는다.

**23** 지구상에서 가장 큰 동물은 흰긴수염고래이다.

**24** 그것은 무게가 180톤까지 나갈 수 있으며 길이는 30미터까지 자랄 수 있다.

**25** 이 고래의 혀의 무게만 해도 아프리카 코끼리의 평균 무게만큼 무겁다.

**26** 사실, 중력은 우주의 어디에나 있다.

**27** 지구에서 멀어 질수록 지구의 중력은 약해지지만, 결코 그것이 완전히 사라지는 것은 아니다.

**28** 당신이 화성이나 금성 같은 다른 행성에 더 가까워진다면, 그들의 중력은 지구의 그것보다 더 강해진다.

**29** 이 퀴즈들 중 어떤 퀴즈가 가장 흥미로웠나요?

**30** 곧 또 다른 퀴즈가 있을 것입니다.

**31** 다음 주제는 무엇일지 맞춰보세요.

**32** 다음 달에 만나요.

• 우리말을 참고하여 본문을 영작하시오.

**1** 흥미로운 사실들은 우리 주위에 있다
➡ _____

**2** "Lawrence 박사에게 물어 보세요"에 오신 것을 환영합니다!
➡ _____

**3** 세상은 흥미로운 것들로 가득 차 있습니다.
➡ _____

**4** 퀴즈를 풀어보고 그것들에 대해 얼마나 아는지 알아보세요.
➡ _____

**5** 준비 됐나요?
➡ _____

**6** 퀴즈
➡ _____

**7** 에펠 타워는 여름에 키가 더 커진다.
➡ _____

**8** 아기들은 어른보다 더 적은 수의 뼈를 가지고 있다.
➡ _____

**9** 암컷 모기만이 사람을 문다.
➡ _____

**10** 번개는 결코 같은 곳을 내리치지 않는다.
➡ _____

**11** 코끼리는 지구에서 가장 큰 동물이다.
➡ _____

**12** 우주에는 중력이 없다.
➡ _____

**13** 금속은 열에 팽창한다.
➡ _____

**14** 여름의 열기 때문에, 에펠 타워의 금속은 팽창한다.
➡ _____

**15** 여름에 에펠 타워는 겨울보다 15센티미터 정도 더 커진다.
➡ _____

**16** 어른은 206개의 뼈를 가지고 있고, 아기는 대략 300개의 뼈를 가지고 있다.
➡ _____

**17** 시간이 흐르면서, 아기의 몇몇 뼈들은 붙는다. 그래서 어른들은 아기보다 더 적은 수의 뼈를 가지고 있다.
➡ _____

**18** 오직 암컷 모기만이 당신을 물 것이다.

➡ _____

**19** 그들은 알을 생산하기 위해서 피가 필요하다.

➡ _____

**20** 암컷 모기는 충분히 흡혈을 한 뒤, 며칠 동안 쉬고 알을 낳는다.

➡ _____

**21** 번개는 같은 곳을 반복해서 칠 수 있다.

➡ _____

**22** 엠파이어스테이트 빌딩은 한 해 평균 스물세 번 번개를 맞는다.

➡ _____

**23** 지구상에서 가장 큰 동물은 흰긴수염고래이다.

➡ _____

**24** 그것은 무게가 180톤까지 나갈 수 있으며 길이는 30미터 까지 자랄 수 있다.

➡ _____

**25** 이 고래의 혀의 무게만 해도 아프리카 코끼리의 평균 무게만큼 무겁다.

➡ _____

**26** 사실, 중력은 우주의 어디에나 있다.

➡ _____

**27** 지구에서 멀어 질수록 지구의 중력은 약해지지만, 결코 그것이 완전히 사라지는 것은 아니다.

➡ _____

**28** 당신이 화성이나 금성 같은 다른 행성에 더 가까워진다면, 그들의 중력은 지구의 그것보다 더 강해진다.

➡ _____

**29** 이 퀴즈들 중 어떤 퀴즈가 가장 흥미로웠나요?

➡ _____

**30** 곧 또 다른 퀴즈가 있을 것입니다.

➡ _____

**31** 다음 주제는 무엇일지 맞춰보세요.

➡ _____

**32** 다음 달에 만나요.

➡ _____

**01** 다음 〈보기〉와 같은 관계가 되도록 빈칸에 주어진 철자로 시작하여 알맞은 말을 쓰시오.

┤ 보기 ├
weaken – strengthen

(1) true – f_____
(2) male – f_____
(3) different – s_____

**02** 다음 괄호 안의 단어를 문맥에 맞게 알맞은 형태로 고쳐 쓰시오.

(1) English has _____ words than any other language. (few)
(2) Alcohol can _____ heart muscle. (weak)

**03** 다음 주어진 우리말에 맞게 빈칸을 채우시오.

(1) 작은 개가 큰 뼈다귀를 갖고 있다.
➡ The small dog has a big _____.
(2) 그것은 완전히 다르다.
➡ It is completely _____.
(3) 모기들은 사람과 동물의 피를 빨아먹는다.
➡ _____ suck the _____ of people and animals.
(4) 시간이 지남에 따라, 그는 그것을 깨달을 것이다.
➡ _____ _____, he will realize it.
(5) 사실, 많은 사람들이 집에서 애완 토끼를 키웁니다.
➡ _____ _____, many people keep pet rabbits at home.

**04** 다음 빈칸에 알맞은 단어를 〈보기〉에서 골라 쓰시오.

┤ 보기 ├
strike   guess   expand   go

(1) The problem will not _____ away.
(2) The ship might _____ a rock in this storm.
(3) Can you _____ what they are talking about?
(4) Metals _____ when they are heated.

**05** 다음 밑줄 친 부분과 바꿔 쓸 수 있는 말을 쓰시오.

The event was delayed for a week because of bad weather.

➡ _____

**06** 주어진 어구를 이용하여 우리말을 영어로 옮기시오.

(1) 여름에 에펠 탑은 겨울보다 15 cm까지 더 커진다. (in summer, the Eiffel Tower, get, tall, than, winter)
➡ _____
_____

(2) 코끼리는 지구에서 가장 큰 동물이다. (the elephant, big, on the Earth)
➡ _____
_____

**07** 다음 문장에서 어법상 틀린 부분을 찾아 바르게 고쳐 쓰시오.

(1) Guess what will the next topic be.

➡ _____

(2) Please tell me who that is girl.

➡ _____

(3) My brother can run the faster in our family.

➡ _____

**08** 다음 빈칸에 알맞은 말을 〈보기〉에서 찾아 쓰시오.

┌─── 보기 ────┐
who    when    what    whether
└──────────────┘

(1) Please tell me _____ you can come to the party.

(2) Do you know _____ the concert starts?

(3) Guess _____ I met yesterday.

[09~10] 다음 글을 읽고 물음에 답하시오.

Some people say that brown eggs are good than white eggs. However, there are no differences in the taste or nutritional value between them. 무엇이 달걀 색깔을 결정하는지 아니? It's the breed of chicken which lay the egg.

**09** 위 글에서 어법상 틀린 부분을 찾아 바르게 고치시오. (두 개)

_____ ➡ _____ , _____ ➡ _____

**10** 위 글의 밑줄 친 우리말에 맞게 주어진 단어를 알맞은 순서로 배열하시오.

┌──────────────────────────────────┐
what, do, the, you, determines, of, know, an egg, color
└──────────────────────────────────┘

➡ _____

_____

[11~13] 다음 글을 읽고 물음에 답하시오.

Welcome to "Ask Dr. Lawrence"! The world is full of interesting things. Take this quiz and find out ⓐ그것들에 대해 얼마나 아는지. Are you ready?

Quiz

1. The Eiffel Tower gets taller (A)[during / for] the summer. Ⓣ Ⓕ

2. ⓑBabies have fewer bones than adults. Ⓣ Ⓕ

3. Only female mosquitoes bite people. Ⓣ Ⓕ

4. (B)[Lightning / Lightening] never strikes the same place twice. Ⓣ Ⓕ

5. The elephant is the (C)[bigest / biggest] animal on the Earth. Ⓣ Ⓕ

6. There is no gravity in space. Ⓣ Ⓕ

**11** 위 글의 밑줄 친 ⓐ의 우리말에 맞게 한 단어를 보충하여, 주어진 어휘를 알맞게 배열하시오.

┌──────────────────────────────────┐
them / know / about / much / you
└──────────────────────────────────┘

➡ _____

**12** 위 글의 괄호 (A)~(C)에서 문맥이나 어법상 알맞은 낱말을 골라 쓰시오.

➡ (A) _____ (B) _____ (C) _____

**13** 위 글의 밑줄 친 ⓑ를 Adults로 시작하여 바꿔 쓰시오.

➡ _____

**01** 출제율 85%

다음 짝지어진 낱말의 관계가 나머지 넷과 <u>다른</u> 것은?

① deep – deepen
② loose – loosen
③ weak – weaken
④ strength – strengthen
⑤ straight – straighten

**02** 출제율 95%

다음 주어진 우리말에 맞게 빈칸을 채우시오.

(1) 엄마는 내가 손톱을 물어뜯곤 했다고 말씀하셨다.

➡ My mom said that I used _____ _____ my nails.

(2) 지구상의 모든 것은 중력의 영향을 받는다.

➡ Everything on Earth is affected by its _____.

(3) Thomas Edison은 위대한 발명가였다.

➡ Thomas Edison _____ a great _____.

(4) 경기장은 사람들로 가득 찼었다.

➡ The stadium _____ full _____ people.

**03** 출제율 95%

다음 빈칸에 알맞은 말이 순서대로 바르게 나열된 것은?

- Let's read and find _____ the topic and situation.
- He plays the same songs over and _____.

① at – over
② out – under
③ as – under
④ out – over
⑤ at – under

**04** 출제율 90%

다음 우리말에 맞게 주어진 단어를 바르게 배열하시오.

(1) 암컷 모기들만 피를 빨아먹는다.

(suck, blood, female, only, mosquitoes)

➡ _____

(2) 피는 물보다 진하다.

(thicker, blood, water, than, is)

➡ _____

(3) 너는 몸무게가 얼마 나가니?

(much, weigh, how, you, do)

➡ _____

(4) 십대의 문화는 성인의 문화와 다르다.

(culture, culture, adult, from, teenage, is, different)

➡ _____

**05** 출제율 95%

다음 〈보기〉의 단어를 사용하여 자연스러운 문장을 만들 수 <u>없는</u> 것은?

┌─ 보기 ─┐
│ to    with    of │
└────────┘

① _____ average, he goes to bed around 12 o'clock.
② I hope this year will be full _____ happiness.
③ Read up _____ page 100.
④ The painting will lose its color _____ time.
⑤ The flight is delayed due _____ bad weather.

출제율 95%

**06** 다음 중 어법상 옳은 것은?

① Take this quiz and find out how much do you know about them.
② The bigger animal on the Earth is the blue whale.
③ Its tongue alone can weigh as more as an average African elephant.
④ Tell me when the dance contest will start.
⑤ This is the difficultest problem in this book.

출제율 100%

**07** 다음 빈칸에 알맞은 것은?

> • Sumi's bag is _____ in our class.
> • Minho gets up _____ in the morning in our class.

① the most heavy – earlier
② the heaviest – earliest
③ heavier – earlier
④ more heavy – the earliest
⑤ the most heaviest – more earlier

출제율 90%

**08** 다음 주어진 두 문장을 〈보기〉처럼 하나의 문장으로 바꾸어 쓰시오.

> ┤ 보기 ├
> • Please tell me.　• Who is that girl?
> ➡ Please tell me who that girl is.

(1) • Can you tell me.
　　• How old is your brother?
　➡ _____

(2) • I know.
　　• Where does she live?
　➡ _____

(3) • Please tell me.
　　• Does he like baseball?
　➡ _____

출제율 95%

**09** 다음 문장의 밑줄 친 부분과 문장의 쓰임이 <u>다른</u> 하나는?

> Welcome to "Ask Dr. Lawrence"! The world is full of interesting things. Take this quiz and find out <u>how much you know about them</u>. Are you ready?

① Tell me <u>when the concert starts</u>.
② Can you tell me <u>who that boy is</u>?
③ <u>How long does it take</u> to go to the bank?
④ I wonder <u>when they will arrive</u>.
⑤ I don't know <u>what I should do</u>.

출제율 90%

**10** 다음 우리말에 맞게 영작한 문장 중 <u>잘못된</u> 것은?

① 이 퀴즈 항목 중에서 어느 것이 가장 흥미로웠나요?
　➡ Which of these quiz items was the most interesting to you?
② 다음 주제가 무엇일지 추측해 보세요.
　➡ Guess what the next topic will be.
③ 이 퀴즈를 풀고 그것들에 관해 얼마나 많이 알고 있는지 알아보세요.
　➡ Take this quiz and find out how much you know about them.
④ 시간이 지남에 따라 아기의 뼈 중 몇몇은 서로 합쳐진다. 그래서 어른들은 아기들보다 더 적은 개수의 뼈를 가지고 있다.
　➡ With time, some of the babies' bones join together, so adults have few bones than babies.
⑤ 그것의 혀의 무게만 해도 아프리카 코끼리의 평균 무게만큼 무겁다.
　➡ Its tongue alone can weigh as much as an average African elephant.

**11** 다음 문장의 밑줄 친 부분 중 어법상 어색한 것은?

> In fact, ①there is gravity everywhere in space. As you ②get farther from the Earth, the gravity of the Earth weakens, but it never goes away ③completely. When you get closer to another planet, such as Mars or Venus, its gravity becomes ④stronger than ⑤those of the Earth.

①      ②      ③      ④      ⑤

**12** 다음 문장의 빈칸에 들어갈 말을 글의 흐름에 맞게 쓰시오.

> Metal expands in heat. Due to summer heat, the metal of the Eiffel Tower expands. In summer, the Eiffel Tower gets 15cm _____ than in winter.

➡ _____

**13** 다음 문장의 괄호 안에 주어진 단어를 알맞은 형태로 고치시오.

> The (A)(big) animal on the Earth is the blue whale. It can weigh up to 180 tons and grow up to 30 meters long. Its tongue alone can weigh as (B)(many) as an average African elephant.

➡ (A) _____ (B) _____

**14** 다음 문장 중 어법상 잘못된 것은?

① He is the strongest man of the three.
② This book is thickest among the books I have ever read.
③ Do you know if she can speak French?
④ She works hardest in my company.
⑤ I like this color most.

**15** 다음 중 형용사의 최상급이 바르게 된 것은?

① fast – most fast    ② large – largeest
③ big – biggest    ④ famous – famousest
⑤ popular – popularest

**16** 다음 빈칸에 알맞은 말을 올바른 형태로 쓰시오.

> My sisters are all pretty. But, among my sisters, Jenny is the _____ girl.

➡ _____

**[17~19]** 다음 글을 읽고 물음에 답하시오.

> Welcome to "Ask Dr. Lawrence"! ⓐThe world is full of interesting things. Take this quiz and find out how much you know about them. Are you ready?
> Quiz
> 1. The Eiffel Tower ⓑgets taller during the summer. Ⓣ Ⓕ
> 2. Babies have fewer bones than adults. Ⓣ Ⓕ
> 3. Only female mosquitoes bite people. Ⓣ Ⓕ
> 4. Lightning never strikes the same place twice. Ⓣ Ⓕ
> 5. ⓒThe elephant is the biggest animal on the Earth. Ⓣ Ⓕ
> 6. There is no gravity in space. Ⓣ Ⓕ

**출제율 90%**

**17** 위 글의 밑줄 친 ⓐ를 다음과 같이 바꿔 쓸 때 빈칸에 들어갈 알맞은 말을 쓰시오.

➡ The world is _____ with interesting things.

**출제율 85%**

**18** 위 글의 밑줄 친 ⓑgets와 바꿔 쓸 수 있는 말을 고르시오.

① brings     ② becomes     ③ makes
④ takes      ⑤ happens

**출제율 95%**

**19** 밑줄 친 ⓒ를 다음과 같이 바꿔 쓸 때 빈칸에 들어갈 알맞은 말을 고르시오.

The elephant is _____ any other animal on the Earth.

① so big as        ② the same as
③ bigger than      ④ as big as
⑤ less big than

[20~23] 다음 글을 읽고 물음에 답하시오.

1. Metal expands in ___ⓐ___. Due to summer heat, the metal of the Eiffel Tower expands. ⓑIn summer, the Eiffel tower gets 15cm shorter than in winter.
2. Adults have 206 bones, but babies have about 300 bones. ___ⓒ___ time, some of the babies' bones join together, so adults have fewer bones than babies.

**출제율 85%**

**20** 위 글의 빈칸 ⓐ에 들어갈 알맞은 말을 본문에서 찾아 쓰시오.

➡ _____

**출제율 95%**

**21** 위 글의 밑줄 친 ⓑ에서 흐름상 어색한 부분을 찾아 고치시오.

_____ ➡ _____

**출제율 95%**

**22** 위 글의 빈칸 ⓒ에 들어갈 알맞은 전치사를 고르시오.

① With     ② On     ③ At
④ To       ⑤ By

**출제율 90%**

**23** 다음 질문에 대한 알맞은 대답을 빈칸에 쓰시오.

Q: Why do adults have fewer bones than babies?
A: Because as time goes by, some of the babies' bones _____ _____.

[24~26] 다음 글을 읽고 물음에 답하시오.

3. Only female mosquitoes will bite you. They need blood to produce eggs. After a female mosquito gets enough blood, she'll ⓐrest for a few days and lay her eggs.
4. Lightning can strike the same place ⓑover and over again. The Empire State Building gets hit ___ⓒ___ lightning 23 times a year ___ⓓ___ average.

**출제율 90%**

**24** 위 글의 밑줄 친 ⓐrest와 같은 의미로 쓰인 것을 고르시오.

① He had a good night's rest.
② Did he rest his chin in his hands?
③ The final decisions rest with you.
④ I want to rest from my work.
⑤ I spent the rest of the day sleeping.

**출제율 95%**

**25** 위 글의 밑줄 친 ⓑover and over again과 바꿔 쓸 수 없는 말을 고르시오.

① again and again      ② time after time
③ step by step         ④ repeatedly
⑤ time and time again

**26** 위 글의 빈칸 ⓒ와 ⓓ에 들어갈 전치사가 바르게 짝지어진 것은?

① in – for
② by – on
③ in – on
④ for – to
⑤ by – for

**[27~29]** 다음 글을 읽고 물음에 답하시오.

Quiz: There is no gravity in space.  Ⓣ Ⓕ
Answer: False

_____ⓐ_____, there is gravity everywhere in space. As you get farther from the Earth, the gravity of the Earth ____ⓑ____, but it never goes away completely. When you get closer to another planet, such as Mars or Venus, ⓒ its gravity becomes stronger than that of the Earth.

**27** 위 글의 빈칸 ⓐ에 들어갈 알맞은 말을 고르시오.

① For example
② Therefore
③ In addition
④ In fact
⑤ In other words

**28** 위 글의 빈칸 ⓑ에 weak을 알맞은 형태로 쓰시오.

➡ _____

**29** 위 글의 밑줄 친 ⓒ가 가리키는 것을 본문에서 찾아 쓰시오.

➡ _____

**[30~32]** 다음 글을 읽고 물음에 답하시오.

3. Only female mosquitoes will bite you. They need blood ⓐto produce eggs. After a female mosquito (A)[will get / gets] enough blood, she'll rest for a few days and (B)[lay / lie] her eggs.

4. Lightning can strike the same place over and over again. The Empire State Building gets hit by lightning 23 times a year on average.

5. The biggest animal on the Earth is the blue whale. It can weigh ____ⓑ____ 180 tons and grow ____ⓒ____ 30 meters long. Its tongue (C)[alone / only] can weigh as much as an average African elephant.

**30** 위 글의 괄호 (A)~(C)에서 문맥이나 어법상 알맞은 낱말을 골라 쓰시오.

➡ (A) _____ (B) _____ (C) _____

**31** 위 글의 밑줄 친 ⓐto produce와 to부정사의 용법이 다른 것을 모두 고르시오.

① I want a chair to sit on.
② He hoped to succeed in life.
③ She was pleased to read the letter.
④ You must be a fool to say so.
⑤ He has too much work to do.

**32** 위 글의 빈칸 ⓑ와 ⓒ에 공통으로 들어갈 알맞은 말을 쓰시오.

➡ _____

# Lesson 5

# Different Countries, Different Cultures

### 🎤 의사소통 기능

- 길 알려 주기
  Go straight one block and turn right. It's on your left.

- 선호 묻기
  Which do you prefer, the London Eye or the Sky Garden?

### 🔧 언어 형식

- 수동태
  Spain **is loved by** lots of tourists.

- so ~ that ... 구문
  It was **so** delicious **that** we all enjoyed it.

# Words & Expressions

교과서

## Key Words

- **abroad** [əbrɔ́ːd] 부 외국으로, 외국에서
- **artist** [áːrtist] 명 화가, 예술가
- **capital** [kǽpətl] 명 수도
- **care** [kɛər] 명 돌봄, 보살핌
- **careful** [kɛ́ərfəl] 형 조심하는, 주의 깊은
- **ceiling** [síːliŋ] 명 천장
- **cheer** [tʃiər] 동 환호하다, 갈채하다 명 환호
- **coaster** [kóustər] 명 (롤러) 코스터
- **column** [káləm] 명 기둥
- **curry** [kɔ́ːri] 명 카레
- **design** [dizáin] 동 설계하다, 디자인하다
- **dish** [diʃ] 명 음식, 접시
- **excuse** [ikskjúːz] 동 ~을 용서하다, 너그러이 봐주다
- **experience** [ikspíəriəns] 명 경험 동 경험하다
- **fan** [fæn] 명 팬, 부채
- **Ferris wheel** 대관람차
- **flamenco** [fləménkou] 명 플라멩코 (스페인 남부 **Andalusia** 지방 집시의 춤)
- **hamburger** [hǽmbəːrgər] 명 햄버거
- **helpful** [hélpfəl] 형 도움이 되는
- **historic** [histɔ́ːrik] 형 역사적인, 역사상 중요한
- **island** [áilənd] 명 섬
- **language** [lǽŋgwidʒ] 명 언어
- **lizard** [lízərd] 명 도마뱀
- **match** [mætʃ] 명 경기, 시합 동 어울리다

- **movement** [múːvmənt] 명 동작
- **near** [niər] 부 근처에
- **paella** [pɑːéijilə] 명 파에야
- **prefer** [prifɔ́ːr] 동 선호하다
- **purple** [pɔ́ːrpl] 명 보라색
- **right** [rait] 형 옳은, 오른쪽의
- **roll** [roul] 동 구르다, 굴리다
- **shine** [ʃain] 동 빛나다
- **slide** [slaid] 동 미끄러지다, 활주하다
- **Spain** [spein] 명 스페인
- **Spanish** [spǽniʃ] 형 스페인의 명 스페인어
- **stadium** [stéidiəm] 명 경기장
- **stop** [stɑp] 명 정거장 동 멈추다, 정지하다
- **tea** [tiː] 명 차
- **theater** [θíːətər] 명 극장
- **title** [táitl] 명 제목
- **tour** [tuər] 명 여행 동 관광하다
- **tourist** [túərist] 명 여행객
- **traditional** [trədíʃənl] 형 전통적인
- **unique** [juːníːk] 형 독특한
- **Vietnamese** [vìètnəmíːz] 명 베트남어 형 베트남의
- **view** [vjuː] 명 전망, 경치
- **wave** [weiv] 동 흔들다 명 파도
- **work** [wəːrk] 동 일하다 명 작품

## Key Expressions

- **across from**: ~의 맞은편에
- **be famous for**: ~로 유명하다
- **be full of**: ~으로 가득 차다
- **be known for**: ~로 알려져 있다
- **by+교통수단**: 교통수단으로 → **by bus**: 버스로, **by subway**: 지하철로, **by taxi**: 택시로
- **cheer for**: ~을 응원하다
- **far from**: ~로부터 멀리
- **get on**: ~에 타다
- **get to** 장소 명사, **get** 장소 부사: ~에 도착하다
- **go on**: (어떤 일이) 계속되다

- **How can I get there?**: 그곳에 어떻게 가니?
- **on foot**: 걸어서
- **on top of**: ~의 위에, ~의 꼭대기에
- **put off**: (시간, 날짜를) 미루다, 연기하다
- **so 형용사/부사 that 주어 동사**: 너무 ~해서 그 결과 …하다
- **take a tour**: 관광하다, 여행을 가다
- **try on**: 입어 보다
- **turn off**: (전기, 가스, 수도 등을) 끄다
- **turn on**: 켜다
- **Which do you prefer, A or B?**: A와 B 중 어느 것을 선호하니?

## Word Power

※ 접미사 '-ful'이 붙어서 형용사가 되는 명사

☐ **pain**(고통) → **painful**(고통스러운)

☐ **color**(색깔) → **colorful**(다채로운)

☐ **hope**(희망, 기대) → **hopeful**(희망에 찬, 기대하는)

☐ **wonder**(놀라움) → **wonderful**(놀랄 만한, 멋진)

☐ **use**(사용) → **useful**(유용한)

☐ **peace**(평화) → **peaceful**(평화로운)

☐ **help**(도움) → **helpful**(도움이 되는)

☐ **care**(조심) → **careful**(조심하는)

※ 'take'를 사용한 다양한 표현들

☐ **take a rest**(쉬다)

☐ **take a walk**(산책하다)

☐ **take a seat**(자리에 앉다)

☐ **take a class**(수업을 받다)

☐ **take a shower**(샤워를 하다)

☐ **take a look (at)**((~을) (한 번) 보다)

☐ **take a chance**((모험삼아) 해 보다)

☐ **take a tour**(여행하다)

☐ **take a picture**(사진을 찍다)

## English Dictionary

☐ **abroad**: 외국으로[에서]
→ in or to a foreign country
외국에서 또는 외국으로

☐ **capital**: 수도
→ the main city of a country where its government is
정부가 있는 한 나라의 주요 도시

☐ **ceiling**: 천장
→ the upper inside surface of a room
방의 위쪽 내부 표면

☐ **cheer**: 환호하다, 갈채하다
→ to give a shout out of pleasure, praise, or support
기쁨, 칭찬 또는 지지를 위해 소리를 지르다

☐ **curry**: 카레
→ a spicy Indian food with meat and vegetables in sauce
소스 안에 고기와 야채가 있는 매운 인도 음식

☐ **excuse**: ~을 용서하다, 너그러이 봐주다
→ to forgive someone for something bad that they have done, especially something that is not very serious
어떤 나쁜 일, 특히 매우 심각하지 않은 어떤 일을 한 사람을 용서하다

☐ **flamenco**: 플라멩코
→ a vigorous rhythmic dance style of the Andalusian Gypsies
안달루시아 집시의 격렬한 리듬을 가진 춤

☐ **lizard**: 도마뱀
→ a reptile that has a rough skin and a long tail
거친 피부와 긴 꼬리를 가진 파충류

☐ **prefer**: 선호하다
→ to like something or someone better than another
다른 것보다 어떤 것이나 어떤 사람을 더 좋아하다

☐ **purple**: 보라색
→ a mixture of blue and red color
파란색과 빨간색을 섞은 색

☐ **shine**: 빛나다
→ to produce bright light
밝은 빛을 만들어 내다

☐ **slide**: 미끄러지다, 활주하다
→ to move along smoothly
부드럽게 움직이다

☐ **Spanish**: 스페인의
→ relating to the language, people or culture of Spain
스페인의 언어, 사람 또는 문화와 관련된

☐ **theater**: 극장
→ a building with a big screen or stage where many people watch movies or plays
많은 사람들이 영화나 연극을 보는 큰 스크린이나 무대를 가진 건물

☐ **tour**: 여행
→ a journey for pleasure during which various places of interest are visited
흥미 있는 다양한 장소를 방문하는 즐거움을 위한 여행

☐ **Vietnamese**: 베트남의
→ relating to the language, people or culture of Vietnam
베트남의 언어, 사람 또는 문화와 관련된

☐ **view**: 전망, 경치
→ an outlook onto, or picture of a scene
어떤 경치의 전망이나 풍경

**01** 다음 밑줄 친 부분과 의미가 가장 가까운 것을 고르시오.

Each character has a <u>unique</u> personality.

① various    ② only    ③ unusual
④ common    ⑤ useful

**02** 다음 빈칸에 들어갈 말로 적절한 것은?

_____ me, which way is the closest subway station?

① Forgive          ② Accuse
③ Watch            ④ Exercise
⑤ Excuse

[03~04] 다음 영영 풀이에 해당하는 단어를 고르시오.

**03**

the upper inside surface of a room

① wall    ② floor    ③ roof
④ closet    ⑤ ceiling

**04**

to produce bright light

① shine    ② shut    ③ rise
④ tear    ⑤ shake

**05** 서답형 다음 주어진 우리말에 맞게 빈칸을 채우시오.

(1) 파리는 프랑스의 수도이다.
　➡ Paris is the _____ of France.
(2) 그녀는 스페인 친구가 있다.
　➡ She has a _____ friend.

**06** 다음 제시된 단어를 사용하여 자연스러운 문장을 만들 수 없는 것은?

┤ 보기 ├
coaster    column    curry    lizard

① The man is riding a roller _____.
② A _____ has four legs and a long tail.
③ The _____ is too spicy for me.
④ I'd like to have a room with a great _____.
⑤ The _____ was made of white marble.

**07** 서답형 다음 밑줄 친 부분과 의미가 가장 가까운 것을 주어진 철자로 시작하여 쓰시오.

(1) What do you think the most <u>typical</u> Korean food is?
(2) Rachel loves the <u>distinctive</u> smell of a rose.

➡ (1) d_____, (2) u_____

**08**  주어진 단어 뒤에 -ful을 붙여 형용사로 만들 수 <u>없는</u> 것을 고르시오.

① help          ② care
③ wonder       ④ friend
⑤ peace

**01** 다음 〈보기〉처럼 짝지어진 두 단어의 관계와 같도록 빈칸에 알맞은 단어를 쓰시오.

┌─ 보기 ─┐

use – useful

(1) tradition : _____
(2) history : _____

**02** 〈보기〉에서 두 문장에 공통으로 들어갈 수 있는 단어를 찾아 쓰시오.

┌─ 보기 ─┐

cheers   match   experience   waves
works

(1)
- My mom always _____ me up when I am about to give up.
- The _____ of the fans filled the stadium.

(2)
- If you like tennis, let's go to watch a tennis _____.
- Her pants _____ the blouse perfectly.

(3)
- He _____ for the company which sells smartphones.
- His paintings are beautiful _____ of art.

(4)
- Surfers are riding the huge _____.
- She _____ her hands to him when she leaves home.

(5)
- We can learn from _____.
- I can _____ different cultures when I travel to other countries.

**03** 다음 우리말에 맞게 주어진 단어를 바르게 배열하시오.

(1) 너는 매일 얼마나 많은 여행객들이 Boston을 방문하는지 아니?
(tourists, every, do, know, how, visit, day, Boston, you, many, ?)
➡ _____

(2) 태양은 빛나고 나무는 자란다.
(grows, the, the, tree, and, shines, sun)
➡ _____

(3) 군중은 그 희소식을 듣고 기운이 났다.
(the, news, the, cheered, at, crowd, good, up)
➡ _____

(4) 나는 외국에서 공부하고 싶다.
(study, I, abroad, to, want)
➡ _____

**04** 다음 빈칸에 알맞은 단어를 〈보기〉에서 골라 쓰시오. (한 단어는 한 번 밖에 사용할 수 없음)

┌─ 보기 ─┐

put   take   try   turn

(1) Do you want to _____ a tour?
(2) Please _____ off the TV. It's past your bedtime.
(3) Is it possible to _____ off my trip until the 25th?
(4) Can I _____ on this jacket?

# Conversation

## ① 길 알려 주기

**Go straight one block and turn right. It's on your left.** 한 블록 직진한 후 우회전하세요. 왼편에 있어요.

■ 'Where is ~?'는 '~가 어디에 있나요?'라는 의미로 길이나 위치를 물어볼 때 사용하는 표현이다. 같은 의미를 가진 표현으로 'How can I get to ~?', 'How do I get to ~?', 또는 'Is there ~ around here?' 등 이 있다. 이에 대한 대답으로 'Go straight.', 'Turn left.', 'It's on your right.' 등의 표현을 이용해서 길을 알려줄 수 있다.

### 길 묻기

- Where is ~? (~가 어디에 있나요?)
- How can/do I get to ~? (~에 어떻게 가나요?)
- Is there ~ around here? (근처에 ~가 있나요?)
- Do you know how to get to ~? (~에 어떻게 가는지 아나요?)
- Can/Could you tell me where ~ is? (어디에 ~가 있는지 말해 줄 수 있나요?)
- Can/Could you tell me how to get to ~? (~에 어떻게 가는지 말해 줄 수 있나요?)

### 길 알려 주기

- Go straight. (직진하세요.)
- Turn left/right. (좌회전/우회전 하세요.)
- It is across from ~. (~ 맞은편에 있어요.)
- It is on your left/right. (왼편/오른편에 있어요.)
- You'll see ~ on your left/right. (왼편에/오른편에 ~이 보일 거예요.)
- It is around the corner. (모퉁이 지나서 있어요.)
- Walk to the end of this block. (이 블록 끝까지 가세요.)
- Go straight until you see ~. (~가 보일 때까지 직진하세요.)
- It takes ten minutes on foot. (걸어서 10분 걸려요.)
- You can't miss it. (꼭 찾을 거예요.)

### 장소나 위치를 나타내는 표현

- around(~ 근처에)
- across from(~ 맞은편에)
- before(~ 전에)
- in front of(~ 앞에)
- near(근처에)
- next to(~ 옆에)
- on the corner(모퉁이에)
- around the corner(모퉁이를 돌아서)

## 핵심 Check

**1.** 다음 우리말과 일치하도록 빈칸에 알맞은 말을 쓰시오.

A: Excuse me. _____ is the _____? (실례합니다. 은행이 어디에 있나요?)

B: _____ until you see a crosswalk. (횡단보도가 보일 때까지 직진하세요.)

A: And then? Should I cross the street? (그 다음엔? 길을 건너야 해요?)

B: Yes. Then, you'll see the bank. It is _____ the school.
(네. 그러면 은행이 보일 거예요. 학교 옆에 있어요.)

## ② 선호 묻기

**Which do you prefer, the London Eye or the Sky Garden?** 런던 아이와 스카이 가든 중 어느 곳을 선호하나요?

■ A와 B 둘 중에 어느 것을 더 좋아하는지 물을 때 'Which do you prefer, A or B?'라는 표현을 사용한다. prefer는 like better[more]로도 바꾸어 쓸 수 있으므로 'Which do you like better[more], A or B?'라고도 할 수 있다. which가 뒤에 나오는 명사를 수식하는 의문형용사로도 쓰일 수 있으므로 'Which place do you prefer, the London Eye or the Sky Garden?'이라고도 할 수 있다.

### 선호 묻기

- Which do you prefer, A or B? (A와 B 중 어느 것을 선호하니?)
- Do you prefer A to B? (너는 B보다 A를 더 좋아하니?)

■ 두 가지 중에서 어느 것을 더 선호하는지 말할 때 'I prefer A to B.', 'I think A is better than B.'로 말할 수 있다. 이때 비교 대상이 되는 than B나 to B는 생략할 수 있다. prefer A to B에서 to가 전치사이므로 뒤에 명사나 동명사가 오는 것에 유의해야 한다.

### 선호 표현하기

- I prefer A (to B). (나는 A를 (B보다) 선호한다.)
- I like A more than B.
- I think A is better than B.
- I think A is preferable to B.

### 핵심 Check

2. 다음 우리말과 일치하도록 빈칸에 알맞은 말을 쓰시오. (철자가 주어진 것도 있음)

(1) A: _____ do you p_____, baseball or tennis? (야구와 테니스 중에 어느 것을 더 좋아하니?)

B: I _____ baseball _____ tennis. (나는 테니스보다 야구가 더 좋아.)

(2) A: Which do you _____ _____, meat or fish?

(너는 고기와 생선 중에 어느 것을 더 좋아하니?)

B: I _____ meat to fish. (나는 생선보다 고기를 더 좋아해.)

**Listen & Speak 1 A-1**

> B: Excuse me. Is the Picasso Museum ❶near here?
>
> G: Yes. It's not ❷far from here.
>
> B: ❸How can I get there?
>
> G: ❹Go straight one block and turn left. It's on your right.

> B: 실례할게. 이 근처에 피카소 박물관이 있니?
> G: 응, 여기서 멀지 않아.
> B: 그곳에 어떻게 가니?
> G: 한 블록 직진한 후 좌회전해. 오른편에 있어.

❶ near: ~ 근처에

❷ far from: ~에서 먼

❸ 'How can I get to 장소 ~?'는 '~에 어떻게 가니?'란 의미로 길을 물어보는 표현이다. 여기서 there는 위에서 언급된 the Picasso Museum을 의미한다. How can I get there? (= Do you know how to get there?)

❹ Go straight.: 직진하세요. Turn left/right.: 좌회전/우회전 하세요. It is on your left/right.: 왼편/오른편에 있어요.

**Check(√) True or False**

(1) The Picasso Museum is near here.      T ☐ F ☐

(2) The girl knows how to get to the Picasso Museum.      T ☐ F ☐

(3) The Picasso Museum is far from here.      T ☐ F ☐

**Listen & Speak 2 A-1**

> B: ❶It's really hot here in Thailand. ❷Let's go to the night market and have some fresh fruit juice.
>
> G: ❸Sounds good. ❹How do we get there?
>
> B: ❺We can go on foot or by bus. ❻Which do you prefer?
>
> G: I ❼prefer the bus.

> B: 태국은 정말 더워. 야시장에 가서 신선한 과일 주스를 마시자.
> G: 좋아. 우리는 그곳에 어떻게 가지?
> B: 우리는 걸어가거나 버스를 탈 수 있어. 어느 것을 선호하니?
> G: 나는 버스를 선호해.

❶ 특정한 주어가 없이 날씨, 계절, 시간 등을 나타내는 문장에서는 주어의 자리에 It을 쓸 수 있다. Thailand: 태국

❷ '~하자'라는 제안을 하고자 할 때 'Let's ~'의 표현을 쓸 수 있다. have(먹다, 마시다)는 접속사 and로 go와 연결되어 있다. night market: 야시장

❸ sound+형용사: ~하게 들리다

❹ get to 장소 명사, get 장소 부사: ~에 도착하다

❺ on foot: 걸어서, by+교통수단: 교통수단으로 → by bus: 버스로, by subway: 지하철로, by taxi: 택시로

❻ 'Which do you prefer'의 뒤에 'on foot or by bus'가 생략되어 있다. A와 B 둘 중에 어느 것을 더 좋아하는지 물을 때 'Which do you prefer, A or B?'라는 표현을 사용한다.

❼ prefer: 선호하다

**Check(√) True or False**

(4) They are going to walk to the night market.      T ☐ F ☐

(5) They are in Thailand.      T ☐ F ☐

(6) They are going to the night market to have fruit juice.      T ☐ F ☐

### Listen & Speak 1 A-2

**B:** Sally, I ❶need to buy some candies for Halloween. Where can I buy ❷them?

**G:** You ❸can buy them at Wendy's Candy Shop.

**B:** ❹Where is it?

**G:** ❺Go straight two blocks and turn right. It's across from the library.

❶ need: ~이 필요하다. need는 뒤에 to부정사(to+동사원형)를 목적어로 취할 수 있다.

❷ them = some candies

❸ can+동사원형: ~할 수 있다. at+장소: ~에서

❹ Where is ~?'는 '~가 어디에 있나요?'라는 의미로 길이나 위치를 물어볼 때 사용하는 표현이다.

❺ Go straight: 직진하세요. Turn left/right: 좌회전/우회전 하세요. across from: ~ 맞은편에

### Listen & Speak 2 A-2

**G:** ❶What is this long dress called?

**M:** ❷It is an Ao dai, a type of traditional clothing from Vietnam.

**G:** Can I ❸try one on?

**M:** Sure. ❹Which do you prefer, the purple one or the yellow one?

**G:** The purple one, please.

❶ 이름을 모르는 물건에 대해 어떻게 말하는지 물어볼 때 'How do you say ~?', 'What is ~ called?', 'What do you call ~?' 등으로 질문할 수 있다.

❷ an Ao dai와 a type of traditional clothing from Vietnam은 동격 관계이다. traditional: 전통적인 clothing: 옷, 의복

❸ try on: 입어 보다

❹ Which do you prefer, A or B?: A와 B 중 어느 것을 선호하니? one은 an Ao dai를 의미한다.

### Conversation A

**M:** Welcome to London City Tour. ❶Today, we'll visit famous places in London. Can you see the London Eye? ❷It's on your right. ❸It's a Ferris wheel near the River Thames. ❹The view from the London Eye is amazing. Many people visit it every year.

❶ we'll = we will (우리는 ~할 것이다) famous: 유명한 place: 장소

❷ It is on your left/right: 왼편/오른편에 있어요.

❸ Ferris wheel: 대관람차 near: ~ 근처에

❹ view: 전망, 경치 amazing: 놀라운

### Conversation B

**Staff:** ❶How may I help you?

**Hana's mom:** We ❷want to enjoy a good view of London.

**Hana:** Where is the best place ❸to go to?

**Staff:** We have two great places. ❹The London Eye is a Ferris wheel and the Sky Garden is a glass garden on top of a tall building. ❺ Which do you prefer?

**Hana's mom:** Hmm... I ❻prefer the London Eye.

**Hana:** Me, too.

**Staff:** Good choice. You can ❼get there by bus.

**Hana's mom:** ❽Where is the nearest stop?

**Staff:** Go straight one block and turn right. It's on your left. ❾Have a good trip!

**Hana:** Wow, I can see all of London. Look! There is a big clock.

**Hana's mom:** I think that's Big Ben. ❿Why don't we go and visit it later?

**Hana:** That sounds great.

❶ 'May I help you?(도와드릴까요?)'에 의문사 How를 붙인 'How may I help you?'는 '무엇을 도와드릴까요?' 또는 '어떻게 도와드릴까요?'의 의미를 지닌다.

❷ want는 뒤에 to부정사(to+동사원형)를 목적어로 취할 수 있지만 동명사는 목적어로 취할 수 없다. view: 전망, 경치

❸ to부정사의 형용사적 용법으로 앞의 the best place를 수식하고 있다. the best place to go to: 가기에 가장 좋은 장소

❹ Ferris wheel: 대관람차 glass: 유리 on top of: ~의 위에, ~의 꼭대기에

❺ 문장 뒤에 'the London Eye or the Sky Garden'이 생략되어 있다. Which do you prefer, A or B?: A와 B 중 어느 것을 선호하니?

❻ prefer: 선호하다

❼ get 장소 부사: ~에 도착하다 by+교통수단: 교통수단으로 → by bus: 버스로

❽ Where is ~?: ~가 어디에 있나요? nearest: near(가까운)의 최상급, 가장 가까운 stop: 정거장

❾ Have a good trip!: 좋은 여행 하세요!

❿ 상대방에게 '함께 ~하자'는 표현으로 'Why don't we ~?'를 사용할 수 있다.

● 다음 우리말과 일치하도록 빈칸에 알맞은 말을 쓰시오.

### Listen & Speak 1 A

1. **B:** Excuse me. _____ the Picasso Museum _____ here?

   **G:** Yes. It's not _____ _____ here.

   **B:** _____ can I get there?

   **G:** _____ _____ one block and turn _____ . It's _____ your right.

2. **B:** Sally, I need _____ _____ some candies for Halloween. _____ _____ I buy them?

   **G:** You can buy _____ _____ Wendy's Candy Shop.

   **B:** _____ _____ _____ ?

   **G:** _____ _____ two _____ and turn right. It's _____ _____ the library.

### Listen & Speak 1 B

1. **A:** Excuse me. _____ _____ the park?

   **B:** _____ _____ _____ _____ and turn left. It's _____ your right.

2. **A:** Excuse me. _____ _____ the school?

   **B:** Go _____ one block and turn left. _____ _____ your right. _____ _____ _____ the restaurant.

### Listen & Talk 2 A

1. **B:** _____ really hot here in Thailand. _____ _____ to the night market and have some fresh fruit juice.

   **G:** Sounds _____ . _____ do we _____ _____ ?

   **B:** We can go _____ _____ _____ _____ _____ . _____ _____ _____ _____ ?

   **G:** I _____ the bus.

2. **G:** _____ _____ this long dress _____ ?

   **M:** It is an Ao dai, a _____ of _____ _____ from Vietnam.

   **G:** Can I _____ _____ _____ ?

   **M:** Sure. _____ _____ _____ _____ , the purple one or the yellow one?

   **G:** The purple one, please.

## Listen & Talk 2 B

1. **A:** _____ _____ _____ _____, hamburgers or spaghetti?

   **B:** I prefer hamburgers.

2. **A:** _____ _____ _____ _____, curry _____ paella?

   **B:** I prefer paella.

## Conversation A

**M:** Welcome to London City Tour. Today, _____ _____ famous places in London. Can you _____ the London Eye? It's _____ _____ _____. It's a Ferris wheel near the River Thames. The _____ _____ the London Eye is amazing. Many people visit it every year.

## Conversation B

**Staff:** _____ may I _____ you?

**Hana's mom:** We _____ _____ _____ _____ a good view of London.

**Hana:** Where is the best place _____ _____ _____?

**Staff:** We have two great places. The London Eye is a Ferris wheel and the Sky Garden is a glass garden _____ _____ _____ a tall building. _____ do you prefer?

**Hana's mom:** Hmm... I _____ the London Eye.

**Hana:** Me, too.

**Staff:** Good choice. You can _____ there _____ _____.

**Hana's mom:** _____ is the _____ _____?

**Staff:** Go _____ one block and _____ _____. It's on your left. Have a good trip!

**Hana:** Wow, I can see all of London. Look! _____ _____ a big clock.

**Hana's mom:** I think that's Big Ben. _____ _____ _____ go and visit it later?

**Hana:** That sounds great.

1. **A:** 햄버거와 스파게티 중 어느 것을 선호하니?
   **B:** 나는 햄버거를 선호해.

2. **A:** 카레와 파에야 중 어느 것을 선호하니?
   **B:** 나는 파에야를 선호해.

**M:** 런던 시티 투어에 오신 걸 환영합니다. 오늘 우리는 런던에서 유명한 장소들을 방문할 거예요. 런던 아이가 보이죠? 오른편에 있어요. 그것은 템스강 근처에 있는 대관람차예요. 런던 아이에서의 전망은 놀라워요. 매년 많은 사람들이 그곳을 방문해요.

직원: 무엇을 도와드릴까요?
엄마: 우리는 런던의 멋진 경치를 즐기고 싶어요.
하나: 가기에 가장 좋은 장소는 어디인가요?
직원: 두 곳이 있습니다. 런던 아이는 대관람차이고 스카이 가든은 높은 건물 꼭대기에 있는 유리 정원이에요. 어느 것을 선호하시나요?
엄마: 흠... 저는 런던 아이가 좋아요.
하나: 저도요.
직원: 좋은 선택이에요. 그곳에 버스로 갈 수 있답니다.
엄마: 가장 가까운 버스 정거장은 어디에 있나요?
직원: 여기서 한 블록 직진한 후 오른쪽으로 도세요. 왼편에 있어요. 좋은 여행하세요!
하나: 와, 런던 전체를 다 볼 수 있어요. 보세요! 커다란 시계가 있어요.
엄마: 내 생각에 저것은 빅벤 같아. 우리 나중에 가서 그곳을 방문해 볼래?
하나: 좋아요.

**01** 다음 대화의 빈칸에 알맞은 말은?

> A: Excuse me. _____ is the park?
> B: Go straight two blocks and turn left. It's on your right.

① When  ② Where  ③ Who
④ What  ⑤ How

**02** 다음 대화의 밑줄 친 부분과 바꾸어 쓸 수 <u>없는</u> 것을 고르시오.

> A: Which do you prefer, hamburgers or spaghetti?
> B: <u>I like hamburgers more than spaghetti.</u>

① I prefer hamburgers.
② I prefer hamburgers to spaghetti.
③ I think hamburgers are better than spaghetti.
④ I think I prefer hamburgers to spaghetti.
⑤ I think hamburgers are less preferable to spaghetti.

**03** 다음 대화의 밑줄 친 부분과 바꾸어 쓸 수 있는 것을 <u>모두</u> 고르시오.

> A: Excuse me. <u>Where is the school?</u>
> B: Go straight one block and turn left. It's on your right. It's across from the restaurant.

① How can I get to the school?
② Do you know when to go to the school?
③ How do I get to the school?
④ Could I tell you where the school is?
⑤ Is there the school around here?

**04** 자연스러운 대화가 되도록 순서대로 배열하시오.

> (A) How can I get there?
> (B) Go straight one block and turn left. It's on your right.
> (C) Excuse me. Is the Picasso Museum near here?
> (D) Yes. It's not far from here.

➡ _____

[01~02] 다음 대화를 읽고 물음에 답하시오.

B: Excuse me. Is the Picasso Museum near here?
G: Yes. It's not far (A)_____ here.
B: (B)_____ can I get there?
G: Go straight one block and turn left. It's on your right.

**01** 빈칸 (A)에 알맞은 말을 고르시오.

① for   ② from   ③ to
④ in   ⑤ into

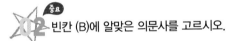

**02** 빈칸 (B)에 알맞은 의문사를 고르시오.

① Where   ② How   ③ What
④ When   ⑤ Who

[03~05] 다음 대화를 읽고 물음에 답하시오.

B: ⓐIt's really hot here in Thailand. (①) ⓑLet's go to the night market and have some fresh fruit juice. (②)
G: Sounds good. (③)
B: ⓒWe can go on foot or by bus. (④) ⓓWhat do you prefer?
G: ⓔI prefer the bus. (⑤)

**03** 위 대화의 ①~⑤ 중 다음 주어진 말이 들어갈 알맞은 곳은?

How do we get there?

①   ②   ③   ④   ⑤

**04** ⓐ~ⓔ 중 어법상 어색한 것을 고르시오.

① ⓐ   ② ⓑ   ③ ⓒ   ④ ⓓ   ⑤ ⓔ

**05** 위 대화의 내용과 일치하지 않는 것을 고르시오.

① The boy wants to drink some fresh fruit juice.
② They are going to go to the night market.
③ They are in Thailand.
④ They are going to take a bus to go to the night market.
⑤ The girl knows how they get to the night market.

**06** 다음 중 짝지어진 대화가 어색한 것은?

① A: Which do you like better, Korean movies or foreign movies?
  B: I think Korean movies are better than foreign movies.
② A: Can you tell me how to get to the hospital?
  B: Of course. Go straight and turn left.
③ A: I prefer the park to the beach.
  B: OK. Let's go to the park.
④ A: Do you know how to get to the library?
  B: I'm a stranger, too. Go straight and turn left. It's next to the bookstore.
⑤ A: Which shirt do you prefer, the red one or the yellow one?
  B: I'd prefer the red one.

[07~09] 다음 대화를 읽고 물음에 답하시오.

B: Jisu, (A)[why / how] don't we watch the movie *Best Friends* on Saturday? (①)

G: Sounds good. (②)

B: (③) On Saturday there are two showings, one at five and the other at seven. Which do you prefer?

G: I prefer the seven showing. (④)

B: Okay. Then (B)[how about / let's] meet at six. (⑤)

G: Sounds good.

**07** 위 대화의 ①~⑤ 중 다음 주어진 말이 들어갈 알맞은 곳은?

What time does it begin?

①     ②     ③     ④     ⑤

서답형
**08** 괄호 (A)와 (B)에서 알맞은 말을 골라 쓰시오.

➡ (A) _____, (B) _____

**09** 위 대화를 읽고 대답할 수 없는 질문을 고르시오.

① What time does the movie *Best Friends* begin on Saturday?

② Where are they going to meet on Saturday?

③ What time does the girl prefer, five or seven?

④ What time are they going to meet on Saturday?

⑤ What movie are they going to watch on Saturday?

[10~12] 그림을 참고하여 다음 대화를 읽고 물음에 답하시오.

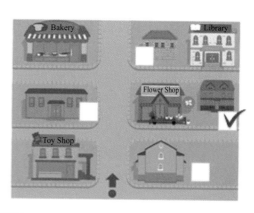

B: Sally, I need to buy some candies for Halloween. (A)_____ can I buy them?

G: You can buy them at Wendy's Candy Shop.

B: (B)_____ is it?

G: (C)_____ It's (D)_____ the library.

서답형
**10** (A)와 (B)에 공통으로 들어갈 의문사를 쓰시오.

➡ _____

중요
**11** 그림에 표시가 되어 있는 곳을 찾아 갈 때 빈칸 (C)에 알맞을 말을 고르시오.

① Go straight one block and turn left.

② Go straight one block and turn right. It's on your right.

③ Go straight two blocks and turn right.

④ Go straight two blocks and turn right. It's on your left.

⑤ Go straight two blocks and turn left.

서답형
**12** 그림을 참고하여 (D)에 들어갈 단어를 쓰시오. (2 단어)

➡ _____

**Conversation** 서술형 시험대비

**01** 다음 대화에서 어색한 부분을 찾아 고치시오.

> A: Which do you prefer, cookies or pie?
> B: Yes, I do. I prefer cookies

➡ _____

[02~03] 그림을 참고하여 다음 대화를 읽고 물음에 답하시오.

B: Excuse me. 나에게 아프리카 박물관에 가는 방법을 말해 줄 수 있니? (how, to, to, African, the, can, me, Museum, you, tell, get, ?)
G: Sure. Go straight two blocks and turn (A) _____.
B: Go straight and turn (A) _____. And then?
G: It's on your (B) _____. It's (C) _____ the shoe store.
B: I got it. Thank you very much.

**02** 밑줄 친 우리말에 맞게 괄호 안에 주어진 단어를 배열하여 영작하시오.

➡ _____

★**03** 그림에 표시된 아프리카 박물관(③번)에 갈 때 (A)~(C)에 알맞은 말을 쓰시오.

➡ (A) _____, (B) _____, (C) _____

[04~05] 다음 대화를 읽고 물음에 답하시오.

B: It's really hot here in Thailand. Let's go to the night market and have some fresh fruit juice.
G: Sounds good. (a)How do we get there?
B: We can go (A)_____ foot or (B)_____ bus. Which do you prefer?
G: I prefer the bus.

**04** 빈칸 (A)와 (B)에 알맞은 전치사를 쓰시오.

➡ (A) _____, (B) _____

**05** 밑줄 친 (a)와 같은 의미가 되도록 주어진 단어를 이용해서 문장을 만드시오.

➡ _____ (can, how)

_____
(how, know)

_____
(how, tell, can)

[06~07] 다음 대화를 읽고 물음에 답하시오.

A: Which do you prefer, curry (A)_____ paella?
B: (B)I prefer paella.

★**06** 빈칸 (A)에 알맞은 접속사를 쓰시오.

➡ _____

★**07** 위 대화의 밑줄 친 (B)에서 생략된 것을 쓰시오.

➡ _____

 교과서

# Grammar

## 1 수동태

Leonardo da Vinci **painted** *Mona Lisa*. 〈능동태〉 Leonardo da Vinci는 모나리자를 그렸다.
*Mona Lisa* **was painted** by Leonardo da Vinci. 〈수동태〉 모나리자는 Leonardo da Vinci에 의해 그려졌다.

- **수동태**는 '**주어+be동사+동사의 과거분사+by+행위자**'의 형식을 가지며 '…에 의해 ~되다[당하다, 받다]'라는 뜻이며, 주어가 동사가 나타내는 행위를 당하거나 행동의 영향을 받는 것을 나타낸다. 수동태 문장의 주어 자리에는 능동태 문장의 목적어가 오고, by 다음에는 능동태 문장의 주어를 쓴다. 이때 능동태 문장의 주어가 일반인이면 'by + 행위자'는 생략할 수 있다. 누가 그 동작을 했는지 중요하지 않거나 잘 모를 때, 수동태 문장으로 표현한다. 수동태는 현재, 과거, 미래 시제로 쓸 수 있고, 'be동사+동사의 과거분사'에서 be동사로 시제를 표현한다.

  - This place **was used** for cooking. 이곳은 요리를 위해 사용되었다.

- 4형식 문장의 수동태는 간접목적어와 직접목적어 각각을 주어로 하는 수동태가 가능하며 직접목적어를 주어로 한 수동태에서는 간접목적어 앞에 특정한 전치사를 써야 한다. 전치사 to를 쓰는 동사에는 'give, send, tell, teach, show, bring' 등이 있고, 전치사 for를 쓰는 동사에는 'buy, make, choose, cook, get' 등이 있으며, 전치사 of를 쓰는 동사는 'ask' 등이 있다. 또한 make, buy, read, write 등은 직접목적어를 주어로 하는 수동태만 가능하다.

  - A book **was given** to Sam by Harry. 책 한 권이 Harry에 의해 Sam에게 주어졌다.

- 조동사가 있는 문장의 수동태는 '조동사+be+p.p.' 형식을 갖는다.

  - A dress **will be bought** for Jennifer by her mom. 옷이 그녀의 엄마에 의해 Jennifer에게 사주어질 것이다.

- 목적격보어가 원형부정사인 경우, 수동태 문장에서는 to부정사로 바뀐다.

  - Jack **was made** to wash the dishes by his mom. Jack은 그의 엄마에 의해 설거지하도록 시켜졌다.

- by 이외의 전치사를 사용하는 수동태에 유의한다.

  - be interested in: ~에 흥미가 있다
  - be covered with: ~로 덮여 있다
  - be made of: ~로 만들어지다(물리적 변화)
  - be satisfied with: ~에 만족하다
  - be filled with: ~로 가득 차다
  - be surprised at: ~에 놀라다
  - be made from: ~로 만들어지다(화학적 변화)
  - be pleased with: ~에 기뻐하다

### 핵심 Check

1. 다음 괄호 안에서 알맞은 말을 고르시오.

   (1) The building was (build / built) last year.
   (2) The book (will / will be) written by Andy.

## 2  so ~ that ... 구문

> It was **so** delicious **that** we all enjoyed it. 너무 맛있어서 우리 모두는 그것을 즐겼다.
> The movie was **so** funny **that** I laughed a lot. 그 영화는 너무 재밌어서 나는 많이 웃었다.

- '**so+형용사[부사]+that+주어+동사**' 구문은 '너무 ~해서 …하다'라는 뜻으로 원인과 결과를 나타낸다. so 뒤에 나오는 내용이 원인을 뜻하고, that 이하가 결과를 나타낸다. 이때 so는 뒤에 나오는 형용사나 부사를 강조한다.
  - I was **so** tired **that** I couldn't go out. 나는 너무 피곤해서 나갈 수 없었다.

- '**so ... that**' 구문에서 that 앞에 형용사나 부사 대신 명사가 오면 so 대신 such를 쓴다.
  - There was **such** a crowd **that** we could hardly move. 사람이 아주 많아서 우리는 거의 움직이지 못했다.

- '**so that+주어+동사**'는 목적을 나타내어 '~하기 위해서' 혹은 '~하도록'이라는 의미로 쓰인다. 'so ~ that ...'과 혼동하지 않도록 유의한다.
  - Record this meeting **so that** people can replay it later. 이 회의를 기록하여 나중에 재생할 수 있도록 하십시오.

- '**so+형용사[부사]+that+주어+can ~**'은 '형용사[부사]+enough+to 동사원형'으로 바꿔 쓸 수 있으며, '**so+형용사[부사]+that+주어+can't ~**'는 'too+형용사[부사]+to 동사원형'으로 바꿔 쓸 수 있다.
  - She was **so** kind **that** she invited me.
    = She was kind **enough to** invite me. 그녀는 너무 친절해서 나를 초대했다.
  - Emma was **so** sick **that** she couldn't lift a finger.
    = Emma was **too** sick **to** lift a finger. Emma는 너무 아파서 손가락도 까딱할 수 없었다.

### 핵심 Check

2. 다음 우리말에 맞게 괄호 안의 어구를 바르게 배열하시오.

(1) 물이 맑아서 밑바닥까지 보였다.

(you, the water, the bottom, could, was, see, clear, so, that)

➡ _____

(2) 그는 매우 열심히 공부해서 변호사가 되었다.

(he, he, a lawyer, became, worked, hard, that, so)

➡ _____

(3) 당신이 그곳에 제시간에 도착할 수 있게 빨리 몰겠습니다.

(you, I'll, there, time, get, drive, can, so, in, fast, that)

➡ _____

**01** 다음 문장에서 어법상 어색한 부분을 바르게 고쳐 쓰시오.

(1) The room cleans by him every day.

_____ ➡ _____

(2) *The Kiss* is painted by Gustav Klimt in 1908.

_____ ➡ _____

(3) Mike felt very happy that he danced.

_____ ➡ _____

(4) She exercises hard so that may stay healthy.

_____ ➡ _____

**02** 다음 중 어법상 바르지 <u>않은</u> 것은?

① The pictures were taken by my sister.
② The bridge was built about 50 years ago.
③ Jessica is loved by everybody.
④ The letter is sent tomorrow.
⑤ *Harry Potter* was written by J.K. Rowling.

**03** 다음 문장의 밑줄 친 부분 중에서 어법상 잘못된 곳을 고르시오.

①It was ②too ③delicious ④that we ⑤all enjoyed it.

**04** 다음 우리말에 맞게 주어진 어구를 바르게 배열하시오. (필요하면 어형을 바꿀 것)

(1) 그 물은 너무 깨끗해서 우리는 그것을 마실 수 있었다. (we, the water, was, drink, could, that, it, clean, so)

➡ _____

(2) 그는 축구 시합 중에 부상을 입었다. (he, injure, during, the soccer match)

➡ _____

**01** 다음 빈칸에 알맞은 것은?

> English _____ all around the world.

① speaks
② spoke
③ spoken
④ is spoken
⑤ to speak

**02** 다음 빈칸에 알맞은 말이 순서대로 바르게 짝지어진 것은?

> • The car _____ by him every Sunday.
> • The cap was _____ small that I couldn't wear it.

① washes – so
② is washed – too
③ is washed – so
④ was washed – too
⑤ was washed – very

**03** 다음 중 수동태로의 전환이 어색한 것은?

① Soccer fans filled the stadium.
　→ The stadium was filled with soccer fans.
② They make a lot of cars in Korea.
　→ A lot of cars are made in Korea.
③ Mom made me a delicious spaghetti last night.
　→ A delicious spaghetti was made for me by Mom last night.
④ King Sejong invented Hangeul.
　→ Hangeul was invented by King Sejong.
⑤ Jenny sent me the pictures drawn in France.
　→ The pictures sent to me were drawn in France by Jenny.

**서답형**
**04** 다음 문장에서 어법상 틀린 부분을 찾아 바르게 고치시오.

> He is weak so that he can't swim across the river.

_____ ➡ _____

**05** 다음 괄호 안에서 알맞은 것을 고르시오.

(1) I was (excited / exciting) because we could watch some of the world's most famous soccer players.
(2) We (consider / are considered) blue whales to be the biggest animals.
(3) English was taught (to / for) us by Ms Green.
(4) Some interesting books were chosen (to / for) me by her.
(5) The way to the station was asked (to / of) me by the old lady.
(6) Angelina is (so / very) shy that she can't speak in front of many people.
(7) Clark was so hungry (that / what) he ate all the food.

**06** 다음 빈칸에 알맞은 말이 바르게 짝지어진 것을 고르시오.

> • I worked _____ hard _____ I passed the test.

① so – that
② that – so
③ too – that
④ that – too
⑤ too – to

**07** 다음 빈칸에 공통으로 들어갈 말로 가장 적절한 것은?

> • Does that mean that you're pleased _____ it?
> • I am not satisfied _____ the service.

① with      ② for      ③ in

④ at      ⑤ of

**08** 다음 우리말에 맞게 영작한 것을 고르시오.
중요

> • 그녀는 너무 화가 나서 얼굴이 빨개졌다.

① She was too angry to turn red.

② She was enough angry to turn red.

③ She was angry so that her face turned red.

④ She was so angry that her face turned red.

⑤ She was angry in order that her face turned red.

**09** 다음 우리말을 영어로 바르게 옮기지 <u>않은</u> 것은?

> Steve는 충분한 수면을 취하려고 어제 일찍 잤다.

① Steve went to bed early yesterday so that he could get plenty of sleep.

② Steve went to bed so early yesterday that he could get plenty of sleep.

③ Steve went to bed early yesterday to get plenty of sleep.

④ Steve went to bed early yesterday in order to get plenty of sleep.

⑤ Steve went to bed early yesterday so as to get plenty of sleep.

**10** 다음 문장을 수동태로 바르게 바꾼 것은?

> Jenny turned off the TV.

① The TV turned off Jenny.

② The TV turned off by Jenny.

③ The TV was turned off Jenny.

④ The TV was turned by Jenny.

⑤ The TV was turned off by Jenny.

**11** 다음 문장을 수동태는 능동태로, 능동태는 수동태로 고치시오.
고난이도

(1) Both were designed by Antoni Gaudi.
➡ _____

(2) This photo was taken by James.
➡ _____

(3) Her mom made her a beautiful dress.
➡ _____

(4) The book fair will be held in Seoul.
➡ _____

(5) By whom is it considered to be dangerous?
➡ _____

**12** 다음 괄호 안에서 알맞은 말을 고르시오.
서답형

(1) Vietnam is (so / such) beautiful that you should come someday.

(2) I was in (so / such) a hurry that I could not pay you a visit.

(3) The park was so noisy that I (shouldn't / couldn't) rest.

➡ (1) _____ (2) _____ (3) _____

**13** 다음 중 두 문장을 서로 바꿔 쓸 수 <u>없는</u> 것은?

① *Romeo and Juliet* was written by Shakespeare.
→ Shakespeare wrote *Romeo and Juliet*.

② Morris bought his son a new suit last week.
→ A new suit was bought for his son by Morris last week.

③ They showed the public the photos taken by him.
→ The photos taken by him were shown to the public.

④ The thief forced Judy to hand over the money.
→ Judy was forced to hand over the money by the thief.

⑤ Our teacher made us do our homework.
→ We were made do our homework by our teacher.

**14** 다음 중 어법상 올바른 문장을 <u>모두</u> 고르시오.

① He was seen put the bag on the table by Ann.

② He was read the storybook every night by his mom.

③ Melbourne is well known for its beautiful ocean roads.

④ It was so a nice day that we went for a walk.

⑤ Julie is so kind that everybody likes her.

**서답형**
**15** 다음 문장에서 어법상 <u>어색한</u> 부분을 바르게 고쳐 다시 쓰시오.

(1) The World Wide Web(www) invented by Tim Berners-Lee in 1989.
_____ ➡ _____

(2) The car accident was happened last night.
_____ ➡ _____

(3) I was too careless to trust such a man.
_____ ➡ _____

[16~18] 다음 두 문장이 같은 의미가 되도록 빈칸에 알맞은 말을 고르시오.

**16**

Harry chose Christine some books.
= Some books _____ Christine by Harry.

① chose
② were choosing
③ were chosen
④ were chosen to
⑤ were chosen for

**17**

I heard him sing.
= He _____ by me.

① heard singing
② was singing
③ was heard sing
④ heard sing
⑤ was heard to sing

**18**

Because she is very sick, she can't move.
= She is _____ she can't move.

① too sick that
② to sick too
③ so sick that
④ sick so that
⑤ very sick that

**01** 다음 문장을 수동태는 능동태로, 능동태는 수동태로 고치시오.

(1) The painting was stolen by someone last week.

　➡ _____

(2) Its size and unique design impressed me.

　➡ _____

(3) Eva heard Peter open the window.

　➡ _____

(4) Angie will give me a present on my birthday.

　➡ _____

(5) Cathy took care of the baby.

　➡ _____

**02** 주어진 두 문장을 한 문장으로 만들 때, 빈칸에 알맞은 말을 3 단어로 쓰시오.

(1) • I was very stupid.

　• I made the mistake.

　➡ I was _____ I made the mistake.

(2) • He is very tall.

　• He can touch the ceiling.

　➡ He is _____ touch the ceiling.

(3) • Alice was really shocked.

　• She couldn't say even a word.

　➡ Alice was _____ say even a word.

**03** 다음 우리말을 so와 that을 이용하여 영어로 쓸 때 빈칸에 알맞은 말을 쓰시오.

(1) Robert는 시험에 합격하기 위해서 열심히 공부했다.

　➡ Robert studied _____ he could pass the exam.

(2) Robert는 열심히 공부해서 시험에 합격할 수 있었다.

　➡ Robert studied _____ he could pass the exam.

**04** 다음 문장에서 어법상 어색한 부분을 바르게 고쳐 다시 쓰시오.

(1) Cake is made of flour, milk, eggs and sugar.

　➡ _____

(2) The shirts are ironed by John tomorrow morning.

　➡ _____

(3) Mike was seen be hit by a car by Ms. Brown.

　➡ _____

(4) Our dog was ran over by a truck.

　➡ _____

(5) The matter will discussed by us tommorrow.

　➡ _____

**05** 다음 문장을 같은 뜻을 갖는 문장으로 바꿔 쓸 때 빈칸을 알맞게 채우시오.

(1) The test was so easy that I could pass it.
→ The test was _____ pass.

(2) Andrew speaks _____ I can't understand him.
→ Andrew speaks too fast for me to understand.

**06** 다음 우리말을 괄호 안에 주어진 어휘를 이용하여 영작하시오.

(1) 그 소설은 Ernest Hemingway에 의해 씌여졌다. (novel, write)
➡ _____

(2) 최초의 월드컵은 1930년 우루과이에서 열렸다. (Uruguay, the first World Cup, take place)
➡ _____

(3) Laura는 그녀의 딸에게 동화책을 읽어 주었다. (read, a fairy tale book) (수동태로 쓸 것.)
➡ _____

(4) Kimberly는 그 소식을 듣고 낙담했다. (disappointed, the news)
➡ _____

(5) 너는 Allie가 노래하는 것을 들었니? (hear, sing) (수동태로 쓸 것.)
➡ _____

(6) 너무나도 추워서 그는 감기에 걸렸다. (cold, catch a cold)
➡ _____

**07** 괄호 안의 어휘를 사용하여 주어진 문장을 같은 의미가 되도록 다시 쓰시오.

(1) Claire got up so late that she couldn't get on the train. (too)
➡ _____

(2) Chuck spoke too low for me to hear. (so, can)
➡ _____

(3) Bill was so smart that he could solve the difficult math problems. (enough)
➡ _____

(4) Juliet is rich enough to buy the house. (so, can)
➡ _____

**08** 다음 문장을 주어진 어휘로 시작하여 다시 쓰시오.

(1) My grandmother made the sweater for me. (the sweater)
➡ _____

(2) Does she clean these rooms every day? (are)
➡ _____

(3) Mariel made Dan prepare dinner. (Dan)
➡ _____

(4) Your recent success pleased Joakim a lot. (Joakim)
➡ _____

# Reading

## My Happy Days in Spain

by Park Jinwoo

My family traveled to Spain this summer. Spain is loved by lots of
tourists. We visited many interesting places.

Our trip started in Madrid. Madrid is the capital and is famous for
soccer. We went to a stadium to watch a soccer match. My sister and I
were excited because we could watch some of the world's most famous
soccer players.

The stadium was full of soccer fans. As we watched the match, we
cheered by singing songs, waving our hands, and shouting with the
other fans.

After we toured Madrid, we went to Seville. While we walked around
the city, we saw many historic buildings. We visited a flamenco
museum and watched a flamenco dance. A woman in a red dress was
dancing the flamenco with wonderful movements.

travel 여행하다
tourist 여행객, 관광객
capital 수도
stadium 경기장
match 경기, 시합
be famous for ~으로 유명하다
be full of ~으로 가득 차다
cheer 응원하다
historic 역사적인
flamenco 플라멩코(격정적인 스페인 춤)
movement 동작

### 확인문제

● 다음 문장이 본문의 내용과 일치하면 T, 일치하지 않으면 F를 쓰시오.

1  Jinwoo's family traveled to Spain last summer. ☐

2  Jinwoo's family trip started in Madrid. ☐

3  Jinwoo's family went to a stadium to watch a soccer match. ☐

4  The stadium was full of the world's most famous soccer players. ☐

5  Jinwoo's family went to Seville after they toured Madrid. ☐

6  Jinwoo's family watched a flamenco dance on the street. ☐

For dinner, we ate paella. It is a traditional Spanish dish with rice, vegetables, meat, and seafood. It tasted like fried rice in Korea. It was so delicious that we all enjoyed it.

In Barcelona, we took a tour of Park Guell and Sagrada Familia. Both were designed by Antoni Gaudi. In Park Guell, we saw some of Gaudi's creative works like a colorful lizard.

After Park Guell, we visited Sagrada Familia. Work on the building started in 1883 and is still going on today. I was impressed by its size and unique design. The ceiling inside Sagrada Familia shone like the night sky with bright stars. Its stone columns stood like big trees. At Park Guell and Sagrada Familia I could feel Gaudi's creativity and his love of nature.

Traveling in Spain was a wonderful experience. While I was there, I learned a lot about Spain. I want to visit the country again.

traditional 전통적인
paella 파에야
Spanish 스페인의
lizard 도마뱀
take a tour 여행하다, 관광하다
still 여전히
unique 특별한
ceiling 천장
shine 빛나다
column 기둥
go on 계속하다
impress 감명을 주다
experience 경험

---

📎 **확인문제**

● 다음 문장이 본문의 내용과 일치하면 T, 일치하지 <u>않으면</u> F를 쓰시오.

**1** For dinner, Jinwoo's family ate paella. ☐

**2** Paella tasted like kimchi pancake in Korea. ☐

**3** Park Guell and Sagrada Familia were designed by Antoni Gaudi. ☐

**4** Jinwoo's family visited Park Guell after Sagrada Familia. ☐

**5** Jinwoo was impressed by the size and unique design of Sagrada Familia. ☐

**6** The ceiling inside Sagrada Familia stood like big trees. ☐

• 우리말을 참고하여 빈칸에 알맞은 말을 쓰시오.

**1** My _____ _____ in Spain – _____ Park Jinwoo

**2** My family _____ _____ Spain this summer.

**3** Spain _____ _____ _____ lots of tourists.

**4** We _____ many _____ places.

**5** _____ _____ started in Madrid.

**6** Madrid is the capital and _____ _____ _____ soccer.

**7** We went to a stadium _____ _____ a soccer match.

**8** My sister and I _____ _____ because we could watch some of _____ _____ _____ _____ _____ _____.

**9** The stadium _____ _____ _____ soccer fans.

**10** As we watched the match, we cheered _____ _____ songs, waving our hands, and _____ with the other fans.

**11** _____ we toured Madrid, we went to Seville.

**12** _____ we _____ _____ the city, we saw many historic buildings.

**13** We _____ a flamenco museum and _____ a flamenco dance.

**14** A woman _____ was dancing the flamenco _____ _____ _____.

| | |
|---|---|
| **1** | 스페인에서의 행복한 날들 – 박진우 |
| **2** | 나의 가족은 이번 여름에 스페인을 여행했다. |
| **3** | 스페인은 수많은 관광객들에게 사랑받는다. |
| **4** | 우리는 여러 흥미로운 장소를 방문했다. |
| **5** | 우리의 여행은 마드리드에서 시작했다. |
| **6** | 마드리드는 수도이며 축구로 유명하다. |
| **7** | 우리는 축구 경기를 보기 위해서 경기장으로 갔다. |
| **8** | 나의 여동생과 나는 세계에서 가장 유명한 축구 선수 몇몇을 볼 수 있었기 때문에 신이 났다. |
| **9** | 경기장은 축구 팬들로 가득 차 있었다. |
| **10** | 우리는 경기를 보는 동안 노래를 부르고, 손을 흔들고, 다른 팬들과 함께 소리를 치며 응원을 했다. |
| **11** | 마드리드를 여행하고 난 후, 우리는 세비야로 갔다. |
| **12** | 우리는 도시를 걸어다니는 동안, 역사상 중요한 많은 건물들을 보았다. |
| **13** | 우리는 플라멩코 박물관을 방문해서 플라멩코 춤을 보았다. |
| **14** | 빨간 드레스를 입은 여자가 멋진 동작으로 플라멩코를 추고 있었다. |

**15** _____ dinner, we ate paella.

**16** It is a _____ _____ _____ _____ rice, vegetables, meat, and seafood.

**17** It _____ _____ fried rice in Korea.

**18** It was _____ delicious _____ we all enjoyed it.

**19** In Barcelona, we _____ _____ _____ _____ Park Guell and Sagrada Familia.

**20** Both _____ _____ _____ Antoni Gaudi.

**21** In Park Guell, we saw some of Gaudi's _____ _____ _____ a colorful lizard.

**22** _____ Park Guell, we visited Sagrada Familia.

**23** Work on the building started in 1883 and _____ _____ _____ _____ today.

**24** I _____ _____ its size and unique design.

**25** The ceiling inside Sagrada Familia _____ _____ the night sky with bright stars.

**26** Its stone columns _____ _____ big trees.

**27** At Park Guell and Sagrada Familia I could feel Gaudi's _____ and _____ _____ _____ _____.

**28** _____ in Spain was _____.

**29** _____ I was there, I learned _____ _____ about Spain.

**30** I want _____ _____ the country again.

**15** 저녁 식사로 우리는 파에야를 먹었다.

**16** 그것은 쌀과 채소, 고기, 해산물이 들어간 전통적인 스페인 요리이다.

**17** 그것은 한국의 볶음밥과 같은 맛이 났다.

**18** 너무 맛있어서 우리 모두는 그것을 즐겼다.

**19** 바르셀로나에서 우리는 구엘 공원과 사그라다 파밀리아를 둘러보았다.

**20** 두 곳 모두 Antoni Gaudi에 의해 설계되었다.

**21** 구엘 공원에서 우리는 형형색색의 도마뱀과 같은 몇몇 Gaudi의 창의적인 작품들을 보았다.

**22** 구엘 공원을 본 다음, 우리는 사그라다 파밀리아를 방문했다.

**23** 건물 공사는 1883년에 시작되었고 오늘날까지도 여전히 진행 중이다.

**24** 나는 건물의 크기와 독특한 디자인에 감명 받았다.

**25** 사그라다 파밀리아 안의 천장은 밝은 별이 있는 밤하늘처럼 빛났다.

**26** 돌기둥은 큰 나무처럼 서 있었다.

**27** 구엘 공원과 사그라다 파밀리아에서 나는 Gaudi의 창의성과 자연에 대한 사랑을 느낄 수 있었다.

**28** 스페인 여행은 훌륭한 경험이었다.

**29** 나는 그곳에서 스페인에 대해 많은 것을 배웠다.

**30** 나는 그 나라를 다시 방문하고 싶다.

● 우리말을 참고하여 본문을 영작하시오.

**1** 스페인에서의 행복한 날들 – 박진우

➡ _____

**2** 나의 가족은 이번 여름에 스페인을 여행했다.

➡ _____

**3** 스페인은 수많은 관광객들에게 사랑받는다.

➡ _____

**4** 우리는 여러 흥미로운 장소를 방문했다.

➡ _____

**5** 우리의 여행은 마드리드에서 시작했다.

➡ _____

**6** 마드리드는 수도이며 축구로 유명하다.

➡ _____

**7** 우리는 축구 경기를 보기 위해서 경기장으로 갔다.

➡ _____

**8** 나의 여동생과 나는 세계에서 가장 유명한 축구 선수 몇몇을 볼 수 있었기 때문에 신이 났다.

➡ _____

**9** 경기장은 축구 팬들로 가득 차 있었다.

➡ _____

**10** 우리는 경기를 보는 동안 노래를 부르고, 손을 흔들고, 다른 팬들과 함께 소리를 치며 응원을 했다.

➡ _____

**11** 마드리드를 여행하고 난 후, 우리는 세비야로 갔다.

➡ _____

**12** 우리는 도시를 걸어다니는 동안, 역사상 중요한 많은 건물들을 보았다.

➡ _____

**13** 우리는 플라멩코 박물관을 방문해서 플라멩코 춤을 보았다.

➡ _____

**14** 빨간 드레스를 입은 여자가 멋진 동작으로 플라멩코를 추고 있었다.

➡ _____

**15** 저녁 식사로 우리는 파에야를 먹었다.

➡ _____

**16** 그것은 쌀과 채소, 고기, 해산물이 들어간 전통적인 스페인 요리이다.

➡ _____

**17** 그것은 한국의 볶음밥과 같은 맛이 났다.

➡ _____

**18** 너무 맛있어서 우리 모두는 그것을 즐겼다.

➡ _____

**19** 바르셀로나에서 우리는 구엘 공원과 사그라다 파밀리아를 둘러보았다.

➡ _____

**20** 두 곳 모두 Antoni Gaudi에 의해 설계되었다.

➡ _____

**21** 구엘 공원에서 우리는 형형색색의 도마뱀과 같은 몇몇 Gaudi의 창의적인 작품들을 보았다.

➡ _____

**22** 구엘 공원을 본 다음, 우리는 사그라다 파밀리아를 방문했다.

➡ _____

**23** 건물 공사는 1883년에 시작되었고 오늘날까지도 여전히 진행 중이다.

➡ _____

**24** 나는 건물의 크기와 독특한 디자인에 감명 받았다.

➡ _____

**25** 사그라다 파밀라아 안의 천장은 밝은 별이 있는 밤하늘처럼 빛났다.

➡ _____

**26** 돌기둥은 큰 나무처럼 서 있었다.

➡ _____

**27** 구엘 공원과 사그라다 파밀리아에서 나는 Gaudi의 창의성과 자연에 대한 사랑을 느낄 수 있었다.

➡ _____

**28** 스페인 여행은 훌륭한 경험이었다.

➡ _____

**29** 나는 그곳에서 스페인에 대해 많은 것을 배웠다.

➡ _____

**30** 나는 그 나라를 다시 방문하고 싶다.

➡ _____

[01~03] 다음 글을 읽고 물음에 답하시오.

My family traveled to Spain this summer. Spain is loved by ⓐlots of tourists. We visited many interesting places.

Our trip started in Madrid. Madrid is the capital and is famous for soccer. We went to a stadium to watch a soccer match. My sister and I were excited because we could watch some of the world's most famous soccer players.　　　　　　　<I = Park Jinwoo>

**01** 위 글의 종류로 알맞은 것을 고르시오.

① review　　　　② essay
③ traveler's journal　④ biography
⑤ article

**02** 위 글의 밑줄 친 ⓐlots of와 바꿔 쓸 수 없는 말을 모두 고르시오.

① a few　　　　② many
③ plenty of　　④ a number of
⑤ much

**03** 위 글의 내용과 일치하지 않는 것은?

① 진우의 가족은 이번 여름에 스페인을 여행했다.
② 수많은 관광객들이 스페인을 사랑한다.
③ 진우의 가족 여행은 마드리드에서 끝났다.
④ 마드리드는 스페인의 수도이다.
⑤ 진우와 여동생은 세계에서 가장 유명한 축구 선수 몇몇을 볼 수 있었다.

[04~06] 다음 글을 읽고 물음에 답하시오.

After we toured Madrid, we went to Seville. ⓐWhile we walked around the city, we saw many historic buildings. We visited a flamenco museum and watched a flamenco dance. A woman in a red dress was ⓑdancing the flamenco with wonderful movements.
　　　　　　<we = Jinwoo's family>

**서답형**
**04** Where did Jinwoo's family see many historic buildings? Fill in the blanks with the suitable words.

➡ They _____.

**05** 위 글의 밑줄 친 ⓐWhile과 같은 의미로 쓰인 것을 고르시오.

① While Tom is very good at science, his brother is hopeless.
② While I was waiting at the bus stop, three buses went by.
③ I've read fifty pages, while he's read only twenty.
④ They chatted for a while.
⑤ The walls are green, while the ceiling is white.

**06** 아래 <보기>에서 위 글의 밑줄 친 ⓑdancing과 문법적 쓰임이 같은 것의 개수를 고르시오.

┤ 보기 ├
① His hobby is collecting stamps.
② They aren't playing tennis.
③ She heard someone calling her name.
④ I like baking cookies.
⑤ The girl standing at the door is my sister.

① 1개　② 2개　③ 3개　④ 4개　⑤ 5개

**[07~10]** 다음 글을 읽고 물음에 답하시오.

For dinner, we ate paella. It is a traditional Spanish dish with rice, vegetables, meat, and seafood. It tasted like fried rice in Korea. ⓐ <u>너무 맛있어서 우리 모두는 그것을 즐겼다.</u>

In Barcelona, we took a tour of Park Guell and Sagrada Familia. Both were designed by Antoni Gaudi. In Park Guell, we saw some of Gaudi's creative ⓑ<u>works</u> like a colorful lizard.                    <we = Jinwoo's family>

**서답형**

**07** 위 글의 밑줄 친 ⓐ의 우리말에 맞게 주어진 어휘를 이용하여 9단어로 영작하시오.

> It, so, delicious

➡ _____

**08** 위 글의 밑줄 친 ⓑworks와 같은 의미로 쓰인 것을 고르시오.

① He works at a small shop.
② She collected Beethoven's piano works.
③ They started engineering works there.
④ This pill works on me.
⑤ The machine works 24 hours a day.

**중요**

**09** 위 글의 주제로 알맞은 것을 고르시오.

① how to make a traditional Spanish dish
② the difference of paella and fried rice
③ the introduction of the dish and places Jinwoo's family enjoyed
④ the historical importance of Park Guell and Sagrada Familia
⑤ the reason why Gaudi designed Park Guell and Sagrada Familia

**서답형**

**10** 다음 빈칸 (A)와 (B)에 알맞은 단어를 넣어 구엘 공원에 대한 소개를 완성하시오.

> It is in (A)_____ and was designed by Antoni Gaudi. Jinwoo's family saw some of Gaudi's creative works such as (B)_____ _____ there.

**[11~13]** 다음 인터뷰를 읽고 물음에 답하시오.

**How much do you know about Vietnam?**

The capital of Vietnam is Hanoi. ⓐ <u>Vietnamese is spoken there.</u> Pho and banh mi are popular dishes in Vietnam. Every year lots of tourists visit Halong Bay and Nha Trang. Halong Bay has 1,969 islands and Nha Trang is well known ⓑ its beautiful beaches. Vietnam is so beautiful that you should come someday.

**서답형**

**11** 위 글의 밑줄 친 ⓐ를 능동태로 바꾸시오.

➡ _____

**12** 위 글의 빈칸 ⓑ에 들어갈 알맞은 전치사를 고르시오.

① to          ② for          ③ by
④ as          ⑤ in

**중요**

**13** 위 글의 내용과 일치하지 않는 것은?

① 베트남의 수도는 하노이이다.
② 베트남에서는 주로 영어를 사용한다.
③ pho와 banh mi가 인기 있는 요리이다.
④ 하롱베이는 1,969개의 섬을 가지고 있다.
⑤ 나트랑은 아름다운 해변으로 잘 알려져 있다.

[14~17] 다음 글을 읽고 물음에 답하시오.

After Park Guell, we visited Sagrada Familia. Work on the building started in 1883 and is still going on today. I was impressed by its size and unique design. The (A)[ceiling / sealing] inside Sagrada Familia shone like the night sky with bright stars. Its stone columns stood like big trees. At Park Guell and Sagrada Familia I could feel Gaudi's creativity and his love of nature. ⓐTraveling in Spain was a wonderful experience. While I was (B)[there / in there], I learned a lot (C)[about / of] Spain. I want to visit the country again. <I = Park Jinwoo>

**서답형**

**14** 위 글의 괄호 (A)~(C)에서 문맥이나 어법상 알맞은 낱말을 골라 쓰시오.

➡ (A)_____ (B)_____ (C)_____

**15** 위 글의 밑줄 친 ⓐ와 바꿔 쓸 수 있는 문장을 모두 고르시오.

① It was a wonderful experience to travel in Spain.

② That was a wonderful experience to travel in Spain.

③ To traveling in Spain was a wonderful experience.

④ To travel in Spain was a wonderful experience.

⑤ That was a wonderful experience traveling in Spain.

**서답형**

**16** 본문의 내용과 일치하도록 다음 빈칸 ⓐ와 ⓑ에 알맞은 단어를 쓰시오.

To Jinwoo, the ⓐ_____ and ⓑ_____ _____ of Sagrada Familia were impressive.

**17** 위 글을 읽고 답할 수 없는 질문은?

① Where did Jinwoo's family visit before they visited Sagrada Familia?

② When did work on Sagrada Familia start?

③ Why is work on Sagrada Familia still going on today?

④ What were the columns of Sagrada Familia made of?

⑤ Where could Jinwoo feel Gaudi's creativity and his love of nature?

[18~19] 다음 글을 읽고 물음에 답하시오.

For dinner, we ate paella. It is a traditional Spanish dish with rice, vegetables, meat, and seafood. (①) It tasted like fried rice in Korea. (②) It was so delicious that we all enjoyed it. (③) In Barcelona, we took a tour of Park Guell and Sagrada Familia. (④) In Park Guell, we saw some of Gaudi's creative works like a colorful lizard. (⑤) <we = Jinwoo's family>

**중요**

**18** 위 글의 흐름으로 보아, 주어진 문장이 들어가기에 가장 적절한 곳은?

Both were designed by Antoni Gaudi.

① ② ③ ④ ⑤

**19** 위 글을 읽고 대답할 수 없는 질문은?

① What are the ingredients of paella?

② What's the recipe of paella?

③ In Barcelona, what did Jinwoo's family do?

④ By whom were Park Guell and Sagrada Familia designed?

⑤ In Park Guell, what did Jinwoo's family see?

**[20~23]** 다음 글을 읽고 물음에 답하시오.

After Park Guell, we visited Sagrada Familia. Work on the building started in 1883 and is still ⓐgoing on today. I was impressed by its size and unique design. The ceiling inside Sagrada Familia shone like the night sky with bright stars. Its stone columns stood like big trees. At Park Guell and Sagrada Familia I could feel Gaudi's __ⓑ__ and his love of nature.

Traveling in Spain was a wonderful experience. While I was there, I learned a lot about Spain. I want to visit the country again.

<I = Park Jinwoo>

**20** 위 글의 밑줄 친 ⓐgoing on과 바꿔 쓸 수 있는 말을 고르시오.

① stopping
② remaining
③ increasing
④ continuing
⑤ staying

서답형
**21** 위 글의 빈칸 ⓑ에 create를 알맞은 형태로 쓰시오.

➡ _____

**22** 위 글의 마지막 부분에서 알 수 있는 진우의 심경으로 가장 알맞은 것을 고르시오.

① satisfied
② frightened
③ bored
④ ashamed
⑤ disappointed

중요
**23** 위 글의 내용과 일치하지 <u>않는</u> 것은?

① 진우의 가족은 사그라다 파밀리아 보다 구엘 공원을 먼저 보았다.
② 사그라다 파밀리아의 건물 공사는 1883년에 시작되었다.

③ 사그라다 파밀리아 안의 천장은 밝은 별이 있는 밤하늘처럼 빛났다.
④ 진우는 구엘 공원에서 Gaudi의 창의성과 자연에 대한 사랑을 느낄 수 있었다.
⑤ 진우는 스페인 여행 중에 스페인에 대해 많은 것을 배웠다.

**[24~26]** 다음 글을 읽고 물음에 답하시오.

**How much do you know about Australia?**
The capital of Australia is Canberra. English __ⓐ__ there. Meat pie and lamington are popular dishes in Australia. Every year lots of tourists visit Sydney and Melbourne. Sydney has the Sydney Opera House and Melbourne is well known for its beautiful ocean roads. ⓑ오스트레일리아는 너무 멋져서 당신은 언젠가 그곳을 꼭 방문해야 합니다.

서답형
**24** 위 글의 빈칸 ⓐ에 speak를 알맞은 형태로 쓰시오.

➡ _____

서답형
**25** 위 글의 밑줄 친 ⓑ의 우리말에 맞게 한 단어를 보충하여, 주어진 어휘를 알맞게 배열하시오.

is / you / that / visit / Australia / someday / wonderful / it / should

➡ _____

서답형
**26** 위 글을 참조하여 다음 빈칸 (A)와 (B)에 들어갈 알맞은 말을 쓰시오.

The tourist attraction of Sydney is (A)_____ _____ _____ _____ and Melbourne is famous for its beautiful (B)_____ _____ .

*tourist attraction: 관광명소

[01~03] 다음 글을 읽고 물음에 답하시오.

My family traveled to Spain this summer. ⓐ Spain is loved by lots of tourists. We (A)[visited / visited to] many interesting places.

Our trip started in Madrid. ⓑMadrid is the capital and is famous for soccer. We went to a stadium (B)[watching / to watch] a soccer match. My sister and I (C)[was / were] excited because we could watch some of the world's most famous soccer players.

**01** 위 글의 밑줄 친 ⓐ를 능동태로 고치시오.

➡ _____

**02** 위 글의 괄호 (A)~(C)에서 어법상 알맞은 낱말을 골라 쓰시오.

➡ (A)_____ (B)_____ (C)_____

**03** 위 글의 밑줄 친 ⓑ를 다음과 같이 바꿔 쓸 때 빈칸에 들어갈 알맞은 말을 쓰시오.

➡ Madrid is the capital and is _____ _____ for soccer.

[04~06] 다음 글을 읽고 물음에 답하시오.

The stadium was full of soccer fans. As we watched the match, we cheered by ⓐsing songs, ⓑwave our hands, and ⓒshout with the other fans.

ⓓ we toured Madrid, we went to Seville. While we walked around ⓔthe city, we saw many historic buildings. We visited a flamenco museum and watched a flamenco dance. A woman in a red dress was dancing the flamenco with wonderful movements.

<we = Jinwoo's family>

**04** 위 글의 밑줄 친 ⓐ~ⓒ를 각각 알맞은 형태로 쓰시오.

➡ ⓐ _____ ⓑ _____ ⓒ _____

**05** 다음과 같은 뜻이 되도록 위 글의 빈칸 ⓓ에 들어갈 알맞은 말을 쓰시오.

We toured Madrid before we went to Seville.

➡ _____

**06** 위 글의 밑줄 친 ⓔthe city가 가리키는 것을 본문에서 찾아 쓰시오.

➡ _____

[07~09] 다음 글을 읽고 물음에 답하시오.

For dinner, we ate paella. It is a traditional ⓐ ____ dish with rice, vegetables, meat, and seafood. ⓑIt felt like fried rice in Korea. It was so delicious that we all enjoyed it.

In Barcelona, we ⓒtook a tour of Park Guell and Sagrada Familia. Both were designed by Antoni Gaudi. In Park Guell, we saw some of Gaudi's creative works like a colorful lizard.

<we = Jinwoo's family>

**07** 위 글의 빈칸 ⓐ에 Spain을 알맞은 형태로 쓰시오.

➡ _____

**08** 위 글의 밑줄 친 ⓑ에서 흐름상 어색한 부분을 찾아 고치시오.

➡ _____

**09** 위 글의 밑줄 친 ⓒtook a tour of를 한 단어로 고치시오.

➡ _____

[10~12] 다음 글을 읽고 물음에 답하시오.

For dinner, we ate paella. It is a traditional Spanish dish with rice, vegetables, meat, and seafood. ⓐ한국의 볶음밥과 같은 맛이 났다. ⓑIt was so delicious that we all enjoyed it.

In Barcelona, we took a tour of Park Guell and Sagrada Familia. Both were designed by Antoni Gaudi. In Park Guell, we saw some of Gaudi's creative works ⓒlike a colorful lizard.

**10** 위 글의 밑줄 친 ⓐ의 우리말에 맞게 한 단어를 보충하여, 주어진 어휘를 알맞게 배열하시오.

Korea / rice / it / fried / in / tasted

➡ _____

**11** 위 글의 밑줄 친 ⓑIt이 가리키는 것을 본문에서 찾아 쓰시오.

➡ _____

**12** 위 글의 밑줄 친 ⓒlike를 두 단어로 바꿔 쓰시오.

➡ _____

[13~14] 다음 글을 읽고 물음에 답하시오.

ⓐAfter Park Guell, we visited Sagrada Familia. Work on the building started in 1883 and is still going on today. I was (A)[impressing / impressed] by its size and unique design. The ceiling inside Sagrada Familia (B)[shone / shined] like the night sky with bright stars. Its stone columns (C)[were stood / stood] like big trees. At Park Guell and Sagrada Familia I could feel Gaudi's creativity and his love of nature.

**13** 위 글의 밑줄 친 ⓐ를 before[Before]를 사용하여 고치시오.

➡ _____

_____

**14** 위 글의 괄호 (A)~(C)에서 문맥이나 어법상 알맞은 낱말을 골라 쓰시오.

➡ (A) _____ (B) _____ (C) _____

[15~17] 다음 글을 읽고 물음에 답하시오.

The stadium was full of soccer fans. As we watched the match, we cheered by singing songs, waving our hands, and shouting with the other fans.

After we toured Madrid, we went to Seville. While we walked around the city, we saw many ⓐ _____ buildings. We visited a flamenco museum and watched a flamenco dance. ⓑ A woman in a red dress was dancing the flamenco with wonderful movements.

<we = Jinwoo's family>

**15** 위 글의 빈칸 ⓐ에 history를 알맞은 형태로 쓰시오.

➡ _____

**16** 위 글의 밑줄 친 ⓑ를 다음과 같이 고칠 때 빈칸에 들어갈 알맞은 관계대명사를 쓰시오.

➡ A woman _____ was wearing a red dress

**17** 위 글을 읽고 진우의 가족이 마드리드와 세비야에서 한 일을 각각 우리말로 쓰시오.

➡ 마드리드: _____

세비야: _____

_____

# 구석구석

## Enjoy Writing

How much do you know about Vietnam?

The capital of Vietnam is Hanoi. Vietnamese is spoken there. Pho and banh
→ 능동태: They speak Vietnamese there.

mi are popular dishes in Vietnam.
요리

Every year lots of tourists visit Halong Bay and Nha Trang.
= a lot of. many

Halong Bay has 1,969 islands and Nha Trang is well known for its beautiful
be well known for: ~으로 잘 알려져 있다

beaches. Vietnam is so beautiful that you should come someday.
so ~ that ...: 너무 ~해서 ...하다

**구문해설** · capital: 수도 · Vietnamese: 베트남어 · popular: 인기 있는 · island: 섬
· someday: 언젠가

해석

당신은 베트남에 대해서 얼마나 많이 알고 있나요? 베트남의 수도는 하노이입니다. 그곳에서는 베트남어가 사용됩니다. 베트남에서는 pho(퍼, 베트남 쌀국수)와 banh mi(반미, 바게트 빵으로 만든 샌드위치)가 인기 있는 요리입니다. 매년 많은 관광객들이 하롱베이와 나트랑을 방문합니다. 하롱베이는 1,969개의 섬을 가지고 있고 나트랑은 아름다운 해변으로 잘 알려져 있습니다. 베트남은 너무 아름다워서 당신은 언젠가 꼭 오셔야 합니다.

## Project Step 3

My group chose Hong Kong for a trip. Hong Kong is loved by many people
choose의 과거형                          love의 수동태 be loved by: ~에 의해서 사랑받다

who want to do fun activities. We'll have great experiences at Mong Kok
주격 관계대명사    want는 to부정사를 목적어로 취한다.

Market, Victoria Peak, and Ocean Park.

**구문해설** · choose 선택하다 · activity 활동 · experience 경험

우리 모둠은 여행 장소로 홍콩을 선택했다. 홍콩은 재밌는 활동을 하고 싶어 하는 많은 사람들에게 사랑받는다. 우리는 몽콕 시장, 빅토리아 피크 그리고 오션 파크에서 멋진 경험을 할 것이다.

## Wrap Up

I was moved by a book. The title of the book is *The Old Man and the Sea*. It
수동태(= A book moved me.)

was written by Ernest Hemingway.
수동태(= Ernest Hemingway wrote it.)

The story was so great that I read it many times.
'so+형용사[부사]+that+주어+동사'의 형태로 원인과 결과를 나타낸다.(= Because the story was very great. I read
it many times.)

**구문해설** · title 제목 · many times 여러 번

나는 어떤 책에 감동을 받았다. 그 책의 제목은 '노인과 바다'이다. 그것은 Ernest Hemingway에 의해 씌여졌다. 그 이야기는 너무도 대단해서 나는 그것을 여러 번 읽었다.

**Words & Expressions**

**01** 다음 중 밑줄 친 부분의 뜻풀이가 바르지 <u>않은</u> 것은?

① Let's <u>cheer for</u> our national team! (응원하다)

② How can I <u>get</u> there? (얻다, 획득하다)

③ I <u>designed</u> my house. (설계했다)

④ The <u>tea</u> has a wonderful flavor. (차)

⑤ What's the <u>title</u> of this song? (제목)

**02** 다음 제시된 단어를 사용하여 자연스러운 문장을 만들 수 없는 것은? (형태 변화 가능)

┌─── 보기 ───
│ prefer   roll   slide   wave
└

① The children are _____ over the frozen lake.

② The baby _____ to her mom.

③ They are _____ a big ball.

④ How about _____ a tour of the city then?

⑤ I _____ tea to coffee.

**[03~04]** 두 문장에 공통으로 들어갈 수 있는 단어를 쓰시오.

**03**
┌
│ • Most people want to be famous _____ something.
│ • He is well known _____ his cool dancing and great music.
└

**04**
┌
│ • Aren't there any ways I can get _____ the next flight to Sydney?
│ • It takes about ten minutes _____ foot.
└

**05** 다음 주어진 우리말에 맞게 빈칸을 채우시오.

(1) King Sejong is a _____ figure. (세종 대왕은 역사상 중요한 인물이다.)

(2) They went to the _____ last night. (그들은 어젯밤 극장에 갔다.)

(3) He looked up at the _____. (그는 천장을 올려다봤다.)

(4) They _____ _____ the players and shake hands with the _____. (그들은 선수들을 응원하고 팬들과 악수합니다.)

**Conversation**

**[06~07]** 다음 대화를 읽고 물음에 답하시오.

B: Sally, I need to buy some candies for Halloween. (A)_____

G: You can buy them at Wendy's Candy Shop.

B: (B)_____

G: Go straight two blocks and turn right. It's across from the library.

**06** 빈칸 (A)와 (B)에 알맞은 것끼리 짝지어진 것을 고르시오.

　　　(A)　/　　(B)

① What can I buy? / Where is it?

② What can I buy? / Is there a candy shop near here?

③ How can I buy them? / What can I buy?

④ Where can I buy them? / What can I buy?

⑤ Where can I buy them? / Where is it?

**07** 위 대화의 내용과 일치하지 <u>않는</u> 것을 고르시오.

① Sally knows where Wendy's Candy Shop is.

② To get to Wendy's Candy Shop, the boy should go straight 2 blocks and turn right.

③ They are going to buy candies at Wendy's Candy Shop.

④ The boy wants to buy some candies for Halloween.

⑤ Wendy's Candy Shop is across from the library.

**08** 다음 그림과 일치하지 <u>않는</u> 대화를 고르시오.

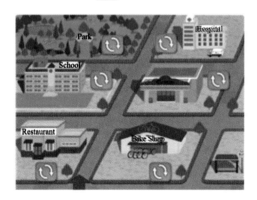

① A: Excuse me. Where is the bike shop?
B: Go straight. It's on your right.

② A: Excuse me. Where is the school?
B: Go straight one block and turn left. It's on your right. It's across from the restaurant.

③ A: Excuse me. Where is the hospital?
B: Go straight two blocks and turn right. It's on your left. It's across from the school.

④ A: Excuse me. Where is the park?
B: Go straight two blocks and turn left. It's on your right.

⑤ A: Excuse me. Where is the cinema?
B: Go straight one block and turn right. It's on your left. It's across from the bike shop.

**[09~11]** 다음 대화를 읽고 물음에 답하시오.

**Staff:** How may I help you?

**Hana's mom:** We want to enjoy a good view of London. (①)

**Hana:** Where is the best place to go to?

**Staff:** We have two great places. (②) Which do you prefer? (③)

**Hana's mom:** Hmm... (④) I prefer the London Eye.

**Hana:** Me, too.

**Staff:** Good choice. You can get there by bus.

**Hana's mom:** <u>가장 가까운 버스 정거장은 어디 있나요?</u>

**Staff:** (⑤) Go straight one block and turn right. It's on your left. Have a good trip!

**Hana:** Wow, I can see all of London. Look! There is a big clock.

**Hana's mom:** I think that's Big Ben. Why don't we go and visit it later?

**Hana:** That sounds great.

**09** 다음 영영풀이에 해당하는 단어를 대화에서 찾아 쓰시오.

> what you can see from a particular place or position, especially beautiful countryside

➡ _____

**10** 위 대화의 ①~⑤ 중 주어진 문장이 들어갈 알맞은 곳은?

> The London Eye is a Ferris wheel and the Sky Garden is a glass garden on top of a tall building.

①      ②      ③      ④      ⑤

**11** 밑줄 친 우리말을 주어진 단어를 이용하여 영작하시오. (5단어)

➡ _____ (stop, near)

**12** 주어진 문장 다음에 이어질 대화의 순서를 바르게 배열하시오.

> Let's go on a trip abroad.

> (A) I prefer Bangkok. The city is so colorful that we should go there.
> (B) Okay. Let's go there.
> (C) Which city do you prefer, Bangkok or Taiwan?

➡ _____

---

**Grammar**

**13** 다음 중 어법상 올바르지 <u>않은</u> 것은?

① The beautiful song was written by my friend.
② The plane stopped flying and turned into a restaurant.
③ Mary wasn't made to clean her room by her sister.
④ It rained so hard that we put off the picnic.
⑤ It was so noisy in the hall that I couldn't hear him speak.

**14** 다음 우리말을 주어진 어휘를 이용하여 영작했을 때 빈칸에 적절한 말을 쓰시오.

> • 그 문제들은 너무 어려워서 우리는 풀 수 없었다. (difficult, solve)
> = (1) The problems were _____
> _____ .
> = (2) The problems were _____
> _____ .

---

**15** 다음 빈칸에 알맞은 말이 바르게 짝지어진 것은?

> • The students were made _____ their homework by the teacher.
> • John started _____ early that he didn't need to hurry up.

① to do – so
② to do – very
③ did – too
④ doing – so
⑤ doing – very

**16** Which is grammatically correct?

① The room was too cold that David turned on the heater.
② This story was so funny which I laughed a lot.
③ Arnold got up so late that he didn't miss the train.
④ The movie was so sad that Rachel cried a lot.
⑤ John is kind so that everyone likes him.

**17** 다음 두 문장의 의미가 같도록 빈칸에 들어갈 알맞은 말을 쓰시오.

> Because the city's night view is so beautiful, we should see it.
> = The city's night view is _____
> we should see it.

**18** 다음 그림을 보고 괄호 안에 주어진 단어를 이용하여 빈칸을 채우시오.

(1) (*The Old Man and the Sea*, write)

→ *The Old Man and the Sea*

_____ Ernest Hemingway.

(2) (The pyramids, build)

→ The pyramids_____ the ancient Egyptians.

**19** 다음 중 밑줄 친 부분의 쓰임이 <u>어색한</u> 것은?

① The ball was <u>caught by</u> Jenny.

② Nha Trang is <u>well known for</u> its beautiful beaches.

③ I <u>was written</u> a long letter by my girl friend.

④ The animals in the cage were <u>looked after by</u> Aybek.

⑤ At first, I <u>was surprised at</u> the number of side dishes.

**20** 괄호 안에 주어진 단어를 이용하여 다음을 영작하시오.

(1) 전화는 누구에 의해 발명되었니? (the telephone, invent, 6 단어)

➡ _____

(2) 그 집의 지붕은 눈으로 덮여 있었다. (the house, the roof, cover, 9 단어)

➡ _____

(3) 너무 어두워서 아무 것도 보이지 않았다. (nothing, see, could, dark, that, 9 단어)

➡ _____

(4) 그 달리기 선수는 너무 빨리 달려서 아무도 그를 따라잡을 수 없었다. (the runner, that, nobody, catch, 12 단어)

➡ _____

**Reading**

[21~23] 다음 글을 읽고 물음에 답하시오.

My family traveled to Spain this summer. Spain is loved by lots of tourists. We visited many interesting places.

Our ⓐtrip started in Madrid. Madrid is the capital and is famous for soccer. We went to a stadium ⓑto watch a soccer match. My sister and I were excited because we could watch some of the world's most famous soccer players.     <I = Park Jinwoo>

**21** 위 글의 밑줄 친 ⓐtrip과 바꿔 쓸 수 있는 단어를 본문에서 찾아 알맞은 형태로 쓰시오. (2개)

➡ _____, _____

**22** 위 글의 밑줄 친 ⓑto watch와 to부정사의 용법이 다른 것을 **모두** 고르시오.

① There's no plan to build a new office.

② He cannot be a gentleman to do such a thing.

③ She lived long to see her son come back.

④ I have lots of homework to do today.

⑤ He promised me to do the dishes.

**23** 위 글의 내용과 일치하도록 다음 빈칸 (A)와 (B)에 알맞은 단어를 쓰시오.

> During their trip to Spain, Jinwoo's family went to (A)_____ _____ in Madrid and watched (B)_____ _____ _____.

---

**[24~25]** 다음 글을 읽고 물음에 답하시오.

The stadium was full of soccer fans. ⓐAs we watched the match, we cheered by singing songs, waving our hands, and shouting with the other fans.

After we toured Madrid, we went to Seville. While we walked around the city, we saw many historic buildings. We visited a flamenco museum and watched a flamenco dance. A woman in a red dress was dancing the flamenco with wonderful movements.

<we = Jinwoo's family>

**24** 위 글의 밑줄 친 ⓐAs와 같은 의미로 쓰인 것을 고르시오.

① As he is honest, everyone liked him.

② Leave the papers as they are.

③ He came up to me as I was speaking.

④ I respect him as a teacher.

⑤ As she grew older, she became more beautiful.

**25** 위 글의 내용과 일치하지 <u>않는</u> 것은?

① Jinwoo's family watched a soccer match in Madrid.

② Jinwoo's family walked around the soccer stadium.

③ Jinwoo's family saw many historic buildings.

④ Jinwoo's family watched a flamenco dance.

⑤ A woman wearing a red dress was dancing the flamenco.

---

**[26~27]** 다음 글을 읽고 물음에 답하시오.

For dinner, we ate paella. It is a traditional Spanish dish with rice, vegetables, meat, and seafood. It tasted like (A)[frying / fried] rice in Korea. It was so delicious that we all enjoyed it.

In Barcelona, we took a tour of Park Guell and Sagrada Familia. ⓐBoth (B)[was / were] designed by Antoni Gaudi. In Park Guell, we saw some of Gaudi's (C)[common / creative] works like a colorful lizard.

**26** 위 글의 괄호 (A)~(C)에서 문맥이나 어법상 알맞은 낱말을 골라 쓰시오.

➡ (A)_____ (B)_____ (C)_____

**27** 위 글의 밑줄 친 ⓐBoth가 가리키는 것을 본문에서 찾아 쓰시오.

➡ _____

**[01~02]** 다음 빈칸에 공통으로 들어갈 수 있는 단어를 쓰시오.

출제율 95%

**01**
- I'd like to _____ a walk with my dog.
- You can _____ a class or join a club together after school.
- They liked to _____ a tour of the castle.

출제율 90%

**02**
- The 'Mona Lisa' was painted _____ Leonardo Da Vinci.
- It took about 5 hours _____ bus.

출제율 95%

**03** 다음 우리말 해석에 맞게 빈칸을 완성하시오. (철자가 주어진 경우 그 철자로 시작할 것)

(1) All the people in the concert hall stood and _____ loudly. (콘서트홀에 있던 모든 사람이 일어나 크게 환호했다.)

(2) Would you like to _____ _____ this? (이걸 입어 보시겠습니까?)

(3) India is f_____ _____ curry. (인도는 카레로 유명하다.)

(4) Can I _____ there _____ _____? (거기까지 걸어서 갈 수 있나요?)

출제율 90%

**04** 다음 영영풀이에 해당하는 말을 주어진 철자로 시작하여 쓰고, 알맞은 것을 골라 문장을 완성하시오.

- f_____: a vigorous rhythmic dance style of the Andalusian Gypsies
- p_____: a mixture of blue and red color
- V_____: relating to the language, people or culture of Vietnam

(1) He enjoys dancing the _____.

(2) She learned _____ to get a job in Vietnam.

(3) She wore a dress of dark _____.

**[05~06]** 다음 대화를 읽고 물음에 답하시오.

B: It's really hot here in Thailand. (①)
G: Sounds good. (②) How do we get there? (③)
B: We can go on foot or by bus. (④) Which do you prefer? (⑤)
G: I prefer the bus.

출제율 100%

**05** 위 대화의 ①~⑤ 중 주어진 문장이 들어갈 알맞은 곳은?

Let's go to the night market and have some fresh fruit juice.

①　　　②　　　③　　　④　　　⑤

출제율 85%

**06** 위 대화를 읽고 대답할 수 없는 질문을 고르시오.

① How will they go to the night market?
② Which does the boy prefer, bus or taxi?
③ Where are they?
④ Where are they going to go?
⑤ What are they going to drink?

**[07~10]** 그림을 참고하여 다음 대화를 읽고 물음에 답하시오.

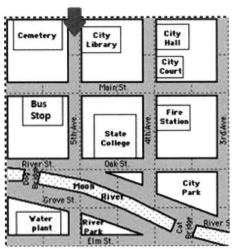

Staff: (A)_____ may I help you?

Hana's mom: We want to enjoy a good view of London. (①)

Hana: <u>가기에 가장 좋은 장소는 어디인가요?</u>

Staff: We have two great places. The London Eye is a Ferris wheel and the Sky Garden is a glass garden on top of a tall building. (B)_____ do you prefer?

Hana's mom: Hmm... (②) I prefer the London Eye.

Hana: Me, too. (③)

Staff: Good choice. You can get there by bus. (④)

Hana's mom: (C)_____ is the nearest stop?

Staff: (D)_____ Have a good trip!

Hana: Wow, I can see all of London. Look! There is a big clock.

Hana's mom: I think that's Big Ben. (⑤)

Hana: That sounds great.

**07** 위 대화의 ①~⑤ 중 주어진 문장이 들어갈 알맞은 곳은?

> Why don't we go and visit it later?

①      ②      ③      ④      ⑤

**08** 빈칸 (A)~(C)에 알맞은 의문사를 쓰시오.

➡ (A)_____ (B)_____ (C)_____

**09** 밑줄 친 우리말과 의미가 같도록 영작하시오. (8단어)

➡ _____

**10** 그림을 보고 빈칸 (D)에 들어갈 말을 주어진 단어를 이용해 두 문장으로 쓰시오.

➡ _____

(block, go, your, turn, it)

**11** 주어진 문장 다음에 이어질 대화의 순서를 바르게 배열하시오.

> Excuse me. Can you tell me how to get to the Africa Museum?

> (A) Go straight and turn right. And then?
> (B) It's on your left. It's across from the shoe store.
> (C) Sure. Go straight two blocks and turn right.
> (D) I got it. Thank you very much.

➡ _____

**12** 다음 중 태의 전환이 <u>잘못된</u> 것은?

① Those pictures were not painted by the artist.
→ The artist did not paint those pictures.

② Frank showed her the album.
→ The album was shown for her by Frank.

③ Edvard Munch painted *The Scream* in 1893.
→ *The Scream* was painted by Edvard Munch in 1893.

④ They saw Marianne dance on the stage.
→ Marianne was seen to dance on the stage by them.

⑤ Teresa took good care of the little babies.
→ Good care was taken of the little babies by Teresa.

**13** 다음 두 문장을 'so ~ that' 구문을 사용하여 한 문장으로 연결하시오.

(1) • The shoes look really great.
  • Sandra wants to buy them.
  ➡ _____

(2) • The stereo was very loud.
  • It was impossible to sleep.
  ➡ _____

**14** 다음 괄호 안의 어휘를 이용하여 빈칸에 알맞은 말을 쓰시오.

(1) The story was _____ I read it many times. (great)

(2) Many soldiers _____ in the war. (kill)

[15~17] 다음 글을 읽고 물음에 답하시오.

My family traveled to Spain this summer. Spain is loved by lots of tourists. We visited many interesting places.

Our trip started in Madrid. Madrid is the ⓐ capital and is famous for soccer. We went to a stadium to watch a soccer match. My sister and I were   (A)   because we could watch some of the world's most famous soccer players.

**15** 위 글의 빈칸 (A)에 들어갈 알맞은 말을 고르시오.

① interesting    ② disappointed
③ upset    ④ excited
⑤ amusing

**16** 위 글의 밑줄 친 ⓐcapital과 같은 의미로 쓰인 것을 고르시오.

① The cause of business failure is lack of capital.

② Paris is the fashion capital of the world.

③ He set up a business with a starting capital of £100,000.

④ I want to invest my capital in your business.

⑤ Please write in capital letters.

**17** What is Madrid well known for? Answer in English in a full sentence. (6 words)

➡ _____

**[18~20]** 다음 글을 읽고 물음에 답하시오.

The stadium was full of soccer fans. As we watched the match, we cheered by ⓐsinging songs, waving our hands, and shouting with the other fans.

ⓑAfter we toured of Madrid, we went to Seville. While we walked around the city, we saw many historic buildings. We visited a flamenco museum and watched a flamenco dance. A woman in a red dress was dancing the flamenco with wonderful movements.

<we = Jinwoo's family>

**18** 위 글의 밑줄 친 ⓐsinging과 문법적 쓰임이 <u>다른</u> 것을 모두 고르시오.

① My son is singing songs on the musical stage.
② She is good at singing songs.
③ Do you know the boy singing songs there?
④ My dream is singing songs on the musical stage.
⑤ They always enjoy singing songs together.

**19** 위 글의 밑줄 친 ⓑ에서 어법상 <u>틀린</u> 부분을 찾아 고치시오.

➡ _____

**20** 위 글을 읽고 대답할 수 <u>없는</u> 질문은?

① Where did Jinwoo's family cheer?
② What did Jinwoo's family do when they cheered?
③ What did Jinwoo's family see while they walked around Seville?
④ How long did Jinwoo's family watch a flamenco dance?
⑤ What was the flamenco dancer wearing?

**[21~24]** 다음 글을 읽고 물음에 답하시오.

____ⓐ____ dinner, we ate paella. It is a traditional Spanish dish ____ⓑ____ rice, vegetables, meat, and seafood. It tasted like fried rice in Korea. It was so delicious that we all enjoyed it.

In Barcelona, we took a tour of Park Guell and Sagrada Familia. Both were designed by Antoni Gaudi. In Park Guell, we saw some of Gaudi's ____ⓒ____ works like a colorful lizard.

**21** 위 글의 빈칸 ⓐ와 ⓑ에 들어갈 전치사가 바르게 짝지어진 것은?

① To – with
② For – by
③ In – from
④ To – by
⑤ For – with

**22** 다음 중 paella의 재료가 <u>아닌</u> 것을 고르시오.

① 쌀
② 채소
③ 고기
④ 국수
⑤ 해산물

**23** 위 글의 빈칸 ⓒ에 create를 알맞은 형태로 쓰시오.

➡ _____

**24** By whom were Park Guell and Sagrada Familia designed? Answer in English.

➡ _____

**01** 밑줄 친 부분에서 어법상 어색한 부분을 찾아 고치시오.

> M: Welcome to London City Tour. Today, we'll visit famous places in London. Can you see the London Eye? It's on your right. It's a Ferris wheel near the River Thames. The view from the London Eye are amazing. Many people visit it every year.

➡ _____

_____

**02** 그림을 보고 (A)와 (B)에 공통으로 들어갈 문장을 쓰시오. (목적지는 표시된 ③) (총 7 단어)

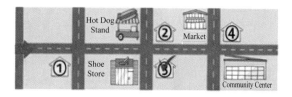

> B: Excuse me. Can you tell me how to get to the Africa Museum?
> G: Sure. (A)_____
> B: (B)_____ And then?
> G: It's on your left. It's across from the shoe store.
> B: I got it. Thank you very much.

➡ _____

**03** 주어진 문장 다음에 이어질 대화의 순서를 바르게 배열하시오.

> Jisu, why don't we watch the movie *Best Friends* on Saturday?

> (A) Sounds good. What time does it begin?
> (B) I prefer the seven showing.

> (C) On Saturday there are two showings, one at five and the other at seven. Which do you prefer?
> (D) Okay. Then let's meet at six.

➡ _____

**04** 그림을 참고하여 어떤 것을 더 선호하는지 묻는 질문을 완성하시오.

**Roller Coaster** | **Scary House**

> A: _____
> _____
> B: I prefer the Scary House.

**05** 주어진 문장이 같은 뜻이 되도록 빈칸에 알맞은 말을 쓰시오.

(1) Because the city is so colorful, we should go there.
= The city is _____ we should go there.

(2) Emily was very tired. So, she couldn't do the dishes.
= Emily was _____ she couldn't do the dishes.
= Emily was _____ do the dishes.

**06** 다음 주어진 문장을 능동태는 수동태로, 수동태는 능동태로 바꾸시오.

(1) Hong Kong is loved by many people who want to do fun activities.

➡ _____

_____

(2) What did she promise to do last weekend?

➡ _____

(3) Ms. Grace taught us physics last year.

➡ _____

_____

**[07~09]** 다음 글을 읽고 물음에 답하시오.

ⓐThe stadium was full of soccer fans. As we watched the match, we cheered by singing songs, waving our hands, and shouting with the other fans.

After we toured Madrid, we went to Seville. While we walked around the city, we saw many historic buildings. We visited a flamenco museum and watched a flamenco dance. ⓑ빨간 드레스를 입은 여자가 멋진 동작으로 플라멩코를 추고 있었다.

&lt;we = Jinwoo's family&gt;

**07** 위 글의 밑줄 친 ⓐ를 다음과 같이 바꿔 쓸 때 빈칸에 들어갈 알맞은 말을 쓰시오.

➡ The stadium _____ _____ _____ soccer fans.

**08** 위 글의 밑줄 친 ⓑ의 우리말에 맞게 한 단어를 보충하여, 주어진 어휘를 알맞게 배열하시오.

movements / the flamenco / was / wonderful / dancing / a red dress / with / a woman

➡ _____

_____

**09** 본문의 내용과 일치하도록 다음 빈칸 (A)와 (B)에 알맞은 단어를 쓰시오.

Jinwoo's family went to (A)_____ after they toured Madrid and they saw (B) _____ _____ _____ while they walked around the city.

**[10~12]** 다음 글을 읽고 물음에 답하시오.

For dinner, we ate paella. It is a traditional Spanish dish with rice, vegetables, meat, and seafood. It tasted ⓐ fried rice in Korea. It was so delicious that we all enjoyed it.

In Barcelona, we took a tour of Park Guell and Sagrada Familia. ⓑBoth were designed by Antoni Gaudi. In Park Guell, we saw some of Gaudi's creative works ⓒ a colorful lizard.

**10** 위 글의 빈칸 ⓐ와 ⓒ에 공통으로 들어갈 알맞은 말을 쓰시오.

➡ _____

**11** 다음 빈칸 (A)~(D)에 알맞은 단어를 넣어 paella에 대한 소개를 완성하시오.

Paella which is a traditional (A)_____ dish tastes like fried rice in (B)_____ and its ingredients are (C)_____, _____, _____ and (D)_____.

**12** 위 글의 밑줄 친 ⓑ를 능동태로 고치시오.

➡ _____

# 창의사고력 서술형 문제

**01** 주어진 정보와 그림을 이용해 빈칸에 알맞은 말을 쓰시오..

```
BANK  POLICE STATION  STORE
          Main Street
LIBRARY  POST OFFICE  DRUGSTORE  MOVIE THEATER  HOSPITAL
         SCHOOL  RESTAURANT
          Central Avenue
First Street          Second Street
         TRAIN STATION          CHURCH
```

<조건>
1. A는 은행을 가고 싶어 한다.
2. 'next'나 'across' 둘 중에서 하나의 단어가 반드시 들어가야 한다.
3. 'know'를 이용해 길을 물어보는 문장을 만든다.

A: Excuse me. _____
B: Of course. _____ It's on your left.
_____ / _____

**02** 주어진 정보를 이용해 호주를 소개하는 글을 쓰시오.

country: Australia
capital: Canberra
language: English
dish: meat pie, lamington
place • Sydney has the Sydney Opera House.
      • Melbourne has beautiful ocean roads.

**How much do you know about Australia?**
The (A)_____ of Australia is Canberra. (B)_____ is spoken there. (C)_____ are popular dishes in Australia. Every year lots of tourists visit Sydney and Melbourne. Sydney has (D)_____ and Melbourne is well known for its (E)_____. Australia is so wonderful that you should visit it someday.

**03** 〈보기〉에 주어진 어휘와 so와 that을 이용하여 3 문장 이상 쓰시오.

보기

| practice dancing hard | thief | cartoon/interesting |
|---|---|---|
| become a B-boy dancer | run away/find | keep reading |

(1) _____
(2) _____
(3) _____

## 단원별 모의고사

**01** 다음 〈보기〉에 짝지어진 두 단어의 관계와 같도록 빈칸에 알맞은 단어를 쓰시오.

┌─ 보기 ─────────────────┐
│         nation – national        │
└──────────────────────┘

(1) use – _____
(2) hope – _____
(3) color – _____

**02** 〈보기〉의 주어진 단어를 이용해 빈칸을 채우시오.

┌─ 보기 ─────────────────┐
│   at   from   in   on   of   to   │
└──────────────────────┘

(1) The department store was full _____ customers.
(2) It's not very far _____ your home.
(3) The lamp is _____ top _____ the television.
(4) Turn _____ that fan.

**03** 다음 우리말 해석에 맞게 빈칸을 완성하시오. (철자가 주어진 경우 그 철자로 시작할 것)

(1) May I _____ _____ this shirt? (제가 이 셔츠를 입어 봐도 될까요?)
(2) The spring sale will g_____ _____ for a week. (봄 세일은 일주일 동안 계속될 것이다.)
(3) The museum is _____ _____ the park. (박물관은 공원 맞은편에 있습니다.)
(4) Melbourne _____ _____ _____ _____ its beautiful ocean roads. (멜버른은 아름다운 해안 도로로 잘 알려져 있다.)

**04** 다음 〈보기〉의 단어를 사용하여 자연스러운 문장을 만들 수 없는 것은?

┌─ 보기 ─────────────────────┐
│ hamburger   match   movement   tour │
└──────────────────────────┘

① They are playing an important _____.
② The animal moved with quick _____s.
③ I can speak three _____s, English, Japanese and Korean.
④ On today's _____, we will see many rare animals.
⑤ They had _____s for lunch yesterday.

**05** 그림을 보고 대화의 빈칸을 완성하시오.

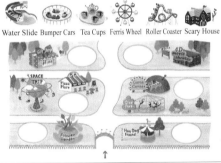

Water Slide  Bumper Cars  Tea Cups  Ferris Wheel  Roller Coaster  Scary House

(1)
A: _____ is the Roller Coaster?
B: Go straight two blocks and turn _____. It's on _____ _____. _____ _____ _____ the 4D Movie Theater.

(2)
A: _____ _____ the Water Slide?
B: Go straight _____ _____ and _____. It's _____. It's _____ from _____ _____.

[06~08] 다음 대화를 읽고 물음에 답하시오.

A: Let's go on a trip abroad.
B: (A)(do, Bangkok, city, prefer, which, or, Taiwan, you?)
A: I prefer Bangkok. The city is (B)[such / so] colorful (C)[what / that] we should go there.
B: Okay. Let's go there.

**06** 다음 영영풀이에 해당하는 단어를 대화에서 찾아 쓰시오.

in or to a foreign country

➡ _____

**07** 괄호 (A) 안의 단어를 배열하여 알맞은 문장을 만드시오.

➡ _____

**08** 괄호 (B)와 (C)에서 알맞은 단어를 골라 쓰시오.

➡ (B)_____, (C)_____

[09~10] 다음 대화를 읽고 물음에 답하시오.

B: Jisu, why don't we (A)[watch / watching] the movie *Best Friends* on Saturday?
G: Sounds good. (B)[What time / Where] does it begin?
B: On Saturday there (C)[is / are] two showings, ⓐ_____ at five and ⓑ_____ at seven. Which do you prefer?
G: I prefer the seven showing.
B: Okay. Then let's meet at six.
G: Sounds good.

**09** (A)~(C)에 알맞은 단어를 골라 쓰시오.

➡ (A)_____ (B)_____ (C)_____

**10** 빈칸 ⓐ와 ⓑ에 들어갈 말로 적절한 것끼리 짝지어진 것을 고르시오.

| | ⓐ | ⓑ |
|---|---|---|
| ① | one | another |
| ② | one | the other |
| ③ | one | other |
| ④ | another | the other |
| ⑤ | another | some |

[11~13] 다음 대화를 읽고 물음에 답하시오.

G: What is this long dress (A)_____(call)?
M: It is an Ao dai, a type of traditional clothing from Vietnam.
G: Can I try one (B)_____?
M: Sure. (C)너는 보라색과 노란색 중 어느 것을 선호하니?
G: The purple one, please.

**11** 빈칸 (A)에 주어진 단어를 어법에 맞게 쓰시오.

➡ _____

**12** 빈칸 (B)에 알맞은 전치사를 쓰시오.

➡ _____

**13** 밑줄 친 (C)의 우리말을 주어진 단어를 이용해 영작하시오.

➡ _____
_____ (one, prefer, which)

**14** 같은 의미가 되도록 빈칸에 알맞은 말을 쓰시오.

(1) I heard Jenny lock the door.

= Jenny _____ .

(2) Because Australia is very wonderful, you should visit it someday.

= Australia is _____ you should visit it someday.

**15** 다음 중 어법상 <u>어색한</u> 것을 고르시오.

① The cake was so delicious that we all enjoyed it.

② This chair was made to Diana by my grandpa.

③ Vietnamese is spoken there.

④ The room was cleaned by Jenny.

⑤ Alex studied so hard that he could enter the university.

**16** 다음 두 문장을 한 문장으로 바르게 연결한 것은?

• Benjamin became very angry.
• His blood was boiling.

① Benjamin became very angry that his blood was boiling.

② Benjamin became angry enough to boil his blood.

③ Benjamin became too angry to boil his blood.

④ Benjamin became angry so that his blood was boiling.

⑤ Benjamin became so angry that his blood was boiling.

**17** 우리말과 일치하도록 괄호 안의 어구를 바르게 배열하시오.

(1) Sharon은 성공하기 위해 열심히 일했다. (Sharon, she, so, succeed, worked, might, hard, that)

➡ _____

(2) 상자가 너무 무거워서 아무도 움직일 수 없었다. (one, the box, it, that, no, heavy, could, was, move, so)

➡ _____

(3) 그 기계는 Kim 선생님에 의해 수리될 것이다. (Mr. Kim, the machine, repaired, will, be, by)

➡ _____

**18** 다음 밑줄 친 부분 중 생략할 수 있는 것은?

① Jessica is loved <u>by everybody</u>.

② I was moved <u>by a book</u>.

③ English is spoken there <u>by them</u>.

④ The apples were eaten <u>by Jenny</u>.

⑤ The room was cleaned <u>by the students</u>.

**[19~20]** 다음 글을 읽고 물음에 답하시오.

My family traveled to Spain (A)[this summer / in this summer]. Spain is loved by lots of tourists. We visited many (B)[interesting / interested] places.

Our trip started in Madrid. Madrid is the capital and is famous for soccer. We went to a stadium to watch a soccer match. My sister and I were (C)[exciting / excited] because we could watch some of the world's most famous soccer players. <I = Park Jinwoo>

**19** 위 글의 괄호 (A)~(C)에서 어법상 알맞은 낱말을 골라 쓰시오.

➡ (A) _____ (B) _____ (C) _____

## 20 위 글을 읽고 대답할 수 없는 질문은?

① When did Jinwoo's family travel to Spain?

② Why did Jinwoo's family trip start in Madrid?

③ What is the capital of Spain?

④ Why did Jinwoo's family go to a stadium?

⑤ How did Jinwoo and his sister feel in the stadium?

**[21~22] 다음 글을 읽고 물음에 답하시오.**

The stadium was full of soccer fans. (①) As we watched the match, we cheered by singing songs, waving our hands, and shouting ⓐ___ the other fans. (②)

After we toured Madrid, we went to Seville. (③) We visited a flamenco museum and watched a flamenco dance. (④) A woman ⓑ___ a red dress was dancing the flamenco ⓐ___ wonderful movements. (⑤)

\<we = Jinwoo's family\>

## 21 위 글의 흐름으로 보아, 주어진 문장이 들어가기에 가장 적절한 곳은?

While we walked around the city, we saw many historic buildings.

①     ②     ③     ④     ⑤

## 22 위 글의 빈칸 ⓐ와 ⓑ에 들어갈 전치사가 바르게 짝지어진 것은?

① with – from     ② for – in

③ in – to     ④ for – to

⑤ with – in

**[23~25] 다음 글을 읽고 물음에 답하시오.**

For dinner, we ate paella. It is a ⓐtradition Spanish dish with rice, vegetables, meat, and seafood. ⓑIt tasted fried rice in Korea. It was so delicious that we all enjoyed it.

In Barcelona, we took a tour of Park Guell and Sagrada Familia. Both were designed by Antoni Gaudi. In Park Guell, we saw some of Gaudi's creative works like a colorful lizard.

\<we = Jinwoo's family\>

## 23 위 글의 밑줄 친 ⓐ를 알맞은 어형으로 고치시오.

➡ _____

## 24 위 글의 밑줄 친 ⓑ에서 어법상 틀린 부분을 고치시오.

➡ _____

## 25 위 글의 내용과 일치하지 않는 것은?

① 진우의 가족은 저녁 식사로 파에야를 먹었다.

② 파에야는 전통적인 스페인 요리이다.

③ 진우의 가족은 바르셀로나에서 구엘 공원과 사그라다 파밀리아를 둘러보았다.

④ Antoni Gaudi는 구엘 공원과 사그라다 파밀리아의 건설 자금을 지원했다.

⑤ 구엘 공원에서 Gaudi의 창의적인 작품들을 볼 수 있다.

# INSIGHT
## on the textbook

교과서 파헤치기

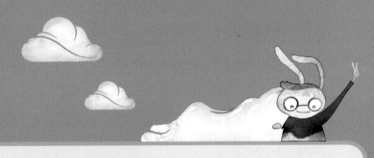

※ 다음 영어를 우리말로 쓰시오.

| | | | |
|---|---|---|---|
| 01 position | | 22 download | |
| 02 pull | | 23 backward | |
| 03 stretch | | 24 put | |
| 04 difficult | | 25 show | |
| 05 nature | | 26 waist | |
| 06 advice | | 27 comfortable | |
| 07 push | | 28 bend | |
| 08 exercise | | 29 lower | |
| 09 understand | | 30 habit | |
| 10 place | | 31 fresh | |
| 11 count | | 32 usually | |
| 12 second | | 33 simple | |
| 13 shoulder | | 34 warm | |
| 14 activity | | 35 each other | |
| 15 however | | 36 team up with | |
| 16 life | | 37 block out | |
| 17 pour | | 38 get over | |
| 18 switch | | 39 from top to bottom | |
| 19 back | | 40 focus on | |
| 20 massage | | 41 loosen up | |
| 21 neck | | 42 straighten up | |
| | | 43 be good for | |

※ 다음 우리말을 영어로 쓰시오.

01 벌써, 이미 _____

02 ~ 뒤에 _____

03 편안한 _____

04 부드럽게 _____

05 걸음 _____

06 길 _____

07 움직이다 _____

08 넘어지다 _____

09 ~을 향하다; 얼굴 _____

10 낚시 _____

11 습관 _____

12 따뜻한 _____

13 둘 다 _____

14 유지하다 _____

15 구부리다 _____

16 운동하다 _____

17 자연 _____

18 어려운 _____

19 활동 _____

20 (근육 등의) 긴장이 풀리다 _____

21 건강한, 건강에 좋은 _____

22 ~을 낮추다 _____

23 간단한, 단순한 _____

24 신선한 _____

25 스트레스를 받다[주다] _____

26 빛 _____

27 ~와 같은, ~처럼 _____

28 줄이다 _____

29 보통, 대개 _____

30 그릇 _____

31 스트레칭하다 _____

32 뒤로 _____

33 목 _____

34 자세 _____

35 준비 운동을 하다 _____

36 위에서 아래까지 _____

37 ~에 집중하다 _____

38 몇 초 동안 _____

39 ~에 대해 걱정하다 _____

40 ~을 준비하다 _____

41 (빛을) 가리다[차단하다] _____

42 똑바로 하다 _____

43 회복[극복]하다 _____

※ 다음 영영풀이에 알맞은 단어를 <보기>에서 골라 쓴 후, 우리말 뜻을 쓰시오.

1 _____ : to say numbers in order: _____

2 _____ : not hard to understand or do: _____

3 _____ : making you feel physically relaxed: _____

4 _____ : to make something smaller in size, amount, number, etc.: _____

5 _____ : an opinion or suggestion about what someone should do: _____

6 _____ : either of the two parts of the body between the top of each arm and the neck : _____

7 _____ : to change or replace something with another thing: _____

8 _____ : the part of the body between the head and the shoulders: _____

9 _____ : to move your body so that it is not straight: _____

10 _____ : the way someone stands, sits, or lies down: _____

11 _____ : to become or to cause something to become less tense, tight, or stiff: _____

12 _____ : something that a person does often in a regular and repeated way: _____

13 _____ : to put your arms, legs, etc., in positions that make the muscles long and tight: _____

14 _____ : to do gentle physical exercises to prepare your body for a sport or other activity: _____

15 _____ : to hold something firmly and use force in order to move it or try to move it toward yourself: _____

16 _____ : the action of rubbing and pressing a person's body with the hands to reduce pain in the muscles and joints: _____

| 보기 | | | |
|---|---|---|---|
| stretch | bend | count | habit |
| advice | position | switch | massage |
| relax | reduce | neck | comfortable |
| warm up | shoulder | pull | simple |

※ 다음 우리말과 일치하도록 빈칸에 알맞은 말을 쓰시오.

### Listen & Speak 1-A-1

B: I want to eat _____ _____ . Do you _____ any _____ ?

G: I _____ _____ fresh salad. It _____ me _____ _____ .

B: Really? Do you know _____ _____ _____ it?

G: Yes, it's quite _____ . First, _____ many vegetables _____ small pieces. Next, _____ them _____ a bowl. Then, _____ some lemon juice on them. Finally, _____ everything together.

B: That's it? I _____ _____ it.

### Listen & Speak 1-A-2

B: People say that we should walk _____ _____ 10,000 _____ every day _____ _____ _____ . I can't _____ the number of my _____ _____ .

G: You _____ _____ this smartphone app. Do you know _____ _____ _____ it?

B: No. _____ you _____ _____ _____ ?

G: Sure. First, _____ the app. Then, walk _____ your smartphone. Later, you can _____ the number of _____ _____ _____ .

B: Thank you. I _____ _____ _____ it today.

### Listen & Speak 2-A-1

G: _____ do you _____ _____ after school?

B: I _____ _____ _____ _____ _____ .

G: _____ cool. What _____ you _____ ?

B: I _____ _____ salad, Bibimbap, and vegetable juice.

### Listen & Speak 2-A-2

B: What do you do _____ _____ ?

G: I _____ _____ .

B: _____ _____ of pictures do you _____ _____ ?

G: I _____ pictures _____ nature, _____ trees and flowers. The beautiful pictures _____ _____ _____ .

해석

B: 나는 건강에 좋은 것을 먹고 싶어. 말해 줄 조언이 있니?

G: 나는 신선한 샐러드를 자주 먹어. 그것은 나를 기분 좋게 만들어.

B: 정말? 그것을 어떻게 만드는지 아니?

G: 응, 아주 간단해. 먼저, 많은 채소들을 작은 조각으로 잘라. 다음으로 그것들을 그릇에 담아. 그런 다음, 레몬 주스를 조금 부어. 마지막으로 모든 것을 함께 섞어.

B: 그게 다야? 한번 해 봐야겠다.

B: 사람들은 우리가 건강해지기 위해서 매일 10,000 걸음 이상을 걸어야 한다고 말해. 나는 내 걸음 수를 쉽게 셀 수 없어.

G: 너는 이 스마트폰 앱을 사용할 수 있어. 어떻게 사용하는지 아니?

B: 아니. 내게 보여줄 수 있니?

G: 물론. 먼저 앱을 다운로드해. 그런 다음 스마트폰을 가지고 걸어. 나중에 네가 걸은 걸음 수를 확인할 수 있어.

B: 고마워. 오늘부터 그것을 쓰기 시작해야겠어.

G: 너는 방과 후에 뭐 하는 걸 즐기니?

B: 나는 건강에 좋은 음식을 요리하는 것을 즐겨.

G: 멋지구나. 너는 무엇을 만들 수 있니?

B: 나는 샐러드, 비빔밥 그리고 야채 주스를 만들 수 있어.

B: 너는 주말에 무엇을 하니?

G: 나는 사진을 찍어.

B: 너는 보통 어떤 종류의 사진을 찍니?

G: 나는 나무와 꽃 같은 자연의 사진을 찍는 것을 좋아해. 그 아름다운 사진들은 내 스트레스를 줄여주거든.

### Listen & Speak 2-A-3

G: Do you _____ _____ _____ ?

B: Yes. _____ name is Coco. I _____ _____ her.

G: _____ do you do _____ _____ ?

B: I _____ _____ a walk with her. It _____ me _____ .

### Conversation A

B: Tomorrow, I _____ an English _____ contest. I started _____ _____ the contest two weeks _____ . I enjoy _____ _____ English, but I _____ _____ _____ the contest. I _____ _____ well.

### Conversation B

Karl: Hana, _____ the _____ ?

Hana: Well, I'm _____ _____ the test _____ _____ .

Karl: I understand. I _____ my longboard _____ I'm stressed. Do you _____ _____ _____ _____ a longboard?

Hana: _____ , I _____ .

Karl: Let's _____ _____ ! I _____ teach you. _____ one foot _____ the board and _____ hard _____ the other.

Hana: _____ this? Wow! This is fun. I _____ _____ already.

Karl: See? I _____ _____ my longboard _____ it _____ my stress.

Hana: That's _____ !

### Wrap Up 1

B: You _____ _____ . _____ the matter?

G: Well, I _____ _____ _____ .

B: Did you _____ _____ _____ ?

G: Not _____ . Do you know how to _____ _____ a cold?

B: Well, I usually drink _____ water _____ I have a cold. It _____ _____ _____ _____ .

G: _____ good. I _____ _____ _____ it.

### Wrap Up 2

B: My family _____ many activities. My dad enjoys _____ . _____ in the morning, he goes to the lake and _____ _____ with some fish. My mom _____ _____ pictures. She likes _____ _____ beautiful mountains and lakes. My brother and I _____ _____ soccer.

G: 너는 강아지를 기르고 있니?

B: 응. 그녀의 이름은 코코야. 난 코코를 아주 좋아해.

G: 너는 코코와 함께 무엇을 하니?

B: 난 코코와 산책하는 걸 즐겨. 그것은 나를 건강하게 만들어.

B: 내일 영어 말하기 대회가 있어. 나는 2주 전에 대회를 준비하기 시작했어. 나는 영어로 말하는 것을 즐기지만, 난 그 대회가 걱정돼. 나는 잠을 잘 못 자.

Karl: 하나야, 무슨 일 있니?

하나: 음. 다음 주에 있을 시험 때문에 스트레스를 받아.

Karl: 난 이해돼. 나는 스트레스를 받을 때 롱보드를 타. 넌 롱보드를 어떻게 타는지 아니?

하나: 아니, 몰라.

Karl: 나가자! 내가 가르쳐 줄 수 있어. 한 발을 보드 위에 올려놓고 다른 한 발로 세게 밀어.

하나: 이렇게? 와! 이거 재밌다. 벌써 기분이 좋아졌어.

Karl: 봤지? 나는 롱보드를 타는 것이 나의 스트레스를 줄여주기 때문에 즐겨.

하나: 정말 멋진데!

B: 너 아파 보여. 무슨 일 있니?

G: 음, 감기에 걸렸어.

B: 병원에 가봤니?

G: 아직. 넌 감기가 나아지는 방법을 아니?

B: 음, 나는 감기에 걸렸을 때 보통 따뜻한 물을 마셔. 그것은 내 기분을 좋아지게 해.

G: 좋아. 한번 해 볼게.

B: 우리 가족은 많은 활동을 즐겨. 우리 아빠는 낚시를 즐기셔. 이른 아침, 그는 호수에 가서서 약간의 물고기를 가지고 돌아오셔. 우리 엄마는 그림 그리기를 즐기셔. 그녀는 아름다운 산과 호수를 그리는 것을 좋아하셔. 나의 형과 나는 축구를 즐겨.

※ 다음 우리말에 맞도록 대화를 영어로 쓰시오.

 해석

### Listen & Speak 1-A-1

B: _____

G: _____

B: _____

G: _____

_____

_____

B: _____

B: 나는 건강에 좋은 것을 먹고 싶어. 말해 줄 조언이 있니?
G: 나는 신선한 샐러드를 자주 먹어. 그것은 나를 기분 좋게 만들어.
B: 정말? 그것을 어떻게 만드는지 아니?
G: 응. 아주 간단해. 먼저, 많은 채소들을 작은 조각으로 잘라. 다음으로 그것들을 그릇에 담아. 그런 다음, 레몬 주스를 조금 부어. 마지막으로 모든 것을 함께 섞어.
B: 그게 다야? 한번 해 봐야겠다.

### Listen & Speak 1-A-2

B: _____

_____

G: _____

B: _____

G: _____

_____

B: _____

B: 사람들은 우리가 건강해지기 위해서 매일 10,000 걸음 이상을 걸어야 한다고 말해. 나는 내 걸음 수를 쉽게 셀 수 없어.
G: 너는 이 스마트폰 앱을 사용할 수 있어. 어떻게 사용하는지 아니?
B: 아니. 내게 보여줄 수 있니?
G: 물론. 먼저 앱을 다운로드해. 그런 다음 스마트폰을 가지고 걸어. 나중에 네가 걸은 걸음 수를 확인할 수 있어.
B: 고마워. 오늘부터 그것을 쓰기 시작해야겠어.

### Listen & Speak 2-A-1

G: _____

B: _____

G: _____

B: _____

G: 너는 방과 후에 뭐 하는 걸 즐기니?
B: 나는 건강에 좋은 음식을 요리하는 것을 즐겨.
G: 멋지구나. 너는 무엇을 만들 수 있니?
B: 나는 샐러드, 비빔밥 그리고 야채 주스를 만들 수 있어.

### Listen & Speak 2-A-2

B: _____

G: _____

B: _____

G: _____

_____

B: 너는 주말에 무엇을 하니?
G: 나는 사진을 찍어.
B: 너는 보통 어떤 종류의 사진을 찍니?
G: 나는 나무와 꽃 같은 자연의 사진을 찍는 것을 좋아해. 그 아름다운 사진들은 내 스트레스를 줄여주거든.

## Listen & Speak 2-A-3

G: _____

B: _____

G: _____

B: _____

## Conversation A

B: _____

_____

_____

## Conversation B

Karl: _____

Hana: _____

Karl: _____

_____

Hana: _____

Karl: _____

_____

Hana: _____

Karl: _____

Hana: _____

## Wrap Up 1

B: _____

G: _____

B: _____

G: _____

B: _____

G: _____

## Wrap Up 2

B: _____

_____

_____

G: 너는 강아지를 기르고 있니?
B: 응. 그녀의 이름은 코코야. 난 코코를 아주 좋아해.
G: 너는 코코와 함께 무엇을 하니?
B: 난 코코와 산책하는 걸 즐겨. 그것은 나를 건강하게 만들어.

B: 내일 영어 말하기 대회가 있어. 나는 2주 전에 대회를 준비하기 시작했어. 나는 영어로 말하는 것을 즐기지만, 난 그 대회가 걱정돼. 나는 잠을 잘 못 자.

Karl: 하나야, 무슨 일 있니?
하나: 음, 다음 주에 있을 시험 때문에 스트레스를 받아.
Karl: 난 이해돼. 나는 스트레스를 받을 때 롱보드를 타. 넌 롱보드를 어떻게 타는지 아니?
하나: 아니, 몰라.
Karl: 나가자! 내가 가르쳐 줄 수 있어. 한 발을 보드 위에 올려놓고 다른 한 발로 세게 밀어.
하나: 이렇게? 와! 이거 재밌다. 벌써 기분이 좋아졌어.
Karl: 봤지? 나는 롱보드를 타는 것이 나의 스트레스를 줄여주기 때문에 즐겨.
하나: 정말 멋진데!

B: 너 아파 보여. 무슨 일 있니?
G: 음, 감기에 걸렸어.
B: 병원에 가봤니?
G: 아직. 넌 감기가 나아지는 방법을 아니?
B: 음, 나는 감기에 걸렸을 때 보통 따뜻한 물을 마셔. 그것은 내 기분을 좋아지게 해.
G: 좋아. 한번 해 볼게.

B: 우리 가족은 많은 활동을 즐겨. 우리 아빠는 낚시를 즐기셔. 이른 아침, 그는 호수에 가셔서 약간의 물고기를 가지고 돌아오셔. 우리 엄마는 그림 그리기를 즐기셔. 그녀는 아름다운 산과 호수를 그리는 것을 좋아하셔. 나의 형과 나는 축구를 즐겨.

※ 다음 우리말과 일치하도록 빈칸에 알맞은 것을 골라 쓰시오.

**1** _____ school you sit _____ many _____ .
A. hours        B. for        C. at

**2** _____ you _____ _____ ?
A. tired        B. get        C. do

**3** Why _____ you massage _____ and _____ ?
A. stretch        B. yourself        C. don't

**4** _____ begin _____ the eyes.
A. with        B. let's

**5** _____ your eyes and _____ them _____ with your fingers.
A. softly        B. massage        C. close

**6** It _____ _____ your eyes.
A. relax        B. will

**7** _____ you finish, _____ your eyes with your hands to _____ _____ the light.
A. out        B. cover        C. block        D. when

**8** It will _____ your eyes _____ more _____ .
A. comfortable        B. feel        C. make

**9** Next, _____ your _____ .
A. neck        B. massage

**10** _____ your fingers _____ the _____ of your neck.
A. back        B. on        C. put

**11** Draw small _____ with your _____ to _____ your neck.
A. massage        B. fingers        C. circles

**12** Massage from _____ to _____ .
A. bottom        B. top

**13** The massage will _____ you _____ _____ .
A. better        B. feel        C. help

**14** _____ work _____ your _____ .
A. waist        B. on        C. let's

**15** _____ _____ with a friend.
A. up        B. team

1 학교에서 너는 오랜 시간에 걸쳐 앉아 있다.

2 여러분은 피곤한가?

3 마사지와 스트레칭을 하는 게 어떤가?

4 눈부터 시작하자.

5 눈을 감고 손가락으로 눈을 부드럽게 마사지해라.

6 그것은 여러분의 눈을 편안하게 해줄 것이다.

7 끝나면, 빛을 차단하기 위해 손으로 눈을 가려라.

8 그것은 여러분의 눈을 더 편안하게 해줄 것이다.

9 다음으로, 여러분의 목을 마사지해라.

10 여러분의 목 뒤에 손가락을 대라.

11 여러분의 목을 마사지하기 위해 손가락으로 작은 원을 그려라.

12 위에서 아래로 마사지해라.

13 마사지는 여러분의 기분이 좋아지도록 도울 것이다.

14 허리 운동을 하자.

15 친구와 짝을 이루어라.

**16** Stand _____ to each _____ and _____ your partner.
    A. face             B. other           C. close

**17** _____ each _____ wrists.
    A. other's           B. hold

**18** Slowly _____ your head and _____ _____.
    A. backward        B. body          C. stretch

**19** _____ that position _____ three _____.
    A. seconds         B. for           C. hold

**20** Then, slowly _____ each other _____ a standing position.
    A. to             B. pull

**21** You and your partner _____ _____ at the same _____.
    A. speed          B. move         C. should

**22** _____ you don't, _____ of you will _____!
    A. fall             B. both          C. if

**23** _____ the _____ of your right foot _____ the desk _____ you.
    A. behind        B. top         C. on         D. place

**24** Then, slowly _____ your left leg and _____ _____.
    A. yourself       B. lower        C. bend

**25** _____ it for a _____ seconds and slowly _____ _____.
    A. up             B. few         C. straighten    D. hold

**26** This _____ will _____ _____ your right leg.
    A. up             B. loosen       C. position

**27** _____ your legs and _____ the _____.
    A. exercise       B. repeat       C. switch

**28** _____ do you _____ now?
    A. feel             B. how

**29** If you _____ yourself and _____ every day, you will _____ _____.
    A. healthier      B. stretch      C. massage      D. feel

**30** Also, you can _____ _____ your _____ better.
    A. studies       B. on         C. focus

**16** 서로 가까이 서서 여러분의 파트너를 마주 보아라.

**17** 서로의 손목을 잡아라.

**18** 천천히 여러분의 머리와 몸을 뒤로 뻗어라.

**19** 3초 동안 그 자세를 유지해라.

**20** 그리고 나서, 천천히 서로 선 자세로 끌어 당겨라.

**21** 너와 너의 파트너는 같은 속도로 움직여야 한다.

**22** 그렇지 않으면, 너희 둘 다 넘어질 것이다!

**23** 여러분의 뒤에 있는 책상 위에 오른쪽 발등을 올려놓아라.

**24** 그리고 나서, 천천히 왼쪽 다리를 구부리고 몸을 낮추어라.

**25** 몇 초 동안 그 자세를 유지하다가 천천히 몸을 펴라.

**26** 이 자세는 여러분의 오른쪽 다리를 풀어 줄 것이다.

**27** 다리를 바꿔서 운동을 반복해라.

**28** 지금 기분이 어떤가?

**29** 매일 마사지와 스트레칭을 하면, 여러분은 더 건강해지는 것을 느낄 것이다.

**30** 또한, 여러분은 공부에 더 집중할 수 있을 것이다.

※ 다음 우리말과 일치하도록 빈칸에 알맞은 말을 쓰시오.

1  _____ _____ you sit _____ many hours.

2  Do you _____ _____ ?

3  _____ _____ you massage _____ and _____ ?

4  _____ _____ _____ the eyes.

5  _____ your eyes and _____ them softly _____ your _____ .

6  It _____ _____ your eyes.

7  _____ you finish, _____ your eyes _____ your hands to _____ _____ the light.

8  It will _____ your eyes _____ _____ _____ .

9  Next, _____ _____ _____ .

10  _____ your fingers _____ the _____ of your neck.

11  _____ small circles _____ your fingers _____ _____ your neck.

12  Massage _____ _____ _____ _____ .

13  The massage will _____ _____ _____ _____ .

14  _____ _____ _____ your _____ .

15  _____ _____ _____ a friend.

1  학교에서 너는 오랜 시간에 걸쳐 앉아 있다.

2  여러분은 피곤한가?

3  마사지와 스트레칭을 하는 게 어떤가?

4  눈부터 시작하자.

5  눈을 감고 손가락으로 눈을 부드럽게 마사지해라.

6  그것은 여러분의 눈을 편안하게 해줄 것이다.

7  끝나면, 빛을 차단하기 위해 손으로 눈을 가려라.

8  그것은 여러분의 눈을 더 편안하게 해줄 것이다.

9  다음으로, 여러분의 목을 마사지해라.

10  여러분의 목 뒤에 손가락을 대라.

11  여러분의 목을 마사지하기 위해 손가락으로 작은 원을 그려라.

12  위에서 아래로 마사지해라.

13  마사지는 여러분의 기분이 좋아지도록 도울 것이다.

14  허리 운동을 하자.

15  친구와 짝을 이루어라.

**16** Stand close to _____ _____ and _____ your partner.

**17** _____ each other's _____.

**18** _____ _____ your head and body _____.

**19** _____ that position _____ _____ _____.

**20** Then, slowly _____ each other _____ a standing position.

**21** You and _____ partner should move _____ the same speed.

**22** _____ you don't, _____ _____ you _____ _____!

**23** _____ the _____ of your right foot _____ the desk _____ you.

**24** Then, _____ _____ your left leg and _____ yourself.

**25** _____ it for _____ _____ _____ and slowly _____ _____.

**26** _____ _____ will _____ _____ your right leg.

**27** _____ your legs and _____ _____ _____.

**28** _____ do you _____ now?

**29** If you _____ yourself and _____ _____ _____, you will _____ _____.

**30** Also, you _____ _____ _____ your studies _____.

16 서로 가까이 서서 여러분의 파트너를 마주 보아라.

17 서로의 손목을 잡아라.

18 천천히 여러분의 머리와 몸을 뒤로 뻗어라.

19 3초 동안 그 자세를 유지해라.

20 그러고 나서, 천천히 서로 선 자세로 끌어 당겨라.

21 너와 너의 파트너는 같은 속도로 움직여야 한다.

22 그렇지 않으면, 너희 둘 다 넘어질 것이다!

23 여러분의 뒤에 있는 책상 위에 오른쪽 발등을 올려놓아라.

24 그러고 나서, 천천히 왼쪽 다리를 구부리고 몸을 낮추어라.

25 몇 초 동안 그 자세를 유지하다가 천천히 몸을 펴라.

26 이 자세는 여러분의 오른쪽 다리를 풀어 줄 것이다.

27 다리를 바꿔서 운동을 반복해라.

28 지금 기분이 어떤가?

29 매일 마사지와 스트레칭을 하면, 여러분은 더 건강해지는 것을 느낄 것이다.

30 또한, 여러분은 공부에 더 집중할 수 있을 것이다.

※ 다음 문장을 우리말로 쓰시오.

**1**  At school you sit for many hours.

➡ _____

**2**  Do you get tired?

➡ _____

**3**  Why don't you massage yourself and stretch?

➡ _____

**4**  Let's begin with the eyes.

➡ _____

**5**  Close your eyes and massage them softly with your fingers.

➡ _____

**6**  It will relax your eyes.

➡ _____

**7**  When you finish, cover your eyes with your hands to block out the light.

➡ _____

**8**  It will make your eyes feel more comfortable.

➡ _____

**9**  Next, massage your neck.

➡ _____

**10**  Put your fingers on the back of your neck.

➡ _____

**11**  Draw small circles with your fingers to massage your neck.

➡ _____

**12**  Massage from top to bottom.

➡ _____

**13**  The massage will help you feel better.

➡ _____

**14**  Let's work on your waist.

➡ _____

**15**  Team up with a friend.

➡ _____

**16** Stand close to each other and face your partner.

➡ _____

**17** Hold each other's wrists.

➡ _____

**18** Slowly stretch your head and body backward.

➡ _____

**19** Hold that position for three seconds.

➡ _____

**20** Then, slowly pull each other to a standing position.

➡ _____

**21** You and your partner should move at the same speed.

➡ _____

**22** If you don't, both of you will fall!

➡ _____

**23** Place the top of your right foot on the desk behind you.

➡ _____

**24** Then, slowly bend your left leg and lower yourself.

➡ _____

**25** Hold it for a few seconds and slowly straighten up.

➡ _____

**26** This position will loosen up your right leg.

➡ _____

**27** Switch your legs and repeat the exercise.

➡ _____

**28** How do you feel now?

➡ _____

**29** If you massage yourself and stretch every day, you will feel healthier.

➡ _____

**30** Also, you can focus on your studies better.

➡ _____

※ 다음 괄호 안의 단어들을 우리말에 맞도록 바르게 배열하시오.

**1** (school / you / at / sit / hours. / many / for)
➡ _____

**2** (get / do / tired? / you)
➡ _____

**3** (you / don't / why / massage / stretch? / and / yourself)
➡ _____

**4** (begin / with / let's / eyes. / the)
➡ _____

**5** (eyes / close / your / and / them / massage / fingers. / with / softly / your)
➡ _____

**6** (will / it / relax / eyes. / your)
➡ _____

**7** (you / finish, / when / your / cover / with / eyes / hands / your / block / to / light. / the / out)
➡ _____

**8** (will / it / make / eyes / your / feel / comfortable. / more)
➡ _____

**9** (next, / neck. / your / massage)
➡ _____

**10** (fingers / put / your / the / on / back / neck. / your / of)
➡ _____

**11** (small / draw / circles / your / with / fingers / massage / neck. / to / your)
➡ _____

**12** (from / bottom. / to / massage / top)
➡ _____

**13** (massage / the / help / will / better. / feel / you)
➡ _____

**14** (work / on / waist. / let's / your)
➡ _____

**15** (up / team / friend. / a / with)
➡ _____

**1** 학교에서 너는 오랜 시간에 걸쳐 앉아 있다.

**2** 여러분은 피곤한가?

**3** 마사지와 스트레칭을 하는 게 어떤가?

**4** 눈부터 시작하자.

**5** 눈을 감고 손가락으로 눈을 부드럽게 마사지해라.

**6** 그것은 여러분의 눈을 편안하게 해줄 것이다.

**7** 끝나면, 빛을 차단하기 위해 손으로 눈을 가려라.

**8** 그것은 여러분의 눈을 더 편안하게 해줄 것이다.

**9** 다음으로, 여러분의 목을 마사지해라.

**10** 여러분의 목 뒤에 손가락을 대라.

**11** 여러분의 목을 마사지하기 위해 손가락으로 작은 원을 그려라.

**12** 위에서 아래로 마사지해라.

**13** 마사지는 여러분의 기분이 좋아지도록 도울 것이다.

**14** 허리 운동을 하자.

**15** 친구와 짝을 이루어라.

**16** (close / to / stand / other / each / and / partner. / your / face)

➡ _____

**17** (each / wrists. / hold / other's)

➡ _____

**18** (stretch / slowly / head / your / and / backward. / body)

➡ _____

**19** (that / hold / for / position / seconds. / three)

➡ _____

**20** (slowly / then, / each / pull / other / to / position. / standing / a)

➡ _____

**21** (your / and / you / partner / move / should / the / at / speed. / same)

➡ _____

**22** (don't, / you / if / of / you / both / fall! / will)

➡ _____

**23** (the / place / of / top / right / your / foot / on / the / desk / you. / behind)

➡ _____

**24** (slowly / then, / your / bend / leg / left / yourself. / lower / and)

➡ _____

**25** (it / hold / a / for / seconds / few / and / slowly / up. / straighten)

➡ _____

**26** (position / this / loosen / will / up / leg. / right / your)

➡ _____

**27** (your / switch / legs / and / exercise. / the / repeat)

➡ _____

**28** (you / do / how / now? / feel)

➡ _____

**29** (you / massage / if / yourself / and / stretch / day, / every / will / you / healthier. / feel)

➡ _____

**30** (can / you / also, / on / focus / better. / studies / your)

➡ _____

**16** 서로 가까이 서서 여러분의 파트너를 마주 보아라.

**17** 서로의 손목을 잡아라.

**18** 천천히 여러분의 머리와 몸을 뒤로 뻗어라.

**19** 3초 동안 그 자세를 유지해라.

**20** 그리고 나서, 천천히 서로 선 자세로 끌어 당겨라.

**21** 너와 너의 파트너는 같은 속도로 움직여야 한다.

**22** 그렇지 않으면, 너희 둘 다 넘어질 것이다!

**23** 여러분의 뒤에 있는 책상 위에 오른쪽 발등을 올려놓아라.

**24** 그리고 나서, 천천히 왼쪽 다리를 구부리고 몸을 낮추어라.

**25** 몇 초 동안 그 자세를 유지하다가 천천히 몸을 펴라.

**26** 이 자세는 여러분의 오른쪽 다리를 풀어 줄 것이다.

**27** 다리를 바꿔서 운동을 반복해라.

**28** 지금 기분이 어떤가?

**29** 매일 마사지와 스트레칭을 하면, 여러분은 더 건강해지는 것을 느낄 것이다.

**30** 또한, 여러분은 공부에 더 집중할 수 있을 것이다.

※ 다음 우리말을 영어로 쓰시오.

**1** 학교에서 여러분은 오랜 시간에 걸쳐 앉아 있다.

➡ _____

**2** 여러분은 피곤한가?

➡ _____

**3** 마사지와 스트레칭을 하는 게 어떤가?

➡ _____

**4** 눈부터 시작하자.

➡ _____

**5** 눈을 감고 손가락으로 눈을 부드럽게 마사지해라.

➡ _____

**6** 그것은 여러분의 눈을 편안하게 해줄 것이다.

➡ _____

**7** 끝나면, 빛을 차단하기 위해 손으로 눈을 가려라.

➡ _____

**8** 그것은 여러분의 눈을 더 편안하게 해줄 것이다.

➡ _____

**9** 다음으로, 여러분의 목을 마사지해라.

➡ _____

**10** 여러분의 목 뒤에 손가락을 대라.

➡ _____

**11** 여러분의 목을 마사지하기 위해 손가락으로 작은 원을 그려라.

➡ _____

**12** 위에서 아래로 마사지해라.

➡ _____

**13** 마사지는 여러분의 기분이 좋아지도록 도울 것이다.

➡ _____

**14** 허리 운동을 하자.

➡ _____

**15** 친구와 짝을 이루어라.

➡ _____

**16** 서로 가까이 서서 여러분의 파트너를 마주 보아라.

➡ _____

**17** 서로의 손목을 잡아라.

➡ _____

**18** 천천히 여러분의 머리와 몸을 뒤로 뻗어라.

➡ _____

**19** 3초 동안 그 자세를 유지해라.

➡ _____

**20** 그리고 나서, 천천히 서로 선 자세로 끌어 당겨라.

➡ _____

**21** 너와 너의 파트너는 같은 속도로 움직여야 한다.

➡ _____

**22** 그렇지 않으면, 너희 둘 다 넘어질 것이다!

➡ _____

**23** 여러분의 뒤에 있는 책상 위에 오른쪽 발등을 올려놓아라.

➡ _____

**24** 그리고 나서, 천천히 왼쪽 다리를 구부리고 몸을 낮추어라.

➡ _____

**25** 몇 초 동안 그 자세를 유지하다가 천천히 몸을 펴라.

➡ _____

**26** 이 자세는 여러분의 오른쪽 다리를 풀어 줄 것이다.

➡ _____

**27** 다리를 바꿔서 운동을 반복해라.

➡ _____

**28** 지금 기분이 어떤가?

➡ _____

**29** 매일 마사지와 스트레칭을 하면, 여러분은 더 건강해지는 것을 느낄 것이다.

➡ _____

**30** 또한, 여러분은 공부에 더 집중할 수 있을 것이다.

➡ _____

※ 다음 우리말과 일치하도록 빈칸에 알맞은 말을 쓰시오.

## Enjoy Writing C

1. My Plan _____ _____ _____

2. _____ _____ my plan to be healthier.

3. I will exercise _____ _____ _____ _____ a week.

4. I will eat breakfast _____ _____.

5. If I exercise more than _____ _____ _____ _____, I will

   _____ _____.

6. Also, _____ I eat breakfast every day, I _____ _____

   _____ in the morning.

7. I will change my _____, and it will _____ _____ _____ a

   healthy life.

1. 더 건강해지기 위한 나의 계획
2. 여기 더 건강해지기 위한 나의 계획이 있다.
3. 나는 일주일에 세 번 이상 운동을 할 것이다.
4. 나는 매일 아침을 먹을 것이다.
5. 일주일에 세 번 이상 운동을 하면 더 강해질 것이다.
6. 또한, 매일 아침을 먹으면 아침에 기분이 나아질 것이다.
7. 나는 습관을 바꿀 것이고, 그것은 나를 건강한 삶을 살게 할 것이다.

## Project - Step 2

1. Do you know _____ _____ _____ your shoulders?

2. Our _____ _____ _____ _____ _____ "Number Stretching."

3. First, make a number "1" _____ your arm _____ _____

   _____.

4. _____, make a number "2" _____ your arms.

5. It _____ _____ your _____.

6. Now, _____ a number "3".

7. If you move your arms _____ _____ _____, it will _____

   _____.

8. _____, make a number "4".

9. It is _____ _____ _____ difficult, but it will _____

   _____ _____ your shoulders.

1. 여러분은 여러분의 어깨를 어떻게 스트레칭하는지 아니?
2. 우리의 스트레칭 운동은 "숫자 스트레칭"이라고 부른다.
3. "첫 번째, 준비 운동을 하기 위해 팔로 숫자 "1"를 만들어라.
4. 그런 다음, 팔로 숫자 2를 만들어라.
5. 그것은 여러분의 어깨를 쫙 펴줄 것이다.
6. 이제 숫자 3을 만들어라.
7. 팔을 동그랗게 움직이면 기분이 좋아질 것이다.
8. 마지막으로, 숫자 4를 만들어라.
9. 그것은 조금 어렵긴 하지만, 여러분의 어깨에 좋을 것이다.

## Wrap Up - Writing

1. Sumi: I feel stressed _____ _____. What _____ I _____?

2. Jiae: When I _____ _____, I listen to music. It _____

   _____ _____ better.

3. If you don't know _____ _____ _____ music, I will show

   you.

1. 수미: 나는 요즘 스트레스를 받고 있어. 어떻게 해야 하지?
2. 지애: 스트레스를 받을 때, 나는 음악을 들어. 그건 내 기분을 좋아지게 해.
3. 음악을 다운로드하는 방법을 모르면, 내가 가르쳐 줄게.

※ 다음 우리말을 영어로 쓰시오.

## Enjoy Writing C

1. 더 건강해지기 위한 나의 계획
➡ _____

2. 여기 더 건강해지기 위한 나의 계획이 있다.
➡ _____

3. 나는 일주일에 세 번 이상 운동을 할 것이다.
➡ _____

4. 나는 매일 아침을 먹을 것이다.
➡ _____

5. 일주일에 세 번 이상 운동을 하면 더 강해질 것이다.
➡ _____

6. 또한, 매일 아침을 먹으면 아침에 기분이 나아질 것이다.
➡ _____

7. 나는 습관을 바꿀 것이고, 그것은 나를 건강한 삶을 살게 할 것이다.
➡ _____

## Project - Step 2

1. 여러분은 여러분의 어깨를 어떻게 스트레칭하는지 아니?
➡ _____

2. 우리의 스트레칭 운동은 "숫자 스트레칭"이라고 부른다.
➡ _____

3. "첫 번째, 준비 운동을 하기 위해 팔로 숫자 "1"를 만들어라.
➡ _____

4. 그런 다음, 팔로 숫자 2를 만들어라.
➡ _____

5. 그것은 여러분의 어깨를 쫙 펴줄 것이다.
➡ _____

6. 이제 숫자 3을 만들어라.
➡ _____

7. 팔을 동그랗게 움직이면 기분이 좋아질 것이다.
➡ _____

8. 마지막으로, 숫자 4를 만들어라.
➡ _____

9. 그것은 조금 어렵긴 하지만, 여러분의 어깨에 좋을 것이다.
➡ _____

## Wrap Up - Writing

1. 수미: 나는 요즘 스트레스를 받고 있어. 어떻게 해야 하지?
➡ _____

2. 지애: 스트레스를 받을 때, 나는 음악을 들어. 그건 내 기분을 좋아지게 해.
➡ _____

3. 음악을 다운로드하는 방법을 모르면, 내가 가르쳐 줄게.
➡ _____

※ 다음 영어를 우리말로 쓰시오.

| | | | |
|---|---|---|---|
| 01 | hunger | 22 | lantern |
| 02 | recycle | 23 | awesome |
| 03 | environment | 24 | global |
| 04 | celebrate | 25 | community |
| 05 | save | 26 | communicate |
| 06 | aim | 27 | garden |
| 07 | education | 28 | poor |
| 08 | far | 29 | alongside |
| 09 | flood | 30 | plate |
| 10 | hurt | 31 | citizen |
| 11 | gather | 32 | protect |
| 12 | produce | 33 | hold |
| 13 | send | 34 | international |
| 14 | adult | 35 | care for |
| 15 | share | 36 | thanks to |
| 16 | join | 37 | watch out (for) |
| 17 | trash | 38 | die of |
| 18 | messy | 39 | go well |
| 19 | nothing | 40 | be good at |
| 20 | raise | 41 | throw away |
| 21 | waste | 42 | in need |
| | | 43 | share A with B |

※ 다음 우리말을 영어로 쓰시오.

| | | |
|---|---|---|
| 01 시민 | | 22 자연환경, 환경 |
| 02 미국의, 미국인 | | 23 모으다 |
| 03 가난한 | | 24 쓰레기 |
| 04 싸움; 싸우다 | | 25 교육 |
| 05 ~ 옆에, 나란히 | | 26 다치게 하다 |
| 06 공동체, 사회 | | 27 어른 |
| 07 굉장한, 감탄할 만한 | | 28 살리다, 구하다 |
| 08 캠페인, 조직적 활동 | | 29 (폐기물을) 재활용하다 |
| 09 정원 | | 30 생산하다 |
| 10 접시 | | 31 홍수 |
| 11 팔다 | | 32 축하하다, 기념하다 |
| 12 업로드하다, 올리다 | | 33 기아, 배고픔 |
| 13 전 세계적인, 지구상의 | | 34 (자금 등을) 모금하다 |
| 14 (회의, 시합 등을) 열다 | | 35 ~에 관심을 가지다 |
| 15 국제적인 | | 36 샤워를 하다 |
| 16 당황한 | | 37 어려움에 처한 |
| 17 남기다 | | 38 (~에 대해서) 조심하다 |
| 18 의사소통하다 | | 39 ~을 버리다 |
| 19 보호하다 | | 40 ~을 잘하다 |
| 20 (컴퓨터의) 사이트 | | 41 ~ 덕분에 |
| 21 가져가다 | | 42 ~을 돌보다, 신경 쓰다 |
| | | 43 ~으로 죽다 |

※ 다음 영영풀이에 알맞은 단어를 <보기>에서 골라 쓴 후, 우리말 뜻을 쓰시오.

1 _____ : a grown-up person: _____

2 _____ : an overflow of water: _____

3 _____ : a place where you can grow plants: _____

4 _____ : untidy or dirty: _____

5 _____ : having very little money: _____

6 _____ : to give goods in exchange for money: _____

7 _____ : to plan or hope to achieve something: _____

8 _____ : including the whole world: _____

9 _____ : to process used or waste materials so as to make suitable for reuse:

     _____

10 _____ : emotionally disturbed or agitated: _____

11 _____ : to fail to use time, money, energy, etc. fully or in the sensible or useful

     way: _____

12 _____ : to collect money for a particular purpose: _____

13 _____ : to do something enjoyable on a special occasion: _____

14 _____ : to bring people together or collect things together: _____

15 _____ : a person who lives in a country or town legally: _____

16 _____ : to share or exchange information or emotion with someone: _____

| 보기 | | | |
|---|---|---|---|
| citizen | recycle | poor | celebrate |
| raise | upset | flood | sell |
| aim | communicate | adult | garden |
| gather | waste | global | messy |

※ 다음 우리말과 일치하도록 빈칸에 알맞은 말을 쓰시오.

### Listen & Speak 1 A

1. **B:** Did you _____ the news _____ _____ _____?
   **G:** Yes, _____ _____. They said _____ _____ _____ people _____ their homes.
   **B:** My club is _____ _____ _____ them some money.
   **G:** _____ can you do that? _____ _____ going _____ _____ money, Andy?
   **B:** Yes. We're _____ _____ _____ pencil cases and _____ them.

2. **B:** Do you have any _____ for the summer _____, Suji?
   **G:** Yes. I'm _____ _____ the Philippines to _____ _____ _____ _____ _____ my family.
   **B:** Oh, I _____ there and _____ some children study last year. _____ _____ _____ _____ _____ that, too?
   **G:** Yes. And I'll _____ _____ walls _____ the children.
   **B:** That _____ _____.

### Listen & Speak 1 B

1. **G:** _____ you _____ _____ _____ _____ a short shower?
   **B:** Yes, I _____, / No, _____ _____.

2. **G:** Are you _____ _____ _____ _____ _____?
   **B:** Yes, _____ _____. / No, _____ _____.

### Listen & Speak 2 A

1. **G:** _____ are you doing, Jason?
   **B:** I'm _____ a poster _____ global _____. Many people are _____ _____ _____.
   **G:** That's _____ _____. I didn't know that.
   **B:** I _____ more people _____ _____ _____ hunger.

1. **B:** 홍수에 대한 뉴스를 보았니?
   **G:** 응, 보았어. 많은 사람들이 집을 잃었다고 하더라.
   **B:** 우리 동아리는 그들에게 약간의 돈을 보낼 거야.
   **G:** 그것을 어떻게 할 수 있니? 돈을 모금할 거니, Andy?
   **B:** 응. 우리는 필통을 만들어서 그것들을 팔 거야.

2. **B:** 여름 방학에 어떤 계획이 있니, 수지야?
   **G:** 응. 나는 나의 가족들과 봉사활동을 하러 필리핀에 갈 거야.
   **B:** 오, 나는 작년에 그 곳에 가서 몇몇 아이들이 공부하는 것을 도와줬어. 너도 그렇게 할 거니?
   **G:** 응, 그리고 나는 또한 아이들과 벽화를 그릴 거야.
   **B:** 정말 좋겠다.

1. **A:** 너는 샤워를 짧게 할 거니?
   **B:** 응, 그럴 거야. / 아니, 그러지 않을 거야.

2. **A:** 너는 병을 재활용할 거니?
   **B:** 응, 그럴 거야. / 아니, 그러지 않을 거야.

1. **G:** 무엇을 하고 있니, Jason?
   **B:** 세계의 기아 문제에 대한 포스터를 만드는 중이야. 많은 사람들이 기아로 죽어가고 있어.
   **G:** 정말 안됐다. 난 몰랐어.
   **B:** 더 많은 사람들이 세계의 기아 문제에 관심을 갖기를 바라.

2. **G:** Dad, my class _____ _____ _____ a vegetable _____.

   **M:** A _____ _____? What _____ you grow there, Sena?

   **G:** Carrots. We'll _____ them and _____ them _____ others.

   **M:** That's a _____ _____.

   **G:** I _____ the carrots _____ _____.

2. **G:** 아빠, 우리 반은 채소밭을 가꾸기로 했어요.

   **M:** 채소밭? 거기서 무엇을 기를 거니, 세나야?

   **G:** 당근이요. 우리는 그것을 길러서 사람들과 나눌 거예요.

   **M:** 좋은 생각이구나.

   **G:** 당근이 잘 자랐으면 좋겠어요.

### Listen & Speak 2 B

1. **A:** I _____ people _____ _____ _____ _____ _____.

   **B:** I _____ _____, too. _____ _____ a Keep the World Clean _____.

   **A:** That's a good idea.

2. **A:** _____ _____ _____ _____ _____ animals.

   **B:** I _____ _____, too. _____ _____ a Love Animals campaign.

   **A:** That's a _____ _____.

1. **A:** 나는 사람들이 쓰레기를 버리지 않기를 바라.

   **B:** 나도 그렇게 생각해. '세상을 깨끗하게 하라'라는 캠페인을 열자.

   **A:** 좋은 생각이야.

2. **A:** 나는 사람들이 동물을 해치지 않기를 바라.

   **B:** 나도 그렇게 생각해. '동물을 사랑하라'라는 캠페인을 열자.

   **A:** 좋은 생각이야.

### Wrap Up

1. **B:** _____ _____ _____ for the weekend, Sumin? _____ you _____ _____ _____ _____ _____?

   **G:** Yes. _____ Saturday, I'm _____ _____ _____ my grandmother.

   **B:** _____ _____ _____ Sunday?

   **G:** I _____ _____ _____ for Sunday. Why?

   **B:** I'm _____ _____ _____ _____ _____ _____ at the library on Sunday. Would you _____ _____ _____ with me?

   **G:** Sure.

2. **G:** My club is _____ _____ _____ a green campaign _____ _____ _____ _____ _____.

   **B:** _____ _____ a green campaign?

   **G:** It's a _____ _____ _____ the environment. Many students _____ _____ _____ the streets. We hope _____ _____ that.

   **B:** I _____ your campaign _____ well.

   **G:** Thanks. I _____ _____, _____.

1. **B:** 너의 주말 계획은 뭐니, 수민아? 특별한 걸 할 거니?

   **G:** 응. 토요일에 할머니를 방문할 거야.

   **B:** 일요일은 어때?

   **G:** 일요일은 아무 계획 없어. 왜?

   **B:** 나는 일요일에 도서관에서 봉사활동을 할 거야. 나와 함께 갈래?

   **G:** 물론이지.

2. **G:** 우리 동아리는 다음 주 금요일에 학교에서 그린 캠페인을 열 거야.

   **B:** 그린 캠페인이 뭐야?

   **G:** 환경을 보호하기 위한 캠페인이야. 많은 학생들이 길에 쓰레기를 버려. 우리는 그걸 멈추길 바라.

   **B:** 네 캠페인이 잘 되길 바라.

   **G:** 고마워. 나도 그러길 바라

※ 다음 우리말에 맞도록 대화를 영어로 쓰시오.

해석

### Listen & Speak 1 A

1. B: _____

   G: _____

   B: _____

   G: _____

   B: _____

2. B: _____

   G: _____

   B: _____

   _____

   G: _____

   B: _____

1. B: 홍수에 대한 뉴스를 보았니?
   G: 응, 보았어. 많은 사람들이 집을 잃었다고 하더라.
   B: 우리 동아리는 그들에게 약간의 돈을 보낼 거야.
   G: 그것을 어떻게 할 수 있니? 돈을 모금할 거니, Andy?
   B: 응. 우리는 필통을 만들어서 그것들을 팔 거야.

2. B: 여름 방학에 어떤 계획이 있니, 수지야?
   G: 응. 나는 나의 가족들과 봉사활동을 하러 필리핀에 갈 거야.
   B: 오, 나는 작년에 그 곳에 가서 몇몇 아이들이 공부하는 것을 도와줬어. 너도 그렇게 할 거니?
   G: 응, 그리고 나는 또한 아이들과 벽화를 그릴 거야.
   B: 정말 좋겠다.

### Listen & Speak 1 B

1. G: _____

   B: _____

2. G: _____

   B: _____

1. A: 너는 샤워를 짧게 할 거니?
   B: 응, 그럴 거야. / 아니, 그러지 않을 거야.

2. A: 너는 병을 재활용할 거니?
   B: 응, 그럴 거야. / 아니, 그러지 않을 거야.

### Listen & Speak 2 A

1. G: _____

   B: _____

   G: _____

   B: _____

1. G: 무엇을 하고 있니, Jason?
   B: 세계의 기아 문제에 대한 포스터를 만드는 중이야. 많은 사람들이 기아로 죽어가고 있어.
   G: 정말 안됐다. 난 몰랐어.
   B: 더 많은 사람들이 세계의 기아 문제에 관심을 갖기를 바라.

2. G: _____

   M: _____

   G: _____

   M: _____

   G: _____

2. G: 아빠, 우리 반은 채소밭을 가꾸기
   로 했어요.
   M: 채소밭? 거기서 무엇을 기를 거
   니, 세나야?
   G: 당근이요. 우리는 그것을 길러서
   사람들과 나눌 거예요.
   M: 좋은 생각이구나.
   G: 당근이 잘 자랐으면 좋겠어요.

## Listen & Speak 2 B

1. A: _____

   B: _____

   A: _____

2. A: _____

   B: _____

   A: _____

1. A: 나는 사람들이 쓰레기를 버리지
   않기를 바라.
   B: 나도 그렇게 생각해. '세상을 깨끗
   하게 하라'라는 캠페인을 열자.
   A: 좋은 생각이야.

2. A: 나는 사람들이 동물을 해치지 않
   기를 바라.
   B: 나도 그렇게 생각해. '동물을 사랑
   하라'라는 캠페인을 열자.
   A: 좋은 생각이야.

## Wrap Up

1. B: _____

      _____

   G: _____

   B: _____

   G: _____

   B: _____

      _____

   G: _____

2. G: _____

   B: _____

   G: _____

      _____

   B: _____

   G: _____

1. B: 너의 주말 계획은 뭐니, 수민아?
   특별한 걸 할 거니?
   G: 응. 토요일에 할머니를 방문할 거
   야.
   B: 일요일은 어때?
   G: 일요일은 아무 계획 없어. 왜?
   B: 나는 일요일에 도서관에서 봉사
   활동을 할 거야. 나와 함께 갈래?
   G: 물론이지.

2. G: 우리 동아리는 다음 주 금요일에
   학교에서 그린 캠페인을 열 거야.
   B: 그린 캠페인이 뭐야?
   G: 환경을 보호하기 위한 캠페인이
   야. 많은 학생들이 길에 쓰레기를
   버려. 우리는 그걸 멈추길 바라.
   B: 네 캠페인이 잘 되길 바라.
   G: 고마워. 나도 그러길 바라

※ 다음 우리말과 일치하도록 빈칸에 알맞은 것을 골라 쓰시오.

**1** _____ Citizenship _____
  A. Education      B. Global

**2** _____ is the Global _____ Education _____.
  A. Citizenship      B. site      C. this

**3** Global Citizenship Education _____ us _____ _____ global citizens.
  A. grow      B. helps      C. as

**4** Global citizens are people who _____ to _____ different _____.
  A. understand      B. cultures      C. try

**5** They also _____ _____ people _____ _____ and work for a better world.
  A. need      B. for      C. in      D. care

**6** Please _____ your _____ citizenship education _____ here.
  A. experiences      B. share      C. global

**7** Hello. I _____ Minhee _____ _____.
  A. Korea      B. from      C. am

**8** I am _____ _____ _____ the Global Community Club.
  A. a      B. of      C. member

**9** My club _____ to _____ _____ people from around the world.
  A. with      B. communicate   C. aims

**10** A week _____ we _____ a video about the _____ festival in our village.
  A. ago      B. produced      C. lantern

**11** We _____ it to the Internet and _____, we got _____ 5,000 _____.
  A. amazingly      B. uploaded      C. hits      D. nearly

**12** _____ here _____ our _____.
  A. video      B. for      C. click

**13** Alice: Wow, _____ lantern festival _____ _____!
  A. fantastic      B. your      C. looks

**14** Sunan: We _____ a water festival _____ our _____.
  A. village      B. have      C. in

**15** I'd like to _____ a video _____ _____.
  A. yours      B. like      C. make

1  세계 시민 교육

2  이곳은 세계 시민 교육 사이트 입니다.

3  세계 시민 교육은 우리가 세계 시민으로 자라도록 도와줍니다.

4  세계 시민은 다른 문화를 이해 하려고 노력하는 사람들입니다.

5  그들은 또한 어려움에 처한 사 람들을 보살피고 더 나은 세상 을 위해서 일합니다.

6  당신의 세계 시민 교육 경험을 이곳에 공유해 주세요.

7  안녕. 나는 한국의 민희야.

8  나는 세계 공동체 동아리의 회 원이야.

9  우리 동아리는 전 세계의 사람 들과 소통하는 것을 목표로 해.

10  일주일 전에 우리는 우리 마을 의 등 축제에 관한 비디오를 제 작했어.

11  우리는 그것을 인터넷에 올렸는 데, 놀랍게도 거의 5,000개의 조 회 수를 획득했어.

12  우리 비디오를 보려면 이곳을 클릭해.

13  Alice: 와, 너희 등 축제는 환상 적으로 보인다!

14  Sunan: 우리 마을에는 물 축제 가 있어.

15  나도 너희 것과 같은 비디오를 만들고 싶어.

**16** Hi, _____ _____ is Jo.

    A. name          B. my

**17** I _____ _____ Australia.

    A. from          B. am

**18** A _____ weeks _____ , my teacher _____ us pictures _____ students in Kenya.

    A. few          B. showed          C. ago          D. of

**19** Sadly, they were _____ _____ plastic bags _____ _____ their books.

    A. using          B. all          C. carry          D. to

**20** My class _____ to _____ money to _____ them new school bags.

    A. raise          B. decided          C. send

**21** We _____ cookies and _____ and _____ 600 dollars.

    A. drinks          B. sold          C. raised

**22** We _____ the Kenyan students are _____ _____ the new bags.

    A. with          B. hope          C. happy

**23** Wang: _____ ! I'm _____ they _____ like the bags.

    A. sure          B. awesome          C. will

**24** Kozo: You did _____ _____ !

    A. wonderful          B. something

**25** I _____ Afig _____ Malaysia.

    A. from          B. am

**26** My school started a wall _____ campaign to _____ our village _____ _____ .

    A. make          B. better          C. look          D. painting

**27** Students who are _____ at painting _____ and _____ on some walls of schools and parks.

    A. good          B. painted          C. gathered

**28** _____ to this campaign, our village looks _____ _____ .

    A. nicer          B. thanks          C. much

**29** Now everyone can enjoy _____ _____ the _____ walls.

    A. walking          B. painted          C. alongside

**30** Junho: _____ _____ _____ idea!

    A. nice          B. what          C. a

**16** 안녕, 내 이름은 Jo야.

**17** 나는 호주 출신이야.

**18** 몇 주 전에, 선생님이 우리에게 케냐에 있는 학생들의 사진을 보여주셨어.

**19** 슬프게도, 그들은 모두 책을 들고 다니기 위해서 비닐 봉지를 사용하고 있었어.

**20** 우리 반은 그들에게 새로운 책 가방을 보내기 위해서 기금을 모금하기로 결정했어.

**21** 우리는 쿠키와 음료를 팔아서 600달러를 모았어.

**22** 우리는 케냐의 학생들이 그들의 새 가방을 좋아하기를 바라.

**23** Wang: 멋지다! 분명 그들이 가방을 좋아할 거야.

**24** Kozo: 훌륭한 일을 했구나!

**25** 난 말레이시아의 Afig야.

**26** 우리 학교는 우리 마을을 좀 더 좋아 보이게 하기 위해서 벽화 캠페인을 시작했어.

**27** 그림을 잘 그리는 학생들이 모여서 학교와 공원 벽에 그림을 그렸어.

**28** 이 캠페인 덕분에, 우리 마을은 훨씬 멋져 보여.

**29** 이제 모든 사람들이 그림이 그려진 벽을 따라서 산책하는 것을 즐길 수 있어.

**30** Junho: 정말 멋진 생각이다!

※ 다음 우리말과 일치하도록 빈칸에 알맞은 말을 쓰시오.

1  _____ Citizenship _____

2  _____ is the Global _____ _____ _____ .

3  Global Citizenship Education _____ us _____ _____ _____ _____ .

4  Global citizens are people who _____ _____ _____ different _____ .

5  They also _____ _____ people _____ _____ and work for _____ _____ _____ .

6  Please _____ your _____ citizenship education _____ here.

7  Hello. I _____ Minhee _____ _____ .

8  I am _____ _____ _____ the Global Community Club.

9  My club _____ _____ _____ _____ people from _____ the world.

10  _____ _____ _____ _____ we produced a video _____ _____ _____ in our village.

11  We _____ it to the Internet and _____ , we _____ _____ 5,000 _____ .

12  _____ here _____ our _____ .

13  Alice: Wow, _____ lantern festival _____ _____ !

14  Sunan: We _____ a water festival _____ our _____ .

15  I'd _____ _____ a video _____ _____ .

1  세계 시민 교육

2  이곳은 세계 시민 교육 사이트 입니다.

3  세계 시민 교육은 우리가 세계 시민으로 자라도록 도와줍니다.

4  세계 시민은 다른 문화를 이해 하려고 노력하는 사람들입니다.

5  그들은 또한 어려움에 처한 사람들을 보살피고 더 나은 세상을 위해서 일합니다.

6  당신의 세계 시민 교육 경험을 이곳에 공유해 주세요.

7  안녕. 나는 한국의 민희야.

8  나는 세계 공동체 동아리의 회원이야.

9  우리 동아리는 전 세계의 사람들과 소통하는 것을 목표로 해.

10  일주일 전에 우리는 우리 마을의 등 축제에 관한 비디오를 제작했어.

11  우리는 그것을 인터넷에 올렸는데, 놀랍게도 거의 5,000개의 조회 수를 획득했어.

12  우리 비디오를 보려면 이곳을 클릭해.

13  Alice: 와, 너희 등 축제는 환상적으로 보인다!

14  Sunan: 우리 마을에는 물 축제가 있어.

15  나도 너희 것과 같은 비디오를 만들고 싶어.

**16** Hi, _____ _____ is Jo.

**17** I _____ _____ Australia.

**18** A _____ weeks _____, my teacher _____ _____ _____ _____ students in Kenya.

**19** _____, they were _____ _____ plastic bags _____ _____ their books.

**20** My class _____ to _____ _____ _____ _____ them new school bags.

**21** We _____ cookies and _____ and _____ 600 dollars.

**22** We _____ the Kenyan students _____ _____ _____ the new bags.

**23** Wang: _____! I'm _____ they _____ _____ the bags.

**24** Kozo: You _____ _____ _____ _____!

**25** I _____ Afig _____ _____.

**26** My school started a _____ _____ campaign _____ _____ our village _____ _____.

**27** Students who _____ _____ _____ painting _____ and _____ on some walls of schools and parks.

**28** _____ _____ this campaign, our village _____ _____ _____.

**29** Now everyone can _____ _____ _____ the _____ walls.

**30** Junho: _____ _____ _____ _____ _____!

---

**16** 안녕. 내 이름은 Jo야.

**17** 나는 호주 출신이야.

**18** 몇 주 전에, 선생님이 우리에게 케냐에 있는 학생들의 사진을 보여주셨어.

**19** 슬프게도, 그들은 모두 책을 들고 다니기 위해서 비닐 봉지를 사용하고 있었어.

**20** 우리 반은 그들에게 새로운 책 가방을 보내기 위해서 기금을 모금하기로 결정했어.

**21** 우리는 쿠키와 음료를 팔아서 600달러를 모았어.

**22** 우리는 케냐의 학생들이 그들의 새 가방을 좋아하기를 바라.

**23** Wang: 멋지다! 분명 그들이 가방을 좋아할 거야.

**24** Kozo: 훌륭한 일을 했구나!

**25** 난 말레이시아의 Afig야.

**26** 우리 학교는 우리 마을을 좀 더 좋아 보이게 하기 위해서 벽화 캠페인을 시작했어.

**27** 그림을 잘 그리는 학생들이 모여서 학교와 공원 벽에 그림을 그렸어.

**28** 이 캠페인 덕분에, 우리 마을은 훨씬 멋져 보여.

**29** 이제 모든 사람들이 그림이 그려진 벽을 따라서 산책하는 것을 즐길 수 있어.

**30** Junho: 정말 멋진 생각이다!

※ 다음 문장을 우리말로 쓰시오.

**1** Global Citizenship Education

➡ _____

**2** This is the Global Citizenship Education site.

➡ _____

**3** Global Citizenship Education helps us grow as global citizens.

➡ _____

**4** Global citizens are people who try to understand different cultures.

➡ _____

**5** They also care for people in need and work for a better world.

➡ _____

**6** Please share your global citizenship education experiences here.

➡ _____

**7** Hello. I am Minhee from Korea.

➡ _____

**8** I am a member of the Global Community Club.

➡ _____

**9** My club aims to communicate with people from around the world.

➡ _____

**10** A week ago we produced a video about the lantern festival in our village.

➡ _____

**11** We uploaded it to the Internet and amazingly, we got nearly 5,000 hits.

➡ _____

**12** Click here for our video.

➡ _____

**13** Alice: Wow, your lantern festival looks fantastic!

➡ _____

**14** Sunan: We have a water festival in our village.

➡ _____

**15** I'd like to make a video like yours.

➡ _____

**16** Hi, my name is Jo.

➡ _____

**17** I am from Australia.

➡ _____

**18** A few weeks ago, my teacher showed us pictures of students in Kenya.

➡ _____

**19** Sadly, they were all using plastic bags to carry their books.

➡ _____

**20** My class decided to raise money to send them new school bags.

➡ _____

**21** We sold cookies and drinks and raised 600 dollars.

➡ _____

**22** We hope the Kenyan students are happy with the new bags.

➡ _____

**23** Wang: Awesome! I'm sure they will like the bags.

➡ _____

**24** Kozo: You did something wonderful!

➡ _____

**25** I am Afig from Malaysia.

➡ _____

**26** My school started a wall painting campaign to make our village look better.

➡ _____

**27** Students who are good at painting gathered and painted on some walls of schools and parks.

➡ _____

**28** Thanks to this campaign, our village looks much nicer.

➡ _____

**29** Now everyone can enjoy walking alongside the painted walls.

➡ _____

**30** Junho: What a nice idea!

➡ _____

※ 다음 괄호 안의 단어들을 우리말에 맞도록 바르게 배열하시오.

**1** (Education / Citizenship / Global)
➡ _____

**2** (is / this / Global / the / site. / Education / Citizenship)
➡ _____

**3** (Citizenship / Global / Education / us / helps / grow / citizens. / global / as)
➡ _____

**4** (citizens / global / people / are / try / who / understand / to / cultures. / different)
➡ _____

**5** (also / they / for / care / people / need / in / and / for / work / world. / better / a)
➡ _____

**6** (share / please / global / your / citizenship / here. / experiences / education)
➡ _____

**7** (hello. // Minhee / am / I / Korea. / from)
➡ _____

**8** (am / I / member / a / the / of / Club. / Community / Global)
➡ _____

**9** (club / my / aims / communicate / to / people / with / around / from / world. / the)
➡ _____

**10** (week / a / ago / produced / we / video / a / about / lantern / the / in / festival / village. / our)
➡ _____

**11** (uploaded / we / to / it / Internet / the / and / we / amazingly, / nearly / got / hits. / 5,000)
➡ _____

**12** (here / click / our / video. / for)
➡ _____

**13** (Alice: your / wow, / lantern / fantastic! / looks / festival)
➡ _____

**14** (Sunan: / have / we / water / a / in / festival / village. / our)
➡ _____

**15** (like / I'd / make / to / a / yours. / like / video)
➡ _____

1 세계 시민 교육

2 이곳은 세계 시민 교육 사이트 입니다.

3 세계 시민 교육은 우리가 세계 시민으로 자라도록 도와줍니다.

4 세계 시민은 다른 문화를 이해 하려고 노력하는 사람들입니다.

5 그들은 또한 어려움에 처한 사 람들을 보살피고 더 나은 세상 을 위해서 일합니다.

6 당신의 세계 시민 교육 경험을 이곳에 공유해 주세요.

7 안녕. 나는 한국의 민희야.

8 나는 세계 공동체 동아리의 회 원이야.

9 우리 동아리는 전 세계의 사람 들과 소통하는 것을 목표로 해.

10 일주일 전에 우리는 우리 마을 의 등 축제에 관한 비디오를 제 작했어.

11 우리는 그것을 인터넷에 올렸는 데, 놀랍게도 거의 5,000개의 조 회 수를 획득했어.

12 우리 비디오를 보려면 이곳을 클릭해.

13 Alice: 와, 너희 등 축제는 환상 적으로 보인다!

14 Sunan: 우리 마을에는 물 축제 가 있어.

15 나도 너희 것과 같은 비디오를 만들고 싶어.

**16** (my / hi, / is / Jo. / name)

➡ _____

**17** (am / I / Australia. / from)

➡ _____

**18** (few / a / ago, / weeks / teacher / my / us / showed / pictures / students / of / Kenya. / in)

➡ _____

**19** (they / sadly, / were / using / all / bags / plastic / carry / to / books. / their)

➡ _____

**20** (class / my / to / decided / money / raise / send / to / new / them / bags. / school)

➡ _____

**21** (sold / we / drinks / and / cookies / and / dollars. / 600 / raised)

➡ _____

**22** (hope / we / Kenyan / the / are / students / with / happy / the / bags. / new)

➡ _____

**23** (Wang: / awesome! / sure / I'm / will / they / bags. / the / like)

➡ _____

**24** (Kozo: / did / you / wonderful! / something)

➡ _____

**25** (am / I / Malaysia. / from / Afig)

➡ _____

**26** (school / my / started / wall / a / campaign / painting / make / to / village / our / better. / look)

➡ _____

**27** (who / students / good / are / painting / at / and / gathered / on / painted / walls / some / parks. / and / schools / of)

➡ _____

**28** (to / thanks / campaign, / this / village / our / nicer. / much / looks)

➡ _____

**29** (everyone / now / enjoy / can / walking / the / alongside / walls. / painted)

➡ _____

**30** (Junho: / a / idea! / what / nice)

➡ _____

**16** 안녕, 내 이름은 Jo야.

**17** 나는 호주 출신이야.

**18** 몇 주 전에, 선생님이 우리에게 케냐에 있는 학생들의 사진을 보여주셨어.

**19** 슬프게도, 그들은 모두 책을 들고 다니기 위해서 비닐 봉지를 사용하고 있었어.

**20** 우리 반은 그들에게 새로운 책가방을 보내기 위해서 기금을 모금하기로 결정했어.

**21** 우리는 쿠키와 음료를 팔아서 600달러를 모았어.

**22** 우리는 케냐의 학생들이 그들의 새 가방을 좋아하기를 바라.

**23** Wang: 멋지다! 분명 그들이 가방을 좋아할 거야.

**24** Kozo: 훌륭한 일을 했구나!

**25** 난 말레이시아의 Afig야.

**26** 우리 학교는 우리 마을을 좀 더 좋아 보이게 하기 위해서 벽화 캠페인을 시작했어.

**27** 그림을 잘 그리는 학생들이 모여서 학교와 공원 벽에 그림을 그렸어.

**28** 이 캠페인 덕분에, 우리 마을은 훨씬 멋져 보여.

**29** 이제 모든 사람들이 그림이 그려진 벽을 따라서 산책하는 것을 즐길 수 있어.

**30** Junho: 정말 멋진 생각이다!

※ 다음 우리말을 영어로 쓰시오.

**1** 세계 시민 교육

➡ _____

**2** 이곳은 세계 시민 교육 사이트입니다.

➡ _____

**3** 세계 시민 교육은 우리가 세계 시민으로 자라도록 도와줍니다.

➡ _____

**4** 세계 시민은 다른 문화를 이해하려고 노력하는 사람들입니다.

➡ _____

**5** 그들은 또한 어려움에 처한 사람들을 보살피고 더 나은 세상을 위해서 일합니다.

➡ _____

**6** 당신의 세계 시민 교육 경험을 이곳에 공유해 주세요.

➡ _____

**7** 안녕. 나는 한국의 민희야.

➡ _____

**8** 나는 세계 공동체 동아리의 회원이야.

➡ _____

**9** 우리 동아리는 전 세계의 사람들과 소통하는 것을 목표로 해.

➡ _____

**10** 일주일 전에 우리는 우리 마을의 등 축제에 관한 비디오를 제작했어.

➡ _____

**11** 우리는 그것을 인터넷에 올렸는데, 놀랍게도 거의 5,000개의 수를 획득했어.

➡ _____

**12** 우리 비디오를 보려면 이곳을 클릭해.

➡ _____

**13** Alice: 와, 너희 등 축제는 환상적으로 보인다!

➡ _____

**14** Sunan: 우리 마을에는 물 축제가 있어.

➡ _____

**15** 나도 너희 것과 같은 비디오를 만들고 싶어.

➡ _____

**16** 안녕, 내 이름은 Jo야.

➡ _____

**17** 나는 호주 출신이야.

➡ _____

**18** 몇 주 전에, 선생님이 우리에게 케냐에 있는 학생들의 사진을 보여주셨어.

➡ _____

**19** 슬프게도, 그들은 모두 책을 들고 다니기 위해서 비닐 봉지를 사용하고 있었어.

➡ _____

**20** 우리 반은 그들에게 새로운 책가방을 보내기 위해서 기금을 모금하기로 결정했어.

➡ _____

**21** 우리는 쿠키와 음료를 팔아서 600달러를 모았어.

➡ _____

**22** 우리는 케냐의 학생들이 그들의 새 가방을 좋아하기를 바라.

➡ _____

**23** Wang: 멋지다! 분명 그들이 가방을 좋아할 거야.

➡ _____

**24** Kozo: 훌륭한 일을 했구나!

➡ _____

**25** 난 말레이시아의 Afig야.

➡ _____

**26** 우리 학교는 우리 마을을 좀 더 좋아 보이게 하기 위해서 벽화 캠페인을 시작했어.

➡ _____

**27** 그림을 잘 그리는 학생들이 모여서 학교와 공원 벽에 그림을 그렸어.

➡ _____

**28** 이 캠페인 덕분에, 우리 마을은 훨씬 멋져 보여.

➡ _____

**29** 이제 모든 사람들이 그림이 그려진 벽을 따라서 산책하는 것을 즐길 수 있어.

➡ _____

**30** Junho: 정말 멋진 생각이다!

➡ _____

※ 다음 우리말과 일치하도록 빈칸에 알맞은 말을 쓰시오.

### Conversation B

1. Karl: Jiho, _____ that _____ _____? Are you _____ _____ eat _____ _____ that?

2. Jiho: I'm _____ _____, but Bulgogi is my _____.

3. Karl: Hey! _____ _____ the campaign poster. "_____, Eat, _____!"

4. Jiho: _____ _____ _____ _____ _____?

5. Karl: _____ _____ "Think first before you eat and save the Earth."

6. Jiho: I _____ I _____ too much Bulgogi. _____ _____ it.

7. Karl: Okay. _____ _____ _____ _____.

8. Jiho: We _____ it _____. My clean plate _____ _____ _____ _____.

9. Karl: _____ _____ _____ food _____ _____ _____. I hope we _____ _____ the Earth.

1. Karl: 지호야, 너무 많지 않니? 너 그걸 다 먹을 거니?
2. 지호: 잘 모르겠어, 그렇지만 불고기는 내가 가장 좋아하는 음식이야.
3. Karl: 저기! 캠페인 포스터를 봐. "생각하라, 먹어라, 구하라!"
4. 지호: 저게 무슨 뜻이야?
5. Karl: 그것은 먹기 전에 먼저 생각하고 지구를 살리자는 뜻이야.
6. 지호: 나 불고기를 너무 많이 담아온 것 같아. 나눠 먹자.
7. Karl: 그래. 좋은 생각이야.
8. 지호: 우리 다 먹었네. 내 깨끗한 그릇을 보니 기분이 좋아.
9. Karl: 이제부터 음식을 낭비하지 말자. 나는 우리가 지구를 살리기를 바라.

### Project

1. A: _____ _____ _____ do you like?

2. B: _____ _____ _____ _____ _____ _____ _____ _____ shoes to poor children?

3. C: Good. I hope they _____ _____ _____ them.

4. D: _____ _____ a poster about the activity _____ _____ _____ _____ _____ _____ _____.

5. Sending _____ _____ _____

6. Why: To help poor _____ _____ _____ _____ _____ _____

7. How: 1. _____ shoes _____ _____.

8. 2. _____ pictures or _____ _____ _____ _____ on them.

9. 3. Send them to children _____ _____.

10. When: _____ _____

11. _____ you want _____ _____ _____ _____ for the world, _____ us!

1. A: 어떤 활동을 하고 싶니?
2. B: 가난한 아이들에게 신발을 보내는 게 어때?
3. C: 좋아. 그들이 그것들을 좋아하길 바라.
4. D: 도움을 주고 싶어 하는 사람들을 찾기 위해서 이 활동에 대한 포스터를 만들자.
5. 희망의 신발 보내기
6. 왜: 신발이 없는 가난한 아이들을 돕기 위해
7. 어떻게: 1. 집에서 신발을 가져오세요.
8. 2. 신발에 그림을 그리거나 배려의 말을 쓰세요.
9. 3. 그것들을 어려움에 처한 아이들에게 보내세요.
10. 언제: 7월 3일
11. 세상을 위해 뭔가 특별한 일을 하고 싶다면, 우리와 함께 해요!

※ 다음 우리말을 영어로 쓰시오.

### Conversation B

1. Karl: 지호야, 너무 많지 않니? 너 그걸 다 먹을 거니?
➡ _____

2. 지호: 잘 모르겠어, 그렇지만 불고기는 내가 가장 좋아하는 음식이야.
➡ _____

3. Karl: 저기! 캠페인 포스터를 봐. "생각하라, 먹어라, 구하라!"
➡ _____

4. 지호: 저게 무슨 뜻이야?
➡ _____

5. Karl: 그것은 먹기 전에 먼저 생각하고 지구를 살리자는 뜻이야.
➡ _____

6. 지호: 나 불고기를 너무 많이 담아온 것 같아. 나눠 먹자.
➡ _____

7. Karl: 그래. 좋은 생각이야.
➡ _____

8. 지호: 우리 다 먹었네. 내 깨끗한 그릇을 보니 기분이 좋아.
➡ _____

9. Karl: 이제부터 음식을 낭비하지 말자. 나는 우리가 지구를 살리기를 바라.
➡ _____

### Project

1. A: 어떤 활동을 하고 싶니?
➡ _____

2. B: 가난한 아이들에게 신발을 보내는 게 어때?
➡ _____

3. C: 좋아. 그들이 그것들을 좋아하길 바라.
➡ _____

4. D: 도움을 주고 싶어 하는 사람들을 찾기 위해서 이 활동에 대한 포스터를 만들자.
➡ _____

5. 희망의 신발 보내기
➡ _____

6. 왜: 신발이 없는 가난한 아이들을 돕기 위해
➡ _____

7. 어떻게: 1. 집에서 신발을 가져오세요.
➡ _____

8. 2. 신발에 그림을 그리거나 배려의 말을 쓰세요.
➡ _____

9. 3. 그것들을 어려움에 처한 아이들에게 보내세요.
➡ _____

10. 언제: 7월 3일
➡ _____

11. 세상을 위해 뭔가 특별한 일을 하고 싶다면, 우리와 함께 해요!
➡ _____

※ 다음 영어를 우리말로 쓰시오.

| | | | |
|---|---|---|---|
| 01 | topic | 22 | female |
| 02 | during | 23 | inventor |
| 03 | male | 24 | enough |
| 04 | toward | 25 | average |
| 05 | again | 26 | guess |
| 06 | gravity | 27 | false |
| 07 | twice | 28 | completely |
| 08 | grow | 29 | blood |
| 09 | bone | 30 | adult |
| 10 | weigh | 31 | bite |
| 11 | Mars | 32 | whale |
| 12 | item | 33 | Venus |
| 13 | lightning | 34 | same |
| 14 | metal | 35 | be full of |
| 15 | fewer | 36 | in fact |
| 16 | produce | 37 | due to |
| 17 | rest | 38 | over and over |
| 18 | mosquito | 39 | such as |
| 19 | tongue | 40 | up to |
| 20 | weaken | 41 | find out |
| 21 | expand | 42 | go away |
| | | 43 | a few |

※ 다음 우리말을 영어로 쓰시오.

| | | | |
|---|---|---|---|
| 01 완전히 | | 22 두 번, 두 배 | |
| 02 고래 | | 23 모기 | |
| 03 피 | | 24 항목, 물품 | |
| 04 거짓의 | | 25 화제, 주제 | |
| 05 여성, 암컷 | | 26 화성 | |
| 06 팽창하다 | | 27 쉬다, 휴식하다 | |
| 07 금성 | | 28 (자식·새끼를) 낳다 | |
| 08 같은, 똑같은 | | 29 혀 | |
| 09 부딪치다, 충돌하다 | | 30 남성, 수컷 | |
| 10 추측하다 | | 31 뼈 | |
| 11 열, 열기 | | 32 금속 | |
| 12 (새·곤충 등이) 알을 낳다 | | 33 (위치·방향) ~쪽으로 | |
| 13 보통, 평균 | | 34 ~ 동안, ~ 중에 | |
| 14 발명가 | | 35 사실상, 실제로 | |
| 15 다음의; 그 다음에 | | 36 평균적으로 | |
| 16 충분한 | | 37 알아보다, 찾아보다 | |
| 17 성인, 어른 | | 38 ~로 가득 차다 | |
| 18 물다 | | 39 ~와 같은 | |
| 19 약화시키다, 약화되다 | | 40 ~ 때문에 | |
| 20 중력 | | 41 사라지다 | |
| 21 번개, 벼락 | | 42 여러 번, 몇 번이고 | |
| | | 43 ~와 이어지다 | |

※ 다음 영영풀이에 알맞은 단어를 <보기>에서 골라 쓴 후, 우리말 뜻을 쓰시오.

1 _____ : a red fluid in living things: _____

2 _____ : not real, because it is not true: _____

3 _____ : the gender which does not give birth: _____

4 _____ : to seize or grasp something with teeth: _____

5 _____ : a hard substance such as lead, iron, gold, etc.: _____

6 _____ : to find how heavy a person or thing is: _____

7 _____ : to increase in size, number, or importance: _____

8 _____ : a small flying insect which bites and sucks blood: _____

9 _____ : the usual amount, extent, quality, number, etc.: _____

10 _____ : a white piece of tissue providing structural support for the body:
_____

11 _____ : a person who creates something that does not exist: _____

12 _____ : to a complete degree or to the full or entire extent: _____

13 _____ : the force that a planet pulls things towards the center of it: _____

14 _____ : the gender which has the ability to give birth to children: _____

15 _____ : to come or bring into heavy contact with someone or something:
_____

16 _____ : the soft organ in the mouth used in tasting, swallowing, etc. and by
people in speaking: _____

보기

| strike | metal | false | inventor |
| expand | female | mosquito | tongue |
| bone | completely | gravity | male |
| blood | weigh | bite | average |

※ 다음 우리말과 일치하도록 빈칸에 알맞은 것을 골라 쓰시오.

**1** _____ _____ Are _____ Us
A. Around     B. Facts     C. Interesting

**2** _____ _____ " _____ Dr. Lawrence"!
A. to     B. ask     C. welcome

**3** The world is _____ _____ interesting _____ .
A. things     B. full     C. of

**4** _____ this quiz and find _____ how _____ you know about them.
A. much     B. out     C. take

**5** _____ you _____ ?
A. ready     B. are

**6** Quiz: The Eiffel Tower _____ _____ _____ the summer.
A. get     B. during     C. taller

**7** Babies have _____ bones _____ adults.
A. than     B. fewer

**8** _____ female mosquitoes _____ people.
A. bite     B. only

**9** Lightning _____ _____ the same place _____ .
A. never     B. twice     C. strikes

**10** The elephant is _____ _____ animal _____ the Earth.
A. on     B. biggest     C. the

**11** _____ is _____ gravity _____ space.
A. no     B. in     C. there

**12** Metal _____ _____ heat.
A. in     B. expands

**13** _____ _____ summer heat, the metal of the Eiffel Tower _____ .
A. expands     B. to     C. due

**14** In summer, the Eiffel tower _____ 15cm _____ _____ in winter.
A. taller     B. gets     C. than

**15** _____ have 206 bones, _____ babies have _____ 300 bones.
A. about     B. but     C. adults

**16** _____ time, some of the babies' bones _____ _____ , so adults have _____ bones than babies.
A. fewer     B. with     C. together     D. join

---

**1** 흥미로운 사실들은 우리 주위에 있다

**2** "Lawrence 박사에게 물어 보세요"에 오신 것을 환영합니다!

**3** 세상은 흥미로운 것들로 가득 차 있습니다.

**4** 퀴즈를 풀어보고 그것들에 대해 얼마나 아는지 알아보세요.

**5** 준비 됐나요?

**6** 퀴즈: 에펠 타워는 여름에 키가 더 커진다.

**7** 아기들은 어른보다 더 적은 수의 뼈를 가지고 있다.

**8** 암컷 모기만이 사람을 문다.

**9** 번개는 결코 같은 곳을 내리치지 않는다.

**10** 코끼리는 지구에서 가장 큰 동물이다.

**11** 우주에는 중력이 없다.

**12** 금속은 열에 팽창한다.

**13** 여름의 열기 때문에, 에펠 타워의 금속은 팽창한다.

**14** 여름에 에펠 타워는 겨울보다 15센티미터 정도 더 커진다.

**15** 어른은 206개의 뼈를 가지고 있고, 아기는 대략 300개의 뼈를 가지고 있다.

**16** 시간이 흐르면서, 아기의 몇몇 뼈들은 붙는다. 그래서 어른들은 아기보다 더 적은 수의 뼈를 가지고 있다.

**17** _____ _____ mosquitoes will _____ you.
A. bite          B. female          C. only

**18** They _____ blood _____ _____ eggs.
A. produce          B. to          C. need

**19** After a female mosquito gets _____ _____, she'll _____ for a few days and _____ her eggs.
A. blood          B. lay          C. enough          D. rest

**20** Lightning _____ _____ the _____ place over and _____ again.
A. same          B. over          C. strike          D. can

**21** The Empire State Building _____ hit _____ lightning 23 times a year _____ _____.
A. by          B. gets          C. average          D. on

**22** _____ _____ animal _____ the Earth is the blue _____.
A. whale          B. biggest          C. the          D. on

**23** It can _____ _____ to 180 tons and _____ up to 30 meters _____.
A. long          B. grow          C. weigh          D. up

**24** Its tongue _____ can weigh as _____ _____ an average African elephant.
A. alone          B. as          C. much

**25** _____ fact, there is _____ everywhere in _____.
A. in          B. space          C. gravity

**26** As you get _____ from the Earth, the gravity of the Earth _____, but it never _____ _____ completely.
A. away          B. weakens          C. farther          D. goes

**27** When you _____ closer to another planet, _____ _____ Mars or Venus, its gravity becomes stronger than _____ of the Earth.
A. as          B. that          C. such          D. get

**28** _____ of _____ quiz items is the _____ interesting to you?
A. most          B. these          C. which

**29** _____ will be _____ quiz _____.
A. another          B. there          C. soon

**30** _____ _____ the next topic will _____.
A. be          B. guess          C. what

**31** _____ you _____ month.
A. next          B. see

**17** 오직 암컷 모기만이 당신을 물 것이다.

**18** 그들은 알을 생산하기 위해서 피가 필요하다.

**19** 암컷 모기는 충분히 흡혈을 한 뒤, 며칠 동안 쉬고 알을 낳는다.

**20** 번개는 같은 곳을 반복해서 칠 수 있다.

**21** 엠파이어스테이트 빌딩은 한 해 평균 스물세 번 번개를 맞는다.

**22** 지구상에서 가장 큰 동물은 흰 긴수염고래이다.

**23** 그것은 무게가 180톤까지 나갈 수 있으며 길이는 30미터까지 자랄 수 있다.

**24** 이 고래의 혀의 무게만 해도 아프리카 코끼리의 평균 무게만큼 무겁다.

**25** 사실, 중력은 우주의 어디에나 있다.

**26** 지구에서 멀어 질수록 지구의 중력은 약해지지만, 결코 그것이 완전히 사라지는 것은 아니다.

**27** 당신이 화성이나 금성 같은 다른 행성에 더 가까워진다면, 그들의 중력은 지구의 그것보다 더 강해진다.

**28** 이 퀴즈들 중 어떤 퀴즈가 가장 흥미로웠나요?

**29** 곧 또 다른 퀴즈가 있을 것입니다.

**30** 다음 주제는 무엇일지 맞춰보세요.

**31** 다음 달에 만나요.

※ 다음 우리말과 일치하도록 빈칸에 알맞은 말을 쓰시오.

**1** _____ _____ Are _____ Us

**2** _____ _____ " _____ Dr. Lawrence"!

**3** The world _____ _____ _____ interesting _____ .

**4** _____ this quiz and _____ _____ _____ _____ you know about them.

**5** _____ you _____ ?

**6** _____

**7** The Eiffel Tower _____ _____ _____ the summer.

**8** Babies have _____ _____ _____ _____ .

**9** _____ _____ mosquitoes _____ people.

**10** Lightning _____ _____ the _____ _____ _____ .

**11** The elephant is _____ _____ animal _____ the Earth.

**12** _____ is _____ _____ _____ space.

**13** Metal _____ _____ _____ .

**14** _____ _____ _____ _____ , the metal of the Eiffel Tower _____ .

**15** In summer, the Eiffel tower _____ 15cm _____ _____ _____ _____ .

**16** _____ have 206 _____ , _____ _____ have _____ 300 bones.

**17** _____ _____ , some of the babies' bones _____ , so adults have _____ _____ _____ _____ .

**1** 흥미로운 사실들은 우리 주위에 있다

**2** "Lawrence 박사에게 물어 보세요"에 오신 것을 환영합니다!

**3** 세상은 흥미로운 것들로 가득 차 있습니다.

**4** 퀴즈를 풀어보고 그것들에 대해 얼마나 아는지 알아보세요.

**5** 준비 됐나요?

**6** 퀴즈

**7** 에펠 타워는 여름에 키가 더 커진다.

**8** 아기들은 어른보다 더 적은 수의 뼈를 가지고 있다.

**9** 암컷 모기만이 사람을 문다.

**10** 번개는 결코 같은 곳을 내리치지 않는다.

**11** 코끼리는 지구에서 가장 큰 동물이다.

**12** 우주에는 중력이 없다.

**13** 금속은 열에 팽창한다.

**14** 여름의 열기 때문에, 에펠 타워의 금속은 팽창한다.

**15** 여름에 에펠 타워는 겨울보다 15센티미터 정도 더 커진다.

**16** 어른은 206개의 뼈를 가지고 있고, 아기는 대략 300개의 뼈를 가지고 있다.

**17** 시간이 흐르면서, 아기의 몇몇 뼈들은 붙는다. 그래서 어른들은 아기보다 더 적은 수의 뼈를 가지고 있다.

**18** _____ _____ mosquitoes _____ _____ you.

**19** They _____ blood _____ _____ _____.

**20** After a female mosquito gets _____ _____, she'll _____ _____ _____ _____ and _____ her eggs.

**21** Lightning _____ _____ the _____ place _____ _____.

**22** The Empire State Building _____ hit _____ lightning 23 _____ _____.

**23** _____ _____ animal _____ the Earth is the blue _____.

**24** It _____ _____ _____ _____ 180 tons and _____ _____ _____ 30 meters _____.

**25** Its tongue _____ can _____ _____ _____ _____ an average African elephant.

**26** _____ _____, there is _____ everywhere in _____.

**27** As you get _____ from the Earth, the gravity of the Earth _____, but it _____ _____ _____ _____.

**28** When you _____ closer to another planet, _____ _____ Mars or Venus, its gravity _____ _____ _____ _____ of the Earth.

**29** _____ of _____ quiz items is _____ _____ _____ to you?

**30** _____ will _____ quiz _____.

**31** _____ _____ the next topic _____ _____.

**32** _____ you _____ _____.

**18** 오직 암컷 모기만이 당신을 물 것이다.

**19** 그들은 알을 생산하기 위해서 피가 필요하다.

**20** 암컷 모기는 충분히 흡혈을 한 뒤, 며칠 동안 쉬고 알을 낳는다.

**21** 번개는 같은 곳을 반복해서 칠 수 있다.

**22** 엠파이어스테이트 빌딩은 한 해 평균 스물세 번 번개를 맞는다.

**23** 지구상에서 가장 큰 동물은 흰 긴수염고래이다.

**24** 그것은 무게가 180톤까지 나갈 수 있으며 길이는 30미터까지 자랄 수 있다.

**25** 이 고래의 혀의 무게만 해도 아프리카 코끼리의 평균 무게만큼 무겁다.

**26** 사실, 중력은 우주의 어디에나 있다.

**27** 지구에서 멀어 질수록 지구의 중력은 약해지지만, 결코 그것이 완전히 사라지는 것은 아니다.

**28** 당신이 화성이나 금성 같은 다른 행성에 더 가까워진다면, 그들의 중력은 지구의 그것보다 더 강해진다.

**29** 이 퀴즈들 중 어떤 퀴즈가 가장 흥미로웠나요?

**30** 곧 또 다른 퀴즈가 있을 것입니다.

**31** 다음 주제는 무엇일지 맞춰보세요.

**32** 다음 달에 만나요.

Step3

※ 다음 문장을 우리말로 쓰시오.

**1** ▶ Interesting Facts Are Around Us

➡ _____

**2** ▶ Welcome to "Ask Dr. Lawrence"!

➡ _____

**3** ▶ The world is full of interesting things.

➡ _____

**4** ▶ Take this quiz and find out how much you know about them.

➡ _____

**5** ▶ Are you ready?

➡ _____

**6** ▶ Quiz

➡ _____

**7** ▶ The Eiffel Tower gets taller during the summer.

➡ _____

**8** ▶ Babies have fewer bones than adults.

➡ _____

**9** ▶ Only female mosquitoes bite people.

➡ _____

**10** ▶ Lightning never strikes the same place twice.

➡ _____

**11** ▶ The elephant is the biggest animal on the Earth.

➡ _____

**12** ▶ There is no gravity in space.

➡ _____

**13** ▶ Metal expands in heat.

➡ _____

**14** ▶ Due to summer heat, the metal of the Eiffel Tower expands.

➡ _____

**15** ▶ In summer, the Eiffel tower gets 15cm taller than in winter.

➡ _____

**16** ▶ Adults have 206 bones, but babies have about 300 bones.

➡ _____

**17** ▶ With time, some of the babies' bones join together, so adults have fewer bones than babies.

➡ _____

**18** ▶ Only female mosquitoes will bite you.

➡ _____

**19** ▶ They need blood to produce eggs.

➡ _____

**20** ▶ After a female mosquito gets enough blood, she'll rest for a few days and lay her eggs.

➡ _____

**21** ▶ Lightning can strike the same place over and over again.

➡ _____

**22** ▶ The Empire State Building gets hit by lightning 23 times a year on average.

➡ _____

**23** ▶ The biggest animal on the Earth is the blue whale.

➡ _____

**24** ▶ It can weigh up to 180 tons and grow up to 30 meters long.!

➡ _____

**25** ▶ Its tongue alone can weigh as much as an average African elephant.

➡ _____

**26** ▶ In fact, there is gravity everywhere in space.

➡ _____

**27** ▶ As you get farther from the Earth, the gravity of the Earth weakens, but it never goes away completely.

➡ _____

**28** ▶ When you get closer to another planet, such as Mars or Venus, its gravity becomes stronger than that of the Earth.

➡ _____

**29** ▶ Which of these quiz items is the most interesting to you?

➡ _____

**30** ▶ There will be another quiz soon.

➡ _____

**31** ▶ Guess what the next topic will be.

➡ _____

**32** ▶ See you next month.

➡ _____

※ 다음 괄호 안의 단어들을 우리말에 맞도록 바르게 배열하시오.

**1** (Facts / Interesting / Us / Around / Are)
➡ _____

**2** (to / welcome / Lawrence"! / Dr. / "Ask)
➡ _____

**3** (world / the / full / is / of / things. / interesting)
➡ _____

**4** (this / take / quiz / and / out / find / much / how / know / you / them. / about)
➡ _____

**5** (ready? / you / are)
➡ _____

**6** (quiz: / Eiffel / The / Tower / taller / gets / the / during / summer.)
➡ _____

**7** (have / babies / bones / fewer / adults. / than)
➡ _____

**8** (female / only / mosquitoes / people. / bite)
➡ _____

**9** (never / lightening / the / strikes / twice. / place / same)
➡ _____

**10** (elephant / the / is / the / animal / biggest / Earth. / the / on)
➡ _____

**11** (no / is / there / gravity / space. / in)
➡ _____

**12** (expands / heat. / in / metal)
➡ _____

**13** (to / due / summer / heat, / metal / the / of / Eiffel / expands. / Tower)
➡ _____

**14** (summer, / in / Eiffel / the / gets / tower / 15cm / in / winter. / than / taller)
➡ _____

**15** (have / adults / bones, / 206 / babies / but / about / have / bones. / 300)
➡ _____

**16** (time, / with / of / some / babies' / the / join / bones / together, / adults / so / fewer / have / bones / babies. / than)
➡ _____

**1** 흥미로운 사실들은 우리 주위에 있다

**2** "Lawrence 박사에게 물어 보세요"에 오신 것을 환영합니다!

**3** 세상은 흥미로운 것들로 가득 차 있습니다.

**4** 퀴즈를 풀어보고 그것들에 대해 얼마나 아는지 알아보세요.

**5** 준비 됐나요?

**6** 퀴즈: 에펠 타워는 여름에 키가 더 커진다.

**7** 아기들은 어른보다 더 적은 수의 뼈를 가지고 있다.

**8** 암컷 모기만이 사람을 문다.

**9** 번개는 결코 같은 곳을 내리치지 않는다.

**10** 코끼리는 지구에서 가장 큰 동물이다.

**11** 우주에는 중력이 없다.

**12** 금속은 열에 팽창한다.

**13** 여름의 열기 때문에, 에펠 타워의 금속은 팽창한다.

**14** 여름에 에펠 타워는 겨울보다 15센티미터 정도 더 커진다.

**15** 어른은 206개의 뼈를 가지고 있고, 아기는 대략 300개의 뼈를 가지고 있다.

**16** 시간이 흐르면서, 아기의 몇몇 뼈들은 붙는다. 그래서 어른들은 아기보다 더 적은 수의 뼈를 가지고 있다.

**17** (female / only / mosquitoes / you. / bite / will)
➡ _____

**18** (need / they / to / blood / eggs. / produce)
➡ _____

**19** (a / after / mosquito / female / enough / gets / blood, / rest / she'll / for / a / days / few / and / eggs. / her / lay)
➡ _____
_____

**20** (can / lightning / strike / same / the / over / place / and / again. / over)
➡ _____

**21** (Empire / the / Building / State / hit / gets / lightning / by / times / 23 / average. / on / year / a)
➡ _____

**22** (biggest / the / animal / the / Earth / on / the / is / whale. / blue)
➡ _____

**23** (can / it / up / weigh / 180 / to / tons / grow / and / to / up / long. / meters / 30)
➡ _____

**24** (tongue / its / can / alone / as / weigh / much / as / an / African / average / elephant.)
➡ _____

**25** (fact, / in / is / there / everywhere / gravity / space. / in)
➡ _____

**26** (you / as / farther / get / the / from / Earth, / gravity / the / of / Earth / the / weakens, / it / but / goes / never / completely. / away)
➡ _____
_____

**27** (you / when / closer / get / another / to / planet, / as / such / Venus, / or / Mars / gravity / its / stronger / becomes / than / of / that / Earth. / the)
➡ _____
_____

**28** (of / these / which / items / quiz / is / most / the / interesting / you? / to)
➡ _____

**29** (will / there / another / be / soon. / quiz / is / most / the / interesting / you? / to)
➡ _____

**30** (what / guess / next / the / be. / will / topic)
➡ _____

**31** (you / see / month. / next)
➡ _____

**17** 오직 암컷 모기만이 당신을 물 것이다.

**18** 그들은 알을 생산하기 위해서 피가 필요하다.

**19** 암컷 모기는 충분히 흡혈을 한 뒤, 며칠 동안 쉬고 알을 낳는다.

**20** 번개는 같은 곳을 반복해서 칠 수 있다.

**21** 엠파이어스테이트 빌딩은 한 해 평균 스물세 번 번개를 맞는다.

**22** 지구상에서 가장 큰 동물은 흰 긴수염고래이다.

**23** 그것은 무게가 180톤까지 나갈 수 있으며 길이는 30미터까지 자 랄 수 있다.

**24** 이 고래의 혀의 무게만 해도 아 프리카 코끼리의 평균 무게만큼 무겁다.

**25** 사실, 중력은 우주의 어디에나 있다.

**26** 지구에서 멀어 질수록 지구의 중력은 약해지지만, 결코 그것이 완전히 사라지는 것은 아니다.

**27** 당신이 화성이나 금성 같은 다 른 행성에 더 가까워진다면, 그 들의 중력은 지구의 그것보다 더 강해진다.

**28** 이 퀴즈들 중 어떤 퀴즈가 가장 흥미로웠나요?

**29** 곧 또 다른 퀴즈가 있을 것입니다.

**30** 다음 주제는 무엇일지 맞춰보세요.

**31** 다음 달에 만나요.

※ 다음 우리말을 영어로 쓰시오.

**1** 흥미로운 사실들은 우리 주위에 있다

➡ _____

**2** "Lawrence 박사에게 물어 보세요"에 오신 것을 환영합니다!

➡ _____

**3** 세상은 흥미로운 것들로 가득 차 있습니다.

➡ _____

**4** 퀴즈를 풀어보고 그것들에 대해 얼마나 아는지 알아보세요.

➡ _____

**5** 준비 됐나요?

➡ _____

**6** 퀴즈

➡ _____

**7** 에펠 타워는 여름에 키가 더 커진다.

➡ _____

**8** 아기들은 어른보다 더 적은 수의 뼈를 가지고 있다.

➡ _____

**9** 암컷 모기만이 사람을 문다.

➡ _____

**10** 번개는 결코 같은 곳을 내리치지 않는다.

➡ _____

**11** 코끼리는 지구에서 가장 큰 동물이다.

➡ _____

**12** 우주에는 중력이 없다.

➡ _____

**13** 금속은 열에 팽창한다.

➡ _____

**14** 여름의 열기 때문에, 에펠 타워의 금속은 팽창한다.

➡ _____

**15** 여름에 에펠 타워는 겨울보다 15센티미터 정도 더 커진다.

➡ _____

**16** 어른은 206개의 뼈를 가지고 있고, 아기는 대략 300개의 뼈를 가지고 있다.

➡ _____

**17** 시간이 흐르면서, 아기의 몇몇 뼈들은 붙는다. 그래서 어른들은 아기보다 더 적은 수의 뼈를 가지고 있다.

➡ _____

**18** 오직 암컷 모기만이 당신을 물 것이다.

➡ _____

**19** 그들은 알을 생산하기 위해서 피가 필요하다.

➡ _____

**20** 암컷 모기는 충분히 흡혈을 한 뒤, 며칠 동안 쉬고 알을 낳는다.

➡ _____

**21** 번개는 같은 곳을 반복해서 칠 수 있다.

➡ _____

**22** 엠파이어스테이트 빌딩은 한 해 평균 스물세 번 번개를 맞는다.

➡ _____

**23** 지구상에서 가장 큰 동물은 흰긴수염고래이다.

➡ _____

**24** 이것은 무게가 180톤까지 나갈 수 있으며 길이는 30미터 까지 자랄 수 있다.

➡ _____

**25** 이 고래의 혀의 무게만 해도 아프리카 코끼리의 평균 무게만큼 무겁다.

➡ _____

**26** 사실, 중력은 우주의 어디에나 있다.

➡ _____

**27** 지구에서 멀어 질수록 지구의 중력은 약해지지만, 결코 그것이 완전히 사라지는 것은 아니다.

➡ _____
_____

**28** 당신이 화성이나 금성 같은 다른 행성에 더 가까워진다면, 그들의 중력은 지구의 그것보다 더 강해진다.

➡ _____
_____

**29** 이 퀴즈들 중 어떤 퀴즈가 가장 흥미로웠나요?

➡ _____

**30** 곧 또 다른 퀴즈가 있을 것입니다.

➡ _____

**31** 다음 주제는 무엇일지 맞춰보세요.

➡ _____

**32** 다음 달에 만나요.

➡ _____

※ 다음 영어를 우리말로 쓰시오.

| | | | |
|---|---|---|---|
| 01 | tourist | | |
| 02 | care | | |
| 03 | abroad | | |
| 04 | wave | | |
| 05 | excuse | | |
| 06 | tour | | |
| 07 | traditional | | |
| 08 | experience | | |
| 09 | historic | | |
| 10 | column | | |
| 11 | island | | |
| 12 | roll | | |
| 13 | capital | | |
| 14 | view | | |
| 15 | cheer | | |
| 16 | work | | |
| 17 | language | | |
| 18 | unique | | |
| 19 | match | | |
| 20 | shine | | |
| 21 | careful | | |

| | |
|---|---|
| 22 | prefer |
| 23 | helpful |
| 24 | stadium |
| 25 | movement |
| 26 | ceiling |
| 27 | slide |
| 28 | purple |
| 29 | Vietnamese |
| 30 | design |
| 31 | near |
| 32 | theater |
| 33 | dish |
| 34 | lizard |
| 35 | be full of |
| 36 | across from |
| 37 | be famous for |
| 38 | try on |
| 39 | be known for |
| 40 | put off |
| 41 | on foot |
| 42 | cheer for |
| 43 | far from |

※ 다음 우리말을 영어로 쓰시오.

01 빛나다

02 역사적인

03 경험; 경험하다

04 섬

05 전통적인

06 구르다, 굴리다

07 돌봄, 보살핌

08 미끄러지다, 활주하다

09 근처에

10 도움이 되는

11 ~을 용서하다

12 보라색

13 여행객

14 조심하는, 주의 깊은

15 흔들다; 파도

16 여행, 관광하다

17 전망, 경치

18 환호하다; 환호

19 음식, 접시

20 경기, 시합

21 수도

22 설계하다

23 동작

24 천장

25 도마뱀

26 기둥

27 선호하다

28 일하다; 작품

29 언어

30 외국으로(에서)

31 독특한

32 극장

33 정거장; 멈추다

34 베트남어; 베트남의

35 ~의 맞은편에

36 ~으로 가득 차다

37 ~의 위에, ~의 꼭대기에

38 ~을 응원하다

39 (시간, 날짜를) 미루다

40 ~로부터 멀리

41 ~로 알려져 있다

42 입어 보다

43 ~로 유명하다

※ 다음 영영풀이에 알맞은 단어를 <보기>에서 골라 쓴 후, 우리말 뜻을 쓰시오.

1 _____ : to produce bright light: _____

2 _____ : in or to a foreign country: _____

3 _____ : to move along smoothly: _____

4 _____ : the upper inside surface of a room: _____

5 _____ : a mixture of blue and red color: _____

6 _____ : the main city of a country where its government is: _____

7 _____ : a reptile that has a rough skin and a long tail: _____

8 _____ : relating to the language, people or culture of Spain: _____

9 _____ : to give a shout out of pleasure, praise, or support: _____

10 _____ : relating to the language, people or culture of Vietnam: _____

11 _____ : a building with a big screen or stage where many people watch movies
      or plays: _____

12 _____ : an outlook onto, or picture of a scene: _____

13 _____ : a spicy Indian food with meat and vegetables in sauce: _____

14 _____ : to like something or someone better than another: _____

15 _____ : a journey for pleasure during which various places of interest are visited:
      _____

16 _____ : to forgive someone for something bad that they have done, especially
      something that is not very serious: _____

| 보기 | | | |
|---|---|---|---|
| theater | abroad | shine | prefer |
| view | cheer | tour | purple |
| curry | lizard | capital | Vietnamese |
| Spanish | ceiling | slide | excuse |

※ 다음 우리말과 일치하도록 빈칸에 알맞은 말을 쓰시오.

### Listen & Speak 1 A

1. **B:** _____ me. _____ the Picasso Museum _____ here?

   **G:** Yes. It's not _____ _____ here.

   **B:** _____ _____ _____ I _____ _____?

   **G:** _____ _____ one block and _____ _____. It's _____
   _____ _____.

2. **B:** Sally, I _____ _____ _____ _____ some candies for Halloween.
   _____ _____ I _____ them?

   **G:** You can _____ _____ _____ _____ Wendy's Candy Shop.

   **B:** _____ _____ _____ _____?

   **G:** _____ _____ two _____ and turn right. It's _____
   _____ _____ _____.

### Listen & Speak 1 B

1. **A:** _____ _____. _____ _____ _____ the park?

   **B:** _____ _____ _____ _____ and turn left. It's _____
   _____ _____.

2. **A:** Excuse me. _____ _____ the school?

   **B:** Go _____ _____ _____ and turn left. _____ _____
   your right. _____ _____ _____ the restaurant.

### Listen & Talk 2 A

1. **B:** _____ really hot here in Thailand. _____ _____ to the
   night market and _____ some _____ _____ _____.

   **G:** Sounds _____. _____ do we _____ _____?

   **B:** We can go _____ _____ _____ _____ _____.
   _____ _____ _____ _____?

   **G:** I _____ the bus.

2. **G:** _____ this long dress _____?

   **M:** It is an Ao dai, a _____ of _____ _____ from Vietnam.

   **G:** Can I _____ _____ _____?

   **M:** Sure. _____ _____ _____ _____, the purple one or the
   _____ _____?

   **G:** The _____ _____, please.

1. **B:** 실례할게. 이 근처에 피카소 박물관이 있니?
   **G:** 응, 여기서 멀지 않아.
   **B:** 그곳에 어떻게 가니?
   **G:** 한 블록 직진한 후 좌회전해. 오른편에 있어.

2. **B:** Sally야, 나는 할로윈에 필요한 사탕을 사야 해. 그것들을 어디서 살 수 있니?
   **G:** 넌 그것들을 Wendy's 사탕 가게에서 살 수 있어.
   **B:** 그곳은 어디에 있니?
   **G:** 두 블록 직진한 후 우회전해. 도서관 맞은편에 있어.

1. **A:** 실례합니다. 공원이 어디에 있나요?
   **B:** 두 블록 직진한 후 좌회전하세요. 오른편에 있어요.

2. **A:** 실례합니다. 학교가 어디에 있나요?
   **B:** 한 블록 직진한 후 좌회전하세요. 오른편에 있어요. 식당 맞은편이에요.

1. **B:** 태국은 정말 더워. 야시장에 가서 신선한 과일 주스를 마시자.
   **G:** 좋아. 우리는 그곳에 어떻게 가지?
   **B:** 우리는 걸어가거나 버스를 탈 수 있어. 어떤 것을 선호하니?
   **G:** 나는 버스를 선호해.

2. **G:** 이 긴 드레스를 뭐라고 부르나요?
   **M:** 그것은 베트남 전통 의상의 한 종류인 아오자이야.
   **G:** 제가 한 번 입어볼 수 있나요?
   **M:** 물론이지. 너는 보라색과 노란색 중 어떤 것을 선호하니?
   **G:** 보라색이요.

**Listen & Talk 2 B**

1. A: _____ _____ _____ _____, hamburgers or spaghetti?

   B: I _____ _____.

2. A: _____ _____ _____ _____, curry _____ paella?

   B: I _____ _____.

**Conversation A**

M: _____ _____ London City Tour. Today, _____ _____ famous places in London. Can you _____ the London Eye? It's _____ _____ _____. It's a Ferris wheel _____ the River Thames. The _____ _____ the London Eye is _____. Many people visit it _____ _____.

**Conversation B**

Staff: _____ _____ I _____ you?

Hana's mom: We _____ _____ a good _____ London.

Hana: Where is the _____ _____ _____ _____ _____ _____?

Staff: We have two _____ _____. The London Eye is a Ferris wheel and the Sky Garden is a glass garden _____ _____ _____ a tall building. _____ _____ you _____?

Hana's mom: Hmm... I _____ the London Eye.

Hana: _____, _____.

Staff: Good choice. You can _____ there _____ _____.

Hana's mom: _____ is the _____ _____?

Staff: Go _____ _____ _____ and _____ _____. It's _____ _____ _____. Have a good trip!

Hana: Wow, I _____ _____ all of London. Look! _____ _____ a big clock.

Hana's mom: _____ _____ that's Big Ben. _____ _____ _____ _____ and _____ it _____?

Hana: That _____ great.

※ 다음 우리말에 맞도록 대화를 영어로 쓰시오.

### Listen & Speak 1 A

1. B: _____

   G: _____

   B: _____

   G: _____

2. B: _____

   G: _____

   B: _____

   G: _____

### Listen & Speak 1 B

1. A: _____

   B: _____

2. A: _____

   B: _____

### Listen & Talk 2 A

1. B: _____

   _____

   G: _____

   B: _____

   G: _____

2. G: _____

   M: _____

   G: _____

   M: _____

   G: _____

해석

1. B: 실례할게. 이 근처에 피카소 박물관이 있니?
   G: 응, 여기서 멀지 않아.
   B: 그곳에 어떻게 가니?
   G: 한 블록 직진한 후 좌회전해. 오른편에 있어.

2. B: Sally야, 나는 할로윈에 필요한 사탕을 사야 해. 그것들을 어디서 살 수 있니?
   G: 넌 그것들을 Wendy's 사탕 가게에서 살 수 있어.
   B: 그곳은 어디에 있니?
   G: 두 블록 직진한 후 우회전해. 도서관 맞은편에 있어.

1. A: 실례합니다. 공원이 어디에 있나요?
   B: 두 블록 직진한 후 좌회전하세요. 오른편에 있어요.

2. A: 실례합니다. 학교가 어디에 있나요?
   B: 한 블록 직진한 후 좌회전하세요. 오른편에 있어요. 식당 맞은편이에요.

1. B: 태국은 정말 더워. 야시장에 가서 신선한 과일 주스를 마시자.
   G: 좋아. 우리는 그곳에 어떻게 가지?
   B: 우리는 걸어가거나 버스를 탈 수 있어. 어떤 것을 선호하니?
   G: 나는 버스를 선호해.

2. G: 이 긴 드레스를 뭐라고 부르나요?
   M: 그것은 베트남 전통 의상의 한 종류인 아오자이야.
   G: 제가 한 번 입어볼 수 있나요?
   M: 물론이지. 너는 보라색과 노란색 중 어떤 것을 선호하니?
   G: 보라색이요.

## Listen & Talk 2 B

1. A: _____

   B: _____

2. A: _____

   B: _____

## Conversation A

M: _____

_____

_____

_____

## Conversation B

Staff: _____

Hana's mom: _____

Hana: _____

Staff: _____

_____

Hana's mom: _____

Hana: _____

Staff: _____

Hana's mom: _____

Staff: _____

Hana: _____

Hana's mom: _____

Hana: _____

1. A: 햄버거와 스파게티 중 어느 것을 선호하니?
   B: 나는 햄버거를 선호해.

2. A: 카레와 파에야 중 어느 것을 선호하니?
   B: 나는 파에야를 선호해.

M: 런던 시티 투어에 오신 걸 환영합니다. 오늘 우리는 런던에서 유명한 장소들을 방문할 거예요. 런던 아이가 보이죠? 오른편에 있어요. 그것은 템스강 근처에 있는 대관람차예요. 런던 아이에서의 전망은 놀라워요. 매년 많은 사람들이 그곳을 방문해요.

직원: 무엇을 도와드릴까요?
엄마: 우리는 런던의 멋진 경치를 즐기고 싶어요.
하나: 가기에 가장 좋은 장소는 어디인가요?
직원: 두 곳이 있습니다. 런던 아이는 대관람차이고 스카이 가든은 높은 건물 꼭대기에 있는 유리 정원이에요. 어느 것을 선호하시나요?
엄마: 흠... 저는 런던 아이가 좋아요.
하나: 저도요.
직원: 좋은 선택이에요. 그곳에 버스로 갈 수 있답니다.
엄마: 가장 가까운 버스 정거장은 어디 있나요?
직원: 여기서 한 블록 직진한 후 오른쪽으로 도세요. 왼편에 있어요. 좋은 여행하세요!
하나: 와, 런던 전체를 다 볼 수 있어요. 보세요! 커다란 시계가 있어요.
엄마: 내 생각에 저것은 빅벤 같아. 우리 나중에 가서 그곳을 방문해 볼래?
하나: 좋아요.

※ 다음 우리말과 일치하도록 빈칸에 알맞은 것을 골라 쓰시오.

**1** My _____ _____ in Spain – _____ Park Jinwoo
   A. Days          B. by          C. happy

**2** My family _____ _____ Spain _____ summer.
   A. to          B. traveled          C. this

**3** Spain is _____ _____ lots _____ tourists.
   A. of          B. by          C. loved

**4** We _____ many _____ _____.
   A. places          B. visited          C. interesting

**5** _____ _____ started _____ Madrid.
   A. in          B. trip          C. our

**6** Madrid is the _____ and is _____ _____ soccer.
   A. for          B. capital          C. famous

**7** We _____ to a stadium to _____ a soccer _____.
   A. match          B. watch          C. went

**8** My sister and I were _____ because we could watch some
   of the _____ _____ _____ soccer player.
   A. most          B. excited          C. famous          D. world's

**9** The stadium was _____ _____ soccer _____.
   A. of          B. full          C. fans

**10** As we watched the match, we cheered _____ _____ songs,
   _____ our hands, and _____ with the other fans.
   A. waving          B. singing          C. shouting          D. by

**11** _____ we _____ Madrid, we _____ to Seville.
   A. went          B. after          C. toured

**12** _____ we _____ _____ the city, we saw many historic
   buildings.
   A. walked          B. while          C. around

**13** We _____ a flamenco _____ and _____ a flamenco
   dance.
   A. museum          B. watched          C. visited

**14** A woman _____ a red dress was _____ the flamenco
   _____ wonderful _____.
   A. with          B. in          C. movements          D. dancing

**1** 스페인에서의 행복한 날들 – 박진우

**2** 나의 가족은 이번 여름에 스페인을 여행했다.

**3** 스페인은 수많은 관광객들에게 사랑받는다.

**4** 우리는 여러 흥미로운 장소를 방문했다.

**5** 우리의 여행은 마드리드에서 시작했다.

**6** 마드리드는 수도이며 축구로 유명하다.

**7** 우리는 축구 경기를 보기 위해서 경기장으로 갔다.

**8** 나의 여동생과 나는 세계에서 가장 유명한 축구 선수 몇몇을 볼 수 있었기 때문에 신이 났다.

**9** 경기장은 축구 팬들로 가득 차 있었다.

**10** 우리는 경기를 보는 동안 노래를 부르고, 손을 흔들고, 다른 팬들과 함께 소리를 치며 응원을 했다.

**11** 마드리드를 여행하고 난 후, 우리는 세비야로 갔다.

**12** 우리는 도시를 걸어다니는 동안, 역사상 중요한 많은 건물들을 보았다.

**13** 우리는 플라멩코 박물관을 방문해서 플라멩코 춤을 보았다.

**14** 빨간 드레스를 입은 여자가 멋진 동작으로 플라멩코를 추고 있었다.

**15** _____ dinner, we _____ paella.

    A. ate            B. for

**16** It is a _____ Spanish _____ rice, vegetables, meat, and seafood.

    A. with         B. dish        C. traditional

**17** It _____ _____ fried rice _____ Korea.

    A. in           B. like        C. tasted

**18** It was _____ delicious _____ we _____ enjoyed it.

    A. that        B. so        C. all

**19** In Barcelona, we _____ a _____ _____ Park Guell and Sagrada Familia.

    A. of          B. tour        C. took

**20** _____ were _____ _____ Antoni Gaudi.

    A. designed      B. both       C. by

**21** In Park Guell, we saw some of Gaudi's _____ works _____ a _____ lizard.

    A. like         B. colorful       C. creative

**22** _____ Park Guell, we _____ Sagrada Familia.

    A. visited       B. after

**23** _____ on the building started in 1883 and is still _____ _____ today.

    A. going        B. work       C. on

**24** I was _____ by _____ size and _____ design.

    A. unique       B. impressed      C. its

**25** The _____ inside Sagrada Familia _____ _____ the night sky _____ bright stars.

    A. with       B. shone      C. ceiling      D. like

**26** Its stone _____ _____ _____ big trees.

    A. like        B. stood      C. colomns

**27** At Park Guell and Sagrada Familia I could _____ Gaudi's _____ and his _____ of _____.

    A. feel        B. nature      C. love      D. creativity

**28** _____ in Spain was a _____ _____.

    A. experience     B. wonderful     C. traveling

**29** _____ I was there, I learned _____ _____ about Spain.

    A. lot        B. while      C. a

**30** I want to _____ the _____ _____.

    A. country      B. visit      C. again

**15** 저녁 식사로 우리는 파에야를 먹었다.

**16** 그것은 쌀과 채소. 고기, 해산물이 들어간 전통적인 스페인 요리이다.

**17** 그것은 한국의 볶음밥과 같은 맛이 났다.

**18** 너무 맛있어서 우리 모두는 그것을 즐겼다.

**19** 바르셀로나에서 우리는 구엘 공원과 사그라다 파밀리아를 둘러보았다.

**20** 두 곳 모두 Antoni Gaudi에 의해 설계되었다.

**21** 구엘 공원에서 우리는 형형색색의 도마뱀과 같은 몇몇 Gaudi의 창의적인 작품들을 보았다.

**22** 구엘 공원을 본 다음. 우리는 사그라다 파밀리아를 방문했다.

**23** 건물 공사는 1883년에 시작되었고 오늘날까지도 여전히 진행 중이다.

**24** 나는 건물의 크기와 독특한 디자인에 감명 받았다.

**25** 사그라다 파밀라아 안의 천장은 밝은 별이 있는 밤하늘처럼 빛났다.

**26** 돌기둥은 큰 나무처럼 서 있었다.

**27** 구엘 공원과 사그라다 파밀리아에서 나는 Gaudi의 창의성과 자연에 대한 사랑을 느낄 수 있었다.

**28** 스페인 여행은 훌륭한 경험이었다.

**29** 나는 그곳에서 스페인에 대해 많은 것을 배웠다.

**30** 나는 그 나라를 다시 방문하고 싶다.

※ 다음 우리말과 일치하도록 빈칸에 알맞은 말을 쓰시오.

**1** My _____ _____ in Spain – _____ Park Jinwoo

**2** My family _____ _____ _____ this summer.

**3** Spain _____ _____ _____ _____ _____ tourists.

**4** We _____ many _____ _____.

**5** _____ _____ _____ _____ _____ Madrid.

**6** Madrid is the _____ and _____ _____ _____ soccer.

**7** We went to a stadium _____ _____ a _____ _____.

**8** My sister and I _____ _____ _____ we could watch some of _____ _____ _____ _____ _____ _____ _____.

**9** The stadium _____ _____ _____ soccer fans.

**10** As we watched the match, we _____ _____ _____ songs, _____ our hands, and _____ with the _____ _____.

**11** _____ we _____ Madrid, we _____ _____ Seville.

**12** _____ we _____ the city, we saw _____ _____ _____.

**13** We _____ a flamenco museum and _____ a flamenco dance.

**14** A woman _____ the flamenco _____ _____ _____.

| | |
|---|---|
| **1** | 스페인에서의 행복한 날들 – 박진우 |
| **2** | 나의 가족은 이번 여름에 스페인을 여행했다. |
| **3** | 스페인은 수많은 관광객들에게 사랑받는다. |
| **4** | 우리는 여러 흥미로운 장소를 방문했다. |
| **5** | 우리의 여행은 마드리드에서 시작했다. |
| **6** | 마드리드는 수도이며 축구로 유명하다. |
| **7** | 우리는 축구 경기를 보기 위해서 경기장으로 갔다. |
| **8** | 나의 여동생과 나는 세계에서 가장 유명한 축구 선수 몇몇을 볼 수 있었기 때문에 신이 났다. |
| **9** | 경기장은 축구 팬들로 가득 차 있었다. |
| **10** | 우리는 경기를 보는 동안 노래를 부르고, 손을 흔들고, 다른 팬들과 함께 소리를 치며 응원을 했다. |
| **11** | 마드리드를 여행하고 난 후, 우리는 세비야로 갔다. |
| **12** | 우리는 도시를 걸어다니는 동안, 역사상 중요한 많은 건물들을 보았다. |
| **13** | 우리는 플라멩코 박물관을 방문해서 플라멩코 춤을 보았다. |
| **14** | 빨간 드레스를 입은 여자가 멋진 동작으로 플라멩코를 추고 있었다. |

**15** _____ _____ , we _____ paella.

**16** It is a _____ _____ _____ _____ rice, vegetables, _____ , and _____ .

**17** It _____ _____ _____ _____ in Korea.

**18** It was _____ delicious _____ we _____ _____ it.

**19** In Barcelona, we _____ _____ _____ _____ Park Guell and Sagrada Familia.

**20** Both _____ _____ _____ Antoni Gaudi.

**21** In Park Guell, we saw some of Gaudi's _____ _____ _____ a _____ _____ .

**22** _____ Park Guell, we _____ Sagrada Familia.

**23** _____ _____ the building started in 1883 and _____ _____ _____ _____ today.

**24** I _____ _____ _____ _____ _____ and unique design.

**25** The ceiling inside Sagrada Familia _____ _____ the night sky _____ _____ _____ .

**26** Its _____ _____ _____ _____ big trees.

**27** At Park Guell and Sagrada Familia I _____ _____ Gaudi's _____ and _____ _____ _____ _____ .

**28** _____ in Spain was _____ _____ _____ _____ .

**29** _____ I was there, I learned _____ _____ about Spain.

**30** I want _____ _____ the country again.

15 저녁 식사로 우리는 파에야를 먹었다.

16 그것은 쌀과 채소, 고기, 해산물이 들어간 전통적인 스페인 요리이다.

17 그것은 한국의 볶음밥과 같은 맛이 났다.

18 너무 맛있어서 우리 모두는 그것을 즐겼다.

19 바르셀로나에서 우리는 구엘 공원과 사그라다 파밀리아를 둘러보았다.

20 두 곳 모두 Antoni Gaudi에 의해 설계되었다.

21 구엘 공원에서 우리는 형형색색의 도마뱀과 같은 몇몇 Gaudi의 창의적인 작품들을 보았다.

22 구엘 공원을 본 다음. 우리는 사그라다 파밀리아를 방문했다.

23 건물 공사는 1883년에 시작되었고 오늘날까지도 여전히 진행 중이다.

24 나는 건물의 크기와 독특한 디자인에 감명 받았다.

25 사그라다 파밀라아 안의 천장은 밝은 별이 있는 밤하늘처럼 빛났다.

26 돌기둥은 큰 나무처럼 서 있었다.

27 구엘 공원과 사그라다 파밀리아에서 나는 Gaudi의 창의성과 자연에 대한 사랑을 느낄 수 있었다.

28 스페인 여행은 훌륭한 경험이었다.

29 나는 그곳에서 스페인에 대해 많은 것을 배웠다.

30 나는 그 나라를 다시 방문하고 싶다.

※ 다음 문장을 우리말로 쓰시오.

**1** My Happy Days in Spain — by Park Jinwoo

➡ _____

**2** My family traveled to Spain this summer.

➡ _____

**3** Spain is loved by lots of tourists.

➡ _____

**4** We visited many interesting places.

➡ _____

**5** Our trip started in Madrid.

➡ _____

**6** Madrid is the capital and is famous for soccer.

➡ _____

**7** We went to a stadium to watch a soccer match.

➡ _____

**8** My sister and I were excited because we could watch some of the world's most famous soccer players.

➡ _____

**9** The stadium was full of soccer fans.

➡ _____

**10** As we watched the match, we cheered by singing songs, waving our hands, and shouting with the other fans.

➡ _____

**11** After we toured Madrid, we went to Seville.

➡ _____

**12** While we walked around the city, we saw many historic buildings.

➡ _____

**13** We visited a flamenco museum and watched a flamenco dance.

➡ _____

**14** A woman in a red dress was dancing the flamenco with wonderful movements.

➡ _____

**15** For dinner, we ate paella.

➡ _____

**16** It is a traditional Spanish dish with rice, vegetables, meat, and seafood.

➡ _____

**17** It tasted like fried rice in Korea.

➡ _____

**18** It was so delicious that we all enjoyed it.

➡ _____

**19** In Barcelona, we took a tour of Park Guell and Sagrada Familia.

➡ _____

**20** Both were designed by Antoni Gaudi.

➡ _____

**21** In Park Guell, we saw some of Gaudi's creative works like a colorful lizard.

➡ _____

**22** After Park Guell, we visited Sagrada Familia.

➡ _____

**23** Work on the building started in 1883 and is still going on today.

➡ _____

**24** I was impressed by its size and unique design.

➡ _____

**25** The ceiling inside Sagrada Familia shone like the night sky with bright stars.

➡ _____

**26** Its stone columns stood like big trees.

➡ _____

**27** At Park Guell and Sagrada Familia I could feel Gaudi's creativity and his love of nature.

➡ _____

**28** Traveling in Spain was a wonderful experience.

➡ _____

**29** While I was there, I learned a lot about Spain.

➡ _____

**30** I want to visit the country again.

➡ _____

※ 다음 괄호 안의 단어들을 우리말에 맞도록 바르게 배열하시오.

**1** (happy / my / in / Days / by / – / Spain / Jinwoo / Park)
➡ _____

**2** (family / my / to / traveled / Spain / summer. / this)
➡ _____

**3** (is / Spain / by / loved / lots / tourists. / of)
➡ _____

**4** (visited / we / interesting / many / places.)
➡ _____

**5** (trip / our / Madrid. / in / started)
➡ _____

**6** (is / Madrid / capital / the / is / and / soccer. / for / famous)
➡ _____

**7** (went / we / a / to / stadium / watch / to / match. / soccer / a)
➡ _____

**8** (sister / my / and / were / I / excited / we / because / could / some / watch / of / world's / the / famous / most / / players. / soccer)
➡ _____

**9** (stadium / the / full / was / fans. / soccer / of)
➡ _____

**10** (we / as / the / watched / match, / cheered / we / singing / by / songs, / waving / hands, / our / and / with / shouting / the / fans. / other)
➡ _____
_____

**11** (we / after / Madrid, / toured / went / we / Seville. / to)
➡ _____

**12** (we / while / walked / the / around / city, / saw / we / many / buildings. / historic)
➡ _____

**13** (visited / we / flamenco / a / museum / and / a / watched / dance. / flamenco)
➡ _____

**14** (woman / a / in / red / a / dress / dancing / was / flamenco / the / movements. / wonderful / with)
➡ _____

**1** 스페인에서의 행복한 날들 – 박진우

**2** 나의 가족은 이번 여름에 스페인을 여행했다.

**3** 스페인은 수많은 관광객들에게 사랑받는다.

**4** 우리는 여러 흥미로운 장소를 방문했다.

**5** 우리의 여행은 마드리드에서 시작했다.

**6** 마드리드는 수도이며 축구로 유명하다.

**7** 우리는 축구 경기를 보기 위해서 경기장으로 갔다.

**8** 나의 여동생과 나는 세계에서 가장 유명한 축구 선수 몇몇을 볼 수 있었기 때문에 신이 났다.

**9** 경기장은 축구 팬들로 가득 차 있었다.

**10** 우리는 경기를 보는 동안 노래를 부르고, 손을 흔들고, 다른 팬들과 함께 소리를 치며 응원을 했다.

**11** 마드리드를 여행하고 난 후, 우리는 세비야로 갔다.

**12** 우리는 도시를 걸어다니는 동안, 역사상 중요한 많은 건물들을 보았다.

**13** 우리는 플라멩코 박물관을 방문해서 플라멩코 춤을 보았다.

**14** 빨간 드레스를 입은 여자가 멋진 동작으로 플라멩코를 추고 있었다.

**15** (dinner, / for / paella. / ate / we)

➡ _____

**16** (is / it / Spanish / traditional / a / with / dish / rice, / meat, / vegetables, / seafood. / and)

➡ _____

**17** (tasted / it / fried / like / Korea. / in / rice)

➡ _____

**18** (was / it / delicious / so / that / all / we / it. / enjoyed)

➡ _____

**19** (Barcelona, / in / took / we / tour / a / Park / of / and / Guell / Familia. / Sagrada)

➡ _____

**20** (were / both / by / designed / Gaudi. / Antoni)

➡ _____

**21** (Guell, / Park / in / saw / we / of / some / creative / Gaudi's / works / a / like / lizard. / colorful)

➡ _____

**22** (Park / after / Guell, / visited / we / Familia. / Sagrada)

➡ _____

**23** (on / work / building / the / in / started / 1883 / is / and / going / still / today. / on)

➡ _____

**24** (was / I / by / impressed / size / its / and / design. / unique)

➡ _____

**25** (ceiling / the / Sagrada / inside / Familia / like / shone / night / the / sky / stars. / bright / with)

➡ _____

**26** (stone / its / stood / columns / trees. / big / like)

➡ _____

**27** (Park / at / and / Guell / Familia / Sagrada / could / I / Gaudi's / feel / creativity / his / and / of / nature. / love)

➡ _____

**28** (in / traveling / Spain / was / experiece. / wonderful / a)

➡ _____

**29** (I / while / there, / was / learned / I / about / a / Spain. / lot)

➡ _____

**30** (I / to / want / the / visit / again. / country)

➡ _____

**15** 저녁 식사로 우리는 파에야를 먹었다.

**16** 그것은 쌀과 채소, 고기, 해산물이 들어간 전통적인 스페인 요리이다.

**17** 그것은 한국의 볶음밥과 같은 맛이 났다.

**18** 너무 맛있어서 우리 모두는 그것을 즐겼다.

**19** 바르셀로나에서 우리는 구엘 공원과 사그라다 파밀리아를 둘러보았다.

**20** 두 곳 모두 Antoni Gaudi에 의해 설계되었다.

**21** 구엘 공원에서 우리는 형형색색의 도마뱀과 같은 몇몇 Gaudi의 창의적인 작품들을 보았다.

**22** 구엘 공원을 본 다음, 우리는 사그라다 파밀리아를 방문했다.

**23** 건물 공사는 1883년에 시작되었고 오늘날까지도 여전히 진행 중이다.

**24** 나는 건물의 크기와 독특한 디자인에 감명 받았다.

**25** 사그라다 파밀리아 안의 천장은 밝은 별이 있는 밤하늘처럼 빛났다.

**26** 돌기둥은 큰 나무처럼 서 있었다.

**27** 구엘 공원과 사그라다 파밀리아에서 나는 Gaudi의 창의성과 자연에 대한 사랑을 느낄 수 있었다.

**28** 스페인 여행은 훌륭한 경험이었다.

**29** 나는 그곳에서 스페인에 대해 많은 것을 배웠다.

**30** 나는 그 나라를 다시 방문하고 싶다.

※ 다음 우리말을 영어로 쓰시오.

**1** 스페인에서의 행복한 날들 – 박진우

➡ _____

**2** 나의 가족은 이번 여름에 스페인을 여행했다.

➡ _____

**3** 스페인은 수많은 관광객들에게 사랑받는다.

➡ _____

**4** 우리는 여러 흥미로운 장소를 방문했다.

➡ _____

**5** 우리의 여행은 마드리드에서 시작했다.

➡ _____

**6** 마드리드는 수도이며 축구로 유명하다.

➡ _____

**7** 우리는 축구 경기를 보기 위해서 경기장으로 갔다.

➡ _____

**8** 나의 여동생과 나는 세계에서 가장 유명한 축구 선수 몇몇을 볼 수 있었기 때문에 신이 났다.

➡ _____

**9** 경기장은 축구 팬들로 가득 차 있었다.

➡ _____

**10** 우리는 경기를 보는 동안 노래를 부르고, 손을 흔들고, 다른 팬들과 함께 소리를 치며 응원을 했다.

➡ _____

**11** 마드리드를 여행하고 난 후, 우리는 세비야로 갔다.

➡ _____

**12** 우리는 도시를 걸어다니는 동안, 역사상 중요한 많은 건물들을 보았다.

➡ _____

**13** 우리는 플라멩코 박물관을 방문해서 플라멩코 춤을 보았다.

➡ _____

**14** 빨간 드레스를 입은 여자가 멋진 동작으로 플라멩코를 추고 있었다.

➡ _____

**15** 저녁 식사로 우리는 파에야를 먹었다.

➡ _____

**16** 그것은 쌀과 채소, 고기, 해산물이 들어간 전통적인 스페인 요리이다.

➡ _____

**17** 그것은 한국의 볶음밥과 같은 맛이 났다.

➡ _____

**18** 너무 맛있어서 우리 모두는 그것을 즐겼다.

➡ _____

**19** 바르셀로나에서 우리는 구엘 공원과 사그라다 파밀리아를 둘러보았다.

➡ _____

**20** 두 곳 모두 Antoni Gaudi에 의해 설계되었다.

➡ _____

**21** 구엘 공원에서 우리는 형형색색의 도마뱀과 같은 몇몇 Gaudi의 창의적인 작품들을 보았다.

➡ _____

**22** 구엘 공원을 본 다음, 우리는 사그라다 파밀리아를 방문했다.

➡ _____

**23** 건물 공사는 1883년에 시작되었고 오늘날까지도 여전히 진행 중이다.

➡ _____

**24** 나는 건물의 크기와 독특한 디자인에 감명 받았다.

➡ _____

**25** 사그라다 파밀라아 안의 천장은 밝은 별이 있는 밤하늘처럼 빛났다.

➡ _____

**26** 돌기둥은 큰 나무처럼 서 있었다.

➡ _____

**27** 구엘 공원과 사그라다 파밀리아에서 나는 Gaudi의 창의성과 자연에 대한 사랑을 느낄 수 있었다.

➡ _____

**28** 스페인 여행은 훌륭한 경험이었다.

➡ _____

**29** 나는 그곳에서 스페인에 대해 많은 것을 배웠다.

➡ _____

**30** 나는 그 나라를 다시 방문하고 싶다.

➡ _____

※ 다음 우리말과 일치하도록 빈칸에 알맞은 말을 쓰시오.

### Enjoy Writing

1. _____ _____ do you _____ _____ Vietnam?

2. The _____ _____ _____ is Hanoi. Vietnamese _____ _____ there.

3. Pho and banh mi _____ _____ _____ in Vietnam.

4. _____ _____ _____ _____ tourists visit Halong Bay and Nha Trang.

5. Halong Bay has 1,969 islands and Nha Trang _____ _____ _____ _____ its beautiful beaches.

6. Vietnam is _____ _____ _____ you _____ come someday.

1. 당신은 베트남에 대해서 얼마나 많이 알고 있나요?
2. 베트남의 수도는 하노이입니다. 그곳에서는 베트남어가 사용됩니다.
3. 베트남에서는 pho(퍼, 베트남 쌀국수)와 banh mi(반미, 바게트 빵으로 만든 샌드위치)가 인기 있는 요리입니다.
4. 매년 많은 관광객들이 하롱베이와 나트랑을 방문합니다.
5. 하롱베이는 1,969개의 섬을 가지고 있고 나트랑은 아름다운 해변으로 잘 알려져 있습니다.
6. 베트남은 너무 아름다워서 당신은 언젠가 꼭 오셔야 합니다.

### Project Step 3

1. My group _____ Hong Kong _____ _____ _____.

2. Hong Kong _____ _____ _____ many people _____ want _____ _____ fun activities.

3. We'll _____ _____ _____ _____ Mong Kok Market, Victoria Peak, and Ocean Park.

1. 우리 모둠은 여행 장소로 홍콩을 선택했다.
2. 홍콩은 재밌는 활동을 하고 싶어 하는 많은 사람들에게 사랑받는다.
3. 우리는 몽콕 시장, 빅토리아 피크 그리고 오션 파크에서 멋진 경험을 할 것이다.

### Wrap Up

1. I _____ _____ _____ a book.

2. The _____ _____ _____ _____ is *The Old Man and the Sea*.

3. It _____ _____ _____ Ernest Hemingway.

4. The story was _____ great _____ I read it _____ _____.

1. 나는 어떤 책에 감동을 받았다.
2. 그 책의 제목은 '노인과 바다'이다.
3. 그것은 Ernest Hemingway에 의해 씌여졌다.
4. 그 이야기는 너무도 대단해서 나는 그것을 여러 번 읽었다.

※ 다음 우리말을 영어로 쓰시오.

### Enjoy Writing

1. 당신은 베트남에 대해서 얼마나 많이 알고 있나요?

 ➡ _____

2. 베트남의 수도는 하노이입니다. 그곳에서는 베트남어가 사용됩니다.

 ➡ _____

3. 베트남에서는 pho(퍼, 베트남 쌀국수)와 banh mi(반미, 바게트 빵으로 만든 샌드위치)가 인기 있는 요리입니다.

 ➡ _____

4. 매년 많은 관광객들이 하롱베이와 나트랑을 방문합니다.

 ➡ _____

5. 하롱베이는 1,969개의 섬을 가지고 있고 나트랑은 아름다운 해변으로 잘 알려져 있습니다.

 ➡ _____

6. 베트남은 너무 아름다워서 당신은 언젠가 꼭 오셔야 합니다.

 ➡ _____

### Project Step 3

1. 우리 모둠은 여행 장소로 홍콩을 선택했다.

 ➡ _____

2. 홍콩은 재밌는 활동을 하고 싶어 하는 많은 사람들에게 사랑받는다.

 ➡ _____

3. 우리는 몽콕 시장, 빅토리아 피크 그리고 오션 파크에서 멋진 경험을 할 것이다.

 ➡ _____

### Wrap Up

1. 나는 어떤 책에 감동을 받았다.

 ➡ _____

2. 그 책의 제목은 '노인과 바다'이다.

 ➡ _____

3. 그것은 Ernest Hemingway에 의해 씌여졌다.

 ➡ _____

4. 그 이야기는 너무도 대단해서 나는 그것을 여러 번 읽었다.

 ➡ _____

# MEMO

영어 기출 문제집

# 적중100

1학기

# 정답 및 해설

시사 | 박준언

중
2

영어 기출 문제집

적중100

1학기

# 정답 및 해설

시사 | 박준언

중 2

## Lesson 3

# Living a Healthy Life

01 ④는 -ive를 붙여 형용사형을 만들고 나머지는 -able을 붙여 형용사형을 만든다.

02 be good for: ~에 좋다 / focus on: ~에 집중하다

03 반의어 관계이다. 강한 : 약한 = 서늘한 : 따뜻한

04 신체적으로 편안함을 느끼게 하는: 편안한(comfortable)

05 both of: ~ 둘 다

06 운동이나 다른 활동을 위해 당신의 몸을 준비하기 위해 가벼운 운동을 하다: 준비 운동을 하다(warm up)

07 get over: 회복하다

08 second: (시간 단위인) 초; 두 번째의

### 서술형 시험대비     p.09

01 (1) forward   (2) increase   (3) advice   (4) uncomfortable
02 (1) each other   (2) more than   (3) a little bit
03 (1) ride   (2) reduce   (3) count   (4) download
04 (1) healthy   (2) movable   (3) comfortable
05 (1) get over   (2) prepare for   (3) am worried about
06 (1) (s)tretch   (2) (h)abit   (3) (s)witch   (4) (r)elax

01 (1) 반의어 관계이다. ~ 전에 : ~ 후에 = 뒤로 : 앞으로 (2) 반의어 관계이다. 잘못된 : 틀린 = 줄다 : 증가하다 (3) 유의어 관계이다. 맛있는 : 맛있는 = 조언 : 조언 (4) 나타나다 : 사라지다 = 편안한 : 불편한

02 (1) each other: 서로 (2) more than: ~ 이상 (3) a little bit: 조금

03 (1) ride: 타다 (2) reduce: 줄이다 (3) count: 세다 (4) download: 다운로드하다

04 (1) healthy: 건강에 좋은 (2) movable: 움직이는 (3) comfortable: 편안한

05 (1) get over: 회복하다 (2) prepare for: ~을 준비하다 (3) be worried about: ~에 대해 걱정하다

06 (1) stretch: 스트레칭하다 (2) habit: 습관 (3) switch: 바꾸다 (4) relax: (근육 등의) 긴장을 풀다

### 교과서 Conversation

#### 핵심 Check     p.10~11

1 (1) how to / not good at   (2) how to make
2 (1) What / like to / riding
  (2) what, enjoy doing / fishing
  (3) do you do / enjoy drawing / How

### 교과서 대화문 익히기

#### Check(√) True or False     p.12

1 T   2 F   3 T   4 F

### 교과서 확인학습     p.14~15

**Listen & Speak 1 A-1**
something healthy, have, adivce / often eat, makes, good / how to / cut, into, put, into, pour, mix / should try

**Listen & Speak 1 A-2**
more than / to be, count, steps / can use, how to use / Can, show / download, with, check / will, using

**Listen & Speak 2 A-1**
What, doing / enjoy cooking / Sounds, can / can make

**Listen & Speak 2 A-2**
on weekends / take / What kind, take / taking, of, like / reduce

**Listen & Speak 2 A-3**
puppy / Her, really / with / enjoy taking, makes, healthy

**Conversation A**
have, speaking, preparing, for, ago, speaking in, about, cannot sleep

**Conversation B**
matter / stressed about / ride, when / how to ride / go out, can, Put, on, push, with / Like, feel better / riding, because

## 시험대비 기본평가　p.16

01 ②　　02 ⑤　　03 ②　　04 ⓒ － ⓑ － ⓐ － ⓓ

01 건강에 좋은 주스를 만드는 방법을 아는지 묻고 있으므로 how to make가 들어가야 한다.

02 건강해지기 위해 하는 것으로 적절하지 않은 것을 고른다

03 Do you know how to + 동사원형 ~?은 능력 여부를 묻는 표현으로 Can you + 동사원형 ~?으로 바꿔 쓸 수 있다.

04 ⓒ 너는 강아지가 있니? - ⓑ 응. 그 강아지의 이름은 코코야. 난 강아지를 정말 좋아해. - ⓐ 너는 강아지와 함께 무엇을 하니? - ⓓ 난 강아지와 산책하는 걸 즐겨. 그것은 나를 건강하게 만들어.

## 시험대비 실력평가　p.17~18

01 ⑤　　02 ⑤　　03 ⓑ to ride　ⓓ riding
04 riding[to ride] my longboard　　05 ②
06 ③　　07 ③　　08 (감기에 걸렸을 때) 따뜻한 물을 마시는 것　09 I want to eat something healthy.
10 Eating[To eat] fresh salad　　11 ①, ③
12 ②　　13 ②　　14 ③

01 주어진 문장은 '난 벌써 기분이 더 좋아졌어.'라는 의미로 롱보드를 타는 것이 재미있다는 문장 다음에 와야 한다.

02 ⓐ be stressed about: ~에 대해 스트레스를 받다 ⓒ with: ~로

03 ⓑ how+to부정사: ~하는 방법 ⓓ enjoy -ing: ~하는 것을 즐기다

04 인칭대명사 it은 riding[to ride] my longboard를 가리킨다.

05 ② 하나가 스트레스를 받을 때 무엇을 하는지는 알 수 없다.

06 How have you been?은 안부를 묻는 표현이고, 나머지는 슬픔, 불만족, 실망의 원인을 묻는 표현이다.

07 Do you know how to ~?: 상대방에게 어떤 일을 할 수 있는지 묻는 표현이다.

08 인칭대명사 It은 drinking warm water를 의미한다.

09 -thing으로 끝나는 부정대명사는 형용사가 뒤에서 수식한다.

10 인칭대명사 It은 Eating[To eat] fresh salad를 가리킨다.

11 능력 여부를 묻는 문장에는 Do you know how to ~?, Can you ~?, Are you good at ~? 등이 있다.

12 ⓐ prepare for: ~을 준비하다 ⓒ be worried about: ~에 대해 걱정하다

13 앞뒤 내용이 상반되므로 but이 알맞다.

14 글쓴이는 내일 있을 영어 시험이 걱정된다고 했으므로 스트레스를 받고 있을 것이다.

## 서술형 시험대비　p.19

01 People say that we should walk more than 10,000 steps.
02 너는 그것(스마트폰 앱)을 어떻게 사용하는지 아니? / [모범답안] Can you use it? / Are you good at using it?
03 app　　04 It is to download the app.
05 taking
06 She enjoys taking pictures of nature, like trees and flowers.
07 such as　　08 (r)educe

01 매일 10,000 걸음 이상을 걸어야 한다고 말한다.

02 Do you know how to + 동사원형 ~?은 능력 여부를 묻는 표현으로 Can you + 동사원형 ~? / Are you good at + (동)명사 ~? 등으로 바꿔 쓸 수 있다.

03 특정한 일을 하도록 고안된 컴퓨터 프로그램, 특히 스마트폰에서 사용할 수 있는 프로그램: app(앱)

04 스마트폰 앱을 사용하는 첫 번째 단계는 앱을 다운로드하는 것이라고 언급되었다.

05 enjoy는 동명사를 목적어로 취한다.

06 소녀는 나무와 꽃 같은 자연의 사진을 찍는 것을 즐긴다고 했다.

07 like: ~ 같은(=such as)

08 어떤 것의 크기, 양, 수 등이 작아지게 하다: reduce(줄이다)

## 교과서
## Grammar

### 핵심 Check　p.20~21

**1** (1) melt　(2) do　(3) ring　(4) to come
**2** (1) will give　(2) If　(3) takes　(4) drink

3

01 (1) If I go to France   (2) If it rains tomorrow
02 (1) to look → look   (2) to write → write
     (3) to go → go
03 (1) Unless you leave   (2) If it doesn't rain
04 (1) me go out after dinner
     (2) the children play outside
     (3) the bear stand on the ball

01 조건의 부사절은 「If+주어+동사 ~」의 어순으로 쓴다.
02 사역동사 have, make, let은 목적격 보어로 동사원형을 취한다.
03 「if+주어+don't[doesn't]+동사원형 ~」은 「unless+주어+동사의 현재형 ~」으로 바꿔 쓸 수 있다.
04 「사역동사(let, have, make)+목적어+동사원형」의 형태에 유의하여 주어진 문장을 「목적어+동사원형」 형태로 완성한다.

01 ③     02 ①     03 ⑤     04 ⑤
05 to do → do     06 ③     07 I helped
my mom (to) do the dishes. 08 ③     09 ③
10 ④     11 ④     12 will rain → rains
13 ③     14 His smile always makes me smile.
15 ③     16 ③     17 ②     18 you
stop     19 ②     20 Judy makes her
brother study math.     21 ③     22 Unless
you like the food     23 My father helped me
carry the heavy bag.     24 ⑤

01 「주어+동사+목적어+목적격보어」로 구성된 5형식 문장이므로 사역동사 have의 목적격보어로 쓰일 수 있는 동사원형의 형태가 알맞다.
02 '만약 ~하면'의 조건절을 이끄는 접속사와 '~인지 아닌지'의 명사절을 이끄는 접속사 역할을 하는 if가 적절하다.
03 make가 5형식 문장에 쓰이면 목적격 보어로 형용사 또는 동사원형이 올 수 있다.
04 가까운 미래의 상황을 가정하거나 조건을 나타낼 때 if절은 현재시제로, 종속절은 미래시제로 써야 한다.
05 사역동사 make는 목적격 보어로 동사원형을 취한다.
06 if 조건절은 의미가 미래이더라도 현재시제를 쓴다.
07 help는 준사역동사로 목적격 보어로 동사원형이나 to부정사 둘 다 취할 수 있다.
08 조건을 나타내는 if절에서는 현재시제가 미래의 일을 나타내므로 ③이 알맞다.
09 let, have, make, help는 모두 목적격보어로 동사원형을 취한다. want는 to부정사를 목적격보어로 취한다.

10 If ~ not은 Unless와 의미가 같다.
11 ④는 4형식 문장에 쓰인 수여동사이며, 나머지는 5형식 문장에 쓰인 불완전 타동사이다.
12 조건을 나타내는 if는 미래시제 will과 쓰지 못한다.
13 조건을 나타내는 if 부사절에서는 미래의 일이라도 현재시제를 사용한다.
14 make+목적어+동사원형
15 두 빈칸 모두 동사의 자리이고, 다음에 him이라는 목적어가 나온다. 목적격보어로 'to+동사원형'이 나왔으므로 get이 들어가야 맞다. 동사원형이 목적격보어로 오는 경우 사역동사는 해당되지 않는다. help는 의미상 어울리지 않는다.
16 if ~ not = unless: 만약 ~하지 않으면
17 첫 번째 빈칸에는 사역동사가 들어가야 하고, 두 번째 빈칸에는 사역동사의 목적격보어인 동사원형이 들어가야 한다. 사역동사 let, have, make는 모두 뒤에 동사원형을 동반한다. take care of: ~를 돌보다
18 if ~ not = unless
19 사역동사 make, let과 help는 모두 목적격보어로 동사원형을 쓴다. (② to go → go) ③ 「ask+목적어+to부정사」 형태이다.
21 ③ 조건을 나타내는 if절에서는 현재시제가 미래시제를 대신한다. will leave → leave
22 '만약 ~하지 않는다면'이라는 의미의 「If+주어+don't [doesn't]+동사원형 ~」은 「Unless+주어+동사의 현재형 ~」으로 바꿔 쓸 수 있다.
23 사역동사 help 다음에는 동사원형이나 to부정사가 쓰인다.
24 대화 속의 밑줄 친 make와 ⑤는 사역동사이다.

01 (1) (to) carry   (2) get   (3) help   (4) to show
02 (1) If   (2) when   (3) Unless
03 (1) to explain → explain   (2) fell → fall
     (3) played → play
04 (1) If I am late for class, my teacher gets very angry.
     (2) If the weather is nice, I always walk to school.
     (3) If it rains on weekends, we watch TV.
05 Mom doesn't let me go out at night.
06 I made my younger[little] brother turn off the TV.
07 (1) If you study hard   (2) If it rains
08 (1) Finally, the police let the thief go.
     (2) Love makes people do unusual things.
     (3) I got my dog to wear strange glasses.
     (4) My English teacher helps us (to) write a diary
       every day.
09 (1) you'll pass → you pass
     (2) I won't be → I'm not / I am not

10 (1) My parents let me play computer games every Friday.

(2) My teacher made me wash my hands.

(3) My mom didn't let me go out.

11 (1) If it rains tomorrow, we won't go hiking.

(2) Unless you hurry, you will miss the train.

12 (1) Eddie lets his brother play with his toys.

(2) She makes her children study English.

(3) Dad has us cook breakfast on Sundays.

13 If she doesn't study hard, she will fail the exam.

---

01 (1) help+목적어+(to)동사원형 (2) get+목적어+to부정사 (3) let+목적어+동사원형 (4) 보여줄 그림들이라는 의미의 to부정사의 형용사적 용법이 적절하다.

02 when은 때, if는 조건을 나타낸다. unless는 if ~ not의 뜻이다.

03 5형식 문장에서 사역동사 let, make, have의 목적격보어는 동사원형을 써야 한다.

04 if는 종속절을 이끄는 접속사이다.

06 「사역동사+목적어+목적격보어(동사원형)」 어순으로 써야 한다.

07 '만약 ~한다면'이라는 의미로 조건을 나타내는 표현은 「if+주어+동사의 현재형」으로 나타낸다.

08 (1), (2) let, make는 사역동사로 목적격보어 자리에는 동사원형이 와야 한다. (3) get은 목적격보어 자리에 'to+동사원형'이 온다. (4) help는 목적격보어로 동사원형 또는 to부정사를 쓴다.

09 조건의 if절에서는 미래의 일을 현재시제로 나타낸다.

10 (1) 「let+목적어+동사원형(…이 ~하도록 허락하다)」 (2) 「make+목적어+동사원형(…이 ~하게 하다)」 (3) 「don't let+목적어+동사원형(…이 ~하도록 허락하지 않다)」

11 (1) if 이하가 조건절이므로, 현재시제가 미래시제를 대신한다. (2) unless는 '만약 ~하지 않으면'의 뜻이므로 not을 붙일 필요가 없다.

12 사역동사 have, make, let은 목적격 보어로 동사원형을 사용한다.

13 콤마가 있으므로 if절을 주절 앞에 둔다.

---

교과서
## Reading

확인문제      p.28

1 T   2 F   3 T   4 T

확인문제      p.29

1 T   2 F   3 F   4 T

---

## 교과서 확인학습 A     p.30~31

01 At, for     02 get tired

03 Why don't, yourself     04 Let's, with

05 Close, massage, with     06 will relax

07 When, cover, with, block out

08 make, feel, comfortable     09 massage

10 Put, on     11 Draw, with, to   12 from, to

13 help, feel     14 Let's, waist     15 Team up

16 each other, faces     17 Hold

18 stretch, backward     19 Hold, for

20 pull, to     21 your, at     22 If, both of

23 Place, on, behind     24 bend, lower

25 Hold, a few, up     26 loosen up

27 Switch, repeat 28 How, feel

29 massage, stretch, feel healthier   30 focus on, better

---

## 교과서 확인학습 B     p.32~33

1 At school you sit for many hours.

2 Do you get tired?

3 Why don't you massage yourself and stretch?

4 Let's begin with the eyes.

5 Close your eyes and massage them softly with your fingers.

6 It will relax your eyes.

7 When you finish, cover your eyes with your hands to block out the light.

8 It will make your eyes feel more comfortable.

9 Next, massage your neck.

10 Put your fingers on the back of your neck.

11 Draw small circles with your fingers to massage your neck.

12 Massage from top to bottom.

13 The massage will help you feel better.

14 Let's work on your waist.

15 Team up with a friend.

16 Stand close to each other and face your partner.

17 Hold each other's wrists.

18 Slowly stretch your head and body backward.

19 Hold that position for three seconds.

20 Then, slowly pull each other to a standing position.

21 You and your partner should move at the same speed.

22 If you don't, both of you will fall!

23 Place the top of your right foot on the desk

behind you.

24 Then, slowly bend your left leg and lower yourself.

25 Hold it for a few seconds and slowly straighten up.

26 This position will loosen up your right leg.

27 Switch your legs and repeat the exercise.

28 How do you feel now?

29 If you massage yourself and stretch every day, you will feel healthier.

30 Also, you can focus on your studies better.

## 시험대비 실력평가 p.34~37

| | | | |
|---|---|---|---|
| 01 ③ | 02 ② | 03 your eyes | 04 stretch |
| 05 ⑤ | 06 ③ | 07 ⓑ for | ⓔ of |
| 08 position | 09 ② | 10 ⑤ | 11 ③ |
| 12 ③ | 13 slowly | 14 ④ | 15 ⓑ → ⓒ |
| → ⓐ | 16 softly | 17 눈을 감고 손으로 눈을 | |

부드럽게 마사지하는 것  18 ③  19 ④
20 make your eyes feel more comfortable  21 ②
22 ③  23 feeling → feel[to feel]  24 waist
25 ③  26 ②  27 ⑤  28 ③
29 yourself  30 switch  31 ⑤

01 for many hours: 오랜 시간 동안 / block out: (빛을) 차단하다

02 get tired: 피곤하다

03 인칭대명사 them은 your eyes를 가리킨다.

04 팔, 다리 등을 근육이 길고 단단해지도록 하는 자세에 놓다: stretch(스트레칭하다)

05 인칭대명사 It은 앞에 나온 문장 cover your eyes with your hands to block out the light를 가리킨다.

06 ⓐ, ③: 마주보다, ①, ④: 얼굴, ②: 직면하다, ⑤: 표면

07 for three seconds: 3초 동안 / both of: ~ 둘 다

08 어떤 사람이 서거나 앉거나 눕는 방식 : position(자세)

09 '만약 ~하면'의 뜻으로 조건절을 이끄는 접속사 if가 알맞다.

10 두 사람이 같은 속도로 움직이지 않으면, 두 사람은 넘어질 것이 라고 언급되어 있다.

11 명령문은 상대방, 즉 2인칭에게 하는 말이므로 재귀대명사는 yourself가 되어야 한다.

12 ③ bend(구부리다): 몸을 움직여 구부리다 ① mix ② switch ④ place ⑤ stretch

13 동사를 수식하는 부사 형태가 되어야 한다

14 straighten up: 똑바로 하다 / loosen up: (몸・근육을) 풀어 주다

15 뒤에 있는 책상 위에 오른쪽 발등을 올려놓고 천천히 왼쪽 다리 를 구부리고 몸을 낮추고 그 상태로 놈을 낮춘 상태로 몇 초 동 안 유지한다.

16 동사를 수식하는 부사 형태가 되어야 한다.

17 인칭대명사 It은 앞 문장 Close your eyes and massage them softly with your fingers.를 가리킨다.

18 빛을 차단하기 위해 눈을 가려라가 문맥상 적절하므로 cover가 알맞다.

19 목적을 나타내는 부사적 용법의 to부정사 형태가 되어야 한다.

20 make + 목적어 + 목적격 보어(동사원형): ~을 …하게 하다 / feel+형용사: ~하게 느끼다

21 목을 마사지하는 방법은 '목 뒤에 손가락을 대고(Put), 목을 마 사지하기 위해 손가락으로 작은 원을 그리고(Draw), 위에서 아 래로 마사지해라(Massage)'는 순서가 알맞다.

22 <보기>와 ③은 목적을 나타내는 부사적 용법의 to부정사이다. 나머지는 명사적 용법이다

23 동사 help는 목적격 보어로 동사원형이나 to부정사를 쓸 수 있 다.

24 갈비뼈와 엉덩이 사이의 신체 중앙 부분: 허리

25 머리와 몸을 뒤로 뻗어라가 알맞다. forward → backward

26 ⓑ, ②: (시간 단위인) 초 ①: 두 번째로 ③,⑤: 두 번째의 ④: 둘 째의[제2의]

27 ⓒ should: ~해야 한다 ⓓ 조건을 나타내는 접속사 if 문장에서 주절에는 미래형을 쓴다.

28 주어진 문장의 it은 왼쪽 다리를 구부리고 몸을 낮춘 자세를 가리 키므로 ③이 알맞다.

29 재귀대명사 yourself가 되어야 한다.

30 어떤 것에서 다른 것으로 바꾸다[전환하다]: 바꾸다 (switch)

31 문맥상 몸을 풀어 주다라는 의미를 가진 loosen up이 알맞다.

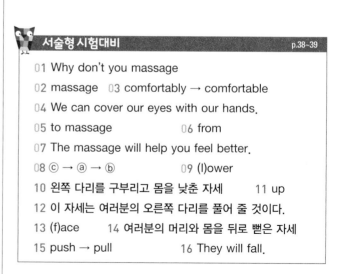

## 서술형 시험대비 p.38~39

01 Why don't you massage

02 massage  03 comfortably → comfortable

04 We can cover our eyes with our hands.

05 to massage  06 from

07 The massage will help you feel better.

08 ⓒ → ⓐ → ⓑ  09 (l)ower

10 왼쪽 다리를 구부리고 몸을 낮춘 자세  11 up

12 이 자세는 여러분의 오른쪽 다리를 풀어 줄 것이다.

13 (f)ace  14 여러분의 머리와 몸을 뒤로 뻗은 자세

15 push → pull  16 They will fall.

01 Why don't you + 동사원형 ~?: ~하는 게 어때?

02 근육의 긴장을 풀어 주거나 근육과 관절의 통증을 완화 시키기

위해 몸을 문지르거나 눌러 주다: 마사지하다 (massage)

03 feel+형용사: ~하게 느끼다

04 빛을 막기 위해 우리는 우리의 눈을 가릴 수 있다고 언급되었다.

05 목적을 나타내는 to부정사의 부사적 용법이다.

06 from A to B: A부터 B까지

07 help+목적어+목적격보어(동사원형/to+동사원형); ~가 …하는 것을 돕다 / feel better: 기분이 나아지다

08 목 뒷부분에 손가락을 대고, 목을 마사지하기 위해 손가락으로 작은 원을 그린 후, 위에서 아래로 마사지한다.

09 뭔가를 위쪽에서 아래로 이동시키다: 낮추다(lower)

11 straighten up: 똑바로 하다

12 loosen up: 몸을 풀어 주다

13 얼굴과 몸을 어떤 것 또는 어떤 사람을 향해 서거나 앉다: 마주 보다

14 밑줄 친 부분은 stretching your head and body backward 를 가리킨다.

15 천천히 서로 서 있는 위치로 끌어당겨라가 문맥상 알맞다. push → pull

16 같은 속도로 움직이지 않으면, 두 사람은 넘어질 것이라고 언급 되어 있다.

### 영역별 핵심문제  p.41~45

| | | | |
|---|---|---|---|
| 01 ④ | 02 ② | 03 team up | |
| 04 massage | 05 ③ | 06 ⑤ | 07 ④ |
| 08 ② | 09 ③ | 10 ③ | 11 (C) – (A) – (D) – (B) |
| | | 12 ⓐ feel ⓑ to make | |
| 13 ④ | 14 ③ | 15 It is to put small pieces of vegetables into a  bowl. | 16 ③ |
| 17 ⑤ | 18 ③ | 19 What will you do if he visits your home tomorrow? | 20 ② |
| | | 21 ② | |
| 22 She has the children play soccer. | | | 23 ④ |
| 24 ③ | 25 changing → change | | 26 If Jenny does not get up now, she will miss the train. 또는 Jenny will miss the train if she does not get up now. |
| | | 27 ⑤ | 28 ② | 29 with |
| 30 ④ | 31 make your eyes feel | | 32 ④ |
| 33 wrists | 34 ④ | 35 ⑤ | 36 how to stretch |
| 37 (A) First  (B) Then  (C) Finally | | | |
| 38 너의 팔로 숫자 2를 만드는 것 | | | 39 ④ |

01 ④는 유의어 관계이고 나머지는 반의어 관계이다.

02 몸을 움직여 구부리다: 구부리다(bend)

03 team up with: ~와 협력하다

04 근육과 관절의 통증을 줄이기 위해 손으로 사람의 몸을 문지르고 누르는 행동: 마사지(massage)

05 • 시청에 가려면 어떤 방법이 가장 좋을까요?. • 나는 경기장으

로 가는 길을 모른다.

06 loosen up: (몸을) 풀어 주다 / block out: (햇빛을) 차단하다

07 방과 후에 무엇을 하는 것을 즐기냐고 물었으므로, 대답으로는 방과 후에 할 수 있는 활동에 대해 말하는 것이 적절하다.

08 '~하는 방법'은 「how to+동사원형」으로 나타낸다.

09 음악의 종류로 답했으므로 '너는 어떤 종류의 음악을 좋아하니?'라고 묻는 것이 알맞다.

10 A: 수학 문제 푸는 것 잘하니? B: 아니, 나 수학 잘 못해.

11 (C) 방과 후에 뭐 하는 걸 즐기니? (A) 나는 건강에 좋은 음식을 요리하 는 것을 즐겨. (D) 멋지구나. 너는 무엇을 만들 수 있니? (B) 나는 샐러드, 비빔 밥 그리고 야채 주스를 만들 수 있어.

12 ⓐ 사역동사 make의 목적격보어로 동사원형을 쓴다. ⓑ how+to부정사: ~하는 방법

13 cut A into B: A를 B로 자르다

14 순서를 열거하는 문장이므로 First, Then, Finally 순으로 오는 것이 알맞다.

15 신선한 샐러드를 만드는 두 번째 단계는 채소의 작은 조각들을 그릇에 담는 것이다.

16 문장의 구조로 보아 목적어와 목적격보어(원형부정사)를 갖는 5형식 문장이므로 사역동사 made가 빈칸에 들어가야 한다.

17 접속사 if가 '~한다면'으로 해석되면 부사절을 이끌고, '~인지 아닌지'로 해석되면 명사절을 이끈다. 주어진 문장과 ⑤ 의 if는 명사절을 이끄는 접속사이다.

18 ①, ②, ④, ⑤의 밑줄 친 동사는 모두 사역동사로 쓰였으나, ③의 have는 '가지고 있다'의 일반동사로 쓰였다.

19 미래의 일이므로 주절에서는 미래시제를 나타낸다.

20 ①, ③, ④, ⑤는 사역동사 구문인데, ②의 told는 목적격보어로 to부정사를 사용하는 동사이다.

21 '만약 ~하면'의 뜻으로 조건절을 이끄는 접속사와 '~인지 아닌지'의 뜻으로 명사절을 이끄는 접속사 역할을 하는 if가 알맞다.

22 사역동사 have는 목적격보어로 동사원형을 쓴다.

23 <보기>와 ④는 사역동사로 '(목적어)를 ~하게 만들다'라는 의미로 쓰였다. ① make it: 해내다 ② make money: 돈을 벌다 ③ make: 만들어 주다(수여동사) ⑤ make an effort: 노력하다

24 ③ 조건을 나타내는 if절에서는 현재시제가 미래시제를 대신한다.

25 어떤 것도 나의 마음을 바꾸게 하지 않을 것이다.

26 첫 문장이 두 번째 문장의 조건이 되므로 접속사 if를 이용하여 연결한다.

27 ①~④는 내용상 조건을 나타내는 접속사 if가 와야 하고, ⑤는 동사 think의 목적어 역할을 하는 접속사 that이 적절하다.

28 (A) for + 숫자를 나타내는 기간 (B) 목적어가 주어 자신이 므로 재귀대명사 yourself가 알맞다. (C) 목적을 나타내는 to부정사 형태가 되어야 한다.

29 ⓐ begin with: ~부터 시작하다 ⓑ with: ~으로

30 빛을 차단하기 위해서 눈을 가리라는 의미가 되는 것이 흐름상 알맞다. open → close

31 make+목적어+목적격 보어(동사원형)

32 team up with: ~와 협력하다

33 손과 팔이 잇닿은 부분: 손목(wrist)

34 that position은 여러분의 머리와 몸을 뒤로 뻗는 것을 가리키므로 ④번이 알맞다.

35 미래를 표현할 때 주절에서는 미래시제를 쓴다.

36 '~하는 방법'이라는 뜻으로 「how to+동사원형」을 쓴다.

37 순서를 열거할 때 First(우선, 먼저), Then(그런 다음), Finally(마지막으로) 순으로 표현한다.

38 인칭대명사 It은 앞 문장의 내용을 받는다.

39 앞뒤 내용이 상반되는 내용이므로 but이 알맞다.

### 단원별 예상문제
p.46~49

01 ③　　01 02 bottom　03 ⑤　　04 ④

05 (1) a few seconds　(2) take a walk　(3) What kind of
06 ③　　07 ②　　08 to be

09 Do you know how to use it?　　10 Later

11 the smartphone app　12 ⑤　　13 ④

14 ②　　15 ④　　16 ⑤　　17 ⑤

18 If it is, will go　　19 had Martin read

20 top　21 ④　22 ⑤　23 ④

24 to　25 warm up　26 for

27 ⓐ Place　ⓑ bend　ⓒ Hold　　28 ①

29 ⑤　　30 ④

01 <보기>와 ③은 -able를 붙여 형용사형이 되는 단어이고, 나머지는 -ive를 붙여 형용사가 되는 단어들이다.

02 반의어 관계이다. 단순한 : 복잡한 = 꼭대기 : 맨 아래

03 focus on: ~에 집중하다 / straighten up: 똑바로 하다

04 어떤 것이 긴장, 팽팽함, 경직성이 줄어들게 하다: relax(근육 등의) 긴장을 풀다

05 (1) for a few seconds: 몇 초 동안 (2) take a walk: 산책하다 (3) what kind of: 어떤 종류의

06 Do you know how to + 동사원형 ~?은 능력 여부를 묻는 표현이다.

07 여가 시간에 무엇을 하느냐는 질문에 나는 영어와 수학 공부하는 것을 싫어한다는 대답은 어색하다.

08 목적을 나타내는 to부정사의 부사적 용법이다.

09 Do you know how to + 동사원형 ~?: ~하는 방법을 아니?(능력 여부를 묻는 표현)

10 later: 나중에

11 인칭대명사 it은 the smartphone app을 가리킨다.

12 사역동사 let은 목적격보어로 동사원형을 취한다.

13 ④ make는 5형식을 이끄는 사역동사이므로 practicing을

14 if로 시작하는 조건절에서는 현재시제가 미래시세를 내신한다.

15 ④ 사역동사 make는 목적어 다음에 목적격보어로 동사원형이 온다.

16 '주말마다'는 반복적인 습관을 나타내므로 현재시제를 사용한다.

17 첫 번째 문장은 이유, 두 번째 문장은 조건을 나타낸다.

18 조건의 부사절에서는 현재시제가 미래시제를 대신한다. 날씨를 말할 때는 비인칭 주어 it을 사용한다.

19 「have+목적어+동사원형」의 사역동사 구문이다.

20 어떤 것의 윗면

21 place A on B: A를 B 위에 놓다

22 a few+복수 명사

23 주어진 문장의 This position은 몇 초 동안 왼쪽 다리를 구부리고 몸을 낮추는 자세를 가리키므로 ④번이 알맞다.

24 ⓐ how to부정사: ~하는 방법 ⓑ 목적을 나타내는 to부정사의 부사적 용법

25 스포츠나 그 밖의 활동을 준비하려고 하는 운동이나 일련의 운동을 하나: 준비 운동을 하다(warm up)

26 be good for: ~에 좋다

27 ⓐ place: 놓다, 두다 ⓑ bend: 구부리다 ⓒ hold: 유지하다

28 straighten up: 똑바로 하다 / focus on: ~에 집중하다

29 문맥상 여러분의 오른쪽 다리를 풀어줄 것이라는 내용이 알 맞다.

30 also: 또한

### 서술형 실전문제
p.50~51

01 Do you know how to massage

02 I enjoy playing catch.

03 I am not good at math.

04 (D) – (C) – (A) – (B)

05 (1) I will have my brother clean my room.
　(2) Inhui made her daughter do the dishes.
　(3) My mother let me watch the TV drama.

06 (1) If you have a fever, you should see a doctor.
　(2) If it rains tomorrow, I will go to a movie.
　(3) If you add yellow to blue, it becomes green.

07 (1) My mother makes me clean my room.
　(2) The librarian helped me find a book.
　(3) They let her go safely.

08 We massage our eyes softly.

09 그것은 여러분의 눈을 더 편안하게 해 줄 것이다.

10 We can draw small circles with our fingers.

11 The massage will help you feel better.

12 are → is

13 He[She] plans to exercise more than three times a week.

14 나의 습관을 바꾸는 것
15 make me live a healthy life

01 Do you know how to + 동사원형 ~?: 너는 ~하는 방법을 아니?

02 I enjoy -ing ~.: 나는 ~하는 것을 즐긴다.

03 능력을 부인하는 표현으로 I'm not good at을 사용할 수 있다.

04 (D) 너는 방과 후에 뭐 하는 걸 즐기니? (C) 나는 건강에 좋은 음식을 요리하는 것을 즐겨. (A) 멋지구나. 너는 무엇을 만들 수 있니? (B) 나는 샐러드, 비빔밥 그리고 야채 주스를 만들 수 있어.

05 have, make, let 등 사역동사는 목적어 다음에 목적격보어로 동사원형을 쓴다.

06 (1) see a doctor: 진찰을 받다 (2) go to a movie: 영화 보러 가다 (3) add A to B: B에 A를 섞다

07 (1) makes가 사역동사이므로 목적격보어로 clean이 들어 가야 한다. (2) help는 목적격보어로 동사원형을 쓴다. (3) let은 사역동사로 목적격보어는 동사원형이 온다.

08 눈을 손가락으로 부드럽게 마사지한다.

09 사역동사 make+목적어+목적격보어(동사원형): ~을 …하게 만들다 / feel+형용사: ~하게 느끼다

10 목을 마사지하기 위해 손가락으로 작은 원을 그릴 수 있다.

11 help+목적어+목적격보어(동사원형/to부정사): ~가 …하는 것을 돕다 / feel better: 기분이 좋아지다

12 Here is + 단수 명사 ~: 여기 ~이 있다

13 글쓴이는 일주일에 세 번 이상 운동할 것이라고 했다.

14 인칭대명사 it은 changing[to change] my habits를 가리킨다.

15 사역동사 make+목적어+목적격보어(동사원형) / live a healthy life: 건강한 삶을 살다

### 창의사고력 서술형 문제
p.52

|모범답안|

01 (1) Do you know how to shop on the Internet? / No, I don't know how to shop on the Internet.

  (2) Do you know how to cook instant noodles? / Yes, I know how to cook instant noodles.

02 (1) If I go to Paris, I can see the Eiffel Tower.

  (2) If it is sunny tomorrow, I will go hiking with my friends.

  (3) If I find an abandoned dog on the street, I will take it to the animal center.

03 (1) My mother let me go to the amusement park.

  (2) Jenny made my brother run fast.

  (3) My friend helped me (to) do my homework.

  (4) My grandparents had me wait so long.

### 단원별 모의고사
p.53~56

| | | | |
|---|---|---|---|
| 01 ⑤ | 02 ③ | 03 ④ | 04 simple |
| 05 (a)dvice | 06 ⑤ | 07 ②, ⑤ | 08 ② |
| 09 ②, ④ | 10 ③ | 11 한쪽 발을 보드 위에 | |

11 올려 놓고 다른 한 발로 세게 민다. 　12 ③

13 feels → feel 　14 ① 　15 ④

16 My brother had me clean[sweep] the room.

17 Unless 　18 ② 　19 ① 　20 ①

21 ④ 　22 ① 　23 Massage from top to bottom. 　24 ④ 　25 ③ 　26 position

27 won't → don't 　28 ⑤ 　29 ②

30 to feel → feel

01 각각의 팔 끝과 목 사이에 있는 신체의 두 부분 중 하나: 어깨 (shoulder)

02 ③ for a few seconds: 수 초 동안

03 face: 얼굴; ~와 마주 보다

04 반의어 관계이다. 배고픈 : 배부른 = 복잡한 : 단순한

05 누군가에게 어떻게 하라고 알려 주는 말이나 제안: 조언, 충고 (advice)

06 능력 여부를 묻는 말에는 Do you know how to ~?, Can you ~?, Are you good at ~? 등이 있다.

07 I enjoy -ing ~는 좋아하는 것을 말하는 표현으로 I like to + 동사원형 ~. / I feel great when I + 동사원형 ~ 으로 바꿔 쓸 수 있다.

08 when: ~할 때 / because: ~이기 때문에

09 Do you know how to + 동사원형 ~?은 능력 여부를 묻는 표현으로 ①, ③, ⑤와 바꿔 쓸 수 있다.

10 the other: (둘 중에서) 다른 하나

11 Put one foot on the board and push hard with the other.에서 알 수 있다.

12 '~하면'이라는 조건의 접속사가 필요하다.

13 make는 사역동사로 목적격보어로 동사원형을 쓴다. 따라서 동사 feels는 원형인 feel로 써야 한다.

14 사역동사 let은 목적격보어로 동사원형(cross)을 쓴다.

15 ④ 조건을 나타내는 if절은 미래의 의미이더라도 현재시제로 써야 한다.

16 사역동사 have+목적어+동사원형: ~하도록 시키다

17 If ~ not은 '~하지 않는다면'이라는 의미로 Unless와 같다.

18 ②는 직접목적어와 간접목적어가 있는 4형식 문장이고 나머지는 모두 5형식 문장이다.

19 ② 미래의 일이므로 조건을 나타내는 문장의 주절은 미래시제를 사용한다.

20 문맥상 오른쪽 발등이 되어야 한다. ⓐ bottom → top

21 loosen up: (근육을) 풀어 주다

9

22 put A on B: A를 B 위에 놓다[대다]

23 from top to bottom: 위에서 아래로

24 파트너를 마주 보고(face), 머리와 몸을 뒤로 뻗고 (stretch), 서로 서 있는 자세로 끌어당긴다(pull)가 옳다.

25 for three seconds: 3초 동안 / at the same speed: 같은 속도로

26 어떤 사람이 서거나 앉거나 눕는 방식: 자세(position)

27 조건의 부사절에서는 미래시제 대신 현재시제를 사용한다.

28 주어진 문장의 It은 massaging[to massage] your eyes softly with your fingers를 가리키므로 ⑤번이 알맞다.

29 block out: (빛을) 차단하다

30 make+목적어+목적격보어(동사원형)

# To Be a Global Citizen

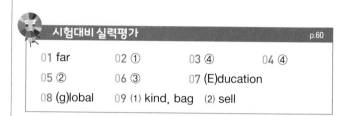

### 시험대비 실력평가 p.60

| | | | |
|---|---|---|---|
| 01 far | 02 ① | 03 ④ | 04 ④ |
| 05 ② | 06 ③ | 07 (E)ducation | |
| 08 (g)lobal | 09 (1) kind, bag (2) sell | | |

01 둘은 반의어 관계이다. more: 더 많이 less: 더 적게 far: 멀리; 먼 near: 가까운

02 flood: 홍수 / 그 폭우로 홍수가 났다.

03 community: 공동체, 지역[공동] 사회 / 매우 큰 지역 사회는 도시라고 불린다.

04 upload: 업로드하다 / 인터넷을 사용해서 문서나 프로그램을 컴퓨터에서 더 큰 시스템으로 보내다

05 citizen: 시민 / 합법적으로 어떤 나라나 마을에 살고 있는 사람

06 ① garden: 정원 / 너는 올해 정원에 장미를 심을 거니? ② Kenyan: 케냐의 / Charlie는 케냐의 중학교에 입학했다. ③ hold: (회의나 시합 등을) 열다 / 올해 그 마을은 축제를 열 것이다. ④ lantern: 랜턴, 제등 / 그녀는 멀리서 랜턴 불빛을 보았다. ⑤ poor: 가난한 / 많은 근로자들은 빈곤 지역 출신이다.

07 education: 교육

08 global: 전 세계적인, 지구상의

09 (1) kind: 종류 bag: 가방 (2) sell: 팔다

### 서술형 시험대비 p.61

01 (1) The cars are moving alongside us.
   (2) Citizens of the same country have the same nationality.
   (3) The heavy rain resulted in the flood.
   (4) We decided to raise money for the needy people.

02 (1) rcommunicate (2) gathered (3) celebrated
   (4) left    03 (1) hunger (2) national   04 care

05 (1) is good at solving  (2) Thanks to  (3) going, turn down  (4) (c)elebrate

01 (1) alongside: ~ 옆에, ~와 나란히 (2) citizen: 시민 (3) flood: 홍수 (4) raise: (자금 등을) 모으다, 모금하다

02 (1) communicate: 의사소통하다 / 우리는 서로 영어로 의사

소통한다. (2) gather: 모으다 / 그는 인터넷에서 정보를 모았다. (3) celebrate: (특별한 날·경사 등을) 축하하다, 기념하다 / 그녀는 작년에 내 생일을 축하해줬다. (4) leave: 남기다 / 그는 어제 접시에 음식을 남겼다.

03 (1) hunger: 기아, 배고픔 / 그들은 굶주림과 공기 오염으로 고통받을 것이다. (2) national: 국가적인 / 이것은 국가적인 문제가 아니라 국제적인 문제이다

04 care for: ~을 돌보다, 신경 쓰다 care about: ~에 관심을 가지다

05 (1) be good at: ~을 잘하다 (2) thanks to: ~ 덕분에 (3) be going to 동사원형: ~할 것이다 turn down the heat: (실내) 온도를 낮추다 (4) celebrate: 기념하다, 축하하다

## 교과서
# Conversation

### 핵심 Check
p.62~63

1 (1) you (p)lanning to / am (2) What are you, to do / I'm, to  2 (B) → (A) → (C)

3 (1) Are you (p)lanning / to swim (2) I hope she

4 ①, ③

### 교과서 대화문 익히기

### Check(√) True or False
p.64

1 F  2 F  3 T  4 T

### 교과서 확인학습
p.66~67

#### Listen & Speak 1 A
1 about the flood / I did, lot, lost / to send / How, Are you, to raise / going to, sell
2 plans, vacation / going to, do, with / went, helped, Are you going to do / paint walls

#### Listen & Speak 1 B
1 to take / am, I'm not
2 going to recycle / I am

#### Listen & Speak 2 A
1 What / making, about, hunger, dying / too bad / hope, care about global

---

2 to make, garden / vegetable garden, will / grow, share, with / hope, grow

#### Listen & Speak 2 B
1 hope, don't throw away / hope so, Let's hold / campaign
2 I hope people don't / so, Let's hold

#### Wrap Up
1 What's your plan, Are, to do anything special / On, going to / about on / have / going to do volunteer work, like to come
2 going to hold, at / What is / protect, throw trash on, to stop / hope, goes

### 시험대비 기본평가
p.68

01 ④        02 ③        03 ①
04 (B) → (C) → (A) → (D)

01 의도나 앞으로의 할 일 물을 때는 Are you going to ~?로 물을 수 있다. 대답을 할 때 긍정이면 Yes, I am., 부정이면 No, I'm not.으로 대답한다.

02 I hope (that) 주어 can 동사 ~.: 나는 ~하기를 바라 hurt: 다치게 하다

03 be going to 동사원형 = be planning to 동사원형: ~할 것이다

04 (B) 반에서 채소밭을 만들기로 했다고 말하자 (C) 채소밭에서 무엇을 기르는지 질문한다. (A) 채소밭에 당근을 길러서 사람들과 나눌 거라고 대답한다. (D) 좋은 생각이라고 상대방의 의견에 동의한다. decide: 결정하다 garden: 정원 will: ~할 것이다 grow: 기르다, 재배하다 share A(사물) with B(사람): A를 B와 나누다[나눠 가지다]

### 시험대비 실력평가
p.69~70

| | | | |
|---|---|---|---|
| 01 ④ | 02 ②, ⑤ | 03 ④ | 04 ④ |
| 05 garden | 06 ④ | 07 ②, ④ | 08 ① |
| 09 ④ | 10 waste | 11 ② | 12 ②, ④ |

01 남자아이가 현재진행형(be동사의 현재형+동사ing)을 사용하여 대답하고 있으므로, 빈칸에는 현재진행형을 사용해 지금 하고 있는 일이 무엇인지 질문한다.

02 많은 사람들이 기아로 죽어가고 있다는 사실에 안타까움을 표현하고 있다.

03 about: ~에 관하여 die of: ~으로 죽다 care about: ~에 관심을 가지다

04 공기가 깨끗해지기를 바라며, '더 많은 나무를 심어라'라는 캠페인을 열자는 말에, '정말 안됐다.'라는 것은 어색하다. That's

too bad. → That's a good idea.

05 식물을 기를 수 있는 장소 / garden: 정원

06 ⓐ, ⓑ, ⓒ, ⓔ: 당근 ⓓ others: 다른 사람들

07 의도나 계획을 묻는 표현으로 'Are you planning to 동사원형 ~?', 'Are you going to 동사원형 ~?', 'Are you trying to 동사원형 ~?' 등이 있으며, '너는 ~할 계획이니?' 또는 '너는 ~할 거니?'의 의미로 쓰인다.

08 공기가 깨끗해지기를 바란다는 말에 어울리는 캠페인은 '더 많은 나무를 심어라'라는 캠페인이다.

09 주어진 문장에서 it은 지호가 가져온 불고기를 의미한다. 불고기를 많이 담아온 것 같아 나눠 먹자는 말의 대답으로, That's a good idea.(좋은 생각이야.)가 어울리므로 ④가 적절하다.

10 시간, 돈, 에너지를 완전히 또는 합리적이거나 유용한 방법으로 사용하지 못하다 / waste: 낭비하다, 허비하다

11 from now on: 앞으로는, 지금부터는

12 ① "생각하라, 먹어라, 구하라!"는 포스터에 쓰여져 있다. ② '불고기를 다 먹을 거니?'라는 질문에 지호는 '잘 모르겠어.'라고 대답했으므로, 다 먹을 거라는 확신이 없었다. ③ 불고기는 지호가 좋아하는 음식이다. ④ 지호와 Karl은 음식을 다 먹었다. ⑤ Karl은 지구를 살리기를 바란다.

### 서술형 시험대비 p.71

01 (1) (g)oing (2) (p)lanning 02 plans
03 she will visit her grandmother, she will do volunteer work at the library
04 Are you going to use your own cup? 05 flood
06 My club is going to send them some money.
07 How 08 I hope people don't throw away trash.

01 의도나 계획을 표현할 때 'I'm planning to 동사원형 ~.(나는 ~할 것이다)' 또는 'I'm going to 동사원형 ~.'을 사용한다.

02 plan: 계획

03 수민이는 토요일에 할머니를 방문하고, 일요일에는 남자아이와 같이 도서관에서 봉사 활동을 할 것이다. do volunteer work: 자원 봉사를 하다

04 의도나 계획을 묻는 표현으로 'Are you going to 동사원형 ~?'을 사용할 수 있으며, '너는 ~할 계획이니?' 또는 너는 ~할 거니?'의 의미로 쓰인다.

05 물의 넘쳐흐름 / flood: 홍수

06 be going to 동사원형: ~할 것이다 send+간접목적어(사람)+직접목적어(사물): ~에게 ~을 보내다

07 홍수로 집을 잃은 사람들에게 돈을 줄 방법을 물어보고 있다. How: 어떻게

08 throw away: ~을 버리다 trash: 쓰레기 I hope (that) 주어 동사 ~: 나는 ~하기를 바라

### 핵심 Check p.72~73

**1** (1) who (2) has (3) that **2** (1) nothing strange
(2) anything delicious (3) something bright
**3** (1) something cool (2) nothing exciting (3) anything sweet

### 시험대비 기본평가 p.74

01 (1) which → who[that]
(2) wonderful something → something wonderful
(3) which → who[that]
(4) delicious anything → anything delicious
02 ④ 03 ②, ④ 04 ③

01 (1) 선행사가 사람인 people이므로 관계대명사는 who가 적절하다. (2) 대명사 something은 형용사가 뒤에서 수식한다. (3) 선행사가 사람인 girl이므로 관계대명사는 who가 적절하다. (4) 대명사 anything은 형용사가 뒤에서 수식한다.

02 선행사가 a huge clock인 사물이고 단수 명사이므로 which is가 적절하다.

03 선행사가 사람인 a woman이고 주격인 she를 대신하므로 주격인 who가 적절하고, that은 who 대신 사용 가능하다.

04 -thing으로 끝나는 대명사는 뒤에서 형용사의 수식을 받는다. 그리고 긍정문에서는 something을 사용하고, 부정문과 의문문에서는 anything을 사용한다.

### 시험대비 실력평가 p.75~77

01 ①
02 (1) Do you know anybody famous?
(2) I want to do something different.
(3) Do you have anything new?
(4) He met someone beautiful yesterday.
03 which / who 04 (1) who (2) who are
(3) who 05 ⑤ 06 ② 07 ④
08 ④ 09 (1) special nothing → nothing special (2) something → anything (3) who are → which[that] is 10 ① 11 ③
12 ⑤ 13 (1) which (2) who (3) which
(4) who 14 ② 15 I want to eat something sweet. 16 someone tall
17 who 18 ① 19 ③ 20 ⑤
21 (1) who (2) that

01 -thing으로 끝나는 대명사는 형용사가 뒤에서 수식을 한다.

02 -thing, -one, -body로 끝나는 대명사는 형용사가 뒤에서 수식을 한다.

03 선행사가 the lion과 doctor이므로 which와 who가 적절하다.

04 (1) 선행사가 사람이므로 who가 적절하다. (2) 선행사가 복수 명사 students이므로 주격 관계대명사 뒤의 동사는 복수동사 are가 적절하다. (3) 동사 was가 관계대명사 뒤에 있기 때문에 주격 who가 적절하다.

05 선행사가 단수명사인 The girl(사람)이므로 관계대명사는 who, 동사는 단수 lives가 적절하다.

06 주격 관계대명사는 뒤에 동사가 온다. 즉, 'who[which/that]+동사 ~'의 형태를 취한다.

07 보기의 who와 같은 쓰임은 ④번의 관계대명사다. 나머지는 모두 의문대명사 who다.

08 선행사가 복수 명사인 two daughters이기 때문에 주격 관계대명사 뒤의 동사는 복수 동사인 are가 되어야 한다.

09 (1) -thing으로 끝나는 대명사는 형용사가 뒤에서 수식한다. (2) 의문문에서는 something이 아니라 anything을 사용한다. (3) 100년 된 집에 산다는 의미로 선행사가 사물이므로 who를 which로 바꾸고, 동사도 단수 동사 is로 바꾼다.

10 many people을 수식하고, 동사 want의 주어 역할을 하는 관계대명사절을 이끄는 who가 적절하다.

11 선행사가 사람이면 who, 사물이면 which를 사용하고, 주격 관계대명사 뒤의 동사는 선행사의 수에 일치시킨다.

12 ①은 선행사가 the girl이므로 who가 적절하다. ②는 선행사가 a book이므로 which를 쓴다. ③은 선행사가 Ms. Ha이고 동사 is의 주어 역할을 하는 who를 쓴다. ④는 선행사가 the phone이고 동사 is의 주어 역할을 하는 which를 쓴다.

13 선행사가 사람이면 who를, 사물이면 which를 사용한다.

14 사물 선행사인 the movie를 수식하는 관계대명사절을 이끄는 주격 관계대명사 which가 적절하다.

15 something은 형용사가 뒤에서 수식한다.

16 someone은 형용사가 뒤에서 수식한다.

17 선행사가 사람 people이기 때문에 관계대명사 that을 who로 바꾸어 쓸 수 있다.

18 something은 형용사가 뒤에서 수식한다.

19 관계대명사를 이용하여 두 문장을 한 문장으로 바꿀 때, 두 번째 문장의 중복되는 명사를 관계대명사로 바꾸어 준다. 중복되는 명사(선행사)가 사물인 stamps이므로 관계대명사 which로 바꾸어 준다.

20 명사는 형용사가 명사 앞에서 수식을 하지만, -thing으로 끝나는 대명사는 형용사가 뒤에서 수식한다.

21 (1), (2)는 모두 선행사가 사람이므로 관계대명사는 who 또는 that을 사용할 수 있다.

01 valuable anything → anything valuable

02 (1) Both paintings show a couple who[that] are dancing
  (2) In 1883, Renoir completed two paintings which[that] look very similar.
  (3) Jake is wearing a hat which[that] looks very old.

03 (1) who → which[that]    (2) who are → which[that] is    (3) whom → who[that]

04 (1) which has    (2) who is
  (3) which has

05 (1) Yesterday I met a girl who is from Mexico.
  (2) I want to buy a smartphone which has a large screen.
  (3) John read an article which was written by his friend.

06 (1) nothing special    (2) something nice

07 (1) The teacher talked about something different.
  (2) Sam is wearing shoes that are too big for him.
  (3) Are you going to do anything special during the summer vacation?

08 which aim → which aims
special something → something special

09 We need someone smarter than us.

10 (1) There is something strange on the roof of the house.
  (2) He liked to draw ballet dancers who[that] were moving.
  (3) He fell in love with a lady who[that] taught music at the nursing home.

01 anything은 형용사가 뒤에서 수식을 한다.

02 (1) 선행사가 a couple이므로 which를 who로 바꾼다. (2) 선행사가 two paintings이므로 whose를 which로 바꾼다. (3) 선행사가 a hat이므로 who를 which로 바꾸고, 동사도 선행사의 수에 맞추어 단수 동사 looks로 고친다.

03 (1) 선행사가 사물인 the tea이므로 who를 which[that]로 고친다. (2) 선행사가 사물인 a house이므로 who를 which[that]으로 고치고, 동사를 단수형인 is로 고친다. (3) 선행사가 사람인 painter이고, 동사 is의 주어 역할을 하는 주격 관계대명사가 필요하므로 whom을 who로 고친다.

04 선행사의 종류에 따라 관계대명사를 선택하고, 주격 관계대명사절의 동사는 선행사의 수에 일치시킨다.

05 두 문장에서 중복되는 명사를 찾고, 사람이 중복되면 who를, 사물이 중복되면 which를 사용한다.

06 대화의 흐름상 B는 주말에 특별한 일이 없다는 것을 알 수 있

다. 그래서 빈칸 (1)은 nothing special이 자연스럽고, (2)는 이번 주말에 Jenny와 근사한 것을 먹을 계획이라고 했으므로 something nice가 적절하다.

07 (1) '~에 관해 말하다'는 talk about이고, 다른 무언가는 something 뒤에 형용사 different를 사용한다. (2) shoes를 수식하는 관계대명사절을 만들 때 선행사가 사물이므로 관계대 명사는 that을 쓰고 동사 are를 사용한다. (3) '~할 것이니?'라 는 표현으로 'are you going to+동사원형'을 이용한다. do의 목적어로 anything을 쓰고 형용사 special이 뒤에서 수식한다. 마지막으로 전치사 during과 명사 the summer vacation을 쓴다.

08 a poster가 선행사이므로 which 뒤에 동사는 단수 동사 aims 가 되어야 한다. 그리고 something은 형용사 special이 뒤에 서 수식해야 한다.

09 '주어(We)+동사(need)+목적어(someone)+형용사 비교급 (smarter) than ~' 어순으로 쓴다.

10 (1) something은 형용사 strange가 뒤에서 수식해야 한다. (2) 선행사가 사람이고 복수 명사인 dancers이므로 who[that] were로 바꾸어야 한다. (3) 선행사가 a lady이기 때문에 관계 대명사 which를 who 또는 that으로 고쳐야 한다.

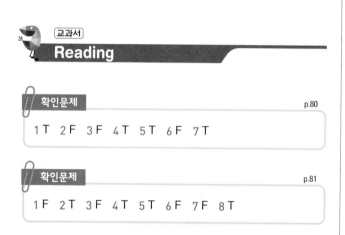

### 교과서 Reading

**확인문제**     p.80

1 T   2 F   3 F   4 T   5 T   6 F   7 T

**확인문제**     p.81

1 F   2 T   3 F   4 T   5 T   6 F   7 F   8 T

### 교과서 확인학습 A    p.82~83

01 Global Citizenship
02 This is
03 helps us grow
04 who try to understand
05 care for, in need
06 share, experiences
07 from Korea
08 a member of
09 to communicate with
10 about the lantern festival
11 uploaded it, 5,000 hits
12 for our video
13 looks fantastic
14 a water festival
15 like yours
16 my name
17 am from
18 showed us pictures
19 they were all, to carry their books

20 to raise money
21 raised 600 dollars
22 are happy with
23 Awesome, I'm sure
24 something wonderful
25 from
26 a wall painting, look better
27 are good at, gathered, painted
28 Thanks to, much nicer
29 walking alongside, painted
30 What a nice idea

### 교과서 확인학습 B    p.84~85

1 Global Citizenship Education
2 This is the Global Citizenship Education site.
3 Global Citizenship Education helps us grow as global citizens.
4 Global citizens are people who try to understand different cultures.
5 They also care for people in need and work for a better world.
6 Please share your global citizenship education experiences here.
7 Hello. I am Minhee from Korea.
8 I am a member of the Global Community Club.
9 My club aims to communicate with people from around the world.
10 A week ago we produced a video about the lantern festival in our village.
11 We uploaded it to the Internet and amazingly, we got nearly 5,000 hits.
12 Click here for our video.
13 Alice: Wow, your lantern festival looks fantastic!
14 Sunan: We have a water festival in our village.
15 I'd like to make a video like yours.
16 Hi, my name is Jo.
17 I am from Australia.
18 A few weeks ago, my teacher showed us pictures of students in Kenya.
19 Sadly, they were all using plastic bags to carry their books.
20 My class decided to raise money to send them new school bags.
21 We sold cookies and drinks and raised 600 dollars.
22 We hope the Kenyan students are happy with the new bags.
23 Wang: Awesome! I'm sure they will like the bags.
24 Kozo: You did something wonderful!

25 I am Afig from Malaysia.

26 My school started a wall painting campaign to make our village look better.

27 Students who are good at painting gathered and painted on some walls of schools and parks.

28 Thanks to this campaign, our village looks much nicer.

29 Now everyone can enjoy walking alongside the painted walls.

30 Junho: What a nice idea!

## 시험대비 실력평가  p.86~89

| | | | |
|---|---|---|---|
| 01 ④ | 02 ③ | 03 Global citizens | |
| 04 ③ | 05 ① | 06 ⑤ | 07 ④ |
| 08 ① | 09 (1) How nice the idea is! | | |
| (2) It is a very nice idea. | | 10 hit(s) | 11 ② |
| 12 ⑤ | 13 ①, ④ | 14 which 또는 that | |
| 15 ③ | 16 ③ | 17 ①, ⑤ | 18 Kenyan |
| 19 ④ | 20 ③ | 21 ③ raising → to raise | |
| 22 students in Kenya | | 23 ② | |
| 24 ① knowing → know | | 25 ⑤ | |
| 26 ①, ③, ⑤ | | | |

01 ④ 위 글은 '웹 사이트에 게시된 글'이다. ② review (책·연극·영화 등에 대한) 논평[비평], 감상문, ③ article (신문·잡지의) 글, 기사, ⑤ summary 요약, 개요

02 ⓐ와 ③번은 ~로서, ~으로, ① 이유, ② ~만큼, ④ ~하다시피[~이듯이], ⑤ ~함에 따라, ~할수록

03 '세계 시민'을 가리킨다.

04 ⓐ와 ②, ④, ⑤는 명사적 용법, ① 부사적 용법, ③ 형용사적 용법

05 ⓑ upload A to ~: A를 ~에 업로드하다, ⓒ for our video: 우리 비디오를 보려면

06 ⑤ 위 글은 민희가 동아리의 목표를 말하면서 마을의 등 축제에 관한 비디오를 제작한 것을 소개하는 내용의 글이므로, 제목으로는 '우리 동아리의 활동을 소개할게'가 적절하다.

07 이 글은 'Afig의 학교가 벽화 캠페인을 시작해서 마을을 더 보기 좋게 만들었다'는 내용의 글이다.

08 very는 비교급을 강조할 수 없다.

09 How+형용사[부사]+주어+동사! (2) What을 very로 고치고 '주어+동사'의 순서로 쓰면 된다.

10 hit: 조회 수, 웹 사이트를 한 번 방문하는 것

11 ② '좋아하다', ⓑ와 나머지는 다 '~와 비슷한', '~와 같이, ~처럼'이라는 뜻이다. ① 그녀는 내 것과 비슷한 드레스를 입고 있다. ③ 그는 술을 많이 마신다. ④ 나는 너처럼 요리를 잘하지

못한다. ⑤ 그녀는 배우처럼 보인다.

12 Sunan은 자기 마을의 물 축제에 관한 비디오를 만든 것이 아니라 만들고 싶다고 했을 뿐이다.

13 ⓐ와 ①, ④번: 즐겁게 보내다, 즐거운 시간을 갖다, ② 놀리다, ③ (음식 등을) 마음대로 드시오. ⑤ 코믹한 표정을 짓다

14 선행사가 사물이고 주어 자리이므로, 주격 관계대명사 which나 that이 적절하다.

15 물싸움을 즐길 수 있다.

16 주어진 문장의 new school bags에 주목한다. ③번 앞 문장의 plastic bags 대신에 쓸 수 있도록 책가방을 보내려는 것이므로 ③번이 적절하다.

17 ⓐ와 ②, ③, ④는 부사적 용법, ① 형용사적 용법, ⑤ 명사적 용법

18 Kenya의 형용사형을 쓰는 것이 적절하다. Kenyan: [형용사, 명사] 케냐의, 케냐인

19 ④ Jo의 반이 어디에서 쿠키와 음료를 팔았는지는 대답할 수 없다. ① From Australia. ② Pictures of students in Kenya. ③ No. ⑤ 600 dollars.

20 위 글은 케냐에 있는 학생들에게 새로운 책가방을 보내기 위해서 기금을 모금하는 것에 관한 글이므로, 주제로는 '새 책가방을 보내기 위해서 기금을 모금하기'가 적절하다.

21 decide는 목적어 자리에 동명사가 아니라 to부정사를 써야 한다

22 '케냐의 학생들'을 가리킨다.

23 ② 'Jo의 선생님이 보여주신 사진의 숫자'는 알 수 없다. ① 호주, ③ 비닐 봉지, ④ 쿠키와 음료를 팔았다. ⑤ 600달러.

24 사역동사 let은 목적격보어 자리에 원형부정사를 쓰는 것이 적절하다.

25 이 글은 Sunan이 친구 민희에게 보내는 송크란 축제의 '초대장'이다. ③ order: 명령하다, ④ force: 강요하다

26 송크란 축제에서는 물싸움, 퍼레이드 구경, 그리고 태국 전통 음식을 맛볼 수 있다.

## 서술형 시험대비  p.90~91

01 (A) site  (B) grow  (C) work

02 (1) 다른 문화를 이해하려고 노력하는 사람들이다.
   (2) 어려움에 처한 사람들을 보살피고 더 나은 세상을 위해서 일하는 사람들이다.

03 take care of 또는 look after

04 we got nearly(또는 almost) 5,000 hits

05 looks like fantastic → looks fantastic

06 (A) make a video  (B) Minhee's club

07 were using plastic bags   08 plastic → school

09 ⑤ to be → are(또는 will be)

10 to send new school bags to them

01 (A) 세계 시민 교육 '(웹)사이트'라고 해야 하므로 site가 적절하다. cite: 인용하다, site: (웹)사이트, 장소, (B) 'help+목적어+원형부정사 또는 to부정사'이므로 grow가 적절하다. (C) care for와 병렬구문을 이루도록 work가 적절하다.

02 '세계 시민'은 다른 문화를 이해하려고 노력하고 또한 어려움에 처한 사람들을 보살피고 더 나은 세상을 위해서 일한다.

03 care for = take care of = look after: 돌보다

04 hits: 조회 수

05 감각동사 look+형용사, look like+명사: ~하게 보이다

06 Sunan은 '민희의 동아리'가 그들 마을의 등 축제에 관한 비디오를 제작한 것처럼 그들 마을의 물 축제에 관한 '비디오를 만들고' 싶어 한다.

07 그들은 비닐 봉지를 사용하고 있었다.

08 Jo의 반은 비닐 봉지 대신 사용할 새로운 '책가방'을 보내기 위해서 기금을 모금했다.

09 'hope+목적어+to부정사'는 쓸 수 없다. 'hope+(that)+주어+동사'로 쓰는 것이 적절하다.

10 send는 'to'를 사용하여 3형식으로 고친다.

11 Afig의 학교는 '그들의 마을을 좀 더 좋아 보이게 하기 위해서' 벽화 캠페인을 시작했다.

12 'at'을 보충하면 된다. be good at: ~에 능숙하다

13 송크란은 태국의 큰 축제이고 전통적인 태국의 '설날'을 축하하기 위해 개최된다. 축제에서 여러분은 큰 '물싸움'을 즐길 수 있고 송크란 퍼레이드를 볼 수 있다.

14 Thai: (형용사) 태국(인, 어)의, (명사) 태국인, 타이어

### 영역별 핵심문제
p.93~97

01 ⑤      02 ①      03 ⑤      04 ③
05 ②      06 (A) going  (B) to do  (C) helped
07 Are you going to do that, too?      08 ④
09 raise
10 We're going to make pencil cases and sell them.
11 (B) → (A) → (D) → (C)    12 (B) → (A) → (C)
13 If you want to do something special for the world
14 (1) He is the student who won the speech contest.
   (2) I know the man who was looking for his dog.
   (3) He wrote a novel which became a best-seller.
15 ②      16 ②      17 ⑤      18 ②

19 helps → help      20 ②      21 ④
22 (1) is → are  (2) which play → who plays
(3) are → is   23 ⑤      24 ④      25 ②, ⑤
26 ⑤      27 (A) the lantern festival  (B) a water festival      28 ③      29 My class decided to raise money to send them new school bag.   30 ①

01 ⑥를 제외한 <보기>의 단어들은 모두 동의어 관계이다. ⓐ gather: 모으다 collect: 모으다 ⓑ global: 전 세계적인, 지구 상의 worldwide: 세계적인 ⓒ save: 살리다, 구하다 rescue: 구출하다, 구조하다 ⓓ upset: 당황한 worried: 걱정스러운, 당황하는 ⓔ far: 멀리, 먼 near: 가까운

02 awesome: 굉장한, 감탄할 만한, 엄청난 impressive: 인상적인, 감동적인

03 finish: (남아 있는 것을) 마저 먹다

04 ① bags, bag: 가방 / 음식 담을 비닐봉지가 필요하세요? ② trash, trash: 쓰레기 / 공원은 10분 후에 폐장합니다. 쓰레기를 남기고 가면 안 됩니다. ③ fight, fight: 싸움, 싸우다 / 너는 너의 친구들과 자주 싸우니? ④ campaign, campaign: 캠페인, 조직적 활동 / 나는 네가 우리의 새로운 캠페인에 참여하기를 원한다. ⑤ garden, garden: 정원 / 너는 정원에 장미를 심을 거니?

05 save: 아끼다, 구하다

06 (A) 현재진행형으로 가까운 미래의 일을 표현하고 있다. (B) to부정사의 부사적 용법 중 목적(~하기 위해서)을 사용한다. to do some volunteer work: 봉사활동을 하기 위해서 (C) 접속사 and로 went와 helped는 병렬구조를 이루고 있다.

07 Are you going 동사원형 ~?: 너는 ~할 거니?

08 ① 남자아이는 필리핀에 작년에 갔었다. ② 여자아이는 이번 여름 방학에 필리핀에 갈 것이다. ③ 남자아이는 필리핀에 가서 아이들이 공부하는 것을 도와줬다. ④ 남자아이의 여름 방학 계획에 대해서는 대화에서 언급되지 않았다. ⑤ 여자아이는 여름 방학에 필리핀에 갈 것이다.

09 특정한 목적을 위한 돈을 모으다 / raise: (자금 등을) 모으다, 모금하다

10 be going to 동사원형: ~할 것이다 sell: 팔다

11 동아리가 다음 주 금요일에 그린 캠페인을 연다는 말에, (B) 그린 캠페인이 무엇인지 질문한다. (A) 환경을 보호하기 위한 캠페인이라고 얘기하며, 많은 학생들이 길에 쓰레기를 버리는 것을 멈추기를 바란다는 희망을 표현하자. (D) 캠페인이 잘되길 빌어주고, (C) 감사를 표하며 캠페인이 잘되기를 바란다고 대답한다.

12 무엇을 하고 있는지 질문하자 (B) 세계 기아 문제에 대한 포스터를 만들고 있다고 말하며, 많은 사람들이 기아로 죽어가고 있다고 말한다. (A) 기아로 많은 사람들이 죽어가는 것에 대해 안타까움을 표현하면서, 그러한 사실을 몰랐다고 얘기한다. (C)

더 많은 사람들이 세계의 기아 문제에 관심을 갖기를 바라는 희망을 표현한다.

13 대명사 something은 형용사의 수식을 뒤에서 받는다.

14 선행사가 사람이면 who를, 사물이면 which를 사용한다.

15 선행사가 a lady이므로 who wants가 적절하다.

16 사람과 사물, 동물을 선행사로 가질 수 있는 관계대명사는 that이다.

17 ①~④는 의문형용사이고 ⑤는 관계대명사이다.

18 ② 선행사가 '사람+동물'일 때는 관계대명사 that을 사용한다. which를 that으로 고쳐야 한다.

19 선행사가 복수 명사 activities이므로 주격 관계대명사절의 동사는 선행사에 일치하여 복수 동사가 되어야 한다.

20 두 번째 문장에서 선행사가 neighbor로 사람이므로 which를 who로 바꾸어야 하며, 마지막 문장에서 선행사가 the cats로 복수 명사이므로 주격 관계대명사절의 동사는 복수형인 don't가 되어야 한다.

21 선행사가 a cat이므로 관계대명사는 which 또는 that이 적절하고 동사는 단수 동사 is가 와야 한다.

22 관계대명사는 선행사의 종류에 따라 결정되므로 (1) 선행사가 students이므로 who나 that을 쓰고 복수 동사 are로 고친다. (2) 선행사가 a person이므로 which를 who로 고치고 단수 동사 plays로 고친다. (3) 선행사가 my friend이므로 that이나 who를 쓰고 단수 동사 is로 고친다.

23 ⑤ nothing은 형용사 interesting이 뒤에서 수식해야 한다.

24 ①, ②, ⑤번은 '–thing+형용사' 형태의 문장이 되어야 한다. ③은 선행사가 an email이므로 who를 which나 that으로 고쳐야 한다.

25 선행사가 사람이고 주어 자리이므로 주격 관계대명사 who나 that이 적절하다.

26 '세계 시민은 교육 경험을 공유하는 사람들이다.'가 아니라, '당신의 세계 시민 교육 경험을 이곳에 공유해 주세요.'라고 했다.

27 민희의 동아리는 그들 마을의 '등 축제'에 관한 비디오를 제작했고, Sunan은 자기 마을의 '물 축제'에 관한 비디오를 만들고 싶어 한다.

28 ③ '등 축제에 관한 비디오를 만드는 데 얼마나 오래 걸렸는지'는 대답할 수 없다. ① To communicate with people from around the world. ② A video about the lantern festival in their village. ④ Nearly 5,000 hits. ⑤ She thinks it looks fantastic.

29 'raise'를 보충하면 된다.

30 이 글은 케냐에 있는 학생들에게 새로운 책가방을 보내기 위해서 기금을 모금하는 것에 관한 글이므로, 제목으로는 '책가방 보내기 위한 모금'이 적절하다.

---

01 (1) American　(2) Kenyan　　　02 (h)urt
03 (1) far　(2) environment　(3) international
04 ⑤　　　05 ⑤　　　06 Are you going to eat all of that?　07 save　　08 environment 09 ④
10 (1) My club is planning to hold a green campaign at school next Friday.
　(2) My club will hold a green campaign at school next Friday.
11 (A) protect　(B) throw　(C) goes
12 (A) lost　(B) send　(C) raise　(C) sell　13 ⑤
14 ②　　　15 ①　　　16 The man who[that] is working in the garden is my friend.　　17 ⑤
18 bad something → something bad
19 I will buy the novels which[that] were written by Ernest Hemingway.
20 ③　　　　21 Global Citizenship Education helps us grow as global citizens.　22 share　23 ②
24 My club aims to communicate with people from around the world.
25 a video about the lantern festival in our village
26 ④　　　27 ⓐ painting　ⓒ painted　28 ②

---

01 China: 중국 Chinese: 중국의 (1) American: 미국의; 미국인 (2) Kenyan: 케냐의

02 hurt: 다치게 하다

03 (1) far: 멀리; 먼 (2) environment: 자연환경, 환경 (3) international: 국제적인

04 ⑤의 영영풀이는 'communicate'이다. gather의 영영풀이는 'to bring people together or collect things together'이다.

05 주어진 문장은 음식을 다 먹고 나서 얘기할 수 있는 말로 ⑤번 다음의 clean plate로 보아 ⑤번이 적절하다.

06 be going to 동사원형: ~할 것이다

07 save: 살리다, 구하다

08 육지, 바다, 공기, 식물 및 동물이 있는 자연 / environment: 자연환경, 환경

09 주어진 문장의 that이 ④번 앞 문장의 내용을 가리키므로 ④번이 적절하다. I hope to 동사원형 ~: 나는 ~하고 싶어

10 'I'm planning to 동사원형 ~.'은 '나는 ~할 계획이다.'라는 의미로 미래의 계획이나 의도에 대해 사용하는 표현으로 to 다음에 동사원형이 온다. 비슷한 표현으로 'I'm going to 동사원형 ~.', 'I'll 동사원형 ~.' 등이 있다.

11 (A) protect: 보호하다 (B) throw: 버리다 (C) go well: 잘 되다

12 (A) lost는 lose의 과거형이다. 과거의 사실을 말하고 있으므로 과거형을 사용해야 한다. (B) send: 보내다 spend는 4형식

17

을 사용할 수 없고, 내용상 집을 잃은 사람들에게 돈을 보낸다는 것이 적절하다. (C) raise: (자금 등을) 모으다, 모금하다 (D) make와 sell은 등위접속사 and에 의해 연결되어 있다.

13 Let's waste food from now on. → Let's not waste food from now on.

14 선행사가 사람이고 주격이므로 관계대명사 who가 적절하다.

15 사물과 사람을 선행사로 가질 수 있는 관계대명사는 that이다.

16 두 문장에서 동일한 대상을 가리키는 단어를 찾는다. 그 다음 뒤 문장의 대명사를 관계대명사(who, which, that)로 바꾼다. 마지막으로 관계대명사가 이끄는 문장을 선행사 바로 뒤에 붙여 쓴다.

17 ⑤ 'something, anything, nothing, everything'은 형용사가 뒤에서 꾸며 준다.

18 'something'은 형용사가 뒤에서 꾸며 준다.

19 주격 관계대명사와 be동사는 동시에 생략할 수 있다.

20 (A)는 선행사가 many pets이므로 which가 적절하고, (B)는 선행사가 a woman이므로 who가 적절하다.

21 help+목적어+원형부정사

22 share: 공유하다, 공통으로 가지다, 공동으로 가지거나 또는 공통으로 사용하다

23 ② 세계 시민 교육이 어떻게 우리가 세계 시민으로 자라도록 도와주는지는 대답할 수 없다. ① It is the Global Citizenship Education site. ③ Different cultures. ④ People in need. ⑤ A better world.

24 'with'를 보충하면 된다.

25 '우리 마을의 등 축제에 관한 비디오'를 가리킨다.

26 ⓒ와 ② 명사적 용법(목적어), ①과 ⑤ 부사적 용법(목적), ③ 형용사적 용법 (It은 비인칭 주어), ④ 형용사적 용법

27 ⓐ 전치사의 목적어이므로 동명사로 쓰는 것이 적절하다. ⓑ '그림이 그려진' 벽이라고 해야 하므로 'painted'가 적절하다.

28 very는 비교급을 수식할 수 없다.

### 서술형 실전문제　　　　　　　p.102~103

01 to recycle　　　　　　02 don't hurt
03 If you finish all the food on your plate, you will get a small gift.
04 (1) something wrong　(2) anything interesting
(3) everything important　05 (1) like → likes
(2) which teach → who[that] teaches
06 (1) I like my house which[that] is by the lake.
(2) Look at my dog which[that] is playing with a ball.
07 Look at the bird flying in the sky.
08 (A) uploaded　(B) nearly　(C) to make
09 (A) aim　(B) uploaded

10 in the world → in their village
11 to make our village look better
12 (A) wall painting　(B) paint
13 very → much[far, even]

01 사용된 재료나 폐기물을 재사용에 알맞게 되도록 처리하다 / recycle: (폐기물을) 재활용하다 be going to 동사원형: ~할 것이다

02 어떤 사람의 신체 일부에 부상을 입히거나 고통을 유발하다 / hurt: 다치게 하다 / 내용상 동물을 해치지 않기를 바란다는 것이 들어가야 하므로, 'don't'를 추가해야 한다.

03 finish: (남아 있는 것을) 마저 먹다

04 'something, anything, nothing, everything'은 형용사가 뒤에서 꾸며 준다.

05 (1) 주격 관계대명사 who의 선행사가 단수 명사 the girl이므로 like를 likes로 고친다. (2) 선행사가 사람인 the man이므로 which를 who로, 그리고 선행사가 단수 명사이므로 동사 teach를 단수 동사 teaches로 고친다.

06 두 문장에서 동일한 대상을 가리키는 단어를 찾는다. 그 다음 뒤 문장의 대명사를 관계대명사(who, which, that)로 바꾼다. 마지막으로 관계대명사가 이끄는 문장을 선행사 바로 뒤에 붙여 쓴다.

07 주격 관계대명사와 be동사는 동시에 생략할 수 있다.

08 (A) 인터넷에 '올렸다'고 해야 하므로 uploaded가 적절하다. download: (데이터를) 다운로드하다[내려받다], (B) '거의' 5,000 조회 수라고 해야 하므로 nearly가 적절하다. near: 가까운, (거리상으로) 가까이, (C) would like는 목적어로 동명사가 아닌 to부정사를 써야 하므로 to make가 적절하다.

09 그것은 전 세계의 사람들과 소통하는 것이 '목표'인 동아리이다. 동아리 회원들이 지역 축제를 소개하는 비디오를 만들어서 그것을 인터넷에 '올렸다.'

10 일주일 전에 민희의 동아리는 '그들 마을의' 등 축제에 관한 비디오를 만들었다.

11 사역동사(make)+목적어+원형부정사(look)

12 그것은 Afig의 학교가 시작한 '벽화' 캠페인이고, '그림을 잘 그리는' 학생들이 모여서 학교와 공원 벽에 그림을 그렸다. who are good at painting = who paint well

13 very는 원급을 강조하고, much, far, even, still 등은 비교급을 강조한다. nicer를 nice로 고치는 것도 가능하지만, 본문의 앞부분에 나오는 look better에 일치시켜 비교급으로 쓰는 것이 더 적절하다.

### 창의사고력 서술형 문제　　　　　　　p.104

|모범답안|

01 the summer vacation / I'm going to make a vegetable garden / I'm planning to do volunteer work at the library

02 (1) A musician is a person who plays music.

(2) A patient is a person who sees a doctor.

(3) A dentist is a person who takes care of your teeth.

(4) A genius is a person who is very intelligent.

03 (A) shoes  (B) Draw  (C) write  (D) need
(E) special

01 summer vacation: 여름 방학 be going to 동사원형 = be planning to 동사원형: ~할 것이다 do volunteer work: 자원 봉사를 하다

### 단원별 모의고사

01 ③  02 (1) (a)dults  (2) (a)imed, late
(3) education  (4) (r)aise, in need
03 (A) leave  (B) hold  (C) finish
04 I hope (that) many students join our campaign.
05 sell  06 ⑤  07 ⑤
08 ⓑ special anything → anything special
ⓓ I was going to → I'm going to
09 do  10 dying  11 I hope (that) more people care about global hunger.
12 ⓐ making → to make  ⓒ it → them  ⓓ by → with  ⓔ good → well
13 (1) She wanted to do something different.
(2) I did nothing special last year.
(3) Your daughter will never do anything stupid again.
14 ④  15 ⑤  16 who[that]
17 whose → which[that] / who live → who lives
18 ④  19 ⑤  20 ③, ④
21 They also care for people in need  22 ③
23 your video  24 (A) look  (B) walking  (C) What
25 ④

01 ③ 잡다, 쥐다 / 이외의 보기는 '(회의, 시합 등을) 열다'의 의미로 사용되었다.
02 (1) adult: 어른 (2) aim: ~을 목표로 삼다, 지향하다 late: 늦은 (3) education: 교육 (4) raise: (자금 등을) 모으다, 모금하다 in need: 어려움에 처한
03 leave: 남기다 hold: (회의, 시합 등을) 열다 finish: (남아 있는 것을) 마저 먹다
04 I hope (that) 주어 동사 ~: 나는 ~하기를 바란다 campaign: 캠페인, 조직적 활동
05 돈과 교환하여 물건을 주다 / sell: 팔다
06 ⑤ 남자아이가 필통을 만들어서 판다는 말은 나왔지만, 여자아

이가 필통을 만들 수 있는지 없는지에 대해서는 언급되어 있지 않다.
07 주어진 문장은 함께 가자고 제안하는 질문이다. 이에 'Sure.(물론이지)'란 긍정의 대답이 어울린다.
08 ⓑ '-thing', '-body', '-one'으로 끝나는 대명사는 형용사가 뒤에서 수식한다. ⓓ 'Are you going to 동사원형 ~? (너는 ~할 거니?)'으로 질문하였으므로, 과거형 동사로 대답하는 것은 어색하다.
09 do volunteer work: 자원 봉사를 하다
10 die의 현재분사형은 dying이다.
11 I hope (that) 주어 동사 ~: 나는 ~하기를 바란다 care about: ~에 관심을 가지다 global: 전 세계적인, 지구상의
12 ⓐ decide는 to부정사를 목적어로 취하는 동사이다. ⓒ carrots를 받기 때문에 복수형 대명사 them이 적절하다. ⓓ share A(사물) with B(사람): A를 B와 나누다[나눠 가지다] ⓔ grow: 자라다, 크다
13 'something, anything, nothing, everything'은 형용사가 뒤에서 꾸며 준다.
14 두 문장을 관계대명사를 이용하여 한 문장으로 만들 때, 두 번째 문장의 중복되는 단어를 관계대명사로 바꾸어 준다. 사물이 중복되므로 which를 사용하고 뒤의 문장은 그대로 쓰면 된다.
15 ⑤ anybody는 형용사가 뒤에서 꾸며준다. anybody strong이 되어야 한다.
16 '아브라함 링컨은 흑인 노예를 해방하는 데 성공한 16대 대통령이었다.' 선행사가 사람이므로 관계대명사는 who 또는 that을 사용할 수 있다.
17 선행사가 the cell phone이고 관계대명사절에 주어가 없이 동사 has가 있기 때문에 주격 관계대명사 which가 적절하다. 두 번째는 My cousin이 선행사이므로 단수 동사 lives가 적절하다.
18 선행사가 a car이므로 관계대명사 which나 that을 이용하여 한 문장으로 만든다.
19 ⑤번의 선행사는 the letter이므로 관계대명사는 which[that]가 적절하다.
20 ⓐ와 ③, ④는 명사적 용법, ①과 ⑤ 부사적 용법, ② 형용사적 용법
21 'in'을 보충하면 된다. in need: 어려움에 처한
22 ③번 다음 문장의 it에 주목한다. 주어진 문장의 'a video about the lantern festival in our village'를 받고 있으므로 ③번이 적절하다.
23 '너희 비디오'를 가리킨다.
24 (A) 사역동사(make)+목적어+원형부정사(look), (B) enjoy는 목적어로 동명사를 취한다. (C) What+a+형용사+명사(+주어+동사)! How+형용사[부사] (+주어+동사)!
25 ④ 몇 명의 학생들이 참가했는지는 대답할 수 없다. ① Malaysia. ② A wall painting campaign. ③ Students who are good at painting. ⑤ On some walls of schools and parks.

# Interesting Facts Are Around Us

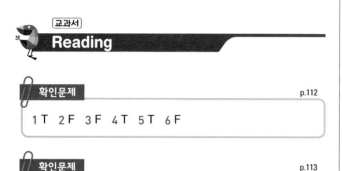

교과서
## Reading

확인문제　　　　　　　　　　　　　　p.112

1 T　2 F　3 F　4 T　5 T　6 F

확인문제　　　　　　　　　　　　　　p.113

1 T　2 F　3 F　4 T　5 T　6 F

### 교과서 확인학습 A　　　　　　　p.114~115

01 Interesting Facts, Around　02 Welcome to
03 is full of　04 how much you know
05 ready　06 Quiz　07 gets taller
08 fewer, than　09 Only, bite　10 never strikes
11 the biggest animal　12 no gravity
13 in heat　14 Due to, expands
15 gets, taller than　16 Adults, about
17 With time, join together
18 Only female mosquitoes　19 to produce eggs
20 enough blood, rest, lay　21 over and over again
22 gets hit by, on average　23 The biggest animal
24 up to, up to, long　25 alone, as much as
26 In fact　27 get farther, weakens, completely
28 get closer, such as, that of
29 Which, the most interesting
30 another quiz　31 what the next topic will be
32 See you

### 교과서 확인학습 B　　　　　　　p.116~117

1 Interesting Facts Are Around Us
2 Welcome to "Ask Dr. Lawrence"!
3 The world is full of interesting things.
4 Take this quiz and find out how much you know about them.
5 Are you ready?
6 Quiz
7 The Eiffel Tower gets taller during the summer.

8 Babies have fewer bones than adults.
9 Only female mosquitoes bite people.
10 Lightning never strikes the same place twice.
11 The elephant is the biggest animal on the Earth.
12 There is no gravity in space.
13 Metal expands in heat.
14 Due to summer heat, the metal of the Eiffel Tower expands.
15 In summer, the Eiffel tower gets 15cm taller than in winter.
16 Adults have 206 bones, but babies have about 300 bones.
17 With time, some of the babies' bones join together, so adults have fewer bones than babies.
18 Only female mosquitoes will bite you.
19 They need blood to produce eggs.
20 After a female mosquito gets enough blood, she'll rest for a few days and lay her eggs.
21 Lightning can strike the same place over and over again.
22 The Empire State Building gets hit by lightning 23 times a year on average.
23 The biggest animal on the Earth is the blue whale.
24 It can weigh up to 180 tons and grow up to 30 meters long.
25 Its tongue alone can weigh as much as an average African elephant.
26 In fact, there is gravity everywhere in space.
27 As you get farther from the Earth, the gravity of the Earth weakens, but it never goes away completely.
28 When you get closer to another planet, such as Mars or Venus, its gravity becomes stronger than that of the Earth.
29 Which of these quiz items is the most interesting to you?
30 There will be another quiz soon.
31 Guess what the next topic will be.
32 See you next month.

### 서술형 실전문제　　　　　　　p.118~119

01 (1) (f)alse　(2) (f)emale　(3) (s)ame
02 (1) fewer　(2) weaken　03 (1) bone　(2) different
(3) Mosquitoes, blood　(4) With time　(5) In fact
04 (1) go　(2) strike　(3) guess　(4) expand　05 due to
06 (1) In summer, the Eiffel Tower gets 15cm taller than in winter.
(2) The elephant is the biggest animal on the Earth.
07 (1) Guess what the next topic will be.
(2) Please tell me who that girl is.
(3) My brother can run the fastest in our family.
08 (1) whether　(2) when　(3) who
09 good → better, lay → lays
10 Do you know what determines the color of an

egg?

11 how much you know about them

12 (A) during    (B) Lightning    (C) biggest

13 Adults have more bones than babies.

01 주어진 보기는 반의어 관계이다. weaken: 약화시키다, 약화되다 strengthen: 강화하다 (1) true: 사실인 false: 거짓의 (2) male: 남성 female: 여성 (3) different: 다른 same: 같은

02 (1) fewer: (few의 비교급) 보다 적은 / 영어는 다른 언어보다 어휘 수가 적다. (2) weaken: 약화시키다, 약화되다 / 알코올은 심장 근육을 약화시킬 수 있다.

03 (1) bone: 뼈 (2) different: 다른 (3) mosquito: 모기 blood: 피 (4) with time: 시간이 지남에 따라 (5) in fact: 사실상, 실제로

04 (1) go away: 사라지다 / 그 문제는 사라지지 않을 것이다. (2) strike: 부딪치다, 충돌하다 / 배는 이 폭풍으로 바위에 부딪칠지도 모른다. (3) guess: 추측하다 / 그들이 무엇에 관해 이야기하고 있는지 추측할 수 있나요? (4) expand: 팽창하다 / 금속은 열을 받으면 팽창한다.

05 because of: ~ 때문에 due to: ~ 때문에 / 그 행사는 나쁜 날씨 때문에 일주일 동안 지연되었다.

06 (1) get+형용사: '~해지다'는 의미이고, '비교급+than' 구문을 이용한다. (2) '가장 ~한'의 의미는 최상급으로, 형태는 'the 최상급+단수명사'이다. big처럼 '단모음+단자음'으로 끝나는 단어는 자음을 한 번 더 쓰고 –est를 붙인다.

07 (1) 'what the next topic will be'는 '의문사(what)+주어(the next topic)+동사(will be)'의 간접의문으로 'guess'의 목적어 역할을 한다. (2) 의문사 who가 이끄는 문장이 tell의 직접목적어 자리에 사용되기 때문에 '의문사+주어+동사'의 어순이 되어야 한다. (3) 셋 이상의 사물과 사람 중에서 '가장 ~한'은 the fastest를 사용한다.

08 (1) 의문사가 없는 의문문은 '~인지 아닌지'를 의미하는 'if'나 'whether'가 명사절을 이끌어 'if[whether]+주어+동사'의 어순으로 쓴다. (2) know의 목적어 자리에 사용된 간접의문문으로 의미상 의문사 when이 적절하다. (3) Guess의 목적어 자리에 사용된 간접의문문으로 의문사 who가 적절하다.

09 than은 비교급과 호응하여 사용하기 때문에 good을 비교급인 better로 고친다. 주격 관계대명사 which 앞의 선행사가 chicken(단수명사)이기 때문에 주격 관계대명사절의 동사 lay는 단수 동사 lays로 고친다.

10 'Do you know'의 목적어 자리에 '의문사+주어+동사' 어순의 간접의문문을 사용한다. 여기서 의문사 what은 의문사이면서 동시에 주어 역할을 한다.

11 'how'를 보충하면 된다.

12 (A) during+특정 기간을 나타내는 명사, for+숫자가 붙은 기간, (B) '번개'라고 해야 하므로 Lightning이 적절하다. lightening: lighten(가볍게 해주다, 밝아지다)의 동명사/현재분사 형태임. (C) '단모음＋단자음'으로 이루어진 1음절 단어는 최상급을 만들 때 마지막 자음을 한 번 더 쓰고 '-est'를 붙여야 하므로 biggest가 적절하다.

13 어른들은 아기들보다 '더 많은' 수의 뼈를 가지고 있다.

01 ④        02 (1) to bite    (2) gravity    (3) was, inventor    (4) was, of        03 ④

04 (1) Only female mosquitoes suck blood.

(2) Blood is thicker than water.

(3) How much do you weigh?

(4) Teenage culture is different from adult culture.

05 ①        06 ④        07 ②

08 (1) Can you tell me how old your brother is?

(2) I know where she lives.

(3) Please tell me if[whether] he likes baseball.

09 ③        10 ④        11 ⑤        12 taller

13 (A) biggest    (B) much    14 ②        15 ③

16 prettiest    17 filled    18 ②        19 ③

20 heat    21 shorter → taller        22 ①

23 join together        24 ④        25 ③

26 ②        27 ④        28 weakens

29 another planet        30 (A) gets    (B) lay (C) alone        31 ①, ②, ⑤    32 up to

01 ④번은 명사와 동사의 관계이고 나머지는 형용사와 동사의 관계이다. ① deep: 깊은 deepen: 깊게 하다 ② loose: 느슨한 loosen: 느슨해지다 ③ weak: 약한 weaken: 약화시키다 ④ strength: 힘 strengthen: 강화하다 ⑤ straight: 똑바른 straighten: 똑바르게 하다

02 (1) used to 동사원형: ~하곤 했다 bite: 물다 (2) gravity: 중력 (3) inventor: 발명가 (4) be full of: ~로 가득 차다

03 find out: 알아보다, 찾아보다 over and over: 여러 번, 몇 번이고

04 (1) female: 여성의, 암컷의 (2) blood: 피 (3) weigh: 무게가 ~ 나가다, 무게를 달다 (4) adult: 성인, 어른

05 ① On, on average: 평균적으로 / 보통 그는 12시쯤에 잔다. ② of, be full of: ~로 가득 차다 / 나는 올해가 행복으로 가득하기를 바란다. ③ to, up to: (특정 수 또는 정도) ~까지 / 100쪽까지 읽어라. ④ with, with time: 시간이 지남에 따라 / 그 그림은 시간이 흐름에 따라 색이 바랠 것이다. ⑤ to, due to: ~ 때문에 / 악천후로 항공기가 지연되고 있습니다.

06 ①은 find out의 목적어 자리에 사용된 간접 의문문으로 Take this quiz and find out how much you know about them.이 되어야 한다. ②는 셋 이상의 사물을 나타낼 때 최상급 형태가 되어야 하므로 the biggest가 적절하다. ③은 'as 원급 as' 형태로 more를 much로 고쳐야 한다. ⑤는 difficult의 최상급 형태는 the most difficult를 쓴다.

07 셋 이상의 사물과 사람 중에서 '가장 ~하다'는 최상급의 의미로 heavy는 heaviest, early는 earliest가 적절하다.

08 간접의문문은 '의문사+주어+동사'의 어순으로 사용되고, 의문사 없는 의문문은 접속사 if나 whether를 사용한다.

09 주어진 문장의 밑줄은 동사의 목적어 자리에 사용된 간접의문문이다. ③번은 직접의문문으로 '의문사+동사+주어 ~?'의 형태로 사용된 문장이다.

10 ④ than이 있으면 앞에는 비교급이 와야 한다. few를 비교급 fewer로 고친다.

21

11 ① 'there is+단수명사'로 맞다. ② get+비교급: 점점 ~해지다, ③ 부사로 동사 goes away를 수식한다. ④ '비교급(stronger) than' 구문이다. ⑤ 지구의 그것(gravity)을 가리키는 단수 명사로 those를 that으로 바꾸어야 한다.

12 첫 번째 문장에서 '금속은 열에 팽창한다.'라고 했으므로 여름에 에펠 탑은 겨울보다 15cm까지 더 커진다는 의미가 적절하다.

13 (A)는 지구상에서 가장 큰 동물이란 의미로 최상급 thickest가 적절하고, (B)는 'as+원급+as' 형태로 동사 weigh를 수식하는 부사 much가 적절하다.

14 ② 최상급 앞에 정관사 the를 사용해서 the longest로 써야 한다. ④, ⑤번의 hardest와 most는 부사의 최상급으로 부사가 최상급이 될 때는 보통 정관사 the를 안 붙인다.

15 ① fastest ② largest ④, ⑤ 3음절어 이상의 형용사나 2음절어 중에서 -ful, -ous, -ive, -less, ing 등으로 끝나는 단어는 최상급을 만들 때 'most+원급' 형태를 사용한다.

16 내 여동생들은 모두 예쁘다. 하지만 내 여동생들 중에서, Jenny가 가장 예쁜 소녀다.

17 be full of = be filled with: ~로 가득 차다

18 'get[become]+비교급'은 '더 ~하게 되다, 더 ~해진다'는 의미로 상태의 변화를 포함하는 표현이다. 여기서는 '더 커진다'는 의미로 쓰였다.

19 '비교급+than any other+단수명사'는 최상급의 뜻을 나타낸다.

20 뒤에 이어지는 문장의 내용과 일치하도록, 금속은 '열'에 팽창한다고 하는 것이 적절하다.

21 여름의 열기 때문에, 에펠 타워의 금속은 팽창한다고 했으므로, 여름에 에펠 타워는 겨울보다 15센티미터 정도 더 '커진다'로 고쳐야 한다.

22 With time: 시간이 흐르면서

23 시간이 흐르면서, 아기의 몇몇 뼈들은 '붙기' 때문에, 어른들은 아기보다 더 적은 수의 뼈를 갖게 된다.

24 ⓐ와 ④번은 쉬다, ① 휴식, 수면, ② (어떤 것에) 받치다[기대다], ③ (결정 등이) ~에 달려 있다, ⑤ (어떤 것의) 나머지

25 ③ 한 걸음 한 걸음, 점차로, ⓑ와 나머지: 반복해서

26 ⓒ gets hit 'by' lightning: 번개를 맞는다, ⓓ 'on' average: 평균적으로

27 앞의 내용을 추가해서 설명하고 있으므로 In fact가 가장 적절하다. ① 예를 들어, ② 그러므로, ③ 게다가, ⑤ 다시 말해

28 weak의 동사 형태를 쓰는 것이 적절하다. 주어가 3인칭 단수(the gravity)이므로 끝에 s를 붙여야 한다.

29 화성이나 금성 같은 '다른 행성'을 가리킨다.

30 (A) 때를 나타내는 부사절에서는 현재시제가 미래시제를 대신하므로 gets가 적절하다. (B) 알을 '낳는다'고 해야 하므로 lay가 적절하다. lay: 놓다, (새, 곤충, 어류가) (알을) 낳다, lie: 눕다, 거짓말하다, (C) 혀의 무게'만' 해도라고 해야 하므로 alone이 적절하다. alone: ~만으로도(명사·대명사 뒤에 쓰여 특정한 그것 하나만을 가리킴을 강조함), only: (명사 앞에 써서) 유일한, 오직[겨우]

31 ⓐ와 ③, ④는 부사적 용법, ①, ⑤ 형용사적 용법, ② 명사적 용법

32 180톤'까지', 30미터'까지'라고 해야 하므로 up to가 적절하다. up to: ~까지

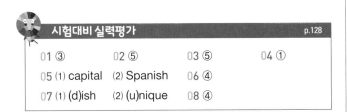

# Different Countries, Different Cultures

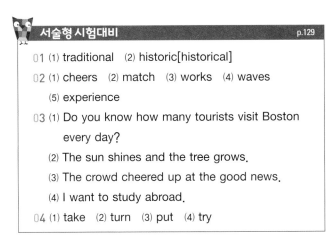

## 시험대비 실력평가
p.128

01 ③  02 ⑤  03 ⑤  04 ①
05 (1) capital (2) Spanish  06 ④
07 (1) (d)ish  (2) (u)nique  08 ④

01 unique: 독특한 unusual: 특이한, 흔치 않은 / 각 등장인물은 독특한 성격을 갖고 있다.

02 Excuse me: (모르는 사람의 관심을 끌려고 할 때) 실례합니다 / 실례지만, 가장 가까운 지하철역이 어느 쪽인가요?

03 ceiling: 천장 / 방의 위쪽 내부 표면

04 shine: 빛나다 / 밝은 빛을 만들어 내다

05 (1) capital: 수도 (2) Spanish: 스페인의

06 ① coaster: (롤러) 코스터 / 그 남자는 롤러 코스터를 타고 있다. ② lizard: 도마뱀 / 도마뱀은 네 개의 다리와 긴 꼬리를 가지고 있다. ③ curry: 카레 / 그 카레는 나한테 너무 맵다. ④ view: 전망, 경치 / 나는 전망이 좋은 방을 원한다. ⑤ column: 기둥 / 그 기둥은 흰 대리석으로 만들어졌다.

07 (1) dish: 음식, 요리 / 가장 대표적인 한국 음식이 무엇이라고 생각하니? (2) unique: 독특한 / Rachel은 장미의 독특한 향기를 사랑한다.

08 ④ friend는 뒤에 ly를 붙여 형용사로 만들 수 있다. friend: 친구 friendly: 친절한 ① help: 도움 helpful: 도움이 되는 ② care: 조심 careful: 조심하는 ③ wonder: 놀라움 wonderful: 놀랄 만한, 멋진 ⑤ peace: 평화 peaceful: 평화로운

## 서술형 시험대비
p.129

01 (1) traditional  (2) historic[historical]
02 (1) cheers  (2) match  (3) works  (4) waves
   (5) experience
03 (1) Do you know how many tourists visit Boston every day?
   (2) The sun shines and the tree grows.
   (3) The crowd cheered up at the good news.
   (4) I want to study abroad.
04 (1) take  (2) turn  (3) put  (4) try

01 둘은 명사와 형용사의 관계이다. use: 사용 useful: 유용한

(1) tradition: 전통 traditional: 전통적인 (2) history: 역사 historic: 역사적인, 역사상 중요한 historical: 역사상, 역사와 관련된

02 (1) cheer: 격려하다, 환호하다, 갈채하다; 환호 (2) match: 경기, 시합; 어울리다 (3) work: 일하다, 작품 (4) wave: 흔들다; 파도 (5) experience: 경험; 경험하다

03 (1) tourist: 여행객 (2) shine: 빛나다 (3) cheer up: 기운을 내다 (4) abroad: 외국으로[에서]

04 (1) take a tour: 관광하다, 여행을 가다 / 너는 여행을 가고 싶니? (2) turn off: (전기, 가스, 수도 등을) 끄다 / TV를 꺼라. 잠잘 시간이 지났어. (3) put off: (시간, 날짜를) 미루다, 연기하다 / 다음 25일까지 여행을 미룰 수 있을까요? (4) try on: 입어 보다 / 이 재킷을 입어 봐도 돼요?

교과서
## Conversation

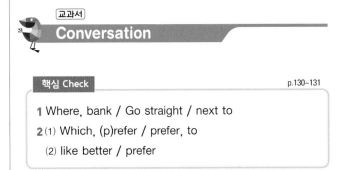

### 핵심 Check
p.130~131

1 Where, bank / Go straight / next to
2 (1) Which, (p)refer / prefer, to
  (2) like better / prefer

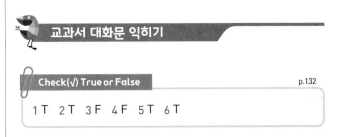

## 교과서 대화문 익히기

### Check(√) True or False
p.132

1 T  2 T  3 F  4 F  5 T  6 T

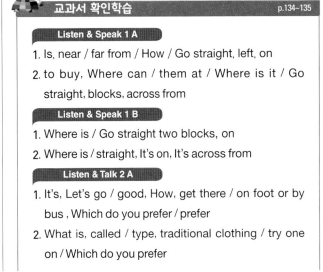

## 교과서 확인학습
p.134~135

### Listen & Speak 1 A
1. Is, near / far from / How / Go straight, left, on
2. to buy, Where can / them at / Where is it / Go straight, blocks, across from

### Listen & Speak 1 B
1. Where is / Go straight two blocks, on
2. Where is / straight, It's on, It's across from

### Listen & Talk 2 A
1. It's, Let's go / good, How, get there / on foot or by bus , Which do you prefer / prefer
2. What is, called / type, traditional clothing / try one on / Which do you prefer

**시험대비 기본평가** p.136

01 ②　　　　　02 ⑤　　　　　03 ①, ③, ⑤

04 (C) → (D) → (A) → (B)

01 'Where is ~?'는 '~가 어디에 있나요?'라는 의미로 길이나 위치를 물어볼 때 사용하는 표현이다.

02 I think hamburgers are less preferable to spaghetti. → I think hamburgers are preferable to spaghetti. less preferable은 덜 선호한다는 의미이므로, less를 빼야 햄버거를 스파게티보다 더 좋아한다는 의미가 된다.

03 ② Do you know when to go to the school? → Do you know where the school is? ④ Could I tell you where the school is? → Could you tell me where the school is?로 바꾸면 길을 물어보는 표현이 될 수 있다.

04 (C) 근처에 피카소 박물관이 있는지 묻는 질문에 (D) 그렇다고 대답한 후 여기서 멀지 않다고 언급한다. (A) 이어서 피카소 박물관을 어떻게 가는지 묻자 (B) 가는 방법을 알려준다.

**시험대비 실력평가** p.137~138

01 ②　　　　02 ②　　　　03 ③　　　　04 ④

05 ⑤　　　　06 ④　　　　07 ②

08 (A) why, (B) let's　　　　09 ②　　　　10 Where

11 ③　　　　12 across from

01 far from: ~에서 먼

02 How can I get there?: 그곳에 어떻게 가니? 'Where is ~?'와 같이 'How can I get ~?'도 길이나 위치를 물어볼 때 사용하는 표현이다.

03 주어진 문장은 야시장에 어떻게 갈 수 있는지 물어보는 질문이다. 이에 대한 대답으로 가는 방법에 대한 언급이 나와야 한다. 그러므로 걸어가거나 버스를 타서 갈 수 있다는 대답 앞에 오는 것이 적절하다.

04 What do you prefer? → Which do you prefer? 걸어가거나 버스를 타는 것 중 하나를 선택하는 것이므로 의문사 Which

가 어울린다.

05 여자아이가 아니라 남자아이가 야시장에 가는 방법을 알고 있다.

06 길을 물어보는 질문에, 'I'm a stranger here, too. (저도 여기 처음이에요.)'라고 말한 후에 길을 알려 주는 것은 어울리지 않는다.

07 주어진 문장은 그것(*Best Friends*)이 언제 시작하는지 시간에 대한 정보를 묻고 있다. 그러므로 5시와 7시에 시작한다는 답이 이어지는 ②번이 적절하다.

08 (A)와 (B)에 사용된 'Why don't we ~?'와 'Let's ~'는 둘 다 '~하자'라고 제안을 할 때 사용할 수 있는 말이다. How about 다음에는 동명사가 나와야 하므로 (B)에는 let's가 적절하다.

09 ① 영화 Best Friends가 토요일 몇 시에 시작하는가? ② 어디서 그들이 토요일에 만날 것인가? ③ 여자아이는 5시나 7시 중 어떤 시간을 선호하는가? ④ 그들은 토요일 몇 시에 만날 것인가? ⑤ 그들은 토요일에 어떤 영화를 볼 것인가?

10 where: 어디서

11 Go straight two blocks: 두 블록 직진하세요. turn right: 우회전하세요.

12 across from: ~의 맞은편에

**서술형 시험대비** p.139

01 'Yes, I do.'를 생략

02 Can you tell me how to get to the African Museum?

03 (A) right, (B) left, (C) across from

04 (A) on, (B) by

05 How can I get there? / Do you know how to get there? / Can you tell me how to get there?

06 or　　　　07 to curry

01 'Which do you prefer, A or B?'는 어느 것을 선호하는지 묻는 표현으로 'Yes.'나 'No.'로 대답할 수 없다.

02 Can you tell me how to get to ~?: ~에 어떻게 가는지 말해 줄 수 있나요? / how to 동사원형: ~하는 방법 / get to 장소 명사: ~에 도착하다

03 그림을 참고해 보면 ③은 두 블록 직진한 후, 우회전하면, 왼편에 있다. across from: ~의 맞은편에

04 on foot: 걸어서, by bus: 버스로

05 How can/do I get to ~?:~에 어떻게 가나요? Do you know how to get to ~?: ~에 어떻게 가는지 아나요? Can you tell me how to get to ~?:~에 어떻게 가는지 말해 줄 수 있나요?

06 Which do you prefer, A or B?: A와 B 중 어떤 것을 선호하니?

07 두 가지 중에서 어떤 것을 더 선호하는지 말할 때 'I prefer A to B.'를 사용한다. to B는 생략할 수 있다.

**1** (1) built   (2) will be

**2** (1) The water was so clear that you could see the bottom.

(2) He worked so hard that he became a lawyer.

(3) I 'll drive fast so that you can get there in time.

**시험대비 기본평가**                              p.142

**01** (1) cleans → is cleaned

(2) is → was

(3) very → so

(4) so that → so that she

**02** ④          **03** ②

**04** (1) The water was so clean that we could drink it.

(2) He was injured during the soccer match.

01 (1) 방이 청소하는 것이 아니라 청소되는 것이므로 수동태가 적절하다. (2) in 1908이라는 과거를 나타내는 부사구가 있으므로 시제를 과거로 써야 한다. (3) 'so+형용사[부사]+that+주어+동사'의 형태로 원인과 결과를 나타내는 것이 적절하다. (4) so that 다음에는 '주어+동사'가 나와야 한다.

02 tomorrow가 있으므로 'will be sent'가 되어야 한다.

03 '…해서 ~하다'의 의미인 'so … that ~' 구문이다.

04 (1) 물이 깨끗해서 그 결과 마실 수 있었던 것이므로 'so … that ~' 구문으로 쓰는 것이 적절하다. (2) 부상을 입은 것이므로 수동태가 적절하다.

**시험대비 실력평가**                              p.143~145

**01** ④          **02** ③          **03** ⑤

**04** weak so → so weak

**05** (1) excited   (2) consider   (3) to   (4) for   (5) of

(6) so   (7) that          **06** ①          **07** ①

**08** ④          **09** ②          **10** ⑤

**11** (1) Antoni Gaudi designed both.

(2) James took this photo.

(3) A beautiful dress was made for her by her mom.

(4) They will hold the book fair in Seoul.

(5) Who considers it to be dangerous?

**12** (1) so   (2) such   (3) couldn't          **13** ⑤

**14** ③, ⑤

**15** (1) invented → was invented

(2) was happened → happened

(3) too careless → careless enough

**16** ⑤          **17** ⑤          **18** ③

01 영어가 말하는 것이 아니라 말해지는 것이므로 수동태가 적절하다.

02 세차되는 것이므로 수동태가 적절하고 원인과 결과를 나타내는 'so+형용사[부사]+that+주어+동사' 구문이 적절하다.

03 The pictures drawn in France were sent to me by Jenny. sent가 능동태의 동사이므로 수동태로 바꾸면 'were sent'가 되어야 한다.

04 'so+형용사[부사]+that+주어+동사'는 원인과 결과를 나타내지만 'so that+주어+동사'는 목적을 나타낸다.

05 (1) 내가 신나게 되는 것이므로 수동태가 적절하다. (2) We가 주어이므로 능동태가 적절하다. (3) 직접목적어를 주어로 한 수동태에서 간접목적어 앞에 teach는 전치사 to를, (4) choose는 전치사 for를, (5) ask는 of를 쓴다. (6), (7) 'so+형용사[부사]+that+주어+동사' 구문이다.

06 원인과 결과를 나타내는 'so ~ that …' 구문이 적절하다.

07 by 이외의 전치사를 사용하는 수동태에 유의한다. be pleased with: ~에 기뻐하다 be satisfied with: ~에 만족하다

08 'so+형용사[부사]+that+주어+동사' 구문은 '너무 ~해서 …하다'라는 뜻으로 원인과 결과를 나타낸다.

09 'so that+주어+동사'는 목적을 나타내어 '~하기 위해서' 혹은 '~하도록'이라는 의미로 쓰인다. 부사적 용법의 '목적'과 바꿔 쓸 수 있다. 원인과 결과를 나타내는 'so ~ that …'과 혼동하지 않도록 유의한다.

10 turn off는 구동사로 하나의 단어처럼 취급하여 be turned off로 나타낸다. off를 빠뜨리지 않도록 주의한다.

11 (3) make는 직접목적어를 주어로 하는 수동태만 가능하며 간접목적어 앞에 전치사 for를 쓴다. (4) 미래 시제의 수동태는 'will be+과거분사'이며 수동태에서 일반인이 행위자일 경우 보통 'by+일반인 주어'를 생략한다. (5) 수동태의 by whom이 who로 바뀌는 것에 주의한다.

12 (1) 원인과 결과를 나타내는 'so ~ that …' 구문이다. (2) 'so ~ that …' 구문에서 that 앞에 형용사나 부사 대신 명사가 오면 so 대신 such를 쓴다. (3) so+형용사[부사]+that+주어+can't+동사원형: 너무 ~하여 …할 수 없다.

13 목적격보어가 원형부정사인 경우, 수동태 문장에서는 to부정사로 바뀐다. We were made to do our homework by our teacher.

14 ① He was seen to put the bag on the table by Ann. ② The storybook was read to him every night by his mom. ④ It was such a nice day that we went for a walk.

15 (1) WWW가 발명되는 것이므로 수동태가 적절하다. (2) happen은 자동사이므로 수동태로 쓰이지 않는다. (3) so+형용

사[부사]+that+주어+can ~ = '형용사[부사]+enough+to 동사원형', so+형용사[부사]+that+주어+can't ~ = too+형용사[부사]+to 동사원형

16 choose는 직접목적어를 주어로 한 수동태에서는 간접목적어 앞에 for를 쓴다.

17 시제가 과거이므로 was heard로 쓰고, 원형부정사인 목적격보어는 to부정사로 쓴다.

18 이유를 나타내는 Because절이므로 'so+형용사[부사]+that+주어+동사' 구문으로 원인과 결과를 나타낼 수 있다

## 서술형 시험대비
p.146~147

01 (1) Someone stole the painting last week.
(2) I was impressed by its size and unique design.
(3) Peter was heard to open the window by Eva.
(4) A present will be given (to) me by Angie on my birthday.
(5) The baby was taken care of by Cathy.

02 (1) so stupid that
(2) tall enough to
(3) too shocked to

03 (1) hard so that (2) so hard that

04 (1) Cake is made from flour, milk, eggs and sugar.
(2) The shirts will be ironed by John tomorrow morning.
(3) Mike was seen to be hit by a car by Ms. Brown.
(4) Our dog was run over by a truck.
(5) The matter will be discussed by us tommorow.

05 (1) easy enough to (2) so fast that

06 (1) The novel was written by Ernest Hemingway.
(2) The first World Cup took place in Uruguay in 1930.
(3) A fairy tale book was read to her daughter by Laura.
(4) Kimberly was disappointed at the news.
(5) Was Allie heard to sing by you?
(6) It was so cold that he caught a cold.

07 (1) Claire got up too late to get on the train.
(2) Chuck spoke so low that I could not hear him.
(3) Bill was smart enough to solve the difficult math problems.
(4) Juliet is so rich that she can buy the house.

08 (1) The sweater was made for me by my grandmother.
(2) Are these rooms cleaned by her every day?
(3) Dan was made to prepare dinner by Mariel.
(4) Joakim was pleased with your recent success a lot.

01 (3) 목적격보어가 원형부정사인 경우 수동태에서는 to부정사로 쓴다. (4) 미래 시제의 수동태는 'will be+과거분사'이다. (5) 구동사(take care of)는 하나의 동사처럼 취급한다는 것에 주의한다.

02 (1) 'so+형용사[부사]+that+주어+동사'의 형태로 원인과 결과를 나타낸다. (2) so+형용사[부사]+that+주어+can ~ = '형용사[부사]+enough+to 동사원형' (3) so+형용사[부사]+that+주어+can't ~ = too+형용사[부사]+to 동사원형

03 (1) 목적을 나타내는 'so that'을 사용한다. (2) 원인과 결과를 나타내는 'so ~ that …'을 사용한다.

04 (1) be made of: ~로 만들어지다(물리적 변화), be made from: ~로 만들어지다(화학적 변화) (2) shirts가 다림질을 하는 것이 아니라 다림질 되는 것이므로 수동태가 적절하며 미래의 일이므로 'will be+pp' 형태가 적절하다. (3) 목적격보어가 원형부정사인 경우, 수동태 문장에서는 to부정사로 바뀐다. (4) run-ran-run (5) 'will be +pp' 형태가 되어야 한다.

05 (1) so+형용사[부사]+that+주어+can ~ = 형용사[부사]+enough+to 동사원형 (2) so+형용사[부사]+that+주어+can't ~ = too+형용사[부사]+to 동사원형

06 (1) 소설이 씌여지는 것이므로 수동태가 적절하다. (2) take place는 자동사로 쓰이므로 수동태로 쓰면 안 된다. (3) read는 직접목적어를 주어로 하는 수동태만 가능하다. fairy tale book: 동화책 (4) be disappointed at: ~에 실망하다, 낙담하다 (5) 목적격보어가 원형부정사인 경우, 수동태 문장에서는 to부정사로 바뀐다 (6) so ~ that: 너무 ~해서 …하다

07 so ~ that 주어 can't … = too ~ to …, ~ enough to부정사 = so ~ that 주어 can … 이때 to부정사 앞에 for 목적격으로 쓰인 것은 to부정사의 의미상의 주어로 that 이하의 절로 바꿀 때는 주격으로 바꿔야 하며, to부정사로 썼을 때 생략된 동사의 목적어는 써 주어야 한다.

08 (1) 직접목적어를 주어로 한 수동태에서 make는 간접목적어 앞에 전치사 for를 쓴다. (2) 의문문을 수동태로 바꿀 때는 평서문으로 바꿔서 고친 후에 다시 의문문으로 바꾸면 쉽다. (3) 목적격보어가 원형부정사인 경우, 수동태 문장에서는 to부정사로 바뀐다. (4) please는 수동태에서 by가 아니라 보통 with를 쓴다. be pleased with: ~로 기뻐하다

교과서

## Reading

확인문제
p.148

1 F  2 T  3 T  4 F  5 T  6 F

1 T   2 F   3 T   4 F   5 T   6 F

## 교과서 확인학습 A    p.150~151

01 Happy Days, by
02 traveled to
03 is loved by
04 visited, interesting
05 Our trip
06 is famous for
07 to watch
08 were excited, the world's most famous soccer players
09 was full of
10 by singing, shouting
11 After
12 While, walked around
13 visited, watched
14 in a red dress, with wonderful movements
15 For
16 traditional Spanish dish with
17 tasted like
18 so, that
19 took a tour of
20 were designed by
21 creative works like
22 After
23 is still going on
24 was impressed by
25 shone like
26 stood like
27 creativity, his love of nature
28 Traveling, a wonderful experience
29 While, a lot
30 to visit

## 교과서 확인학습 B    p.152~153

1 My Happy Days in Spain by Park Jinwoo

2 My family traveled to Spain this summer.

3 Spain is loved by lots of tourists.

4 We visited many interesting places.

5 Our trip started in Madrid.

6 Madrid is the capital and is famous for soccer.

7 We went to a stadium to watch a soccer match.

8 My sister and I were excited because we could watch some of the world's most famous soccer players.

9 The stadium was full of soccer fans.

10 As we watched the match, we cheered by singing songs, waving our hands, and shouting with the other fans.

11 After we toured Madrid, we went to Seville.

12 While we walked around the city, we saw many historic buildings.

13 We visited a flamenco museum and watched a flamenco dance.

14 A woman in a red dress was dancing the flamenco with wonderful movements.

15 For dinner, we ate paella.

16 It is a traditional Spanish dish with rice, vegetables, meat, and seafood.

17 It tasted like fried rice in Korea.

18 It was so delicious that we all enjoyed it.

19 In Barcelona, we took a tour of Park Guell and Sagrada Familia.

20 Both were designed by Antoni Gaudi.

21 In Park Guell, we saw some of Gaudi's creative works like a colorful lizard.

22 After Park Guell, we visited Sagrada Familia.

23 Work on the building started in 1883 and is still going on today.

24 I was impressed by its size and unique design.

25 The ceiling inside Sagrada Familia shone like the night sky with bright stars.

26 Its stone columns stood like big trees.

27 At Park Guell and Sagrada Familia I could feel Gaudi's creativity and his love of nature.

28 Traveling in Spain was a wonderful experience.

29 While I was there, I learned a lot about Spain.

30 I want to visit the country again.

## 시험대비 실력평가    p.154~157

01 ③
02 ①, ⑤
03 ③
04 saw them in Seville
05 ②
06 ③
07 It was so delicious that we all[all of us] enjoyed it.
08 ②
09 ③
10 (A) Barcelona   (B) a colorful lizard
11 They speak Vietnamese there.
12 ②
13 ②
14 (A) ceiling   (B) there   (C) about
15 ①, ④
16 ⓐ size, ⓑ unique design
17 ③
18 ④
19 ②
20 ④
21 creativity   22 ①
23 ④
24 is spoken
25 Australia is so wonderful that you should visit it someday.
26 (A) the Sydney Opera House, (B) ocean roads

01 위 글은 '기행문'이다. ① (책·연극·영화 등에 대한) 논평[비평], 감상문, ② 수필, ④ 전기, ⑤ (신문·잡지의) 글, 기사

02 ① 약간의, ④ a number of: (수가) 많은, ⑤ (양이) 많은, lots of = a lot of = plenty of: (수와 양이) 많은

03 ③ 진우의 가족 여행은 마드리드에서 '시작했다.'

04 '세비야'에서 많은 역사상 중요한 건물들을 보았다.

05 ⓐ와 ②번: …하는 동안, ① …인 데 반하여(둘 사이의 대조를 나타냄), ③과 ⑤ [주절 뒤에서 반대·비교·대조를 나타내어] 그런데, 한편(으로는), ④ 잠깐, 잠시

06 ⓑ와 ②, ③, ⑤번: 현재분사, ①, ④: 동명사

07 so ~ that ...: 너무 ~해서 ...하다

08 ⓑ와 ②번: 작품들(명사), ① 근무하다, 취직해 있다(동사), ③ (건설) 공사[작업](명사), ④ (약 따위가) 작용하다, 듣다[on] (동사), ⑤ (기계 따위가) 움직이다, 작동하다(동사)

09 ③ 위 글은 '진우의 가족이 즐긴 요리와 장소를 소개'하는 글이다.

10 그것은 '바르셀로나'에 있고 Antoni Gaudi에 의해 설계되었다. 그곳에서 진우의 가족은 '형형색색의 도마뱀'과 같은 몇몇 Gaudi의 창의적인 작품들을 보았다.

11 일반인을 나타내는 They를 주어로 해서 바꾸는 것이 적절하다.

12 be well known for: ~으로 잘 알려져 있다

13 ② 베트남에서는 '베트남어'가 사용된다.

14 (A) 사그라다 파밀리아 안의 '천장'이라고 해야 하므로 ceiling이 적절하다. ceiling: 천장, sealing: (봉투 등을) 밀봉[밀폐]하기, (B) there는 부사이므로 전치사 없이 쓰는 것이 적절하다. (C) 스페인에 '대해' 많은 것을 배웠다고 해야 하므로 about이 적절하다. a lot of: 많은

15 ① 가주어 It을 사용하여 바꾸거나, ④ to부정사를 주어로 하여 바꾸는 것이 적절하다.

16 진우에게, 사그라다 파밀리아의 '크기'와 '독특한 디자인'은 인상적이었다. impressive: 인상적인, 인상[감명] 깊은

17 ① They visited Park Guell. ② It started in 1883. ③ 사그라다 파밀리아의 건물 공사가 오늘날까지도 여전히 진행 중인 이유는 알 수 없다. ④ Stone. ⑤ At Park Guell and Sagrada Familia.

18 주어진 문장의 Both에 주목한다. ④번 앞 문장의 Park Guell과 Sagrada Familia를 받고 있으므로 ④번이 적절하다.

19 ② paella의 조리법이 무엇인지는 대답할 수 없다. ① Rice, vegetables, meat, and seafood. ingredient: 재료, ③ They took a tour of Park Guell and Sagrada Familia. ④ Both were designed by Antoni Gaudi. ⑤ They saw some of Gaudi's creative works like a colorful lizard.

20 ④ go on = continue: 계속하다, ② remain: (처리·이행 등을 해야 할 일이) 남아 있다

21 소유격 다음에 명사를 써야 하는데, creation은 '창조, 창작'의 뜻이므로 creativity(창의성, 독창력)를 쓰는 것이 적절하다.

22 스페인 여행은 훌륭한 경험이었다며, 그 나라를 다시 방문하고 싶다고 했으므로 '만족한' 심경이라고 하는 것이 적절하다. ① 만족한, ② 겁먹은, 무서워하는, ③ 지루한, ④ 부끄러운, ⑤ 실망한

23 ④ '사그라다 파밀리아'에서 Gaudi의 창의성과 자연에 대한 사랑을 느낄 수 있었다.

24 영어가 '사용된다'고 해야 하므로 수동태로 쓰는 것이 적절하다.

25 'so'를 보충하면 된다.

26 시드니의 관광명소는 '시드니 오페라하우스'이고 멜버른은 아름다운 '해안 도로들'로 유명하다.

---

**서술형 시험대비** p.158~159

01 Lots of tourists love Spain.
02 (A) visited (B) to watch (C) were
03 well known
04 ⓐ singing ⓑ waving ⓒ shouting
05 After
06 Seville
07 Spanish
08 felt → tasted
09 toured
10 It tasted like fried rice in Korea.
11 paella
12 such as
13 We visited Park Guell before Sagrada Familia. 또는 Before Sagrada Familia, we visited Park Guell.
14 (A) impressed (B) shone (C) stood
15 historic
16 who[that]
17 축구 경기장에서 경기를 보며 응원했다 / 도시를 걸어다니는 동안 많은 역사상 중요한 건물들을 보았고, 플라멩코 박물관을 방문해서 플라멩코 춤을 보았다.

---

01 by 다음의 'lots of tourists'를 주어로 해서 고치는 것이 적절하다.

02 (A) visit는 타동사이므로 전치사 없이 바로 목적어를 쓰는 것이 적절하다. (B) 축구 경기를 '보기 위해서'라고 해야 하므로 to watch가 적절하다. (C) 'My sister and I'가 주어이므로 were가 적절하다.

03 be famous for = be well known for: ~로 유명하다, ~로 잘 알려져 있다

04 전치사 by 뒤에 동명사로 쓰는 것이 적절하다.

05 우리는 세비야로 가기 '전에' 마드리드를 관광했다. = 마드리드를 관광하고 난 '후', 우리는 세비야로 갔다..

06 '세비야'를 가리킨다.

07 형용사 Spanish로 쓰는 것이 적절하다. Spanish: 스페인의

08 한국의 볶음밥과 같은 '맛이 났다'고 하는 것이 적절하다. feel like: (촉감이) …하다

09 tour = take a tour of

10 'like'를 보충하면 된다.

11 '파에야'를 가리킨다.

12 like = such as: ~와 같은

13 '사그라다 파밀리아를 보기 전에 우리는 구엘 공원을 방문했다' 라고 고치는 것이 적절하다.

14 (A) '감명 받았다'고 해야 하므로 impressed가 적절하다. impressing: 감동시키는, (B) 밤하늘처럼 '빛났다'고 해야 하므로 shone이 적절하다. shine - shone: 빛나다, 반짝이다, shine - shined: 윤[광]을 내다, 닦다, (C) stand는 자동사라서 수동태를 만들 수 없으므로 stood가 적절하다.

15 'history'의 형용사형 historic을 쓰는 것이 적절하다. historic: 역사적으로 중요한, 역사적인, historical은 '역사에 바탕을 둔'이라는 뜻으로, 보통 과거와 관련된 것, 역사 연구와 관련된 것 또는 과거에 실제 있었던 일을 묘사할 때 사용하므로 적절하지 않다.

16 주격 관계대명사 'who'나 'that'을 쓰는 것이 적절하다.

17 마드리드의 축구 경기장에서 경기를 보며 응원했고, 세비야를 걸어 다니는 동안 많은 역사상 중요한 건물들을 보았고 플라멩코 박물관을 방문해서 플라멩코 춤을 보았다.

### 영역별 핵심문제

p.161~165

01 ②　　　02 ④　　　03 for　　　04 on

05 (1) historic　(2) theater　(3) ceiling　(4) cheer for, fans

06 ⑤　　　07 ③　　　08 ③　　　09 view

10 ②　　　11 Where is the nearest bus stop?

12 (C) → (A) → (B)　　　13 ②

14 (1) so difficult that we couldn't solve them

　　(2) too difficult for us to solve　　　15 ①

16 ④　　　17 so beautiful that

18 (1) was written by　(2) were built by　　　19 ③

20 (1) By whom was the telephone invented?

　　(2) The roof of the house was covered with snow.

　　(3) It was so dark that nothing could be seen.

　　(4) The runner ran so fast that nobody could catch up with him.

21 travel, tour　22 ①, ④, ⑤

23 (A) a stadium, (B) a soccer match

24 ③　　　25 ②

26 (A) fried　(B) were　(C) creative

27 Park Guell and Sagrada Familia

01 ① cheer for: ~을 응원하다 / 우리의 국가 대표팀을 응원해요! ② get 장소 부사: ~에 도착하다 / 그곳에 어떻게 가니? ③ design: 설계하다, 디자인하다 / 나는 나의 집을 설계했다. ④ tea: 차 / 그 차는 훌륭한 맛을 지니고 있다. ⑤ title: 제목 / 이 노래의 제목이 무엇이니?

02 ① sliding, slide: 미끄러지다, 활주하다 / 아이들은 얼어붙은 호수에서 미끄럼을 타고 있다. ② waved, wave: 흔들다 / 아기는 엄마에게 손을 흔들었다. ③ rolling, roll: 구르다, 굴리다 / 그들은 큰 공을 굴리고 있다. ④ taking, take a tour: 관광하다, 여행을 가다 / 그때 시내 구경을 하시는 게 어때요? ⑤ prefer: 선호하다 / 나는 커피보다 차를 선호한다.

03 be famous for: ~로 유명하다 be well known for: ~로 잘 알려져 있다

04 get on: ~에 타다 on foot: 걸어서

06 (A) 할로윈에 필요한 사탕을 사야 하는데 그것을 어디서 살 수 있는지 물어보고, 이에 대한 대답으로 Wendy's 사탕 가게에서 살 수 있다는 대답을 들었다. (B) Wendy's 사탕 가게가 어디 있는지 질문하고 이에 대한 대답을 듣는 것이 적절하다.

07 할로윈에 필요한 사탕을 사기 위해 Wendy's 사탕 가게에 가야 할 사람은 남자아이이다.

08 ③ It's across from the school. → It's across from the cinema. 병원은 영화관 맞은편에 있다.

09 view: 전망, 경치 / 어떤 특정한 장소나 위치에서 볼 수 있는 것, 특히 아름다운 전원

10 주어진 문장은 런던 아이와 스카이 가든에 대해서 간략히 설명하고 있다. 직원이 런던의 멋진 경치를 즐기기에 좋은 장소가 두 곳 있다고 먼저 말한 후, 이에 대해 설명하는 것이 자연스러우므로 ②가 적절하다.

11 Where is ~?: ~가 어디에 있나요? the 최상급(형용사+est): 가장 ~한 stop: 정거장

12 해외 여행을 가자는 말에. (C) 어떤 도시(방콕이나 대만)를 선호하는지 묻는다. (A) 방콕을 더 좋아한다고 대답하고, 너무 화려해서 가야 한다고 말한다. (B) 그곳(방콕)에 가자고 대답한다.

13 비행기가 식당으로 바뀐 것이므로 수동태가 적절하다. The plane stopped flying and was turned into a restaurant.

14 'so+형용사[부사]+that+주어+can't ~'는 'too+형용사[부사]+to 동사원형'으로 바꿔 쓸 수 있다. 이때 to부정사의 목적어가 주어와 같을 경우 따로 써주지 않는 것에 유의한다.

15 첫 번째 문장에서는 목적격보어가 원형부정사인 경우, 수동태 문장에서는 to부정사로 바뀐다. 두 번째 문장에서는 'so+형용사[부사]+that+주어+동사'의 형태로 원인과 결과를 나타내는 것이 적절하다.

16 ① The room was so cold that David turned on the heater. ② This story was so funny that I laughed a lot. ③ Arnold got up so late that he missed the train. ⑤ John is so kind that everyone likes him.

17 'so+형용사[부사]+that+주어+동사'의 형태로 원인과 결과를 나타낸다.

18 (1) 책이 씌여진 것이고 (2) 피라미드가 건설된 것이므로

'be+pp' 형태의 수동태로 쓴다.

19 ③ write는 직접목적어를 주어로 하는 수동태만 가능하다. A long letter was written to me by my girl friend.

20 (1) 수동태의 의문문은 능동태의 평서문을 수동태로 고친 후에 다시 의문문으로 바꾸면 쉽다. (2) be covered with: ~로 덮여 있다 (3), (4) 'so+형용사[부사]+that+주어+동사' 구문은 '너무 ~해서 …하다'라는 뜻으로 원인과 결과를 나타낸다.

21 trip = travel = tour: 여행

22 ⓑ와 ②, ③번은 부사적 용법, ①, ④ 형용사적 용법 ⑤ 명사적 용법

23 진우의 가족은 스페인 여행 도중에 마드리드에 있는 '경기장'에 가서 '축구 경기'를 보았다.

24 ⓐ와 ③번: …할 때(접속사), ① …이므로, …이기 때문에(접속사), ② …하는 대로(접속사), ④ (자격·기능 등이)

25 ② 진우의 가족은 '세비야'를 걸어다녔다.

26 (A) 한국의 '볶음밥'과 같은 맛이 났다고 해야 하므로 fried가 적절하다. fried rice: 볶음밥, frying: (기름에) 굽는, 튀기는, (B) Both는 복수로 취급하므로 were가 적절하다. (C) Gaudi의 '창의적인' 작품들을 보았다고 해야 하므로 creative가 적절하다. common: 흔한, 공통의, creative: 창의적인

27 '구엘 공원'과 '사그라다 파밀리아'를 가리킨다.

### 단원별 예상문제

01 take    02 by
03 (1) cheered  (2) try on  (3) (f)amous for
   (4) get, on foot
04 (f)lamenco, (p)urple, (V)ietnamese
   (1) flamenco  (2) Vietnamese  (3) purple
05 ①    06 ②    07 ⑤
08 (A) How  (B) Which  (C) Where
09 Where is the best place to go to?
10 Go straight one block and turn right. It's on your left.    11 (C) → (A) → (B) → (D)    12 ②
13 (1) The shoes look so great that Sandra wants to buy them.
   (2) The stereo was so loud that it was impossible to sleep.
14 (1) so great that  (2) were killed    15 ④
16 ②    17 It is well known for soccer.
18 ①, ③
19 toured of → toured 또는 took a tour of
20 ④    21 ⑤    22 ④
23 creative
24 They were designed by Antoni Gaudi.

01 take a walk: 산책하다 / 나는 나의 개와 산책하고 싶다. take a class: 수업을 받다 / 방과 후에 너는 수업을 듣거나 함께 클럽

에 가입할 수 있어. take a tour: 관광하다, 여행을 가다 / 그들은 그 성을 관광했던 것을 좋아했다.

02 수동태(be+p.p+by 행위자): …에 의해서 ~되다, by+교통수단: 교통수단으로 → by bus: 버스로

03 (1) cheer: 환호하다, 갈채하다 (2) try on: 입어 보다 (3) be famous for: ~로 유명하다 (4) on foot: 걸어서 get 장소 부사: ~에 도착하다

04 (1) flamenco: 플라멩코 (스페인 남부 Andalusia 지방 집시의 춤) / 안달루시아 집시의 격렬한 리듬을 가진 춤 / 그는 플라멩코 춤을 즐겨 춘다. (2) Vietnamese: 베트남어; 베트남의 / 베트남 언어, 사람 또는 문화와 관련된 / 그녀는 베트남에서 일자리를 구하기 위해 베트남어를 배웠다. (3) purple: 보라색 / 파란색과 빨간색을 섞은 색 / 그녀는 짙은 보라색 옷을 입었다.

05 주어진 문장은 야시장에 가서 신선한 과일 주스를 마시자고 제안하는 말이다. 날씨가 정말 덥다고 얘기하면서 이러한 제안을 하고, 이 제안에 대해서 'Sounds good.(좋아)'이라고 대답을 하고 있으므로 ①이 적절하다.

06 ② 위의 대화에서는 버스와 걷는 것 중의 선호를 물었기 때문에 버스와 택시 중에 무엇을 더 좋아하는지에 대해 대답할 수 없다. ① 그들은 야시장에 어떻게 갈 것인가? ② 남자아이는 버스와 택시 중 어떤 것을 선호하니? ③ 그들은 어디에 있는가? ④ 그들은 어디에 갈 것인가? ⑤ 그들은 무엇을 마실 것인가?

07 주어진 문장은 나중에 그곳을 방문하자고 제안하는 말이다. 여기서 그곳으로 지칭할 수 있는 장소는 런던 아이와 빅벤이며, 제안에 수락이나 거절하는 표현이 나와야 한다. 그러므로 'That sounds great.(좋아요)'라고 제안을 수락한 문장 앞에 들어가는 것이 적절하다.

08 (A) How may I help you?: 무엇을 도와드릴까요? (B) Which do you prefer(, A or B)?: (A와 B 중) 어떤 것을 선호하니? (C) Where is ~?: ~가 어디에 있나요?

09 'to go to'는 앞의 the best place를 꾸며주는 형용사적 용법으로 쓰인 to부정사이다. Where is ~?: ~가 어디에 있나요? best: 최고의, 가장 좋은

10 Go straight: 직진하세요. Turn right: 우회전하세요. It is on your left: 왼편에 있어요.

11 아프리카 박물관에 가는 방법을 물어보는 질문에 (C) 물론 가르쳐 준다고 대답하며 두 블록 직진한 후 우회전하라고 얘기한다. (A) 두 블록 직진한 후 우회전하고 그 다음에는 어떻게 하는지 질문하자. (B) 아프리카 박물관이 왼편에 있고, 신발 가게 맞은 편에 있다는 추가적인 정보를 준다. (D) 길을 알려 준 것에 대해 감사를 표한다.

12 ③ 간접목적어 앞에 for 대신 to를 써야 한다.

13 (1), (2) 'so+형용사[부사]+that+주어+동사' 구문을 이용하여 원인과 결과를 나타낸다.

14 (1) 'so+형용사[부사]+that+주어+동사'로 원인과 결과를 나타낸다. (2) 누가 그 동작을 했는지 중요하지 않거나 잘 모를 때,

**30** 정답 및 해설

수동태 문장으로 표현한다.

**15** ④ 세계에서 가장 유명한 축구 선수 몇몇을 볼 수 있었기 때문에 '신이 났다'고 하는 것이 적절하다. ① 재미있는, 흥미로운, ② 실망한, ③ 속상한, 마음이 상한, ⑤ 재미있는, 즐거운, amused(재미있어하는, 즐거워하는)

**16** ⓐ와 ②번: 수도, ①, ③, ④ 자본금, 자본 ⑤ 대문자

**17** 마드리드는 '축구'로 유명하다. be famous for = be well known for: ~로 유명하다, ~로 잘 알려져 있다

**18** ⓐ와 ②, ④, ⑤번: 동명사, ①, ③번: 현재분사

**19** tour = take a tour of

**20** ④ 진우의 가족이 얼마나 오래 플라멩코 춤을 보았는지는 대답할 수 없다. ① At the soccer stadium. ② They sang songs, waved their hands, and shouted with the other fans. ③ They saw many historic buildings. ⑤ She was wearing a red dress.

**21** ⓐ For dinner: 저녁 식사로, ⓑ with: '~로, ~이 있는'이라는 뜻의 전치사

**22** 파에야는 '쌀'과 '채소', '고기', '해산물'이 들어간 전통적인 스페인 요리이다.

**23** 뒤의 명사를 수식하는 형용사로 쓰는 것이 적절하다.

## 서술형 실전문제 p.170~171

**01** The view from the London Eye are amazing. → The view from the London Eye is amazing.

**02** Go straight two blocks and turn right.

**03** (A) → (C) → (B) → (D)

**04** Which do you prefer, the Roller Coaster or the Scary House?

**05** (1) so colorful that  (2) so tired that, too tired to

**06** (1) Many people who want to do fun activities love Hong Kong.
(2) What was promised to do by her last weekend?
(3) We were taught physics by Ms. Grace last year. 또는 Physics was taught (to) us by Ms. Grace last year.

**07** was filled with

**08** A woman in a red dress was dancing the flamenco with wonderful movements.

**09** (A) Seville  (B) many historic buildings

**10** like

**11** (A) Spanish  (B) Korea  (C) rice, vegetables, meat (D) seafood

**12** Antoni Gaudi designed both.

**01** The view가 문장의 주어로 단수형이기 때문에 are가 아니라 is가 적절하다.

**02** Go straight.: 직진하세요. Turn right.: 우회전하세요.

**03** 지수에게 토요일에 영화를 보자고 제안한다. (A) 좋다고 대답하며 영화가 몇 시에 시작하는지 질문하자 (C) 토요일에 5시와 7시가 있다고 말하며 어떤 시간을 더 선호하는지 물어본다. (B) 7시를 더 선호한다고 대답하고 (D) 그러면 6시에 만나자고 약속 시간을 정한다.

**04** Which do you prefer, A or B?: A와 B 중 어떤 것을 선호하니?

**05** 'so+형용사[부사]+that+주어+동사' 구문을 이용하여 원인과 결과를 나타낸다.

**06** (2) 의문문의 수동태는 능동태의 의문문을 평서문으로 바꾼 후 이것을 수동태로 고치고, 다시 의문문으로 바꾸면 쉽다. (3) 4형식 문장의 수동태는 간접목적어와 직접목적어 각각을 주어로 하는 수동태가 가능하며 직접목적어를 주어로 한 수동태에서 teach 동사는 간접목적어 앞에 전치사 to를 쓴다. 이때의 to는 생각할 수도 있다.

**07** be full of = be filled with: ~로 가득 차 있다

**08** 'in'을 보충하면 된다.

**09** 진우의 가족은 마드리드를 여행하고 난 후, '세비야'로 가서 도시를 걸어다니는 동안, '많은 역사상 중요한 건물들'을 보았다.

**10** ⓐ tasted like: ~와 같은 맛이 났다, ⓒ like: ~와 같은

**11** 전통적인 '스페인' 요리인 파에야는 '한국'의 볶음밥과 같은 맛이 나고, 그것의 재료는 '쌀'과 '채소', '고기', '해산물'이다. ingredient: (특히 요리 등의) 재료[성분]

**12** Antoni Gaudi를 주어로 해서 고치는 것이 적절하다.

## 창의사고력 서술형 문제 p.172

|모범답안|

**01** (A) Do you know how to get to the bank?
(B) Go straight two blocks and turn right. / It's next to the police station. / It's across from the post office.

**02** (A) capital
(B) English
(C) Meat pie and lamington
(D) the Sydney Opera House
(E) beautiful ocean roads

**03** (1) He practiced dancing so hard that he became a B-boy dancer.
(2) The thief ran away so that no one could find him.
(3) The cartoon was so interesting that I kept reading it.

**01** Do you know how to get to ~?: ~에 어떻게 가는지 아나요? Go straight: 직진하세요. Turn right: 우회전 하세요. next to: ~옆에 across from: ~의 맞은편에

01 (1) useful  (2) hopeful  (3) colorful
02 (1) of  (2) from  (3) on, of  (4) on
03 (1) try on  (2) (g)o on  (3) across from
　　(4) is well known for
04 ③
05 (1) Where / right, your left. It's next to
　　(2) Where is / one block, turn left, on your right,
　　　across, the Flower Garden  06 abroad
07 Which city do you prefer, Bangkok or Taiwan?
08 (B) so, (C) that
09 (A) watch  (B) What time  (C) are
10 ②　　　　11 called　　　12 on
13 Which do you prefer, the purple one or the
　　yellow one?
14 (1) was heard to lock the door by me
　　(2) so wonderful that
15 ②　　　　16 ⑤
17 (1) Sharon worked hard so that she might succeed.
　　(2) The box was so heavy that no one could move it.
　　(3) The machine will be repaired by Mr. Kim.
18 ③
19 (A) this summer  (B) interesting  (C) excited
20 ②　　　　21 ③　　　　22 ⑤
23 traditional　　　　　24 tasted → tasted like
25 ④

01 주어진 두 단어의 관계는 명사와 형용사의 관계이다. use, hope, color는 모두 명사이고 뒤에 ful을 붙여서 형용사가 된다. (1) use: 사용 useful: 유용한 (2) hope: 희망, 기대 hopeful: 희망에 찬, 기대하는 (3) color: 색깔 colorful: 다채로운

02 (1) be full of: ~으로 가득 차다 (2) far from: ~로부터 먼 (3) on top of: ~의 위에, ~의 꼭대기에 (4) turn on: ~을 켜다

03 (1) try on: 입어 보다 (2) go on: (어떤 일이) 계속되다 (3) across from: ~의 맞은편에 (4) be well known for: ~로 잘 알려져 있다

04 ① match: 경기, 시합 / 그들은 중요한 시합을 하는 중이다. ② movement: 동작 / 그 동물은 빠른 동작으로 움직였다. ③ language: 언어 / 나는 영어, 일본어, 한국어 세 가지 언어를 할 수 있다. ④ tour: 여행 / 오늘 여행에서 우리는 많은 희귀 동물을 볼 것이다. ⑤ hamburger: 햄버거 / 그들은 어제 점심으로 햄버거를 먹었다.

05 Where is ~?: ~가 어디에 있나요? Go straight: 직진하세요. Turn left/right: 좌회전/우회전 하세요. next to: ~옆에 across from: ~의 맞은편에

06 abroad: 외국으로[에서] / 외국에서 또는 외국으로

07 Which do you prefer, A or B?: A와 B 중 어떤 것을 선호하니?

08 so 형용사/부사 that 주어 동사: 너무 ~해서 그 결과 ~하다

09 (A) Why don't we 동사원형 ~?: ~할래?(제안하기) (B) What time: 몇 시에, 질문에 대한 대답이 '토요일에는 5시와 7시 두 번 상영해.'라는 것으로 보아 시간에 대해 질문하고 있다. (C) 'There be ~'는 be동사 다음에 주어가 나온다. two showings가 주어이므로 복수동사 are가 적절하다.

10 토요일에 영화가 5시와 7시로 2개를 선택할 수 있다. 이렇게 2개가 있을 때 먼저 언급한 것은 one, 나머지는 the other로 받는다.

11 긴 드레스가 이름이 뭐라고 불리는지 묻고 있는 것이므로 수동태가 어울린다.

12 try ~ on: ~을 입어 보다

13 Which do you prefer, A or B?: A와 B 중 어느 것을 선호하니? 대명사 one은 앞서 나온 Ao dai를 의미한다.

14 (1) hear는 지각동사이므로 목적격보어로 원형부정사를 쓰지만 수동태에서는 원형부정사를 to부정사로 바꿔 주어야 한다. (2) 원인과 결과를 나타내는 'so ~ that …' 구문이 적절하다.

15 ② 직접목적어를 주어로 한 수동태에서 make는 간접목적어 앞에 전치사 for를 쓴다.

16 'so … that ~'은 '너무[매우] …해서 ~하다'의 의미로 원인과 결과를 나타낸다.

17 (1) 'so that+주어+동사' 구문은 목적을 나타내어 '~하기 위해서' 혹은 '~하도록'이라는 의미로 쓴다. (2) 'so+형용사[부사]+that+주어+동사' 구문은 '너무 ~해서 …하다'라는 뜻으로 원인과 결과를 나타낸다. (3) 조동사가 있는 문장의 수동태는 '조동사+be+p.p.' 형식을 갖는다.

18 일반 사람이 주어인 능동태를 수동태로 바꿀 때 'by+일반 사람'은 생략 가능하다.

19 (A) 때를 나타내는 this, last, next 등의 앞에는 전치사를 붙이지 않으므로 this summer가 적절하다. (B) 감정을 나타내는 동사가 무생물을 수식할 때는 보통 현재분사를 쓰므로 interesting이 적절하다. (C) 감정을 나타내는 동사가 사람을 수식할 때는 보통 과거분사를 쓰므로 excited가 적절하다.

20 진우의 가족 여행이 왜 마드리드에서 시작했는지는 대답할 수 없다. ① This summer. ③ Madrid. ④ To watch a soccer match. ⑤ They felt excited.

21 주어진 문장의 the city에 주목한다. ③번 앞 문장의 Seville를 받고 있으므로 ③번이 적절하다.

22 ⓐ with the other fans: 다른 팬들과 함께, with wonderful movements: 멋진 동작으로, ⓑ in: '착용'을 나타내는 전치사

23 명사를 수식하므로 형용사가 되어야 한다. traditional: 전통적인

24 한국의 볶음밥과 같은 맛이 났다고 해야 하므로 tasted like로 고치는 것이 적절하다. taste like+명사: ~와 같은 맛이 나다

25 ④ Antoni Gaudi는 구엘 공원과 사그라다 파밀리아를 '설계했다.'

# 교과서 파헤치기

Lesson 3

1 count, 세다　2 simple, 간단한　3 comfortable, 편안한

4 reduce, 줄이다　5 advice, 조언　6 shoulder, 어깨

7 switch, 바꾸다　8 neck, 목　9 bend, 구부리다

10 position, 자세　11 relax, (근육 등의) 긴장을 풀다

12 habit, 습관　13 stretch, 스트레칭하다

14 warm up, 준비 운동을 하다　15 pull, 당기다

16 massage, 마사지

| | | |
|---|---|---|
| 01 자세 | 02 끌다, 당기다 | 03 스트레칭하다 |
| 04 어려운 | 05 자연 | 06 조언, 충고 |
| 07 밀다 | 08 운동하다 | 09 이해하다, 알다 |
| 10 놓다, 두다 | 11 세다 | 12 (시간 단위인) 초 |
| 13 어깨 | 14 활동 | 15 그러나 |
| 16 삶 | 17 붓다 | 18 바꾸다 |
| 19 뒤쪽, 뒷부분 | 20 마사지; 마사지를 하다 | |
| 21 목 | 22 다운로드하다 | 23 뒤로 |
| 24 놓다, 두다 | 25 보여[가르쳐] 주다 | |
| 26 허리 | 27 편안한 | 28 구부리다 |
| 29 ~을 낮추다, ~을 낮게 하다 | | 30 습관 |
| 31 신선한 | 32 보통, 대개 | 33 간단한, 단순한 |
| 34 따뜻한 | 35 서로 | 36 ~와 협력하다 |
| 37 (빛을) 가리다[차단하다] | | 38 회복[극복]하다 |
| 39 위에서 아래까지 | 40 ~에 집중하다 | 41 몸을 풀어 주다 |
| 42 똑바로 하다 | 43 ~에 좋다 | |

| | | |
|---|---|---|
| 01 already | 02 behind | 03 comfortable |
| 04 softly | 05 step | 06 way |
| 07 move | 08 fall | 09 face |
| 10 fishing | 11 habit | 12 warm |
| 13 both | 14 hold | 15 bend |
| 16 exercise | 17 nature | 18 difficult |
| 19 activity | 20 relax | 21 healthy |
| 22 lower | 23 simple | 24 fresh |
| 25 stress | 26 light | 27 like |
| 28 reduce | 29 usually | 30 bowl |
| 31 stretch | 32 backward | 33 neck |
| 34 position | 35 warm up | |
| 36 from top to bottom | | 37 focus on |
| 38 for a few seconds | | 39 be worried about |
| 40 prepare for | 41 block out | 42 straighten up |
| 43 get over | | |

**Listen & Speak 1 A-1**

something healthy, have, adivce / often eat, makes, feel / how to make / simple, cut, into, put, into, pour, mix / should try

**Listen & Speak 1 A-2**

more than / steps, to be healthy, count, steps easily / can use, how to use / Can, show me / download, with, check, steps you took / will start using

**Listen & Speak 2 A-1**

What, enjoy doing / enjoy cooking healthy food / Sounds, can, make / can make

**Listen & Speak 2 A-2**

on weekends / take pictures / What kind, usually take / enjoy taking, of, like / reduce my stress

**Listen & Speak 2 A-3**

have a puppy / Her, really like / What, with her / enjoy taking, makes, healthy

**Conversation A**

have, speaking, preparing, for, ago, speaking in, am worried about, cannot sleep

**Conversation B**

what's matter / stressed about, next week / ride, when / know how to ride / No, don't / go out, can, Put, on, push, with / Like, feel better / enjoy, riding, because, reduces / great

**Wrap Up 1**

look sick, What's / have a cold / see a doctor / yet, get over / warm, when, makes me feel better / Sounds, will try

**Wrap Up 2**

enjoys, fishing, Early, comes back, enjoys drawing, to draw, enjoy playing

**Listen & Speak 1 A-1**

B: I want to eat something healthy. Do you have any

adivce?

G: I often eat fresh salad. It makes me feel good.

B: Really? Do you know how to make it?

G: Yes, it's quite simple. First, cut many vegetables into small pieces. Next, put them into a bowl. Then, pour some lemon juice on them. Finally, mix everything together.

B: That's it? I should try it.

**Listen & Speak 1 A-2**

B: People say that we should walk more than 10,000 steps every day to be healthy. I can't count the number of my steps easily.

G: You can use this smartphone app. Do you know how to use it?

B: No. Can you show me?

G: Sure. First, download the app. Then, walk with your smartphone. Later, you  can check the number of steps you took.

B: Thank you. I will start using it today.

**Listen & Speak 2 A-1**

G: What do you enjoy doing after school?

B: I enjoy cooking healthy food.

G: Sounds cool. What can you make?

B: I can make salad, Bibimbap, and vegetable juice.

**Listen & Speak 2 A-2**

B: What do you do on weekends?

G: I take pictures.

B: What kind of pictures do you usually take?

G: I enjoy taking pictures of nature, like trees and flowers. The beautiful pictures  reduce my stress.

**Listen & Speak 2 A-3**

G: Do you have a puppy?

B: Yes. Her name is Coco. I really like her.

G: What do you do with her?

B: I enjoy taking a walk with her. It makes me healthy.

**Conversation A**

B: Tomorrow, I have an English speaking contest. I started preparing for the contest two weeks ago. I enjoy speaking in English, but I am worried about the contest. I cannot sleep well.

**Conversation B**

Karl: Hana, what's the matter?

Hana: Well, I'm stressed about the test next week.

Karl: I understand. I ride my longboard when I'm stressed. Do you know how to ride a longboard?

Hana: No, I don't.

Karl: Let's go out! I can teach you. Put one foot on the board and push hard with the other.

Hana: Like this? Wow! This is fun. I feel better already.

Karl: See? I enjoy riding my longboard because it reduces my stress.

Hana: That's great!

**Wrap Up 1**

B: You look sick. What's the matter?

G: Well, I have a cold.

B: Did you see a doctor?

G: Not yet. Do you know how to get over a cold?

B: Well, I usually drink warm water when I have a cold. It makes me feel better.

G: Sounds good. I will try it.

**Wrap Up 2**

B: My family enjoys many activities. My dad enjoys fishing . Early in the morning, he goes to the lake and comes back with some fish. My mom enjoys drawing pictures. She likes to draw beautiful mountains and lakes. My brother and I enjoy playing soccer.

**본문 TEST** Step 1                    p.09~10

01 At, for, hours   02 Do, get tired

03 don't, yourself, stretch        04 Let's, with

05 Close, massage, softly          06 will relax

07 When, cover, block out

08 make, feel, comfortable

09 massage, neck                   10 Put, on, back

11 circles, fingers, massage       12 top, bottom

13 help, feel better

14 Let's, on, waist                15 Team up

16 close, other, faces             17 Hold, other's

18 stretch, body backward

19 Hold, for, seconds              20 pull, to

21 should move, speed              22 If, both, fall

23 Place, top, on, behind

24 bend, lower yourself

25 Hold, few, straighten up

26 position, loosen up

27 Switch, repeat, exercise        28 How, feel

29 massage, stretch, feel healthier

30 focus on, studies

01 At school, for   02 get tired

03 Why don't, yourself, stretch

04 Let's begin with

05 Close, massage, with, fingers   06 will relax

07 When, cover, with, block out

08 make, feel more comfortable

09 massage your neck     10 Put, on, back

11 Draw, with to massage

12 from top to bottom

13 help you feel better

14 Let's work on, waist     15 Team up, with

16 each other, faces     17 Hold, wrists

18 Slowly stretch, backward

19 Hold, for three seconds     20 pull, to

21 your, at     22 If, both of, will fall

23 Place, top, on, behind

24 slowly bend, lower

25 Hold, a few seconds, straighten up

26 The position, loosen up

27 Switch, repeat the exercise     28 How, feel

29 massage, stretch every day, feel healthier

30 can focus on, better

1 학교에서 여러분은 오랜 시간에 걸쳐 앉아 있다.

2 여러분은 피곤한가?

3 마사지와 스트레칭을 하는 게 어떤가?

4 눈부터 시작하자

5 눈을 감고 손가락으로 눈을 부드럽게 마사지해라.

6 그것은 여러분의 눈을 편안하게 해줄 것이다.

7 끝나면, 빛을 차단하기 위해 손으로 눈을 가려라.

8 그것은 여러분의 눈을 더 편안하게 해줄 것이다.

9 다음으로, 여러분의 목을 마사지해라.

10 여러분의 목 뒤에 손가락을 대라.

11 여러분의 목을 마사지하기 위해 손가락으로 작은 원을 그려라.

12 위에서 아래로 마사지해라.

13 마사지는 여러분의 기분이 좋아지도록 도울 것이다.

14 허리 운동을 하자.

15 친구와 짝을 이루어라.

16 서로 가까이 서서 여러분의 파트너를 마주 보아라.

17 서로의 손목을 잡아라.

18 천천히 여러분의 머리와 몸을 뒤로 뻗어라.

19 3초 동안 그 자세를 유지해라.

20 그리고 나서, 천천히 서로 선 자세로 끌어 당겨라.

21 너와 너의 파트너는 같은 속도로 움직여야 한다.

22 그렇지 않으면, 너희 둘 다 넘어질 것이다!

23 여러분의 뒤에 있는 책상 위에 오른쪽 발등을 올려놓아라.

24 그리고 나서, 천천히 왼쪽 다리를 구부리고 몸을 낮추어라.

25 몇 초 동안 그 자세를 유지하다가 천천히 몸을 펴라.

26 이 자세는 여러분의 오른쪽 다리를 풀어 줄 것이다.

27 다리를 바꿔서 운동을 반복해라.

28 지금 기분이 어떤가?

29 매일 마사지와 스트레칭을 하면, 여러분은 더 건강해지는 것을 느낄 것이다.

30 또한, 여러분은 공부에 더 집중할 수 있을 것이다.

1 At school you sit for many hours.

2 Do you get tired?

3 Why don't you massage yourself and stretch?

4 Let's begin with the eyes.

5 Close your eyes and massage them softly with your fingers.

6 It will relax your eyes.

7 When you finish, cover your eyes with your hands to block out the light.

8 It will make your eyes feel more comfortable.

9 Next, massage your neck.

10 Put your fingers on the back of your neck.

11 Draw small circles with your fingers to massage your neck.

12 Massage from top to bottom.

13 The massage will help you feel better.

14 Let's work on your waist.

15 Team up with a friend.

16 Stand close to each other and face your partner.

17 Hold each other's wrists.

18 Slowly stretch your head and body backward.

19 Hold that position for three seconds.

20 Then, slowly pull each other to a standing position.

21 You and your partner should move at the same speed.

22 If you don't, both of you will fall!

23 Place the top of your right foot on the desk behind you.

24 Then, slowly bend your left leg and lower yourself.

25 Hold it for a few seconds and slowly straighten up.

26 This position will loosen up your right leg.

27 Switch your legs and repeat the exercise.

28 How do you feel now?

29 If you massage yourself and stretch every day, you will feel healthier.

30 Also, you can focus on your studies better.`

### Enjoy Writing C

1. to Be Healthier
2. Here is
3. more than three times
4. every day
5. three times a week, become stronger
6. if, will feel better,
7. habits, make me live

### Project - Step 2

1. how to stretch
2. stretching exercise is called
3. with, to warm up
4. Then, with
5. will stretch, shoulders
6. make
7. in a circle, feel nice
8. Finally
9. a little bit, be good for

### Wrap Up - Writing

1. these days, should, go
2. get stressed, makes me feel
3. how to download

### Enjoy Writing C

1. My Plan to Be Healthier
2. Here is my plan to be healthier
3. I will exercise more than three times a week.
4. I will eat breakfast every day.
5. If I exercise more than three times a week, I will become stronger.
6. Also, if I eat breakfast every day, I will feel better in the morning.
7. I will change my habits, and it will make me live a healthy life.

### Project - Step 2

1. Do you know how to stretch your shoulders?
2. Our stretching exercise is called "Number Stretching."
3. First, make a number "1" with your arm to warm up.
4. Then, make a number "2" with your arms. 5
5. It will stretch your shoulders.
6. Now, make a number "3".
7. If you move your arms in a circle, it will feel nice.
8. Finally, make a number "4".
9. It is a little bit difficult, but it will be good for your shoulders.

### Wrap Up - Writing

1. Sumi: I feel stressed these days. What should I do?
2. Jiae: When I get stressed, I listen to music. It makes me feel better.
3. If you don't know how to download music, I will show you.

## 단어 TEST Step 1  p.21

01 기아, 배고픔  02 (폐기물을) 재활용하다
03 자연환경, 환경  04 (특별한 날·경사 등을) 축하하다, 기념하다
05 살리다, 구하다  06 ~을 목표로 삼다, 지향하다
07 교육  08 멀리; 먼  09 홍수
10 다치게 하다  11 모으다  12 생산하다
13 보내다, 전하다  14 어른  15 같이 쓰다, 공유하다
16 참여하다  17 쓰레기  18 엉망진창의
19 아무것도 ~ 아니다  20 (자금 등을) 모금하다
21 낭비하다, 허비하다  22 랜턴, 등불, 등
23 굉장한, 감탄할 만한, 엄청난  24 전 세계적인 지구상의
25 공동체, 사회  26 의사소통하다  27 정원
28 가난한  29 ~ 옆에, 나란히  30 접시
31 시민  32 보호하다  33 (회의, 시합 등을) 열다
34 국제적인  35 ~을 돌보다, 신경 쓰다
36 ~ 덕분에  37 (~에 대해서) 조심하다
38 ~으로 죽다  39 잘 되다  40 ~을 잘하다
41 ~을 버리다  42 어려움에 처한
43 A를 B와 나누다[나눠 가지다]

## 단어 TEST Step 2  p.22

01 citizen  02 American  03 poor
04 fight  05 alongside  06 community
07 awesome  08 campaign  09 garden
10 plate  11 sell  12 upload
13 global  14 hold  15 international
16 upset  17 leave  18 communicate
19 protect  20 site  21 take
22 environment  23 gather  24 trash
25 education  26 hurt  27 adult
28 save  29 recycle  30 produce
31 flood  32 celebrate  33 hunger
34 raise  35 care about  36 take a shower
37 in need  38 watch out (for)
39 throw away  40 be good at  41 thanks to
42 care for  43 die of

## 단어 TEST Step 3  p.23

1 adult, 어른  2 flood, 홍수  3 garden, 정원
4 messy, 엉망진창의  5 poor, 가난한  6 sell, 팔다

---

7 aim, ~을 목표로 삼다, 지향하다
8 global, 전 세계적인, 지구상의
9 recycle, 폐기물을 재활용하다  10 upset, 당황한
11 waste, 낭비하다, 허비하다
12 raise, (자금 등을) 모금하다
13 celebrate, (특별한 날·경사 등을) 축하하다, 기념하다
14 gather, 모으다  15 citizen, 시민
16 communicate, 의사소통하다

## 대화문 TEST Step 1  p.24~25

### Listen & Speak 1 A
1 watch, about the flood / I did, a lot of, lost / going to send / How, Are you, to raise / going to make, sell
2 plans, vacation / going to, do some volunteer work with / went, helped, Are you going to do / also paint, with / sounds nice

### Listen & Speak 1 B
1 Are, going to take / am, I'm not
2 going to recycle bottles / I am, I'm not

### Listen & Speak 2 A
1 What / making, about, hunger, dying of hunger / too bad / hope, care about global
2 decided to make, garden / vegetable garden, will / grow, share, with / good idea / hope, grow well

### Listen & Speak 2 B
1 hope, don't throw away trash / hope so, Let's hold / campaign
2 I hope people don't hurt / hope so, Let's hold / good idea

### Wrap Up
1 What's your plan, Are, going to do anything special / On, going to visit / How about on / have no plans / going to do volunteer work, like to come
2 going to hold, at school next Friday / What is / campaign to protect, throw trash on, to stop / hope, goes / hope so, too

## 대화문 TEST Step 2  p.26~27

### Listen & Speak 1 A
1 B: Did you watch the news about the flood?
  G: Yes, I did. They said a lot of people lost their homes.

37

B: My club is going to send them some money.

G: How can you do that? Are you going to raise money, Andy?

B: Yes. We're going to make pencil cases and sell them.

2 B: Do you have any plans for the summer vacation, Suji?

G: Yes. I'm going to the Philippines to do some volunteer work with my family.

B: Oh, I went there and helped some children study last year. Are you going to do that, too?

G: Yes. And I'll also paint walls with the children.

B: That sounds nice.

### Listen & Speak 1 B

1 G: Are you going to take a short shower?

B: Yes, I am. / No, I'm not.

2 G: Are you going to recycle bottles?

B: Yes, I am. / No, I'm not.

### Listen & Speak 2 A

1 G: What are you doing, Jason?

B: I'm making a poster about global hunger. Many people are dying of hunger.

G: That's too bad. I didn't know that.

B: I hope more people care about global hunger.

2 G: Dad, my class decided to make a vegetable garden.

M: A vegetable garden? What will you grow there, Sena?

G: Carrots. We'll grow them and share them with others.

M: That's a good idea.

G: I hope the carrots grow well.

### Listen & Speak 2 B

1 A: I hope people don't throw away trash.

B: I hope so, too. Let's hold a Keep the World Clean campaign.

A: That's a good idea.

2 A: I hope people don't hurt animals.

B: I hope so, too. Let's hold a Love Animals campaign.

A: That's a good idea.

### Wrap Up

1 B: What's your plan for the weekend, Sumin? Are you going to do anything special?

G: Yes. On Saturday, I'm going to visit my grandmother.

B: How about on Sunday?

G: I have no plans for Sunday. Why?

B: I'm going to do volunteer work at the library on Sunday. Would you like to come with me?

G: Sure.

2 G: My club is going to hold a green campaign at school next Friday.

B: What is a green campaign?

G: It's a campaign to protect the environment. Many students throw trash on the streets. We hope to stop that.

B: I hope your campaign goes well.

G: Thanks. I hope so, too.

### 본문 TEST Step 1 p.28~29

01 Global Citizenship
02 This, Citizenship, site
03 helps, grow as
04 try, understand, cultures
05 care for, in need
06 share, global, experiences
07 am, from Korea
08 a member of
09 aims, communicate with
10 ago, produced, lantern
11 uploaded, amazingly, nearly, hits
12 Click, for, video
13 yours, looks fantastic
14 have, in, village
15 make, like yours
16 my name
17 am from
18 few, ago, showed, of
19 all using, to carry
20 decided, raise, send
21 sold, drinks, raised
22 hope, happy with
23 Awesome, sure, will
24 something wonderful
25 am, from
26 painting, make, look better
27 good, gathered, painted
28 Thanks, much nicer
29 walking alongside, painted
30 What a nice

### 본문 TEST Step 2 p.30~31

01 Global, Education
02 This, Citizenship Education site
03 helps, grow as global citizens
04 try to understand, cultures
05 care for, in need, a better world
06 share, global, experiences
07 am, from Korea
08 a member of
09 aims to communicate with, around
10 A week ago, about the lantern festival
11 uploaded, amazingly, got nearly, hits

12 Click, for, video    13 your, looks fantastic

14 have, in, village    15 like to make, like yours

16 my name    17 am from

18 few, ago, showed us pictures of

19 Sadly, all using, to carry

20 decided, raise money to send

21 sold, drinks, raised

22 hope, are happy with

23 Awesome, sure, will like

24 did something wonderful

25 am, from Malaysia

26 wall painting, to make, look better

27 are good at, gathered, painted

28 Thanks to, looks much nicer

29 enjoy walking alongside, painted

30 What a nice idea

---

1 세계 시민 교육

2 이곳은 세계 시민 교육 사이트입니다.

3 세계 시민 교육은 우리가 세계 시민으로 자라도록 도와줍니다.

4 세계 시민은 다른 문화를 이해하려고 노력하는 사람들입니다.

5 그들은 또한 어려움에 처한 사람들을 보살피고 더 나은 세상을 위해서 일합니다.

6 당신의 세계 시민 교육 경험을 이곳에 공유해 주세요.

7 안녕. 나는 한국의 민희야.

8 나는 세계 공동체 동아리의 회원이야.

9 우리 동아리는 전 세계의 사람들과 소통하는 것을 목표로 해.

10 일주일 전에 우리는 우리 마을의 등 축제에 관한 비디오를 제작했어.

11 우리는 그것을 인터넷에 올렸는데, 놀랍게도 거의 5,000개의 조회 수를 획득했어.

12 우리 비디오를 보려면 이곳을 클릭해.

13 Alice: 와, 너희 등 축제는 환상적으로 보인다!

14 Sunan: 우리 마을에는 물 축제가 있어.

15 나도 너희 것과 같은 비디오를 만들고 싶어.

16 안녕, 내 이름은 Jo야.

17 나는 호주 출신이야.

18 몇 주 전에, 선생님이 우리에게 케냐에 있는 학생들의 사진을 보여주셨어.

19 슬프게도, 그들은 모두 책을 들고 다니기 위해서 비닐 봉지를 사용하고 있었어.

20 우리 반은 그들에게 새로운 책가방을 보내기 위해서 기금을 모금하기로 결정했어.

21 우리는 쿠키와 음료를 팔아서 600달러를 모았어.

22 우리는 케냐의 학생들이 그들의 새 가방을 좋아하기를 바라.

---

23 Wang: 멋지다! 분명 그들이 가방을 좋아할 거야.

24 Kozo: 훌륭한 일을 했구나!

25 난 말레이시아의 Afig야.

26 우리 학교는 우리 마을을 좀 더 좋아 보이게 하기 위해서 벽화 캠페인을 시작했어.

27 그림을 잘 그리는 학생들이 모여서 학교와 공원 벽에 그림을 그렸어.

28 이 캠페인 덕분에, 우리 마을은 훨씬 멋저 보여.

29 이제 모든 사람들이 그림이 그려진 벽을 따라서 산책하는 것을 즐길 수 있어.

30 Junho: 정말 멋진 생각이다!

---

1 Global Citizenship Education

2 This is the Global Citizenship Education site.

3 Global Citizenship Education helps us grow as global citizens.

4 Global citizens are people who try to understand different cultures.

5 They also care for people in need and work for a better world.

6 Please share your global citizenship education experiences here.

7 Hello. I am Minhee from Korea.

8 I am a member of the Global Community Club.

9 My club aims to communicate with people from around the world.

10 A week ago we produced a video about the lantern festival in our village.

11 We uploaded it to the Internet and amazingly, we got nearly 5,000 hits.

12 Click here for our video.

13 Alice: Wow, your lantern festival looks fantastic!

14 Sunan: We have a water festival in our village.

15 I'd like to make a video like yours.

16 Hi, my name is Jo.

17 I am from Australia.

18 A few weeks ago, my teacher showed us pictures of students in Kenya.

19 Sadly, they were all using plastic bags to carry their books.

20 My class decided to raise money to send them new school bags.

21 We sold cookies and drinks and raised 600 dollars.

22 We hope the Kenyan students are happy with the

new bags.

23 Wang: Awesome! I'm sure they will like the bags.

24 Kozo: You did something wonderful!

25 I am Afig from Malaysia.

26 My school started a wall painting campaign to make our village look better.

27 Students who are good at painting gathered and painted on some walls of schools and parks.

28 Thanks to this campaign, our village looks much nicer.

29 Now everyone can enjoy walking alongside the painted walls.

30 Junho: What a nice idea!

---

**구석구석지문 TEST** Step 1                                    p.38

**Conversation B**

1. isn't, too much, going to, all of

2. not sure, favorite

3. Look at, Think, Save

4. What does that mean

5. It means

6. think, took, Let's share

7. That's a good idea

8. ate, all, makes me feel good

9. Let's not waste, from now on, can save

**Project**

1. What kind activity

2. What do you think about sending

3. are happy with

4. Let's make, to find people who want to help

5. Shoes of Hope

6. children who don't have shoes

7. Bring, from home

8. Draw, write caring words

9. in need

10. July 3rd

11. If, to do something special, join

---

**구석구석지문 TEST** Step 2                                    p.39

**Conversation B**

1. Karl: Jiho, isn't that too much? Are you going to eat all of that?

2. Jiho: I'm not sure, but Bulgogi is my favorite.

3. Karl: Hey! Look at the campaign poster. "Think, Eat, Save!"

4. Jiho: What does that mean?

5. Karl: It means "Think first before you eat and save the Earth."

6. Jiho: I think I took too much Bulgogi. Let's share it.

7. Karl: Okay. That's a good idea.

8. Jiho: We ate it all. My clean plate makes me feel good.

9. Karl: Let's not waste food from now on. I hope we can save the Earth.

**Project**

1. A: What kind activity do you like?

2. B: What do you think about sending shoes to poor children?

3. C: Good. I hope they are happy with them.

4. D: Let's make a poster about the activity to find people who want to help.

5. Sending Shoes of Hope

6. Why: To help poor children who don't have shoes

7. How: 1. Bring shoes from home.

8. 2. Draw pictures or write caring words on them.

9. 3. Send them to children in need.

10. When: July 3rd

11. If you want to do something special for the world, join us!

11 inventor, 발명가　12 completely, 완전히

13 gravity, 중력　14 female, 여성, 암컷

15 strike, 부딪치다, 충돌하다　16 tongue, 혀

## 단어 TEST Step 1　　　　　　　　　p.40

01 화제, 주제　02 ~ 동안, ~ 중에　03 남성, 수컷

04 (위치·방향) ~쪽으로　05 다시

06 중력　07 두 번, 두 배

08 (사람·동식물 등이) 자라다, 성장하다　09 뼈

10 무게가 ~ 나가다, 무게를 달다　11 화성

12 항목, 물품　13 번개, 벼락　14 금속

15 (few의 비교급) 보다 적은　16 (자식·새끼를) 낳다

17 쉬다, 휴식하다　18 모기　19 혀

20 약화시키다, 약화되다　21 팽창하다　22 여성, 암컷

23 발명가　24 충분한　25 보통, 평균

26 추측하다　27 거짓의　28 완전히

29 피　30 성인, 어른　31 물다

32 고래　33 금성　34 같은, 똑같은

35 ~로 가득 차다　36 사실상, 실제로　37 ~ 때문에

38 여러 번, 몇 번이고　39 ~와 같은　40 (특정한 수 또는 정도) ~까지　41 알아보다, 찾아보다　42 사라지다

43 약간의, 조금

## 단어 TEST Step 2　　　　　　　　　p.41

01 completely　02 whale　03 blood

04 false　05 female　06 expand

07 Venus　08 same　09 strike

10 guess　11 heat　12 lay

13 average　14 inventor　15 next

16 enough　17 adult　18 bite

19 weaken　20 gravity　21 lightning

22 twice　23 mosquito　24 item

25 topic　26 Mars　27 rest

28 produce　29 tongue　30 male

31 bone　32 metal　33 toward

34 during　35 in fact　36 on average

37 find out　38 be full of　39 such as

40 due to　41 go away　42 over and over

43 join together

## 단어 TEST Step 3　　　　　　　　　p.42

1 blood, 피　2 false, 거짓의　3 male, 남성, 수컷

4 bite, 물다　5 metal, 금속

6 weigh, 무게가 ~나가다, 무게를 달다　7 expand, 팽창하다

8 mosquito, 모기　9 average, 보통, 평균　10 bone, 뼈

## 본문 TEST Step 1　　　　　　　　　p.43~44

01 Interesting Facts, Around

02 Welcome to, Ask　03 full of, things

04 Take, out, much　05 Are ready

06 gets taller during　07 fewer, than

08 Only, bite　09 never strikes, twice

10 the biggest, on　11 There, no, in

12 expands in　13 Due to, expands

14 gets, taller than

15 Adults, but, about

16 With, join together, fewer

17 Only female, bite　18 need, to produce

19 enough blood, rest, lay

20 can strike, same, over

21 gets, by, on average

22 The biggest, on, whale

23 weigh up, grow, long　24 alone, much as

25 In, gravity, space

26 farther, weakens, goes away

27 get, such as, that　28 Which, these, most

29 There, another, soon　30 Guess what, be

31 See, next

## 본문 TEST Step 2　　　　　　　　　p.45~46

01 Interesting Facts, Around

02 Welcome to, Ask　03 is full of, things

04 Take, find out how much　05 Are, ready

06 Quiz　07 gets taller during

08 fewer bones than adults

09 Only female, bite

10 never strikes, same place twice

11 the biggest, on

12 There, no gravity in　13 expands in heat

14 Due to summer heat, expands

15 gets, taller than in winter

16 Adults, bones, but babies, about

17 With time, join together, fewer bones than babies

18 Only female, will bite

19 need, to produce eggs

20 enough blood, rest for a few days, lay

21 can strike, same, over and over again

22 gets, by, times a year on average

23 The biggest, on, whale

24 can weigh up to, grow up to, long

25 alone, weigh as much as    26 In fact, gravity, space

27 farther, weakens, never goes away completely

28 get, such as, becomes stronger than that

29 Which, these, the most interesting

30 There, be another, soon    31 Guess what, will be

32 See, next month

---

1 흥미로운 사실들은 우리 주위에 있다

2 "Lawrence 박사에게 물어 보세요"에 오신 것을 환영합니다!

3 세상은 흥미로운 것들로 가득 차 있습니다.

4 퀴즈를 풀어보고 그것들에 대해 얼마나 아는지 알아보세요.

5 준비 됐나요?

6 퀴즈

7 에펠 타워는 여름에 키가 더 커진다.

8 아기들은 어른보다 더 적은 수의 뼈를 가지고 있다.

9 암컷 모기만이 사람을 문다.

10 번개는 결코 같은 곳을 내리치지 않는다.

11 코끼리는 지구에서 가장 큰 동물이다.

12 우주에는 중력이 없다.

13 금속은 열에 팽창한다.

14 여름의 열기 때문에, 에펠 타워의 금속은 팽창한다.

15 여름에 에펠 타워는 겨울보다 15센티미터 정도 더 커진다.

16 어른은 206개의 뼈를 가지고 있고, 아기는 대략 300개의 뼈를 가지고 있다.

17 시간이 흐르면서, 아기의 몇몇 뼈들은 붙는다. 그래서 어른들은 아기보다 더 적은 수의 뼈를 가지고 있다.

18 오직 암컷 모기만이 당신을 물 것이다.

19 그들은 알을 생산하기 위해서 피가 필요하다.

20 암컷 모기는 충분히 흡혈을 한 뒤, 며칠 동안 쉬고 알을 낳는다.

21 번개는 같은 곳을 반복해서 칠 수 있다.

22 엠파이어스테이트 빌딩은 한 해 평균 스물세 번 번개를 맞는다.

23 지구상에서 가장 큰 동물은 흰긴수염고래이다.

24 그것은 무게가 180톤까지 나갈 수 있으며 길이는 30미터 까지 자랄 수 있다.

25 이 고래의 혀의 무게만 해도 아프리카 코끼리의 평균 무게만큼 무겁다.

26 사실, 중력은 우주의 어디에나 있다.

27 지구에서 멀어 질수록 지구의 중력은 약해지지만, 결코 그것이 완전히 사라지는 것은 아니다.

28 당신이 화성이나 금성 같은 다른 행성에 더 가까워진다면, 그들의 중력은 지구의 그것보다 더 강해진다.

29 이 퀴즈들 중 어떤 퀴즈가 가장 흥미로웠나요?

30 곧 또 다른 퀴즈가 있을 것입니다.

31 다음 주제는 무엇일지 맞춰보세요.

32 다음 달에 만나요.

---

1 Interesting Facts Are Around Us

2 Welcome to "Ask Dr. Lawrence"!

3 The world is full of interesting things.

4 Take this quiz and find out how much you know about them.

5 Are you ready?

6 Quiz: The Eiffel Tower gets taller during the summer.

7 Babies have fewer bones than adults.

8 Only female mosquitoes bite people.

9 Lightning never strikes the same place twice.

10 The elephant is the biggest animal on the Earth.

11 There is no gravity in space.

12 Metal expands in heat.

13 Due to summer heat, the metal of the Eiffel Tower expands.

14 In summer, the Eiffel tower gets 15cm taller than in winter.

15 Adults have 206 bones, but babies have about 300 bones.

16 With time, some of the babies' bones join together, so adults have fewer bones than babies.

17 Only female mosquitoes will bite you.

18 They need blood to produce eggs.

19 After a female mosquito gets enough blood, she'll rest for a few days and lay her eggs.

20 Lightning can strike the same place over and over again.

21 The Empire State Building gets hit by lightning 23 times a year on average.

22 The biggest animal on the Earth is the blue whale.

23 It can weigh up to 180 tons and grow up to 30 meters long.

24 Its tongue alone can weigh as much as an average African elephant.

25 In fact, there is gravity everywhere in space.

26 As you get farther from the Earth, the gravity of the Earth weakens, but it never goes away completely.

27 When you get closer to another planet, such as Mars or Venus, its gravity becomes stronger than that of the Earth.

28 Which of these quiz items is the most interesting to you?

29 There will be another quiz soon.

30 Guess what the next topic will be.

31 See you next month.

---

정답은 p.116~117 Reading 교과서 확인학습 B와 동일

10 Vietnamese, 베트남의　11 theater, 극장

12 view, 전망, 경치　13 curry, 카레　14 prefer, 선호하다

15 tour, 여행　16 excuse, ~을 용서하다, 너그러이 봐주다

## 단어 TEST Step 1　p.53

01 여행객　02 돌봄, 보살핌　03 외국으로(에서)

04 흔들다; 파도　05 ~을 용서하다, 너그러이 봐주다

06 여행　07 전통적인　08 경험; 경험하다

09 역사적인, 역사상 중요한　10 기둥

11 섬　12 구르다, 굴리다　13 수도

14 전망, 경치　15 환호하다, 갈채하다; 환호

16 일하다; 작품　17 언어　18 독특한

19 경기, 시합; 어울리다　20 빛나다

21 조심하는, 주의 깊은　22 선호하다

23 도움이 되는　24 경기장　25 동작

26 천장　27 미끄러지다, 활주하다

28 보라색　29 베트남어; 베트남의

30 설계하다, 디자인하다　31 근처에

32 극장　33 음식, 접시　34 도마뱀

35 ~으로 가득 차다　36 ~의 맞은편에　37 ~로 유명하다

38 입어 보다　39 ~로 알려져 있다

40 (시간, 날짜를) 미루다, 연기하다　41 걸어서

42 ~을 응원하다　43 ~로부터 멀리

## 단어 TEST Step 2　p.54

01 shine　02 historic　03 experience

04 island　05 traditional　06 roll

07 care　08 slide　09 near

10 helpful　11 excuse　12 purple

13 tourist　14 careful　15 wave

16 tour　17 view　18 cheer

19 dish　20 match　21 capital

22 design　23 movement　24 ceiling

25 lizard　26 column　27 prefer

28 work　29 language　30 abroad

31 unique　32 theater　33 stop

34 Vietnamese　35 across from　36 be full of

37 on top of　38 cheer for　39 put off

40 far from　41 be known for　42 try on

43 be famous for

## 단어 TEST Step 3　p.55

1 shine, 빛나다　2 abroad, 외국으로(에서)

3 slide, 미끄러지다, 활주하다　4 ceiling, 천장

5 purple, 보라색　6 capital, 수도　7 lizard, 도마뱀

8 Spanish, 스페인의　9 cheer, 환호하다, 갈채하다

## 대화문 TEST Step 1　p.56~57

**Listen & Speak 1 A**

1 Excuse, Is, near / far from / How can, get there / Go straight, turn left, on your right

2 need to buy, Where can, buy / buy them at / Where is it / Go straight, blocks, across from the library

**Listen & Speak 1 B**

1 Excuse me, Where is / Go straight two blocks, on your right

2 Where is / straight one block, It's on, It's across from

**Listen & Talk 2 A**

1 It's, Let's go, have, fresh fruit juice / good, How, get there / on foot or by bus, Which do you prefer / prefer

2 What is, called / type, traditional clothing / try one on / Which do you prefer, yellow one / purple one

**Listen & Talk 2 B**

1 Which do you prefer / prefer hamburgers

2 Which do you prefer, or / prefer paella

**Conversation A**

Welcome to, we'll visit, see, on your right, near, view from, amazing, every year

**Conversation B**

How may, help / want to enjoy, view of / best place to go to / great places, on top of, Which do, prefer / prefer / Me, too / get, by bus / Where, nearest stop / straight one block, turn right, on your left / can see, There is / I think, Why don't we go, visit, later / sounds

## 대화문 TEST Step 2　p.58~59

**Listen & Speak 1 A**

1 B: Excuse me. Is the Picasso Museum near here?

G: Yes. It's not far from here.

B: How can I get there?

G: Go straight one block and turn left. It's on your right.

2 B: Sally, I need to buy some candies for Halloween. Where can I buy them?

G: You can buy them at Wendy's Candy Shop.

B: Where is it?

G: Go straight two blocks and turn right. It's across from the library.

1 A: Excuse me. Where is the park?

  B: Go straight two blocks and turn left. It's on your right.

2 A: Excuse me. Where is the school?

  B: Go straight one block and turn left. It's on your right. It's across from the restaurant.

1 B: It's really hot here in Thailand. Let's go to the night market and have some fresh fruit juice.

  G: Sounds good. How do we get there?

  B: We can go on foot or by bus. Which do you prefer?

  G: I prefer the bus.

2 G: What is this long dress called?

  M: It is an Ao dai, a type of traditional clothing from Vietnam.

  G: Can I try one on?

  M: Sure. Which do you prefer, the purple one or the yellow one?

  G: The purple one, please.

1 A: Which do you prefer, hamburgers or spaghetti?

  B: I prefer hamburgers.

2 A: Which do you prefer, curry or paella?

  B: I prefer paella.

M: Welcome to London City Tour. Today, we'll visit famous places in London. Can you see the London Eye? It's on your right. It's a Ferris wheel near the River Thames. The view from the London Eye is amazing. Many people visit it every year.

Staff: How may I help you?

Hana's mom: We want to enjoy a good view of London.

Hana: Where is the best place to go to?

Staff: We have two great places. The London Eye is a Ferris wheel and the sky Garden is a glass garden on top of a tall building. Which do you prefer?

Hana's mom: Hmm... I prefer the London Eye.

Hana: Me, too.

Staff: Good choice. You can get there by bus.

Hana's mom: Where is the nearest stop?

Staff: Go straight one block and turn right. It's on your left. Have a good trip!

Hana: Wow, I can see all of London. Look! There is a big clock.

Hana's mom: I think that's Big Ben. Why don't we go and visit it later?

Hana: That sounds great.

01 Happy Days, by　　　02 traveled to, this

03 loved by, of　04 visited, interesting places

05 Our trip, in　06 capital, famous for

07 went, watch, match

08 excited, world's most famous

09 full of, fans　10 by singing, waving, shouting

11 After, toured, went

12 While, walked around

13 visited, museum, watched

14 in, dancing, with, movements　15 For, ate

16 traditional, dish with　17 tasted like, in

18 so, that, all　19 took, tour of

20 Both, designed by

21 creative, like, colorful　22 After, visited

23 Work, going on

24 impressed, its, unique

25 ceiling, shone like, with

26 columns stood like

27 feel, creativity, love, nature

28 Traveling, wonderful experience　29 While, a lot

30 visit, country  again

01 Happy Days, by

02 traveled to Spain

03 is loved by lots of

04 visited, interesting places

05 Our trip started in

06 capital, is famous for

07 to watch, soccer match

08 were excited because, the world's most famous soccer players

09 was full of

10 cheered by singing, waving, shouting, other fans

11 After, toured, went to

12 While, walked around, many historic buildings

13 visited, watched

14 in a red dress was dancing, with wonderful movements

15 For dinner, ate

16 traditional Spanish dish with, meat, seafood

17 tasted like fried rice

18 so, that, all enjoyed　19 took a tour of

20 were designed by

21 creative works like, colorful lizard

22 After, visited　23 Work on, is still going on

24 was impressed by its size

25 shone like, with bright stars

26 stone columns stood like

27 could feel, creativity, his love of nature

28 Traveling, a wonderful experience

29 While, a lot      30 to visit

1 스페인에서의 행복한 날들 - 박진우

2 나의 가족은 이번 여름에 스페인을 여행했다.

3 스페인은 수많은 관광객들에게 사랑받는다.

4 우리는 여러 흥미로운 장소를 방문했다.

5 우리의 여행은 마드리드에서 시작했다.

6 마드리드는 수도이며 축구로 유명하다.

7 우리는 축구 경기를 보기 위해서 경기장으로 갔다.

8 나의 여동생과 나는 세계에서 가장 유명한 축구 선수 몇몇을 볼 수 있었기 때문에 신이 났다.

9 경기장은 축구 팬들로 가득 차 있었다.

10 우리는 경기를 보는 동안 노래를 부르고, 손을 흔들고, 다른 팬들과 함께 소리를 치며 응원을 했다.

11 마드리드를 여행하고 난 후, 우리는 세비야로 갔다.

12 우리는 도시를 걸어다니는 동안, 역사상 중요한 많은 건물들을 보았다.

13 우리는 플라멩코 박물관을 방문해서 플라멩코 춤을 보았다.

14 빨간 드레스를 입은 여자가 멋진 동작으로 플라멩코를 추고 있었다.

15 저녁 식사로 우리는 파에야를 먹었다.

16 그것은 쌀과 채소, 고기, 해산물이 들어간 전통적인 스페인 요리이다.

17 그것은 한국의 볶음밥과 같은 맛이 났다.

18 너무 맛있어서 우리 모두는 그것을 즐겼다.

19 바르셀로나에서 우리는 구엘 공원과 사그라다 파밀리아를 둘러보았다.

20 두 곳 모두 Antoni Gaudi에 의해 설계되었다.

21 구엘 공원에서 우리는 형형색색의 도마뱀과 같은 몇몇 Gaudi 의 창의적인 작품들을 보았다.

22 구엘 공원을 본 다음, 우리는 사그라다 파밀리아를 방문했다.

23 건물 공사는 1883년에 시작되었고 오늘날까지도 여전히 진행 중이다.

24 나는 건물의 크기와 독특한 디자인에 감명 받았다.

25 사그라다 파밀리아 안의 천장은 밝은 별이 있는 밤하늘처럼 빛났다.

26 돌기둥은 큰 나무처럼 서 있었다.

27 구엘 공원과 사그라다 파밀리아에서 나는 Gaudi의 창의성과 자연에 대한 사랑을 느낄 수 있었다.

28 스페인 여행은 훌륭한 경험이었다.

29 나는 그곳에서 스페인에 대해 많은 것을 배웠다.

30 나는 그 나라를 다시 방문하고 싶다.

1 My Happy Days in Spain – by Park Jinwoo

2 My family traveled to Spain this summer.

3 Spain is loved by lots of tourists.

4 We visited many interesting places.

5 Our trip started in Madrid.

6 Madrid is the capital and is famous for soccer.

7 We went to a stadium to watch a soccer match.

8 My sister and I were excited because we could watch some of the world's most famous soccer players.

9 The stadium was full of soccer fans.

10 As we watched the match, we cheered by singing songs, waving our hands, and shouting with the other fans.

11 After we toured Madrid, we went to Seville.

12 While we walked around the city, we saw many historic buildings.

13 We visited a flamenco museum and watched a flamenco dance.

14 A woman in a red dress was dancing the flamenco with wonderful movements.

15 For dinner, we ate paella.

16 It is a traditional Spanish dish with rice, vegetables, meat, and seafood.

17 It tasted like fried rice in Korea.

18 It was so delicious that we all enjoyed it.

19 In Barcelona, we took a tour of Park Guell and Sagrada Familia.

20 Both were designed by Antoni Gaudi.

21 In Park Guell, we saw some of Gaudi's creative works like a colorful lizard.

22 After Park Guell, we visited Sagrada Familia.

23 Work on the building started in 1883 and is still going on today.

24 I was impressed by its size and unique design.

25 The ceiling inside Sagrada Familia shone like the night sky with bright stars.

26 Its stone columns stood like big trees.

27 At Park Guell and Sagrada Familia I could feel Gaudi's creativity and his love of nature.

28 Traveling in Spain was a wonderful experience.

29 While I was there, I learned a lot about Spain.

30 I want to visit the country again.

**Enjoy Writing**

1. How much, know about
2. capital of Vietnam, is spoken
3. are popular dishes
4. Every year lots of
5. is well known for
6. so beautiful that, should

**Project Step 3**

1. chose, for a trip
2. is loved by, who, to do
3. have great experiences at

**Wrap Up**

1. was moved by
2. title of the book
3. was written by
4. so, that, many times

**Enjoy Writing**

1. How much do you know about Vietnam?
2. The capital of Vietnam is Hanoi. Vietnamese is spoken there.
3. Pho and banh mi are popular dishes in Vietnam.
4. Every year lots of tourists visit Halong Bay and Nha Trang.
5. Halong Bay has 1,969 islands and Nha Trang is well known for its beautiful beaches.
6. Vietnam is so beautiful that you should come someday.

**Project Step 3**

1. My group chose Hong Kong for a trip.
2. Hong Kong is loved by many people who want to do fun activities.
3. We'll have great experiences at Mong Kok Market, Victoria Peak, and Ocean Park.

**Wrap Up**

1. I was moved by a book.
2. The title of the book is *The Old Man and the Sea*.
3. It was written by Ernest Hemingway.
4. The story was so great that I read it many times .

MEMO

# MEMO